The British Polity

Other books by Philip Norton:

Law and Order in British Politics (editor) (1984)
The Constitution in Flux (1982)
The Commons in Perspective (1981)
Conservatives and Conservatism (with A. Aughey, 1981)
Dissension in the House of Commons 1974–1979 (1980)
Conservative Dissidents (1978)
Dissension in the House of Commons 1945–74 (1975)

The British Polity

Philip Norton

Longman

New York and London

THE BRITISH POLITY

Longman Inc., 1560 Broadway, New York, N.Y. 10036
Associated companies, branches, and representatives
throughout the world.

Developmental Editor: Irving E. Rockwood
Editorial and Design Supervisor: Thomas Bacher
Production/Manufacturing: Ferne Y. Kawahara
Composition: Composing Room
Printing and Binding: The Alpine Press, Inc.

Library of Congress Cataloging in Publication Data

Norton, Philip.
  The British polity.

  Bibliography: p.
  Includes index.
  1. Great Britain—Politics and government. I. Title.
JN231.N669 1984   320.941   83-19952
ISBN 0-582-28271-3
ISBN 0-582-28272-1 (pbk.)

Manufactured in the United States of America
Printing: 9 8 7 6 5 4 3 2 1   Year: 92 91 90 89 88 87 86 85 84

To Mr. and Mrs. R. A. Bradel

Contents

Illustrations and Tables

FIGURES

MAPS

TABLES

Preface

WHEN IN THE UNITED STATES, I have always been struck by the interest, sometimes the fascination, shown in Britain and its history, politics, and culture. However, for the serious student of British politics, a desire to understand and know more about the subject is difficult to satisfy because of limited sources. Coverage of British events by television and newspapers in the United States is extremely limited and often superficial. There are a number of introductory texts on British politics, but the most popular and most recent are texts by British scholars written primarily for British students. When I was invited to write the volume on British politics in Longman's *Polity* series, I avidly grasped the opportunity to produce a book that appeared to be much needed: an introductory text on British politics written primarily for American students. Although I hope that the book may prove of interest to British readers as well, not least because of the comparisons it introduces, it has been written principally for the American reader.

The plan of the work is simply stated. The first three chapters (Part I) provide an introduction to Britain and its political culture and history. Parts II through V identify and analyze the main features of the contemporary British polity. Governments do not operate in a political vacuum. Part II considers the political environment created by the constitution, the electoral system, political parties, and interest groups. Part III dissects and studies the different levels of government: central government, local government, and the institutions of the European Communities. Government in Britain is politically accountable to Parliament and legally accountable to the monarch. Both institutions constitute the focus of Part IV. The assent of both is necessary for the enactment of legislation. Once passed, legislation is interpreted by the courts and enforced by the different agencies of the state, most notably by the police in the case of criminal law. The effects of law and of government activities are communicated to the lawmakers through various channels. The most important media of communication are television and newspapers, and by their reporting they can have a significant impact on political behavior. The courts, the police, and the mass media constitute the concern of Part V. The final chapter draws out the themes of the book and comprises my own analysis of the strengths and weaknesses of the contemporary British polity.

In each of the chapters in Parts II through V I have tried to provide a common structure. As far as possible, each embodies an illustrative comparison with the equivalent United States institution, a brief historical sketch, an analysis of the current position, and a discussion of the debate that surrounds the institution. Because the book is designed as a student text for class use, I have sought to construct chapters that are sufficiently self-contained to be read independent of one another. Where necessary, important points are repeated or a cross-reference is provided. I have avoided terms that are probably unfamiliar to American readers or, where unavoidable, I have provided an explanation of them. Also, important terms are defined in the glossary that is located at the end of the text. Where financial figures are mentioned, the sterling amount is followed by the approximate dollar equivalent, based on the July 1983 exchange rate of £1 = $1.50, unless otherwise stated.

In writing the book, I have incurred a number of debts. My intellectual debts will be apparent from the footnotes. For reading and commenting on all or part of the manuscript, my thanks are due to John Vanderoef, Jorgen Rasmussen, Ed Page, and Ken Batty. Irving Rockwood of Longman not only read and commented on the text but also provided valuable and considerate editorial guidance. Catherine Davies, Enid Tracy, and Melanie Bucknell provided much-appreciated help in typing the manuscript. It would not have been possible for me to write a work of this nature, designed for American students, without my own experiences of the United States. For these experiences my gratitude goes to the Thouron family and Scholarship Committee for the award of a Thouron Scholarship, allowing me to study at the University of Pennsylvania in 1974–1975, to Fairleigh Dickinson University for the opportunity in 1977 to teach American students, and to Mr. and Mrs. Robert Bradel for their unstinting hospitality on my regular visits to the United States. On this side of the Atlantic, my thanks go to colleagues and friends for continued support. Many of my ideas on British politics have been developed and refined as a result of teaching the subject at the University of Hull. The comments of students have proved an invaluable stimulus to my thoughts and have served to reinforce my long-held view that teaching and research are complementary rather than conflicting pursuits. I have learned a great deal myself through writing this book. Doubtless I shall learn more from student reaction to it.

My thanks are also owing to Professor Samuel H. Beer for his recent work *Britain Against Itself*. As will be clear from my conclusion, I profoundly disagree with his analysis. However, the appearance of his work has provided me with the opportunity to develop and think through my own analysis, and for that I am grateful.

Although I have drawn on the help and work of others, no one else can be held responsible for any faults, misguided interpretations, or omissions that follow. That responsibility is mine alone. I would be pleased to hear from any reader who spots errors or wishes to express comment on the work.

Philip Norton

Introduction

The Contemporary Landscape

British Society and Political Socialization

CONTINUITY AND CHANGE are features of every political system. What makes each significant is the nature and the extent of that change. Some systems are characterized by rapid and sometimes revolutionary change. Others are noted for continuity with past experience and structures. The task of the student of politics is to discern the distinctive features of that continuity and change, to generate concepts, and, if possible, to construct models and theories that will aid understanding of and serve to explain those distinctive features and the relationship among them.

The distinctive features of a political system can be recognized by comparing that system with another or, better still, with many others. In discussing the merits of comparative politics, a student in a class of mine once objected to the whole exercise. "There's no point in comparing one country with another," he argued. "Every country is unique." As others in the class were quick to respond, the only way by which one knows that a country is unique is by comparing it with others. Just as one can know whether one is short or tall only by comparing oneself with others, so one can know whether one's own political system is "short" or "tall" only by putting it alongside other systems and noting the differences.

3

Space and resources preclude an exhaustive or even an extensive comparative study in this work. Instead, I propose to illustrate the distinctive nature of the British polity by comparing it, where appropriate, with the American. They are similar in many respects, with a shared language; advanced industrial economies; similar but not always identical political, social, and economic values; and some mutual needs. Each has a sense of affinity with the other. As we shall see, however, there are significant dissimilarities: dissimilarities that make a comparative exercise useful. Such an exercise will serve not only to sensitize the American reader to the distinctive features of the British polity but also to make readers more aware of the features of their own polity. That, at least, is the hope.

In order to understand continuity and change within the British polity, I propose to stress the significance of the political culture. This emphasis will form the basis of the next chapter as well as the book's conclusion. Before we proceed to an analysis of that culture, a brief sketch of the salient features of contemporary Britain is necessary. This outline is especially pertinent for comparative purposes. There are important dissimilarities between the United States and Britain in terms of geography, demography, and social history. Britain is a small, crowded island, largely oriented in terms of industry and population to England (and especially the Southeast of England), with a class-based society that has superseded but by no means discarded the characteristics of a status-based feudal society. The purpose of this chapter is to highlight those features and, for convenience, consider also the media of political socialization in Britain. Such a study is prerequisite for a consideration of the political culture and the institutions and processes that culture nurtures.

CONTEMPORARY BRITAIN

Land and Population

Looked at from the perspective of land distribution and usage, Great Britain could be described as a predominantly agricultural kingdom based on the three countries of England, Scotland, and Wales. (The United Kingdom comprises these three countries plus Northern Ireland: see Map. 1.1.) In terms of the distribution and activities of the population, it is predominantly English, nonagricultural, and town- or suburban-based.

Great Britain occupies a total area of 88,798 square miles. This compares with an area of 3,615,123 square miles for the United States. (The USSR occupies more than 8 million square miles. The small principality of Monaco, by contrast, comprises but a modest 368 acres.) Within the United States, 10 states each have a greater land area than Britain: Alaska (586,412

MAP 1.1 The United Kingdom.

square miles), Texas (267,339 square miles), and California (158,693) being the most notable. England has approximately the same land area as New York State, Scotland the same area as South Carolina, and Wales the same as Massachusetts.

The disparity in population size is not quite so extreme. In 1980, the United Kingdom population was 56 million, up from 19.7 million at the turn of the century. The United States population in 1980 was 226 million, up from just under 76 million in 1900 (see Table 1.1). There is a more significant difference, however, in population growth. In the 1970s, the United Kingdom population increased by a mere 0.5%, a figure matched only by West Germany. The increase in the United States was one of 10.4%. In the USSR it was 8.8%, in China 13.9%, and in Brazil, nearly 30%.

When the population is put in the context of land size, Britain emerges clearly as a crowded island. The number of people per square kilometer in 1980 was 229. By European standards, this is not exceptional: Belgium, the Netherlands, and West Germany are even more densely populated. The number of people per square kilometer in the United States in 1980 was a modest 24. By worldwide standards, this is a low but not exceptional density. The USSR, Brazil, New Zealand, Australia, and Canada were among the nations with lower population density. In Australia and Canada there were 2 people per square kilometer.

Within the United Kingdom, the population is heavily concentrated in one country. In 1980, more than 46.5 million people lived in England,

TABLE 1.1
United States and United Kingdom Populations, 1900–1980

Year*	United Kingdom Population (Millions)	United States Population (Millions)
1900/1901	38.2	75.99
1910/1911	42.1	91.97
1920/1921	44.0	105.7
1930/1931	46.1	122.77
1940/1941	48.3	131.67
1950/1951	50.6	150.69
1960/1961	53.0	179.2
1970/1971	55.7	203.2
1980	56.0	226.5

*0, United States; 1, United Kingdom.
SOURCES: Adapted from Central Statistical Office, *Social Trends 12* (Her Majesty's Stationery Office, 1981) and *New Statesman's Year Book 1981–82* (Macmillan, 1981).

compared with a little over 5 million in Scotland, 3 million in Wales and 1.7 million in Northern Ireland. The number of people per square kilometer in England in 1980 was 356—the highest population density of European countries and greater even than that of Japan. Within England, the greatest concentration of inhabitants was in the southeast of the country (that is, Greater London and the surrounding counties), with a population of nearly 17 million.

The population resides predominantly in areas classed as urban for local government purposes. Nearly 80% of the population in England, and more than 70% in Scotland and Wales, live in urban areas. [1] The shift from rural to urban areas has been marked in England, the proportion of the population living in nonurban areas declining from a little over 35% in 1951 to not much more than 20% 20 years later.

Although more than three-quarters of the land surface is used for agriculture, very few people are employed in the agricultural industry. There has been a persistent drift from land work since industrialization in the eighteenth and nineteenth centuries, a trend that continues. More than 700,000 people were employed in agriculture, forestry, and fishing in 1961. By 1979, the figure was down to 367,000. Increased efficiency and greater mechanization have in part facilitated this development. (Britain has one of the heaviest tractor densities in the world.) There are more than 250,000 "statistically significant farming units" in Britain, [2] with three-fifths of the full-time farms being devoted mainly to dairying or beef cattle and sheep. Farms devoted to arable crops are predominant in the eastern part of England. Sheep and cattle rearing is a feature of the hills and moorland areas of Scotland, Wales, and northern and southwest England.

Despite the importance and extent of agriculture, nearly half of Britain's food supply has to be imported. Indeed, Britain is heavily dependent on imports for its raw materials. Compared with other large industrialized (and some developing) nations, Britain is notably lacking in natural resources. It is largely self-sufficient in coal, chemicals, and fish, and the recent discovery and exploitation of oil in the North Sea has made it a net exporter of the substance. Other than that, though, it is dependent on other nations either wholly or in part for products such as bauxite, copper, lead, tungsten, tin, nickel, phosphates, potash, rice, corn, cotton, silk, coffee, tobacco, and forestry products, among others. The United States, by contrast, is self-sufficient in most of these products, with surplus supply in several cases. Only in coffee and silk is it wholly dependent on imports. The USSR is even better served in its natural supply of raw materials. France, Germany, Canada, Japan, and India are also more self-sufficient than Britain. This lack of raw materials not only is important for an understanding of British industry but also provides a partial explanation for some of Britain's internationalist and imperial history.

Employment

Britain was the first major nation to experience industrialization. Most of the population moved from the land to find jobs in manufacturing industries in the towns and cities. Most of the economically active population came to be employed in primary industries and manufacturing. In the twentieth century and especially in the period since 1945, more and more workers have moved into service industries. In the 1980s, Britain can be described as having a service economy. Of the people in employment in 1979, over 13 million worked in service industries, compared with 7 million in manufacturing; 1 million in construction; 367,000 in agriculture, fisheries, and forestry; 346,000 in mining and quarrying; and 346,000 in the gas, electricity, and water industries. Table 1.2 shows the changes that have taken place in the period since 1961.

TABLE 1.2
Employment by Industry, 1961–1979

Industry	Number in Employment (Thousands)		
	1961	1971	1979
Agriculture, forestry, and fishing	710	432	367
Mining and quarrying	727	396	346
Construction	1,485	1,262	1,292
Gas, electricity, and water	389	377	346
Manufacturing			
Food, drink, and tobacco	793	770	698
Chemicals, coal, and petroleum products	499	482	482
Metal manufacture	643	557	444
Engineering and allied industries	3,654	3,615	3,270
Textiles, leather, and clothing	1,444	1,319	898
Rest of manufacturing	1,508	1,511	1,386
Total Manufacturing	8,540	8,058	7,176
Services			
Transport and communication	1,678	1,568	1,494
Distributive trades	2,767	2,610	2,826
Insurance, banking, and finance	684	976	1,233
Professional and scientific services	2,124	2,989	3,729
Miscellaneous services	1,819	1,946	2,493
Public administration	1,311	1,509	1,619
Total Services	10,382	11,597	13,394
All Industries and Services	22,233	22,122	22,920

In all the categories other than the service industries, male employees outnumber females. In the service industries, more than half the workers are women. In terms of sector, 7.4 million workers were employed in the public sector in 1980, compared with 17.3 million in the private sector.

As to employment, the service industries clearly represent the growth industries. The other main area of growth is in unemployment. In the 1950s and early 1960s, very few workers were unemployed. In 1961 only 1.5% of the workforce was registered as unemployed, but by 1971 it had risen to 3.5%—a total of 792,000 people. The figure increased throughout the decade, reaching 7.4% in 1980. The following year, the figure exceeded 10% and in 1982, 12.3% of the workforce was unemployed—over 3 million individuals in all. Critics of official statistics argued that not all those out of work were registered as unemployed and that the real figure was therefore higher than that given by the Department of Employment, which is responsible for compiling the data.

Within the United Kingdom, the extent of unemployment is greater the further one moves from London and the Southeast. In 1980, the percentage of the workforce out of work in the Southeast was 4.8%. In the North of England it was 10.9%, in Wales it was 10.3%, in Scotland 10.0%, and in Northern Ireland, traditionally the place with the highest level of unemployment, nearly 14%. Within the workforce, unemployment was greater among immigrants from the New Commonwealth and Pakistan than it was among native-born citizens or those from other European countries. It was also most marked among the younger age groups, those aged under 24 years.[3] There was also a marked increase during the 1980s in the number of long-term unemployed. In April 1972, the proportion unemployed for more than a year accounted for one-sixth of the total unemployed; by April 1981, the proportion had risen to one-fifth.

The level of unemployment in Britain is high in both absolute and comparative terms. In 1982, the United Kingdom had the highest level of unemployment among the seven major countries in the Organization for Economic Cooperation and Development (OECD). Britain's unemployment rate of 12.3% compared with 11% for Canada, 9.5% for the United States, 9.3% for Italy, 8.5% for France, 7% for Germany, and 2.3% for Japan. The average among other OECD countries was 10%. In 1983, the governing Conservative Party in Britain was keen to point out that the rate of increase in unemployment from 1982 to 1983 was higher in the United States, Germany, the Netherlands, and Canada than it was in the United Kingdom (a 23.1% increase in the United States compared with 11.8% in the United Kingdom) and that unemployment would be higher in other countries were it not in some cases for conscription and a retirement age for men of 60. Britain does not have conscription (compulsory national service in the armed services was ended in 1961), and the retirement age for men is 65.[4]

Linguistic and Racial Differences

The population is predominantly English in birth as well as residence. It is concomitantly white and English-speaking. However, it is not totally homogeneous. Not only is there a division among the English, the Scottish, and the Welsh; there is also a division between Gaelic-speaking Scots and those who do not speak Gaelic, and between those who do and do not speak the Welsh language in Wales. In both cases, those who speak the old traditional language are in a small minority. In 1971, only 19.8% of the inhabitants of Wales could speak the Welsh language (down from 27.5% in 1951) and only 1.7% of Scots could speak Gaelic, most of the Gaelic speakers being concentrated in the Scottish highlands and islands. There is a further division when one includes Northern Ireland, where the community is divided along mutually exclusive lines (see Chapter 9): a few families in the province still speak the Irish form of Gaelic. The influx of immigrants into Britain, especially in the 1950s and early 1960s, has also added to the diversity of the population and to linguistic differences.

The number of people in Britain who are from, or whose parents are from, the New Commonwealth countries and Pakistan—a category close to but not quite identical to that of the black population—is just over 2 million, just under 4% of the population. The number has increased gradually from 1,087,000 in 1968, though natural increase (excess of births over death) accounted for more than half the rise in 1979–1980, the last year for which figures are available. The problem of racial tension in Britain has been exacerbated by the fact that, though the total black population is small, it is largely concentrated in certain urban areas, notably London, Leicester, Birmingham, and other West Midlands towns.

By contrast, the United States has experienced analogous problems of concentration but has a much larger black population. In 1970, blacks accounted for well in excess of 10% of the American population (22.5 million out of 203 million); other nonwhite races accounted for nearly a further 3 million citizens. Unlike Britain, the black population in the United States is largely indigenous. The United States also has a far greater ethnic mix than Britain. The hyphen in American society (German-Americans, Polish-Americans) has no significant equivalent in Britain.

Class

The United States does not have a feudal history. The significance of this fact was well drawn out by Louis Hartz in his incisive work on the Lockean basis of American society.[5] Britain, by contrast, most certainly does have a feudal past. Furthermore, unlike some of its European neighbors with feudal histories, it has witnessed no revolutionary break with past experience. As a result, the class patterns of a capitalist society have been superimposed on the hierarchical social structure of a departing feudal society.

Status derives from the tendency of people to accord positive and negative values to human attributes and to distribute respect accordingly. In feudal society, a superior status was accorded to the land-owning aristocracy and gentry. They were deemed to have breeding and to be the best people to run the land. They were accorded deference as a socially superior body. It was a status that was passed on by inheritance, not one that could be acquired by merit or work.

Whereas status is essentially the product of social structure, class is the product of the economic.[6] Defining the concept of class is not an easy task. Marx distinguished two classes, bourgeois and proletarian, based on the ownership of the means of production. This is not a particularly useful definition given the significant distinction between ownership and control. The problem is compounded by the fact that the term means different things to different people. How social scientists define class and how others perceive it (not least in terms of self-ascription) are often far from congruent. The most useful definition is that of groups formed on the basis of occupational difference. In Britain, there are essentially two classes, the middle and the working (a characteristically British distinction, as A. H. Halsey has observed).[7] Within each, there are further divisions. Table 1.3 provides a simple delineation of them.

Class grew out of industrialization and the development of a capitalist economy. It did not displace status; it usurped it. In the nineteenth century, the upper class comprised the traditional landed aristocracy, but it was an aristocracy that had absorbed largely if not wholly the new men of wealth

TABLE 1.3
Social Classes in Britain

Class	Market Research Designation	Encompassing
Middle class		
Upper-middle	A	Higher managerial and professional
Middle	B	Lower managerial and administrative
Lower-middle	C1	Skilled or supervisory nonmanual, lower nonmanual
Working class		
Upper-working	C2	Skilled manual
Working	D	Unskilled manual
	E	Residual, pensioners

who had made their money out of trade and industry. These new men were drawn into the new class until eventually, they overwhelmed it.[8]

This combination of class and status was carried into the twentieth century. In recent decades, however, it has been weakened. Some of the features of a status society, such as peerages, can be passed from father to son: the inheritance is founded in law. Class can be inherited but it is an inheritance based on the market. The market is less predictable than the law. Recent years have witnessed a growing social mobility. The children of many working-class parents have been upwardly mobile socially. The children of some middle-class parents have taken up working-class occupations. Indeed, a few members of that institutional survivor of a feudal era, the House of Lords, pursue manual occupations. Writes Halsey, "Men and women, moving and marrying between different occupational levels, both over the generations and also within their own working lives or careers, have become an increasingly common feature of British social life in the past half century."[9] The general pattern of change has been one of upward mobility. Greater mobility and affluence have eroded the claims to status. Mobility deprives one of claims to breeding. Acceptance of the principal of meritocracy is discordant with claims of inherited worth. Status remains important but it is no longer the central feature of British society that it was in preceding centuries.

The importance of class in contemporary society was confirmed by Butler and Stokes in their study of political change in Britain. In a 1970 survey, they asked respondents to name the main social classes and the class to which they would ascribe themselves. They found that "virtually everyone accepted the conventional class dichotomy between middle and working class."[10] In terms of self-ascription, 77% spontaneously described themselves as middle- or working-class, while a further 5% added only a slight qualification such as "upper-middle" class. All but 1% of the remainder were willing to assign to themselves, when prompted, a middle- or working-class label. As Butler and Stokes point out, "It is difficult not to see this as evidence of the acceptance of the view that British society is divided into two primary classes. This is much more than a sociologist's simplification; it seems to be deeply rooted in the mind of the ordinary British citizen."[11] Most respondents characterized class as being based on occupation, and most (Table 1.4) identified themselves as being in the class suggested by the occupation of the head of their household.

The importance of class is political as well as social. For most of the twentieth century, there has been a significant relationship between class and politics. The Labour party has attracted largely but not wholly the support of the working class, and the Conservative party that of the middle class. The significance of the class–party nexus will be explored in more detail shortly. In recent years, there is some evidence of decline in class identifications and in the correlation between class and party. Such decline,

TABLE 1.4

Class Self-Image by Occupational Status of Head of Household, 1970

	Higher Managerial	Lower Managerial	Supervisory Nonmanual	Lower Nonmanual	Skilled Manual	Unskilled Manual
Middle-class	80%	60%	57%	46%	26%	20%
Working-class	20%	40%	43%	54%	74%	80%

SOURCE: D. Butler and D. Stokes, *Political Change in Britain*, 2nd ed. (Macmillan, 1974), p. 72. Copyright 1974 Macmillan and 1974 St. Martin's Press. Reprinted by permission.

though, has been relative. Class remains a principal feature of British society. Most Britons continue to ascribe themselves to a particular class. Politicians analyze their support in class terms, and sociologists would be lost without it.

Education

Education in Britain is best seen in pyramidal terms. All children receive a primary and secondary school education. Thereafter, only a minority proceed to institutions of further education and but a small percentage enter university. For children receiving education at private schools, the structure is less pyramidal: A greater proportion of those educated at private schools proceed to university than those attending state schools.

After entering primary school at the age of 5, children in England receive a common education until the age of 11, when they enter secondary schools. Most pupils now attend what are termed comprehensive schools, schools whose enrollment criteria are geographic rather than academic.

In the two decades following the Second World War, secondary schools were divided into grammar and secondary modern schools. In the former, scholastic skills were stressed, with a large proportion of students staying beyond the minimum school-leaving age (then 15) and proceeding to university. In the latter, emphasis was placed on practical skills such as technical drawing and woodwork, with some pupils going on to some form of technical college but with most leaving at 15 years of age and few if any achieving university entrance. Selection for grammar schools was based on an intelligence test known as the "Eleven-plus" examination, taken, as the name suggests, when primary schoolchildren reached the age of 11, i.e., at the end of their primary education. Labour party politicians came to view this examination and the consequent dichotomy between grammar and secondary modern schools as educationally questionable and socially divisive: those attending secondary modern schools were seen as "failures" and their subsequent job opportunities limited by virtue of their education. Grammar school pupils were drawn disproportionately from middle-class families.

In 1965, the then Labour government introduced a scheme of reform requiring local authorities to take steps to dispense with the Eleven-plus and introduce a scheme of comprehensive education. Many authorities responded reluctantly, some resisting the government's wishes, and only in the 1970s did the number of pupils in comprehensive schools exceed the number attending selective schools. In 1971, only 38% of secondary schoolchildren attended comprehensive schools; in 1980, the proportion was 83%.

From school, a small proportion proceed to institutions of further and higher education. Only a small fraction of pupils achieve the two Advanced

Level (A-Levels) examination passes that constitute the minimum requirement for university entrance. In 1979–1980, fewer than 30% of girls leaving
school and under 20% of boys entered full-time further education. Fewer
than 10% (8.6% of boys, 6.5% of girls) went on to study full-time for a
degree.

Although secondary education is compulsory, parents are not required
to send their children to state schools. They can opt instead to send children
to private schools. Here the enrollment criterion is more financial than
geographic. Private schools tend to stress scholastic skills and concentrate on
developing the capacity to pass examinations and on building self-confidence. Believing their children will receive a better and more disciplined
education, with a greater prospect of university entry than from a state
school, many parents who can afford it send their children to such private
institutions, known (confusingly) as "public schools." Fees at such schools
will vary, depending on the status of the school. The more prestigious such
as Eton, Harrow, and Winchester can afford to charge annual fees in excess
of £4,000 (more than $6,000 in 1983 terms), whereas some less prestigious
day schools may charge less than £1,000 per year. In 1980, fewer than 6% of
the total school population were attending assisted and independent
schools—yet more than a quarter of University entrants continued to be
drawn from private schools.

There are various forms of higher and further education. There are
various technical colleges and colleges of further education, as well as the
institutions at the top of the pyramid—polytechnics and universities. Polytechnics stress more vocational, practical subjects, often providing sandwich
courses (part teaching, part practical job experience), while universities tend
to stress more academic subjects. Relative to the United States, there are
few universities in the United Kingdom: a total of 46. Of these, 20 have been
founded since 1960. The most prestigious tend to be the oldest: Oxford,
Cambridge, and, in Scotland, St. Andrew's. The Open University is notable
for being a nonresidential university, providing tuition by correspondence
and through special television and radio programs; it is the only university
that requires no formal academic qualifications in order to enroll. The new-
est university, at Buckingham, is the only one to receive no support from
public funds—it is the only wholly private university.

Of the more than half-million students in full-time higher education in
1980, fewer than 200,000 were at a university. A university education continues to provide occupational advantage. Of graduates, more than 80% have
ended up in the professional and managerial classes. As such, they constitute
fewer than one-third of those in these classes, but it is these classes that will
provide more children than any other for university entry. The professional
and managerial classes made up 18% of the population in 1971: their children formed 51% of university entrants in 1975 and 54% in 1979.[12]

Personal Wealth and Taxation

The distribution of marketable wealth among the population is skewed in favor of a minority. Marketable wealth comprises stocks and shares, cash, bank deposits, consumer durables, buildings, trade assets, land, and dwellings net of mortgage debt. In 1971, approximately one-third of the total marketable wealth in Britain was owned by 1% of the population. Two-thirds was owned by the most wealthy 10%. These figures showed a decline during the next three years (the result of a decline in the price of stocks and shares) and little change thereafter. In 1979, just under 25% of the marketable wealth was owned by 1% of the population, and 59% was owned by 10% of the population.

When occupational and state pension rights are added to marketable wealth, there is a change in the pattern of distribution (see Table 1.5). In 1979, only 13% of this aggregate wealth was owned by 1% of the population and 37% by 10% of the population. Over the 1970s, there was a shift in the distribution of wealth in favor of slightly more equality, though most wealth clearly remains in the hands of the minority.

In income, approximately two-thirds of the total household income before tax comes from wages and salaries. In 1980, the average gross weekly earnings of a male manual employee was £112 (approximately $175 at 1983 exchange rates) and of a nonmanual employee, £141 (about $220). The equivalent figures for female workers were £68 and £83 respectively.

Given the progressive nature of taxation, the proportion of earnings paid

TABLE 1.5
Distribution of Wealth, 1971–1979

Percentage of Population	Percentage Owned of Marketable Wealth			Percentage Owned of Marketable Wealth plus Occupational and State Pension Rights		
	1971	1975	1979	1971	1975	1979
1	31	24	24	21	13	13
2	39	31	32	27	18	18
5	52	44	45	37	27	27
10	65	58	59	49	37	37
25	86	83	82	69–72	58–61	58–61
50	97	93	95	85–89	81–85	79–83

SOURCE: Central Statistical Office, Social Trends 12 (HMSO, 1981), p. 99. Copyright 1981 Social Trends. Reproduced by permission of the Controller of Her Majesty's Stationery Office.

in direct taxation varies. In 1980–1981 the highest 10% of earners paid approximately one-quarter of their earnings in direct taxation. Those who were in the lowest 10% of earners paid fifteen per cent.

Expressed as a percentage of the gross national product (GNP), total taxes in Britain in 1978 accounted for 39% of the GNP. Compared with other countries in the OECD, this was not an exceptional proportion. It was unusual compared with the other countries in that it actually represented a decline (of 2%) from the 1971 figure. In 1978, total taxes as a percentage of the GNP exceeded 40% in Germany, France, and the Scandinavian countries (it was 60% in Sweden). They were less than 40% in Canada, the USA (34%), Italy, Japan, and Switzerland.

A slightly different relationship emerges when only direct taxes are expressed as a proportion of the GNP. Britain moves further down the table. In 1978, direct taxes represented 23% of the GNP. This was a lower percentage than in Germany, France, the Scandinavian countries (44% in Sweden's case), Italy, Switzerland, and the United States (24%).[13] Japan and Canada were the only major OECD countries with percentages lower than that for Britain.

POLITICAL SOCIALIZATION

The various values and beliefs that coalesce to maintain, reinforce, or sometimes modify the political culture are not generated in a vacuum; they are acquired through a process of socialization. In that process, the most important influences are usually family, education, occupation, and geographic location. Such influences serve to instill an awareness of one's place in or relationship to society and the political system.

Family

Although much influence is placed on the individual, the family remains the most important social unit in Britain. Most households in Britain comprise married couples with dependent children. The second largest proportion comprise married couples with no children, then married couples with independent children.[14] In 1980, only 8% of people lived on their own (double the percentage in 1961), though this does not signify social detachment from a family. For many people living on their own, their social world may revolve around visits from or to relatives. Family units are also provided by couples living together but not married. In 1979, the General Household Survey found that 10% of nonmarried women were cohabiting. (The question was addressed only to women.) Although marriages are becoming less stable in that divorce rates continue to rise,[15] many divorcees remarry or cohabit with another partner. In 1979, one-third of all marriages constituted remarriages for one or both partners. Of divorced or separated women, 18% were cohabiting.

It is from parents that children inherit social and political values. Indeed, children often acquire their class orientation from parents not only in taught but also in practical terms. Children are more likely to obtain jobs in the class bracket of their fathers than they are to be socially mobile. In the Butler and Stokes survey of 1970, most working-class respondents came from families in which the father was also working-class. Fewer than one-fifth of respondents had experienced upward mobility and slightly fewer than one-tenth had experienced downward mobility.[16] A study of the earnings of children in York in the 1970s compared with their fathers' earnings in the 1950s found a coefficient of earnings of nearly 0.5.[17]

That this should be so is not surprising. Children raised in a middle-class family in which the parents and grandparents were university-educated are likely to be brought up in an environment in which reading and learning are stressed and going to university is encouraged. A university education is likely to result in a better-paying job than is a nonuniversity education. Hence, graduates are more likely to obtain middle-class occupations than are nongraduates. Working-class families, by contrast, are less likely to provide an environment that encourages scholastic skills. This may not be out of unwillingness but rather ignorance on the part of parents: they do not know how to go about encouraging such skills. In some cases they may not wish to. The need to supplement the family income motivates some parents to encourage children to go out and earn a wage as soon as possible. Years spent at university are financially unrewarding from the parents' perspective. An attachment to class may also limit the ambitions of both parents and children. Existing in a working-class milieu reinforced by the still-existing perception of status can create a cocooning effect: it provides a sense of the familiar and the comfortable (in psychological if not financial terms). To leave a working-class environment is to head for the unknown. From parents, children can acquire habits and tastes that are peculiar if not exclusive to a particular class. Certain sports are working-class sports (for example, darts), others middle-class (squash, for instance). Such tastes are passed from one generation to the other, reinforced by the environment in which a family exists.

Among the habits and values passed from parent to child are political ones. Children are more likely to be politically interested and active if their parents have been similarly interested or active.[18] Most important, children tend to inherit their parents' partisan preferences. Butler and Stokes write, "Partisanship over the individual's lifetime has some of the quality of a photographic reproduction that deteriorates with time: it is a fairly sharp copy of the parents' original at the beginning of political awareness, but over the years it becomes somewhat blurred, although remaining easily recognizable."[19] The influence of parents is strongest when both parents share the same partisan preference. In Butler and Stokes' survey, of children whose parents had both been Conservative, 89% expressed a first preference for the Conservative party.[20] This partisanship is reinforced when parents' preferences are congruent with the influences to be identified below.

There is evidence that this parent–party nexus is declining. In the 1983 general election, nearly 8 million people voted for a political ticket (Liberal/Social Democratic Party Alliance) for which their parents could not previously have voted. Nonetheless, family remains the most important primary influence in the process of political socialization. Divergent influences may modify or dispel values imbued as a result of parental influence. But in seeking to make sense of the social and political environment in which he or she lives, an individual's first and foremost point of reference is provided by father (in terms of partisan preference, more likely father) and mother.

Education

Formal education is important in political socialization, less for its effect on partisan support (family remains the predominant influence) than for helping shape awareness of the political system and explicitly or, more often, implicitly, the values that underpin it.

In their study of the civic culture, Almond and Verba found that there were differences in attitude toward government between those with different levels of education, and between those who had received some formal education and those who had received none. The more extensive the education, up to university level, the greater the perceived significance of government action.[21] Nonetheless, the overwhelming majority of those with some formal education, primary or above, considered that national government had some effect. In the countries studied in which a proportion of the population had received no formal education (Italy and Mexico), only a small proportion of those without an education felt that national government had some effect. (The proportion of those with a formal education ascribing influence to the government was lower than that in the United States and in Britain, albeit still a majority among the university-educated.) From this, one may infer the importance of education for the purposes of political socialization.

The correlation between education and political socialization in Britain is not greatly dissimilar to that in the United States. Those with higher levels of education are more likely than those with only a primary education to attach significance to the action of government, to believe that they can have some influence on government, to pay attention to politics and election campaigns, to take the view (though not necessarily to practice it) that citizens should be active in their local community, to hold opinions on a wide range of political subjects, and to be actively involved in politics.[22] In Britain, a little over 3% of the adult population have degrees. Of the members of Parliament (MPs) who sat in the Parliament of 1979–1983, over 62% were graduates.

Where Britain and the United States differ is in the way that the subject of politics is taught. In Britain, manifest teaching of the subject, insofar as it is manifest, can best be described as subtle. There is little emphasis on symbolic acts (there is no obvious English equivalent to saluting the flag) and little formal teaching of politics as such. The media of other subjects are employed. Stradling writes, "Until comparatively recently the prevailing view on political education in England was either that it was already adequately taken care of through History, Geography, Social or General Studies or that it was a wholly unsuitable subject for the school curriculum."[23] Only recently has the opportunity to study politics as a distinct and legitimate subject been expanded within secondary schools. Relative to other disciplines, it remains a little-taught subject. However, the implications of this are not as great as might be thought. Almond and Verba found that having been taught about government increases a sense of subjective political competence.[24] Against this, some studies in the United States, where formal study of "civics" is more extensive than in Britain, found that taking such courses had little impact on political knowledge and attitudes.[25] Similar findings have resulted from a recent survey of British school pupils.[26] What is more important is the length of period in education. In the British study, pupils staying on at school until the age of 18 achieved much higher scores on political knowledge than did those leaving school at 16. From this, one might hypothesize that education is important in developing the intellectual skills necessary to absorb and make sense of political material communicated by other media.

Attendance at school, and particlarly at certain schools, can be important also in providing an environment that can serve to reinforce certain norms and traditions. At leading public schools, most notably Eton, there is a tradition of providing MPs, government ministers, and prime ministers. At such schools, a pupil is more likely to consider pursuing a political career than is the case with pupils attending an inner-city comprehensive school with no such tradition. In most cases, the school environment tends to reinforce the influence of the home background.

Occupation and Class

Occupation and class, as we have seen, are closely related. The former is usually employed as the primary criterion for assessing the latter. Both are important in the context of political socialization.

Certain occupations are important in terms not only of class but also of status. A doctor of medicine is in the same social class as a company director but is more likely than the director to be accorded some degree of deference by the local community. Holding a position of responsibility gives one standing in the community. Holding jobs that are well paying and/or rewarding in terms of personal self-satisfaction may increase one's contentment with the society in which one exists. Conversely, pursuing a mundane, poorly paid job or no job at all may provoke a sense of alienation from society. Certain jobs by their nature may lead to greater social awareness or to a greater degree of social intercourse than others.

Class is an abstraction and the concept acquires meaning only as a result of the socialization process just outlined. From one's parents, education, occupation, and associated life-style one acquires an awareness of social class. Such awareness becomes important in helping clarify one's place in society and, thus, one's relationship to others in that society. It serves to give some meaning and shape to one's social existence.

There is an important but not complete relationship between class and partisan support. That this should be so is not surprising. Those in middle-class occupations are more likely to be better paid and pursue a preferred life-style than those in working-class occupations (though the emphasis should be on the likelihood, not the certainty). Hence, one might expect the middle class to opt for the political party most likely to conserve the existing state of affairs. Those in working-class jobs and those with no jobs at all might be expected to opt for a party that offers some degree of social change and appears more empathic toward the "have-nots" than toward the "haves." This hypothesis is largely but not wholly borne out by the empirical evidence. Middle-class voters have tended to support the Conservative party in Britain, and working-class voters the Labour party. The relationship has never been a complete one. Some middle-class voters have supported the Labour Party and about one-third of working-class voters have traditionally cast their ballots for Conservative candidates. In recent years, the significance of the class–party tie has declined. Nonetheless, as we shall see, class provides the most important indicator of partisan support. No other indicator has proved so reliable.

Location

Location can be important in the process of political socialization in a number of senses. The location of one's residence is important. Living in an area of expensive detached houses can serve to reinforce one's sense of being middle-class. The area provides a social milieu that reinforces that awareness. Conversely, living in an area of less expensive terraced accommodation or of council houses (estates composed of houses rented from the local authority are common) reinforces one's identification with the working class. Within such areas, there is often a particular lifestyle.

The independent influence of location is borne out when correlated with partisan support. Voters who live in class-specific communities are more likely to vote for the relevant class-specific party than are those not living in such communities. As Rose observes, "Working-class voters in safe Labour seats are much more likely to vote Labour than those in the same class, but living in a marginal or Conservative constituency. Environment affects middle-class voters in Conservative areas, but the effect is not so strong."[27] Moving into such specific areas, with changes in the pattern of home ownership, can effect a change in partisan support.[28]

There is also a correlation between partisan support and urban versus rural location. This pattern became more pronounced in the 1960s and 1970s, as did the division between North and South. Increasingly, the Labour party became the dominant party of the North of England, and the Conservative party that of the South. That this should be so is not surprising, given changes in employment and demographic patterns. In 1980, Curtice and Steed pointed out that "the peripheral areas of Britain, with their higher unemployment, and the declining inner parts of conurbations, have become steadily more Labour; while the expanding, more prosperous areas have become more Conservative."[29] In the 1983 general election, the Labour vote declined in all regions by between 6% and 12%. The lowest regional decline took place in Scotland. In urban areas, the swing against Labour was half what it was in rural and mixed areas. Labour, as one analysis showed, remained the party of the traditional working class of the council estates, of Scotland, and of the North.[30]

The Mass Media

The mass media of communication are also important. They are significant not only as media for transmitting material, television now being the main source of political information for most people, but also for the choice of what material to transmit. By choosing to transmit some stories rather than others, those in control of television and newspapers can have some impact on political perceptions and values. In Britain, the national orientation of the broadcasting media and of newspapers is important. The size of the country and the dual position of London as the nation's capital and its largest city has facilitated a national orientation—primarily a London orientation—not possible in the United States.

The partisan influence of the media in Britain is unclear. The broadcasting media are statutorily required to be impartial. Newspapers can and do express partisan preferences. Newspapers with a significant political reporting are not widely read, whereas television news programs are often among the most-watched programs. Research into the impact of the media in Britain is not extensive. What research has been done on their effects, especially in the United States, suggests that their importance is primarily as a reinforcing rather than a realigning agent.[31] The significance of this role should not be underestimated.

A Complex Mix

The process by which an individual becomes politically socialized is a complex one. The influences just outlined are in most cases the more important ones but they are by no means the only ones—nor are they exclusive. They clearly interact with one another, as has been obvious from the foregoing. It has been virtually impossible to discuss one influence without drawing out the impact of another. Also, these influences are far from static. Changes in family structures, the educational system, the nature of employment, and demographic and housing patterns may affect the socialization process. As we have seen, children staying longer in formal education appear to acquire more political knowledge than those leaving school earlier. More children than before are now acquiring a formal education beyond the minimum school-leaving age. Unemployment may generate a sense of political alienation. As we have seen, unemployment has risen steeply in Britain in recent years.

The importance of some of these changes will be touched on later in this work, particularly in the context of partisan support. However, such changes are relative. In terms of the basic values being transmitted in the process of political socialization, the most significant feature is not change but rather continuity. The media for political socialization in Britain are not dissimilar to those in the United States and many other polities. To know this is useful, but to identify those media is to identify the means for transmitting the values and beliefs that coalesce to form the political culture, and not to identify the political culture itself. That is a separate exercise, undertaken in the next chapter. Having identified some of the salient features of contemporary Britain and, as a prerequisite, the process of political socialization, we can now progress to the more analytically useful study of the British political culture.

NOTES

1. R. Rose and I. McAllister, *United Kingdom Facts* (Macmillan, 1982), p. 145.

2. *Britain 1978: An Official Handbook* (Her Majesty's Stationery Office, 1978), p. 266.

3. *Social Trends 12* HMSO, 1981, pp. 72–3.

4. See Conservative Research Department, *The Campaign Guide* (Conservative Central Office, 1983), pp. 75–76. The statistics are drawn from the OECD and the British *Employment Gazette*.

5. L. Hartz, *The Liberal Tradition in America* (Harcourt, Brace & World, 1955).

6. See A. H. Halsey, *Change in British Society,* 2nd ed. (Oxford University Press, 1981). This section draws heavily on this work.

7. Ibid.

8. Ibid., p. 47.

9. Ibid., pp. 53–54.

10. D. Butler and D. Stokes, *Political Change in Britain,* 2nd ed. (Macmillan, 1974), p. 69.

11. Ibid.

12. Halsey, p. 133.

13. Direct taxes encompass taxes on income, social security contributions, motor vehicle license duties paid by households, and taxes on capital gains. The figures are taken from *Social Trends 12,* p. 87.

14. *Social Trends 12,* p. 29.

15. In the United Kingdom in 1980 a total of 158,000 divorces were granted, constituting 12 people per 1,000 married couples. In 1961 only 27,000 divorces were granted. Since that time, the facility for obtaining divorces has been eased through legislation.

16. Butler and Stokes, pp. 96–97.

17. B. Atkinson, A. K. Maynard, and C. G. Trinder, *Parents and Children* (Heinemann, 1983).

18. Butler and Stokes, p. 50.

19. Ibid., p. 51.

20. Ibid., p. 52.

21. G. Almond and S. Verba, *The Civic Culture* (Princeton University Press, 1963), pp. 86–87.

22. Ibid., pp. 380–81.

23. R. Stradling, *The Political Awareness of School Leavers* (Hansard Society, 1977), p. 1.

24. Almond & Verba, p. 361.

25. See K. P. Langton and M. Kent Jennings, "Political Socialisation and the High School Curriculum in the United States," *American Political Science Review,* 62, 1968, pp. 852–67.

26. Stradling, p. 37.

27. R. Rose, *The Problem of Party Government* (Penguin, 1976), pp. 39–40.

28. See Butler and Stokes, pp. 110–14.

29. J. Curtice and M. Steed, "An analysis of the voting," in D. Butler and D. Kavanagh, *The British General Election of 1979* (Macmillan, 1980), p. 402.

30. I. Crewe, *The Guardian,* June 13, 1983.

31. See J. T. Klapper, *The Effects of Mass Communication* (The Free Press, 1960).

Continuity and Change

The British Political Culture

CONTINUITY AND CHANGE, as we have observed, are features of every political system. In order to understand the extent and nature of that change one has to generate some analytically useful framework. What the opening chapter did was to provide largely descriptive material of the society with which we are concerned. It did not generate a framework that would help us understand the nature of continuity and change in Britain. The purpose of this chapter is to provide such a framework.

The emphasis of the chapter will be on the political culture. As I shall seek to show, however, that culture cannot be divorced from the constraints of history and of physical and spatial resources. Each has had a significant impact on the other. The impact has not been in one direction only: the political culture has served to shape political perceptions and actions, and hence to influence the nation's political history. Conversely, those actions have been constrained by the experiences of history. They have also been constrained by Britain's geographic location and limited resources.

A number of problems have to be borne in mind. As we shall see, there are problems inherent in trying to give shape to such an abstract concept as political culture. There is the danger of tautology and of failing to distinguish between how a system operates and the way in which people believe it should operate. There is the problem also of attempting to discern the cause-

and-effect relationships among culture, history, and resources. The problem here is analogous to that embodied in the familiar conundrum "Which came first, the chicken or the egg?" The existence of a stable political culture in Britain has been ascribed by some to the effectiveness of government. But what has enabled government to be effective? Has it been a distinctive political culture, citizens being prepared to acquiesce in and, when called on, to support the demands made of them by government? If so, what explains the existence of such a political culture? Is not a partial explanation the effectiveness of government? The problem is an acute one in the case of Britain, given the absence of any clear point of departure. Where does English, Scottish, or Welsh history begin? At what point is a political culture discernible? The problem is largely an insuperable one, and all we can do at this stage is to bear it in mind. Fortunately, it does not present an insurmountable obstacle; as I shall seek to show, the importance of the relationship is one of mutual reinforcement.

What, then, is the British political culture? How important have been the constraints of history and of resources? How does it compare with other polities? And is it, as some writers have suggested, in a state of collapse?

THE POLITICAL CULTURE

Political culture is a vague abstract concept that has been subject to various definitions.[1] In its simplest form, it may be described as denoting the emotional and attitudinal environment within which a political system operates.[2] Various political scientists have sought to define and identify different types of political culture. Almond and Verba, for example, identified three ideal types: participant, subject, and parochial.[3] Others have sought to generate criteria by which to assess the distinctive features of a political culture.

In his work on political oppositions in western democracies, Robert Dahl observed that patterns of opposition may have something to do with widely shared cultural premises. He noted that four kinds of culturally derived orientations toward politics seem to have a bearing on the pattern of opposition.[4] Those four orientations can usefully be employed to help understand and explain attitudes not just toward political opposition in Britain but to the political culture as a whole. They enable one to draw out the distinctive features of that culture, in a more useful manner than does the framework provided by others, and to consider the impact of both history and resources. Those four orientations, listed not in the order provided by Dahl but in the order I believe to be most significant to an understanding to British political culture, are toward (1) problem-solving, (2) the political system, (3) cooperation and individuality, and (4) other people.

Orientation toward Problem-Solving

Giovanni Sartori has distinguished two approaches to problem-solving: the empirical and the rational.[5] The empirical approach is concerned with what is and what can be seen and touched, proceeding on the basis of testing and retesting and largely rejecting dogma and abstract or coherent grand designs for change. The rationalist approach, by contrast, is concerned with abstraction rather than facts, stressing the need for deductive consistency and tending to be dogmatic and definitive. Dahl states: "While the empirical approach takes the attitude that if a program does not work in practice there must be something wrong about the theory, the rationalist will retort that what is true in theory must also be true in practice—that it is the practice, not the theory, that is wrong."[6]

France has been identified as employing a rationalist approach. Germany and Italy, to some extent, tend also to find such an approach useful. Britain and the United States, by contrast, are seen as the exemplars of an empirical approach. Indeed, it is my contention that this approach is most marked in the British case and that it constitutes the most significant aspect of British political culture.

Although more oriented toward an empirical approach, the United States has exhibited some elements of the rationalist. While tempered by experience and (according to Beard) self-interest, the framers of the United States Constitution were informed by Lockean values and sought to impose a political framework in line with a Lockean conception of society.[7] Those values and that conception of society have permeated the American consciousness, so much so that they have largely gone unstated. They have been so pervasive and so self-evident that there has been little point in articulating them. Hence, the United States might be described as being oriented toward a mix of the empirical and the rationalist, albeit with the former being clearly the more dominant of the two.

Britain, by contrast, has a distinct orientation toward the empirical approach. Even the political system, however strong the attachment to it, tends to be justified in pragmatic terms. Democracy, having been implemented in largely pragmatic fashion, has been lauded on the grounds that "it works." The point has been well put by Vivien Hart in comparing American and British approaches: "In America," she wrote, "the emphasis has been on what democracy is and *should* be, while Britain has been characterised by a more pragmatic and less urgent emphasis on what democracy is and *can* be."[8] Empiricism seems appropriate to the English consciousness. Instinct, trial and error, and incremental change are the essence of the English approach to problem-solving. "I believe in the instinctive wisdom of our well-tried democracy," declared Churchill in 1945—shortly before going down to election defeat.[9]

Such an orientation to problem-solving has been a distinctive feature of English political culture for many centuries, discernible, I would suggest, since at least the thirteenth century. It is an approach that has informed political actions and hence the political history of the country. An empirical orientation has in turn been reinforced by the experience of history—it is the approach that has always been employed and no external constraints have managed to force themselves on the nation to generate conditions in which a rationalist approach would be possible. In the wake of the War of Independence, Americans were able to sit down and generate a political system from first principles. Invasions by foreign powers and subsequent liberation (or absence of liberation) have put other states in similar positions. England, by contrast, has never been faced with or sought such an opportunity. The closest it came was during the Protectorate of Oliver Cromwell in the seventeenth century. When that failed, the country resorted as far as possible to the conditions prevailing prior to its creation. English history is scattered with philosophers generating theories that have failed to find congenial soil in the nation's consciousness. Ideologies have been either discarded or else molded to fit with the experience of history. Prevailing theories, once they no longer seem appropriate, have been dispensed with. The act of dispensing with them has not always met with common assent nor has it always been smooth—the English historical landscape is scattered with periods of violence and upheaval—but once the dispensing process is achieved, it has largely been accepted. Hankering after the old order is congenial to some minds, but seeking to revert by force or civil unrest to the *status quo ante* is not. In the English perception, empiricism is both a descriptive and a prescriptive term. To the Englishman, it is both what is and what he believes always has been.

Orientation toward the Political System

Orientation toward the political system may be classified as allegiant when attitudes, feelings, and evaluations are favorable to the political system; apathetic or detached when feelings and evaluations are neutral; and alienated when such feelings and evaluations are unfavorable.[10] Italy and France have been cited as examples of political cultures that generate alienation and a large measure of apathy. West Germany has been put forward as having a culture that generates detachment. In contrast, Britain and the United States are among those countries cited as exhibiting a strong allegiant orientation.[11]

Almond and Verba found that evaluation of the political system in Britain was the product of a mix of participant and deferential orientations. A participant orientation was developed in Britain (citizens being oriented to the input as well as the output side of the political system, believing that they enjoyed access to it), but it was one adapted to an existing deference to the independent authority of government. The participant orientation in Britain, unlike that in the United States, did not displace the deferential;[12] it remained important.

The participant orientation finds expression in citizens' beliefs that they can influence government at both the national and local level. Although Almond and Verba found few people in their survey who actually sought to exert such influence, the proportion who believed that they *could* exert influence was significant. Of British respondents, 57% said that they could influence national and local government. (The figure for the United States was 67%.) Only 19% of those questioned felt that they had no influence at national and local levels. (The figure for the United States was 15 per cent.) By contrast, of Germans, Italians, and Mexicans interviewed, more believed they had no influence at national and local level than believed that they had. Only 25% of Italians, for example, believed that they could influence national and local government, and 47% said they had no such influence.[13]

Deference to the authority of government has found expression in a number of ways. It has been shown in a voluntary compliance with basic political laws. Criminal acts tend to be antisocial rather than conscious acts against "the state." (Indeed, the concept of "the state" is one that is not well entrenched in English consciousness.) There has been little overt opposition to the parliamentary form of government in Britain. Some may want to modify its form but do not challenge the principle of it, nor do they seek to change its form through unlawful and certainly not violent means. When government authority has been challenged, citizens have expressed themselves in favor of maintaining that authority. When called on by government to act in time of war, citizens have been prepared to respond.

Such deference has often been seen as allied with a social deference, citizens according certain skills of government to those drawn from a particular group. Walter Bagehot, in his classic work *The English Constitution*, identified England as a "deferential nation," one that had a structure of its own. "Certain persons," he wrote, "are by common consent agreed to be wiser than others, and their opinion is, by consent, to rank for much more than its numerical value."[14] Such deference, though possibly weakened, survived into the era of mass suffrage and the democratic ideal. It has been seen as a significant feature of contemporary Britain and has been variously offered as a partial explanation of the continuing success of the Conservative party and its socially atypical leadership.[15]

Such deference, though, has been contingent rather than certain. It has been based on a reciprocity between governors and governed. The populace has deferred to the independent authority of government and to those who occupy government in return for the satisfaction of expectations. Those expectations have covered the substance of policies (improving material well-being, for example) as well as the form of government. Almond and Verba, for example, found that an overwhelming majority of Britons expected equal treatment from politicians and from bureaucrats.[16] Conversely, those to whom citizens accord deference have been characterized by having an in-bred sense of duty. A stress on responsibilities as well as rights has been a significant and long-standing feature of the British culture and has been well imbued by a large part of the nation's political elite. A paternalistic concern for the well-being of the nation has been a feature of most if not all monarchs and has been associated with a particular and often predominant tradition within the Conservative party.

As long as the political system has been able to maintain the capacity to meet the demands and expectations of citizens, an allegiant orientation has been demonstrated by citizens. The longer the system has been able to do this and the longer people have been socialized into accepting the efficacy of the system, the stronger and more enduring the allegiance has been. In Almond and Verba's survey, more Britons expressed pride in their govern-mental and political institutions than in any other feature of the nation that was mentioned.[17] The same pride was found in Americans, on a larger scale. (Of Americans, 85% expressed pride in their institutions, compared with 46% of Britons.) In stark contrast, only 7% of Germans expressed pride in their governmental and political institutions, and the figure for Italians was 3%.[18]

Orientation toward Cooperation and Individuality

Some cultures emphasize the values of cooperating with others, conciliating opposing views, and being prepared to compromise and submerge one's own ideas in a broader and more popularly acceptable solution. Others, by con-trast, stress the virtues of maintaining the distinctiveness, ideas, and integ-rity of the individual, such virtues being considered superior to those of compromise and cooperation.[19]

France and Italy have been cited as examples of countries in which the maintenance of group and individual integrity is stressed in both the general culture and in political life.[20] Britain and the United States are included among those countries in which the political culture emphasizes the virtues of compromise and conciliation, without threatening personal integrity.

The Anglo-American perception was well expressed by Edmund Burke in 1775. "All government, indeed every human benefit and enjoyment, every virtue, and every prudent act," he declared, "is founded on compro-mise and barter."[21]

In Britain there is an almost instinctive distaste for conflict, both in personal relationships and in political life. The formal political framework facilitates an adversary relationship among political parties, but the underly-ing reality is a quest for compromise. Parties play according to the rules of the constitutional game. Similar observations can be made about groups in industry and in society generally. There is a penchant, almost, for resolving disputes by discussion, by sitting around a table and ironing out one's differences. It is an orientation compatible with the others already identified and it is eminently congenial to a society that stresses the responsibilities as well as the rights of the individual. It remains an orientation that Britons not only find congenial but also take as the source of a certain pride.

Orientation toward Other People

A belief that one can have faith and confidence in others has been put forward as a culturally rooted phenomenon, with potentially important implications for political life. Research by Morris Rosenberg has shown that "faith in people" is related to democratic and internationalist values and attitudes.[22] In their study, Almond and Verba found that the Americans and the British "tend to be consistently most positive about the safety and responsiveness of the human environment."[23] The Germans and the Italians, by contrast, were found to be more negative, and the Mexicans inconsistent.

Trust in one's fellow countrymen remains a significant feature of contemporary British society. A Gallup Poll in 1980 found that 85% of respondents considered other Britons to be very or fairly trustworthy.[24] The experience of history may have helped to consolidate such a sense of trust. Britons have stood successfully shoulder-to-shoulder in order to win battles abroad and to repel foreign invaders from their shores. During the Second World War, the nation did not have to contend with a significant fifth column or with the equivalent of Vichy collaborators. There is little or nothing in recent history that would give Britons cause to distrust their compatriots.

Similarly, the experience of history, island isolation, and shared values may serve to explain differing levels of trust that Britons have in other people. Britons tend to retain trust in the inhabitants of countries in which Britain has had or retains colonial interests; countries that share a common language, values, and (in some cases) ancestry; and countries that have stood together in times of crisis. There are strong emotional ties to old Commonwealth countries such as New Zealand, Canada, and Australia. There is also a strong sense of closeness to the United States. Of respondents in the Gallup Poll in 1980, 70% regarded Americans as very or fairly trustworthy. (Only the Swiss and the Dutch received marginally higher ratings.)[25] Another poll a year later asked respondents the extent to which they thought they could trust certain countries as allies in the event of war. The proportion responding that they thought they could trust the United States "a great deal" was 62% (up from 45% in 1975), a figure not matched by any other country: the closest was Norway, which 37% thought they could trust to the same extent.[26]

The two polls revealed lower levels of trust in those countries and people that historically have been Britain's enemies. To the island inhabitants of Britain, such peoples remain distant (though the English Channel constitutes now more a psychological than a physical barrier), with alien cultures, different interests, and different thought processes. Englishmen and Scotsmen, as Anthony King observed, have tended not to think like Europeans nor to think of themselves as Europeans.[27] In the 1980 Gallup Poll, only 32% of the Britons questioned regarded the French as very or fairly trustworthy. The Russians scored 18%. (The West Germans, perhaps surprisingly, scored 60%.) Only 6% of those questioned would trust the French a great deal as allies in time of war, 4% would trust the Spanish, 4% the Italians, and only 3% the Turks. Again, the Germans did better, 22% being prepared to trust them a great deal. Finally, 47% said they would trust the Italians "not at all," and 45% gave a similar response for the French.

Despite British membership of the European Communities, there is an important sense in which Britain and certainly the British still look westward across the Atlantic rather than eastward over the English channel. And despite the travails of recent times, trust in one's fellow countryman and a discriminating, possibly confident, perception of other people remain significant features of the British political culture.

A DECLINING CULTURE?

The political culture of Britain may then be characterized, in broad terms, as having the four orientations identified: empirical in terms of problem-solving and change, allegiant in terms of the political system, cooperative in making decisions, and trusting with relation to fellow countrymen and allies. These, it is important to stress, are generalizations—there are always individuals or subcultures that may not have such orientations. What is important is that they are and remain the orientations of most Britons, both at the mass and the elite level.

The strength of the culture may be said to lie in the convergence of these orientations—that is, they are compatible with and reinforce one another, and similarly are compatible with and are reinforced by the experience of history. The stress on cooperation and compromise, an emphasis compatible with an empirical approach to change, has facilitated the integration of groups and individuals into the political system. Such integration may be seen as reinforcing an allegiant rather than a neutral or alienated orientation to the political system. History, as we have mentioned, has been kind: the country has staved off invasion by its enemies, and the resources have been available for government to make and meet commitments in response to changing demands and expectations. As a result, it has been possible to interpret the experience of history as justifying or reinforcing an attachment to empirical problem-solving and to the virtues of cooperation and trust. The interplay of these variables generated what Almond and Verba characterized as "the civic culture," "a pluralistic culture based on communication and persuasion, a culture of consensus and diversity, a culture that permitted change but moderated it."[28]

What of the civic culture today? My argument is simply stated: Although subject to modification, the civic culture remains. What has been the subject of radical, almost revolutionary, change over the past decade or so has not been the civic culture but the perceptions of that culture. In short, it has not changed as much as observers think it has.

I do not argue that the political culture of Britain remains unchanged. The culture not only allows for change, usually incremental but occasionally radical, but itself can and does change. In good British fashion, however, that change has tended to be piecemeal rather than comprehensive. Some values, attitudes and emotions have been subject to modification over time, but the essential orientations outlined above have not been discarded. They remain the orientations that converge to form the predominant element of the British political culture.

What has changed, and changed radically over the period from the late 1960s to the early 1980s, has been the perception of that culture. Analyses of the British political culture have swung, pendulum fashion, from one extreme to the other. At times of apparent stability, contentment, and political success, there has been a tendency to see the political culture in idealized terms, to hold it aloft and laud it as a culture to be admired and possibly even envied. Although Almond and Verba drew attention to some of the inconsistencies and problems inherent in the civic culture, it was nonetheless difficult not to ascribe positive connotations to that culture.

There are a number of problems inherent in the political culture. A disposition to incremental change can deflect one from considering or even comprehending wider and more fundamental problems. The combination of an empirical orientation and historical continuity has produced a political system that is complex and disparate. While the American federal system has been likened to a marble cake, the British political system can be likened to a patchwork quilt. It may look to some extent like the original, it may even retain traces of the original, but the many pieces that make the whole were added at different times and have been the subject of change and much repair work. It includes structures that (according to some observers) have facilitated policy discontinuity—a discontinuity not incompatible with an empirical orientation to change—yet comprises such an interdependent complex of political bodies that it has become increasingly difficult for government to govern and to initiate radical and comprehensive change. Such difficulty has been exacerbated by the desire to resolve problems by compromise. Problems that cannot be resolved by reasoned debate have tended to be ignored in the hope that they will go away.

Such inherent problems tend to be discounted, ignored, or even interpreted in a favorable light at times when the political system appears to be successfully meeting the demands and expectations of the populace. When the system appears to be malfunctional, usually at times of economic difficulty for the country, some commentators identify such inherent problems as providing at least a partial explanation for the system's poor showing. In the latter half of the 1970s, for example, policy discontinuity arising from an electoral and political system that encouraged an "adversary style" of politics was offered as a partial explanation for Britain's poor economic performance.[29]

Other commentators have sought to identify the nation's problems not in terms of the effect of some aspects of the political culture but as agents generating and reflecting a decline in the culture itself. In the 1970s and early 1980s, a number of observers began to chart a decline in the civic culture.[30] In 1982, on the basis of some survey evidence, Samuel Beer concluded that "it is no exaggeration to speak of the decline in the civic culture as a 'collapse'".[31] He argued that as old institutions failed to meet new expectations, so legitimacy in government would falter and trust in its equity and effectiveness would decline. He hypothesized and sought to show that the consequences of this included a greater self-assertion by participants, a decline of leadership, a weakening of party government, and a loosening of the nexus of class and party. "In an ironic sense," Beer declared, "Britain is maintaining its leadership. As it once showed the way toward democratic success, today it blazes the trail toward democratic failure."[32]

While Beer's hypothesis is plausible as to the effect of institutions that fail to meet new expectations on legitimacy in government, it is arguable as to the extent to which such a failure to meet expectations has taken place. This is a point to which I shall return in the concluding chapter. Although government capacity to meet expectations has declined, its capacity to meet expectations in the past built up a body of diffuse support, support that now exists independently of particular failures to meet demands.[33] Furthermore, there is evidence that the expectations themselves may be changing, converging more with the capacity of the system to meet them.

Certainly, it will be my case that the political culture has neither declined nor been threatened to the extent suggested by Beer and other Jeremiahs.[34] Certain institutions may be under threat (as subsequent chapters will show) but not in a manner inconsistent with the existing political culture. The civic culture may be weakened but it has not collapsed. Its position is similar to that of Mark Twain: reports of its death would be greatly exaggerated. As I shall seek to show, the political culture remains predominantly an allegiant one, and the important question to be addressed is not "why has there been a decline in the civic culture?" but rather "why has that decline not been greater?"

NOTES

1. See D. Kavanagh, *Political Culture* (Macmillan, 1972), pp. 10–11.
2. Ibid., p. 10.
3. G. Almond and S. Verba, *The Civic Culture* (Princeton University Press, 1963), Ch. 1.
4. R. A. Dahl (ed.), *Political Oppositions in Western Democracies* (Yale University Press, 1966), p. 353.
5. G. Sartori, *Democratic Theory* (Wayne State University Press, 1962), p. 233, cited in Dahl, p. 354.
6. Dahl, p. 355.
7. L. Hartz, *The Liberal Tradition in America* (Harcourt, Brace & World, 1955). For the Beard analysis, see C. Beard, *An Economic Interpretation of the Constitution* (Macmillan, 1913).
8. V. Hart, *Distrust and Democracy* (Cambridge University Press, 1978), pp. 202–3.
9. Eve of election broadcast, July 4, 1945.
10. Dahl, p. 353.
11. Almond and Verba, Ch. 14.
12. Ibid., pp. 455–6.
13. Almond and Verba, p. 186.
14. W. Bagehot, *The English Constitution* (first published 1867; Fontana, 1963 ed.).
15. See, e.g., R. McKenzie and A. Silver, *Angels in Marble* (Heinemann, 1968).
16. Almond and Verba, p. 108.
17. For example, the economic system, the characteristics of the people, the contribution to arts/sciences, social legislation, and spiritual values. Almond and Verba, p. 102.
18. Ibid.
19. Dahl, p. 354.
20. Ibid.
21. Speech on conciliation with America, March 22, 1775.
22. M. Rosenberg, "Misanthropy and Political Ideology," *American Sociological Review,* 21, pp. 690–95 and "Misanthropy and attitudes towards International Affairs," *Journal of Conflict Resolution,* 1, 1957, pp. 340–45, cited in Almond and Verba, p. 266.
23. Almond and Verba, p. 268.
24. N. Webb and R. Wybrow, *The Gallup Report* (Sphere Books, 1981), pp. 103–4.
25. Ibid.
26. N. Webb and R. Wybrow, *The Gallup Report: Your Opinions in 1981* (Sphere Books, 1982), pp. 91–92.
27. A. King, *Britain Says Yes* (American Enterprise Institute, 1977), p. 6. See also L. Barzini, *The Impossible Europeans* (Weidenfeld and Nicolson, 1983).
28. Almond and Verba, p. 8.
29. See, e.g., S. E. Finer, *Adversary Politics and Electoral Reform* (Wigram, 1975) and below, Ch. 5.

30. See, e.g., D. Kavanagh, "Political Culture in Great Britain: The Decline of the Civic Culture" in G. Almond and S. Verba (eds.), *The Civic Culture Revisited* (Little, Brown, 1980).

31. S. H. Beer, *Britain Against Itself* (Faber, 1982), p. 119.

32. Ibid., pp. xiv–xv.

33. For the concept of "diffuse support," see D. Easton, *A Systems Analysis of Political Life* (Wiley, 1965), p. 273.

34. I take the term *Jeremiahs* from William Gwyn's succinct chapter, "Jeremiahs and Pragmatists: Perceptions of British Decline" in W. B. Gwyn and R. Rose (eds.), *Britain: Progress and Decline* (Tulane University Press, 1980).

Past and Present

*Historical Perspective and
Contemporary Problems*

A NUMBER OF INTRODUCTORY TEXTS on British politics do not have chapters devoted specifically to political history. The omission is a surprising one. When the proposal for this book was under consideration by the publishers, a number of American professors were asked for their comments. One responded with this advice: "Make sure you incorporate as much historical detail as possible. American students don't know much about British history." It was a shrewd response. The need for such detail, however, is not confined to Americans interested in the subject; it encompasses all those who seek to make some sense of the institutions and complex relationships that form the British polity in the 1980s.

There has been no point in British history at which the prevailing method of government has been completely swept away, allowing those in power to sit down and create from first principles a new and clearly delineated form of government. The country has witnessed continuous and sometimes dramatic change. In the past 300 years alone, the nation has experienced industrialization, the advent of democracy, and the introduction and growth of the welfare state—yet the changes have never been such as to be described as revolutionary. They have been built upon and have adapted that which already existed. The body politic may have undergone radical surgery and it may have aged considerably, but it has continued to endure.

What, then, are the significant features of British history that help us understand the contemporary political system and the political culture? Limitations of space preclude a lengthy dissertation on what is a vast subject. That vastness is apparent when put in comparative perspective. The Magna Carta, for instance, was signed more than two centuries before Christopher Columbus set sail. A Parliament was summoned more than 500 years before the United States Congress first assembled. And an American president, unlike a British monarch, cannot trace his presidential forebears back more than 1,000 years. Nonetheless, it is possible to provide a brief but structured sketch that furthers our understanding of contemporary British politics. This can be done under two headings: one is the emergence of parliamentary government, and the other is the development of the welfare state and the managed economy.

The structure and relationships of the contemporary organs of government can be understood only in historical context. A study of the emergence of the welfare state highlights the increased demands and responsibilities borne by government. Both studies provide a necessary background to understanding some of the problems now faced by government. They serve also to highlight certain features of the political culture.

HISTORICAL PERSPECTIVE

The Emergence of Parliamentary Government

One of the essential features of the British Constitution is a parliamentary government under a limited, or symbolic, monarchy. The formal elements of this type of government will be more fully outlined in the next chapter. For the moment, what concerns us is that this government is the product of change extending over several centuries, coming to fruition only in the past century. Its development has sometimes been characterized as being evolutionary, but in practice, it is the outgrowth of piecemeal change.

Let us begin in the thirteenth century. Traditionally, the sovereign power in England resided in the monarch. Nonetheless, the king was expected to consult with his tenants-in-chief (the earls, barons, and leading churchmen of the kingdom) in order to discover and declare the law and to have their counsel before any levies of extraordinary taxation were made. This expectation was to find documented expression in the Magna Carta of 1215, by which the king recognized it as a right of his subjects "to have the Common Council of the Kingdom" for the assessment of extraordinary aids—that is, taxation. Such consultation was undertaken through a Great Council, from which evolved what was to be recognized as a *parlement* or Parliament. The Great Council itself was essentially the precursor of the House of Lords. The House of Commons evolved from the summoning to council, in the latter half of the thirteenth century on a somewhat sporadic basis, of knights and burgesses as representatives of the counties and towns. At various times in the fourteenth century the Commons deliberated separately from the Lords, and there developed a formal separation of the two bodies.

During the period of the Tudor monarchs in the sixteenth century, Parliament acquired enhanced status. It was generally supportive of the monarch but became more powerful because of the dependence upon it for that support, especially during the reign of Elizabeth I. The relationship between Crown and Parliament under the subsequent Stuart dynasty was one of conflict. The early Stuart kings James I and Charles I sought to assert the doctrine of the divine right of kings and to deny many of the privileges acquired or asserted by Parliament. This conflict was to lead to the civil war and the beheading of Charles I in 1642. With the abolition of the monarchy came a brief period of rule by a Council of State elected by what was termed the Rump Parliament. (Some attempts were actually made to formulate a form of written constitution, but they came to nothing.)[1] Rule by the Council of State was succeeded by Oliver Cromwell's unsuccessful military dictatorship, and in 1660 Charles' son returned to assume the throne as Charles II. The period between 1642 and 1660 proved an aberration in British history. The Restoration witnessed an attempt to return, unconditionally, to the country's position as it was at the beginning of 1642.[2] Through this attempt the Restoration lent itself to a repetition of the earlier struggle between King and Commons. Relations between the two gradually deteriorated during the reign of Charles II and became severe in the reign of his successor, James II. James sought to reassert the divine right of kings, and Parliament combined against him. In 1688 James fled the country. At the invitation of Parliament, the throne was taken by William and Mary of Orange, James' son-in-law and daughter. The new occupants of the throne owed their position to Parliament, and the new relationship between them was asserted by statute in the Bill of Rights. Although the Bill of Rights was important for enumerating various "Liberties of this Kingdom" (some of which were to be similarly expressed during the following century in the Bill of Rights of the United States Constitution),[3] its essential purpose was to assert the position of Parliament in relation to the Crown. The raising of taxes or the dispensing of laws without the assent of Parliament was declared to be illegal. The monarch was expected to govern, but to do so only with the consent of Parliament. The Act of Settlement of 1701, which determined the succession to the throne, affirmed that the laws of England "are the Birthright of the People thereof and all the Kings and Queens who shall ascend the Throne of this Realm ought to administer the Government of the same according to the said Laws and all their Officers and Ministers ought to serve them respectively according to the same."

The monarch thus became formally dependent on Parliament for consent to the raising of taxes and for the passage of legislation. In practice, he or she became increasingly dependent also on ministers for advice. The importance of ministers grew especially in the eighteenth century. The Hanoverian kings were not uninterested in political life but they had difficulty comprehending the complexities of domestic and foreign affairs. According to the historian J. H. Plumb, both George I and George II were "crassly stupid" and "incapable, totally incapable, of forming a policy."[4] During the period of their reigns, the leading body of the king's ministers, generally known as the cabinet, began to meet without the king being present.[5] The period also witnessed the emergence of a minister who was to become popularly known as the prime minister. (Not until the twentieth century was the office of prime minister to be mentioned in a statute.) The relationship among Crown, ministers, and Parliament in that century was one in which the king relied on his ministers to help formulate policy. Those ministers were chosen by the king on the basis of his personal confidence in them, and they remained responsible to him. They also were responsible to Parliament in order to achieve their ends, a fact recognized by both the king and his ministers. Nonetheless, parliamentary support was not difficult to obtain; the king and his ministers had sufficient patronage and position usually to ensure such support. A ministry that enjoyed royal confidence could generally take the House of Lords for granted, and provided it did not prove incompetent or seek to impose excessive taxation, "its position was unassailable in the Commons."[6] The position was to change significantly in the nineteenth century.

Britain underwent what has been popularly referred to as an industrial revolution in the period from the middle of the eighteenth century to the middle of the nineteenth. Seymour Martin Lipset has characterized the United States as the "first new nation," but Britain has been described as "the first industrial nation."[7] Industry became more mechanized, improvements took place in agricultural production techniques, and there were improvements in transport and in the organization of trade and banking. There was a notable growth in the size of cities, particularly in the early part of the nineteenth century. Men of industry and commerce began to emerge as men of some wealth. In 1813, Robert Owen referred to the "working class," a term brought into common speech by Lord Brougham.[8] By the 1830s, a nonlanded middle class, artisans, and an industrial workforce were important constituents of the country's population.

Parliament remained dominated by the aristocracy and by the landed gentry. Representation in the House of Commons was heavily weighted in favor of the rural counties. Some parliamentary constituencies had only a handful of electors: known as "rotten boroughs," they were often in the pocket of an aristocrat or local landowner.[9] Pressure for some parliamentary reform, with a redistribution of seats and a widening of the franchise, began to develop. It was argued that a Parliament full of men of wealth and property was unlikely to view industry, trade, and agriculture from the point of view of the laboring classes. Rotten boroughs were criticized as being used by the ministry to help maintain a majority. Unrest in a number of areas, both agricultural and industrial, and the French Revolution of 1830 (a spur to radical action) increased the pressure for change. One political group in particular, the Whigs, who had been the "outs" in politics for the 25 years prior to 1830, began to see the need for some response to this pressure. The concession of some parliamentary reform was seen as necessary in order to prevent worse happenings. The result was to be the Reform Act of 1832.

The Reform Act, introduced, ironically, by the most aristocratic government of the century, reorganized parliamentary constituencies and extended the franchise. The electorate increased in size from a little under 500,000 to 813,000 electors.[10] Although much remained the same as before—the new electorate constituted but one-thirtieth of the population, 31 boroughs still had fewer than 300 electors in each, voting remained by open ballot (secret ballots were considered rather un-English), and the aristocracy still held great sway politically—the act precipitated important changes both within and outside the House of Commons.

The redistribution of seats and the extension of the franchise helped loosen the grip of the aristocracy and of ministers on the House of Commons. The size of the new electorate encouraged the embryonic development of political organizations. Members of Parliament (MPs) became less dependent on aristocratic patrons without acquiring too great a dependence on the growing party organizations. The result was to be a House of Commons with a greater legitimacy in the eyes of MPs and electors and one with an ability to assert itself in its relationship with government. The House proved willing to amend or reject legislation put before it as well as to remove individual ministers and on the occasion the government itself. In his classic work on the constitution, Walter Bagehot attached much importance to this "elective function"; the House of Commons, he declared, was "a real choosing body: it elects the people it likes. And it dismisses whom it likes too."[11] Debates in the House really counted for something and, with the exception of the period from 1841 to 1846, party cohesion was almost unknown. The House of Commons did not itself govern, but government was carried on within the confines of its guidance and approval.

The period after 1832 witnessed also important changes in the relationships within and among the different elements of Crown, government, and Parliament. The monarch retained the formal prerogative power to appoint the prime minister, but the changed political circumstances essentially dictated that the person chosen should be able to command a majority in the House of Commons. Royal favor ceased to be an essential condition for forming the Government. Within Parliament, the relationship between the two Houses also changed. Members of the House of Lords sat by virtue of birth, holding hereditary peerages. The acceptance of the Commons as the "representative" chamber undermined the authority of the peers to challenge or negate the wishes of the other House. After the 1830s, the Lords tended to be somewhat restrained in their attacks on government measures. "This followed," writes Mackintosh, "from the view that while a ministry retained the confidence of the elected representatives it was entitled to remain in office. The peers on the whole accepted these assumptions, though many found the explicit recognition of the situation hard to bear."[12] The Lords' remaining authority was in practice to be removed in consequence of the 1867 Reform Act, though not until the twentieth century was the House forced formally to accept its diminished status.

Whereas the 1832 Act helped ensure the dominance of the House of Commons within the formal political process, the passage of the Reform Act of 1867 began a process of the transfer of power from Parliament to Ministers. The act itself was the product of demands for change because of the limited impact of the 1832 Act and because of more immediate political considerations.[13] Its effect was to increase the size of the electorate from 1,358,000 to 2,477,000. (The number had grown since 1832 because of increased wealth and population.) Other significant measures followed in its wake. Secret voting was introduced by the Ballot Act of 1870. Other acts sought to prohibit as far as possible corrupt practices and limited the amount of money a candidate could spend on election expenses. Single-member districts (known in Britain as constituencies) of roughly equal electoral size were prescribed as the norm.[14] The 1884 Representation of the People Act extended the franchise to householders and tenants and to all those who occupied land or tenements with an annual value of not less than 10 pounds. The effect of the act was to bring into being an electorate in which working men were in a majority. The consequence of these developments was to be party government.

The size of the new electorate meant that the voters could be reached only through some well-developed organization, and the result was to be the growth of organized and mass-membership political parties. The Conservative National Union and the National Liberal Federation were formed in order to facilitate and encourage the support of the new electors. However, contact with the voters was insufficient in itself to entice their support. Not only had a large section of the population been enfranchised, it was a notably different electorate from that which had existed previously. The new class of electors had different and greater demands than those of the existing middle-class electors. If the votes of working men were to be obtained, the parties had to offer them something. And the parties could fulfil their promises only if they presented a uniform program to the electorate and achieved a cohesive majority in the House of Commons to carry through that program. What this was to produce was a shift of power away from the House of Commons to the cabinet and to the electorate, with political parties serving as the conduit for this transfer.

The electorate proved too large and too politically unsophisticated to evaluate the merits of an individual MP's behavior. Political parties provided the labels with which electors could identify, and elections became gladiatorial contests between parties rather than between individual candidates. The all-or-nothing spoils of an election victory and the method of election encouraged (if it not always produced) a contest between two major parties.[15] And having voted for party candidates, the electors expected the members returned to Parliament to support the program offered by their leaders at the election. Party cohesion soon became a feature of parliamentary life.[16] The House of Commons in effect lost two of the most important functions ascribed to it by Bagehot, those of legislation and of choosing the government: the former passed to the cabinet and the latter to the electorate. The cabinet constituted the leaders of the party enjoying a parliamentary majority. It assumed the initiative for the formulation and introduction of measures of national policy and became increasingly reluctant to be overruled by the House. The growth in the number and complexity of bills further limited the influence of the individual MP. Increasingly, his role became one of supporting his leaders. The cabinet had previously rested its authority on the support of the House; now it derived its authority from the electors. As Mackintosh states, "The task of the House of Commons became one of supporting the Cabinet chosen at the polls and passing its legislation. . . . By the 1900s, the Cabinet dominated British government."[17]

Further modifications and addenda took place in the first half of the twentieth century. The House of Lords was forced by statute in 1911 to accept its diminished status. The franchise was variously extended, most notably to half the population previously excluded because of their sex. The monarch's political influence further receded. The growth and increasing economic weight of groups generated more extensive and complex demands of government. And the size of government grew as its responsibilities expanded.

Basically, though, the essential features of the political system were those established in the preceding century. The responsibility for making public policy rested with the government, a government derived from and resting its support upon a political party. That same party's majority in the House of Commons ensured that the government's measures were approved. Formal and political constraints limited the effect of any opposition from the House of Lords. The monarch gave formal assent to any legislative measure approved by the two houses. Thus, within the formal framework of deciding public policy, the government was dominant. The role of Parliament became largely but not wholly one of legitimating the measures put before it. For the monarch, that became the exclusive role (that is, in respect of legislation). Government, as we shall see, operated within a political environment that imposed important constraints, but the limitations imposed formerly by Parliament and the monarch were largely eroded. Britain retained a parliamentary form of government, but what that meant was not government by Parliament but government through Parliament.

The Welfare State and the Managed Economy

To comprehend some of the problems faced by British government in the 1980s it is necessary to know not only the structure and relationships of the political system but also the popular expectations and the burden of responsibilities borne by government. Those expectations and responsibilities have not been static. Just as the governmental structure has been modified in response to political demands, so the responsibilities of government have grown as greater social and economic demands have been made of it.

Toward the end of the nineteenth century and more especially in the twentieth, the responsibilities of government expanded. In part this was attributable to the growth of the Empire. It was also attributable to the increasing demands and expectations of the newly enfranchised working population. Government began to conceive its duties as extending beyond those of maintaining law and order and of defending the realm. The statute book began to expand, with the addition of measures of social reform. Various such measures were enacted in the years prior to 1867, though the most notable were to be enacted in the remaining decades of the century. They included measures to limit working hours for women and children, to improve housing and public health, to make education for children compulsory, to provide for the safety of workers (including the payment of compensation by employers in the event of accidents at work), and even to extend the right to strike.[18] Such measures, exploited for electoral advantage, were within the capabilities of the government to provide. They did not create too great an economic burden; they were not themselves economic measures.

The growth of expectations and the greater willingness of government to intervene in areas previously considered inviolate was to be continued and become more marked in the twentieth century. The general election of 1906 was something of a watershed in British politics. It was the first election to be fought essentially on national issues and it witnessed the return not only of a reforming Liberal government but also, and in some respects more significantly, of 27 Labour MPs. The Labour party had been created for the purpose of ensuring working-class representation in Parliament, and from 1906 onward class became a significant influence in voting behavior. The nature of electoral conflict changed as the Labour party succeeded the Liberal as the main opposition party to the Conservatives. The franchise was further extended, notably in 1918 and 1928, and new expectations were generated by the experience of the two world wars.

During the First World War (1914–1918), socialists within the Labour party argued the case for the conscription of wealth (public ownership) to accompany the conscription of labor (the drafting of men into the armed forces). Politicians fueled rather than played down the belief that Britain should become, in the words of one politician, "a land fit for heroes" once "the war to end all wars" was won—in other words, that provision should be made for those who had fought for King and Country. The period of the Second World War (1939–1945) witnessed a significant shift of attitudes by a sizable fraction of the electorate. One informed estimate was that by December 1942, about two out of every five people had changed their political outlook since the beginning of the war.[19] The direction in which opinion was moving was toward the left of the political spectrum. There was a reaction against (Conservative) government unpreparedness for war in the 1930s and against those who had not done more to solve the nation's problems during the Depression. There was support for calls for equality of sacrifice. There was some degree of goodwill toward the Soviet Union as a wartime ally. There was also, very importantly, the enhanced position of the Labour party. It had entered into Coalition in 1940 (its leader, Clement Attlee, became deputy prime minister to Churchill) and had demonstrated its claim to be a capable partner in government. As the 1940s progressed, there developed a notable movement, including within the Conservative party, for a greater degree of social and economic intervention by government. This was to find some authoritative expression during the war years themselves and more especially in the years after 1945, when a general election resulted in the return of the first Labour government with a clear working majority in the House of Commons. The period of the 1940s and the 1950s was to produce what Samuel Beer has referred to as the welfare state and the managed economy, or what some commentators have referred to as the period of the social democratic consensus.

The welfare state and the managed economy did not suddenly emerge full-blown in this period. The preceding decades had not witnessed governments unresponsive to electoral expectations and the nation's problems. The Liberal government before the First World War had made the first tentative steps in the introduction of old-age pensions (1908) and national health and unemployment insurance (1911). The interwar years had seen the introduction of a number of significant measures of social reform, especially those associated with Neville Chamberlain as minister of health. He proposed to the cabinet 25 measures and secured the enactment of 21 of them. These included unemployment insurance, public health and housing, and the extension of old-age pensions. Much of this legislation, as one biographer noted, "has an important place in the development of the Welfare State."[20] The government also began to engage in certain measures of economic management. It embarked on a protectionist policy and in return for the grant of a tariff to an industry, demanded that its major producers should reorganize themselves. Such producers were encouraged to reduce capacity and maintain prices. The gold standard was abandoned, the pound was devalued, and interest rates were lowered. The government even proved willing to take certain industries into public ownership: broadcasting, overseas airways, and the electricity-generating industry. By indulging in such policies, Professor Beer has contended, government was beginning to move in the direction of a managed economy.[21] The movement, though, was modest. Government adhered to the prevailing orthodoxy that balanced budgets were necessary and desirable and that deficit financing was neither. Ministers showed little desire to emulate the innovative approach adopted in the United States by Franklin Roosevelt during the period of the first New Deal. (Indeed, Conservative leader Stanley Baldwin commented at one point that the United States Constitution had broken down and was giving way to dictatorship.)[22] Britain and the United States were similar, though, in that both were to be brought out of the Depression of the 1930s not by government economic policies but by rearmament and the Second World War.

Two major documents published in the war years provided the planks for the final emergence of the welfare state and managed economy. These were the Report on Social Insurance and Allied Services by Sir William Beveridge (the so-called Beveridge Report), published in November 1942, and the White Paper on Full Employment, published in 1944. The former proposed a comprehensive scheme of social security, one to provide "social insurance against interruption and destruction of earning power and for special expenditure arising at birth, marriage or death."[23] The latter was significant because of its opening pledge: "The Government accepts as one of their primary aims and responsibilities the maintenance of a high and stable level of employment after the war." There was also one particularly significant measure of social reform enacted during wartime: the 1944 Education Act, pioneered by R. A. Butler. The Act provided for the division among primary, secondary, and higher education—and, within secondary education, between secondary modern and grammar schools—that was to form the basis of the educational system for more than a generation.

The welfare state was brought to fruition by the establishment of the National Health Service (NHS) in 1948, entailing the nationalization of hospitals and the provision of free medical treatment, and by the passage of the 1945 Family Allowance Act, the 1946 National Insurance Act, and the 1948 National Assistance Act. The principle enunciated by the Beveridge Report was largely put into practice. National insurance ensured a certain level of benefit in the event of unemployment or sickness. For those who required special help there was "national assistance," the provision of noncontributory benefits dispensed on the basis of means-testing. There were family allowances for those with children. The state now provided something of a protective safety net from the cradle to the grave. It was still possible to pay for private treatment in the health service, but for most people it was a case of having treatment "on the national health." The NHS became a feature of some pride at home and of considerable interest abroad.

Acceptance and usage of techniques pioneered by the economist J. M. Keynes ushered in the managed economy. Government accepted responsibility for keeping aggregate monetary demand at a level sufficient to ensure full employment or what was considered as far as possible to constitute full employment (an unemployment rate of 1% or 2% was considered acceptable), and the annual Budget was to be used as the main instrument of economic policy. The Labour government proved unwilling to pursue a more overtly socialist approach; physical controls acquired during wartime were eventually discarded and those industries that were nationalized, such as steel and the railways, were basically essential and loss-making concerns. Government was prepared to pursue a managed rather than a controlled economy.

The Conservative party was returned to office in 1951 and was to remain there until 1964. It accepted, or appeared to accept, both the welfare state and Keynesian techniques of demand management. Indeed, it gave the impression of making a success of both. As heir to the Disraelian belief in elevating the condition of the people and as a party seeking to enhance its image among working class voters, the Conservative Party could claim both a principled as well as a practical motive for maintaining the innovations of its predecessor. At the same time, it was reluctant to pursue policies that would increase the tax burden or the public sector of the economy. Good fortune was with the government: world economic conditions improved and heralded a period of sustained growth in industrial output and trade. Government revenue was such that not only was it possible to sustain and indeed expand expenditure on the national health service, it was possible to do so without substantial increases in taxation. Indeed, reductions rather than increases in tax rates were a feature of the period. There was an extensive and successful house-building program. Economic prosperity allowed government to maintain peace with the labor unions by allowing high wage settlements. It was also possible finally to abandon many of the controls maintained since wartime. Government was able to claim to have maintained full employment, an expanding economy, stable prices, and a strong pound. Despite the agonies of withdrawing from Empire and various undulations in economic performance, the decade of the 1950s was seen more than anything as "an age of affluence."[24] In July 1957, Prime Minister Harold Macmillan was able to declare that, for most of the people, "You've never had it so good."

The 1960s witnessed a downturn in economic performance and a growing realization that, in comparative terms, Britain was faring less well than many of her continental neighbors. The Conservative government of Harold Macmillan responded with various novel proposals, including indicative economic planning and an application to join the European Economic Community. The succeeding Labour government of Harold Wilson, returned to office in 1964, sought a more comprehensive method of national economic planning as part of its grand design of modernization. Inflation and unemployment became more visible problems.

Despite the economic problems and some unrelated political problems of the 1960s, the country remained a relatively prosperous one. Living conditions continued to improve. The rise in wages exceeded the rise in inflation. Where economic conditions impinged on the ability to maintain the welfare state, it was essentially at the margin: government imposed nominal charges for medicines obtained on NHS prescriptions. Parties tended to argue more about means rather than ends. The consensus that developed in the 1950s remained intact.

POLITICAL CULTURE AND CONTEMPORARY PROBLEMS

This brief survey not only provides some historical depth to an understanding of contemporary British government—its structure, responsibilities, and political dominance—it also serves to reinforce our grasp of the political culture and to provide in part an explanation for some of the problems now associated with government.

History and Political Culture

From the foregoing sketch one can recognize not only the features of the political culture outlined in the preceding chapter but also the convergence of those features and their interplay with the experience of history. An empirical orientation to change and a conditional relationship between governors and governed are long-standing characteristics of political life. Clearly, government has been shaped by no grand design. Change has been piecemeal and largely incremental. Although the governed have been largely prepared to defer to those in power, their deference has been conditional. If presumed rights and privileges were ignored or dispensed with, the appropriate action was taken to restore them (e.g., the Magna Carta, the beheading of Charles I). The other orientations can be identified from the experience of reform in the nineteenth and early twentieth centuries.

The reforms of the nineteenth century were facilitated not only by an empirical orientation to change but also by the paternalism of political leaders. *Noblesse oblige* (privilege entails responsibility) is a foreign phrase but it embodies a very British concept. Many of the country's aristocratic leaders believed that they had a duty to help improve the condition of the working man. The point should not be overemphasized, since on occasion this sense of duty was not so much a cause of action but a post hoc justification of it. Nonetheless, it was important. It combined with need (to avoid social unrest) and political expediency (to steal the thunder of one's opponents) to produce franchise extension.

Increasingly, change was more easily accommodated as political relationships changed. By the twentieth century, the hegemony of government in the political process ensured that measures could be carried through Parliament without too much difficulty. Equally important, once approved by Parliament, reforms were accepted by the populace and by those at whom they were directed. The widening of the franchise in the nineteenth century, House of Lords reform, and votes for women in the twentieth—these are issues that aroused great emotion and were fiercely opposed but on which reform was accepted once the government of the day had got the measure accepted by Parliament. This in part reflects the orientation toward cooperation. It also may be seen as the product of an allegiant orientation to the political system. The widening of the franchise extended the input of citizens into the political system. The passage of measures of social and economic reform appeared to be meeting their needs.

Equally important, Britons have been taught that the political system works. Although the media of political socialization have changed over time, the content has not. There has been an emphasis on, and lauding of, the continuity and stability. Historically, as we have seen, the country has been rent by various upheavals, sometimes of a quite violent nature. The English Civil War was far from bloodless. The opinion of foreigners, wrote an English scholar in 1704, is "that there have been more shakes and convulsions in the government of England than in that of any other nation."[25] There have been various shakes since—social, economic, and political. In the popular mind, though, such convulsions have not figured largely. "What makes the history of England so eminently valuable," wrote T. H. Buckle, "is that nowhere else has the national progress been so little interfered with, either for good or evil."[26] British government has been accepted as the product of the collected wisdom of many generations, indeed of many centuries. It flatters the British mind, and certainly the English mind, to look upon it as the envy of the world. The Constitution has been lauded as "a living organism in a condition of perpetual growth."[27] George III described it as "the most perfect of human formations."[28] Only recently, in 1981, one member of Parliament declared that, distinguished from other constitutions, "our constitution is the envy of the world."[29] The virtues of the Westminster model of government have been widely extolled. They became embodied in what was taught in British schools. They became part of received wisdom, and to some extent, they remain so.

The British have not been alone in such teaching. British parliamentary government has found its admirers abroad as well, and not least in the United States.[30] Especially in the 1950s and 1960s, the capacity of the party in government to enact a party program was compared with the brokered politics of the American system. It was a comparison that generated some calls for reform; most notable among these was James MacGregor Burns in *The Deadlock of Democracy* published in 1963, arguing the case essentially for the equivalent in the United States of a "responsible party system." Such calls were to extend into the following decade. Charles Hardin cited British experience in contending that "party government—if it can be attained— provides the best hope that our government will be able to meet its problems."[31] Although not all observers wished to emulate British experience, their analyses appeared edged with a touch of envy. In more recent years, such perceptions have waned.

Contemporary Ills and Analyses

In the 1970s, conditions in Britain began to change. Economic indicators worsened considerably, and unemployment rose dramatically (see Chapter 1). By 1973, Britain had the lowest growth rate of the major industrialized nations. Between 1974 and 1978 there was an annual rate of increase in retail prices in excess of 17%. Industrial disputes became more serious: there were more working days lost through such disputes in the period from 1970 to 1978 than there were in the whole of the period from 1946 to 1969.[32] In less than 30 years, the British economy had declined from being one of the strongest to one of the weakest in Europe. Successive governments encountered problems in responding to the changed conditions and in raising resources to meet public expectations. Britain was overshadowed by a body of which, until 1973, it was not a member—the European Communities. Government was increasingly constrained by the activities of economically powerful groups, both at home and abroad (notably, in the latter case, the International Monetary Fund). Although parliamentary government did not cease to work, it no longer appeared to be working in the way that it had in the past. The positive picture of British government began to lose its gloss; academics who had previously written about the political system in positive terms now turned their attention to the problem inherent in that system. British parliamentary government began to assume the status of a rejected lover.

The diagnoses of Britain's problems have been as varied as the problems themselves. Some diagnoses are primarily economic. A number of economists have placed some of the blame for poor economic performance on a failure to modernize (there has been a tendency to retain old plants and to support traditional but declining industries, such as textiles); on the emphasis given to maintaining a balance of payments surplus in order to fund overseas military spending and foreign investments, pursued at the expense of economic growth;[33] and on a failure of postwar economic management to manipulate supply as well as demand.[34] Others have stressed the legacies of former international glory, attitudes, and institutions derived from the days when Britain was at the center of the world economy, acting as a barrier to necessary change.[35]

Some diagnoses have been primarily sociological. As we have seen (Chapter 1), class did not displace status in British society. Preindustrial aristocratic attitudes were carried over into an industrial age. These attitudes included looking down on the pursuit of trade and commerce as somewhat inferior socially. Low priority was given to industry and science and, so the analysis goes, a tendency grew for those with wealth and some ability to avoid management in favor of professional pursuits such as the law.[36] Some blame has also been imputed to the egalitarianism of the labor movement, harboring dislike of profits and risk-taking as well as the values of thrift and self-reliance that underpin the operation of the free market.[37] In short, the attitudes of both the social elite and the labor movement have served to hinder economic growth.

The other diagnoses are essentially political. They are important in the context of later chapters and hence deserve some attention. The historical background provided in this chapter helps us understand some of these diagnoses as well as some of the prescriptions. The three main diagnoses are those of government overload, adversary politics, and pluralist stagnation. Prescriptions have included decentralization, electoral reform, and more radical economic policies.

The thesis of government overload is that as the responsibilities of government have increased, its capacity to meet them has decreased: the combination of these two features has resulted in an overloading of government.[38] A government White Paper in 1970 declared that government had been attempting to do too much. "This has placed an excessive burden on industry, and on the people of the country as a whole, and has also overloaded the government machine itself. . . . The weakness has shown itself in the apparatus of policy formulation and in the quality of many government decisions over the past 25 years."[39] Some writers have argued that the problem of overload has been made worse by the centralization of government decision-making.[40] Centralized government, so the argument goes, has proved too large and too far removed from the problems with which it seeks to cope. Distance from those affected by government decisions has had the effect of increasing their indifference and sense of alienation, especially in the economically disadvantaged regions furthest from London. Government, according to the Royal Commission on the Constitution in 1973, was viewed as being too remote.[41]

A compatible but independent thesis is that of adversary politics. It contends that attempts to generate institutions capable of dealing with Britain's long-term economic problems are thwarted by a political system that encourages an adversary relationship between the two main political parties, one that enables them to alternate in office so that each undoes the work of the other.[42] The consequence, it is argued, is policy discontinuity, making it difficult if not impossible for industrialists and investors to plan ahead. The adversary relationship also encourages a constant escalation of promises by the parties, each seeking to out-promise the other in order to win the all-or-nothing spoils of a general election victory. When, as happened in the 1970s, the resources are no longer available to meet the promises made, disenchantment with the political system begins to develop. Furthermore, the parties are unable to respond adequately to such developments because of an unwillingness to tamper with a system that works to their mutual advantage. In short, Britain has a political system that is malfunctional and not amenable to radical reform.

Pluralist stagnation suggests that the problem lies with the growth of groups in British society, each group pursuing its own interest. Those groups have brought pressure to bear on government to provide resources or pursue policies to the benefit of their members. Such has been the economic leverage of some groups that the role of government has become increasingly one of arbiter between the demands of groups rather than one of policy leader.[43] The tendency of government to wish to avoid conflict has resulted in political inertia, government being unwilling to pursue policies that would generate sustained opposition from well-entrenched groups.[44] The problem has been made worse, according to Samuel Beer, by the numerical growth of such groups. Because there are so many, self-restraint in making demands of government would bring no discernible benefit to any one group. As a result, even though recognizing the need for restraint, a group is tempted to raise its own claims. Other groups then compete to raise theirs. "The source of the problem," argues Beer, "is not a lack of knowledge, but the structure of the situation, which continues to have compelling force even when participants recognise its tendencies. Their numerical pluralism makes it difficult, if not impossible, to make and enforce a bargain, tacit or explicit, that would achieve moderation. If there were only a few, each could know what the others were doing and all would be aware of being watched. But pluralism destroys the basis for such a self-enforcing social contract."[45] For government the problem is thus an acute one. It has fewer benefits to dispense than previously, yet is faced with a plethora of interests, each of which is unwilling to moderate its demands in the interests of all.

These constitute the main political analyses that see the problem as a structural one. There are others that do not see it as structural. The two largest parties in Britain, the Conservative and Labour parties, view Britain's problems as stemming from the pursuit in the past of inadequate policies (Chapter 6). There are other analyses that go beyond the structural or policy analyses, providing somewhat more complex explanations. The most important of these is that provided by Professor Beer in his recent work *Britain Against Itself*. He argues that there is no single causal explanation for

Britain's decline; rather, it has to be seen as resulting from a convergence of pluralist stagnation, a decline of class, and a revolt against authority. The result has been fragmentation in political life. "The outcome has been incoherence and immobilism; drift, not mastery. It is not hyperbole to call it a paralysis of public choice."[46]

I shall return to these analyses in appropriate chapters, responding in particular to Beer's sophisticated analysis in the conclusion. For the moment, two concluding points need to be made. The first, rather obviously, is that no one approach is without its detractors. Each approach has its limitations and these I shall seek to draw out at appropriate points in the text. The second equally obvious point is that, given the disparate analyses, a variety of prescriptions have been offered for dealing with the presumed causes of the nation's ills. Exponents of the government overload thesis tend to favor reform of central government machinery and decentralization of government. Those who adhere to the adversary politics thesis support, for reasons that will be explained later, a reform of the electoral system. Pluralist stagnation, according to Beer's analysis, can be overcome only by mobilizing popular consent through restoring trust in government.[47] For the Conservative and Labour parties the answer lies in (different) radical economic policies. So wide are the analyses and the prescriptions that one is tempted to wonder whether the concept of pluralist stagnation might itself be applied to the political analysis of Britain's ills.

My own argument I will draw together in the conclusion. For the moment, suffice it to say that I take a skeptical view of the structural analyses offered. They are unproven and overexaggerated and they miss the essential point. The problem is not primarily a structural one—structures are dependent variables. The independent variable on which one has to focus is the political culture. The political culture may have helped generate problems of political structure, but Britain's problems, I will argue, are not essentially political: they are economic and social. And the political culture is one that provides government with the breathing space necessary to address itself to those problems. Government may not succeed, but the opportunity is there and in order to understand that one has to understand the political culture and the extent to which it endures. The decline in the culture detected by Beer is relative. The orientations of the political culture identified in the preceding chapter remain. I concluded that chapter by suggesting that the important question was not "why had there been a decline in the civic culture," but rather "why had that decline not been greater?" The answer to that question, and the implications of it for the British polity of the 1980s, will form the basis of the final chapter. My conclusion will not necessarily be an optimistic one—it will emphasize potential rather than expectation—but it will lack the negative connotations attached to the foregoing analyses. It will also forgo structural change as the primary prescription. What is important is attitudes, not structures.

NOTES

1. See A. H. Dodd, *The Growth of Responsible Government* (Routledge & Kegan Paul, 1956), pp. 43–44.

2. B. Kemp, *King and Commons 1660–1832* (Macmillan, 1957), p. 3.

3. Its provisions included, for example, "That excessive Baile ought not to be required nor excessive Fines imposed nor cruell and unusuall Punishments inflicted." Compare this with the Eighth Amendment to the United States Constitution, which prescribes that "Excessive bail shall not be required, nor excessive fines imposed, nor cruel and unusual punishments inflicted."

4. J. H. Plumb, *England in the Eighteenth Century* (Penguin, 1950), p. 50.

5. J. Mackintosh, *The British Cabinet,* 2nd ed. (Methuen, 1968), pp. 50–51.

6. Ibid., p. 64.

7. S. M. Lipset, *The First New Nation* (Heinemann, 1964); P. Mathias, *The First Industrial Nation* (Methuen, 1969).

8. Sir L. Woodward, *The Age of Reform 1815–1870,* 2nd ed. (Oxford University Press, 1962), p. 3.

9. A table compiled in 1815 revealed that 144 peers, along with 123 commoners, controlled 471 seats (more than two-thirds of the total number) in the House of Commons. M. Ostrogorski, *Democracy and the Organisation of Political Parties,* Vol. 1: England (Macmillan, 1902), p. 20.

10. J. B. Conacher (ed.), *The Emergence of British Parliamentary Democracy in the Nineteenth Century* (Wiley, 1971), p. 10. Different authors cite different figures.

11. W. Bagehot, *The English Constitution* (first published 1867; Fontana ed., 1963), p. 150.

12. Mackintosh, p. 113.

13. See Conacher, pp. 68–69, for a summary.

14. See H. J. Hanham, *Elections and Party Management,* 3rd ed. (Harvester Press, 1978), p. xii.

15. Similarly, in the United States the all-or-nothing spoils of presidential victory have encouraged two rather than many parties. See M. Vile, *Politics in the USA* (Hutchinson, 1976 ed.), pp. 62–63.

16. A. L. Lowell, *The Government of England,* Vol. II (Macmillan, 1924), pp. 76–78.

17. Mackintosh, p. 174.

18. Many of the reforms were introduced by Conservative governments. See C. E. Bellairs, *Conservative Social and Industrial Reform* (Conservative Central Office, 1977).

19. P. Addison, *The Road to 1945* (Quartet, 1977), p. 127.

20. I. Macleod, *Neville Chamberlain* (Muller, 1961), p. 123.

21. S. H. Beer, *Modern British Politics* (Faber, 1969 ed.), pp. 278–87.

22. Addison, p. 29.

23. *Social Insurance and Allied Services—Report by Sir William Beveridge,* Cmnd. 6404 (Her Majesty's Stationery Office, 1942), para. 17, p. 9.

24. Based on the title of Vernon Bogdanor and Robert Skidelsky (eds.), *The Age of Affluence 1951–1964* (Macmillan, 1970).

25. G. Botero, *The Reason of State,* quoted in K. Thomas, "The United

Kingdom" in R. Grew (ed), *Crises of Political Development in Europe and the United States* (Princeton University Press, 1978), pp. 45–46.

26. H. T. Buckle, *History of Civilization in England,* quoted in Thomas, p. 44.

27. S. Low, *Governance of England* (1904), quoted in G. Marshall and G. Moodie, *Some Problems of the Constitution,* 4th rev. ed. (Hutchinson, 1967), p. 18.

28. Quoted in P. Norton, *The Constitution in Flux* (Martin Robertson, 1982), p. 23.

29. *House of Commons Debates,* Sixth Series, Vol. 2, col. 1213.

30. See L. D. Epstein, "What Happened to the British Party Model?" *American Political Science Review,* 74 (1), March 1980, pp. 9–22.

31. C. M. Hardin, *Presidential Power and Accountability: Towards a New Constitution* (University of Chicago Press, 1974), p. 139.

32. The total number of working days lost in 1970–1978 inclusive was 98,974. The figure for 1946–1969 inclusive was 76,409. Figures calculated from D. Butler and A. Sloman, *British Political Facts 1900–1979* (Macmillan, 1980), p. 341.

33. See, e.g., W. A. P. Manser, *Britain in Balance* (Penguin, 1973).

34. A. Gamble, "Explanations of Economic Decline." Paper presented at the Political Studies Association Conference, Newcastle-upon-Tyne, 1983, p. 5. This paragraph draws heavily on this paper.

35. See A. Gamble, *Britain in Decline* (Macmillan, 1981).

36. See, e.g., M. Postan, *An Economic History of Western Europe 1945–64* (Methuen, 1967); and A. Gamble, "Explanations of Economic Decline," pp. 13–14.

37. See Sir K. Joseph, *Stranded on the Middle Ground* (Centre for Policy Studies, 1976).

38. See A. King, "The Problem of Overload" in A. King (ed.), *Why Is Britain Becoming Harder to Govern?* (BBC, 1976), pp. 8–30.

39. *The Reorganisation of Central Government,* Cmnd. 4506 (Her Majesty's Stationery Office, 1970), p. 3.

40. See, for example, D. Owen, *Face the Future* (Oxford University Press, 1981).

41. *The Royal Commission on the Constitution 1969–1973,* Vol. 1: Report. Cmnd. 5460 (Her Majesty's Stationery Office, 1973), p. 30.

42. See especially S. E. Finer (ed.), *Adversary Politics and Electoral Reform* (Anthony Wigram, 1975).

43. See S. H. Beer, *Modern British Politics* (Faber, 1969 ed.).

44. See I. Gilmour, *The Body Politic,* rev. ed. (Hutchinson, 1971); J. E. S. Hayward, *Political Inertia* (University of Hull, 1975).

45. S. H. Beer, *Britain Against Itself* (Faber, 1982), p. 31.

46. Ibid., p. 2.

47. Ibid., Conclusion.

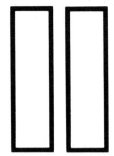

The Political Environment

The Uncodified Constitution

A CONSTITUTION MAY BE DEFINED as a body of laws, customs, and conventions that define the composition and powers of organs of the state and that regulate the relations of the various state organs to one another and to the private citizen.[1]

The United States has a constitution; so does the United Kingdom. Expressed in purely formal terms (Table 4.1) there is very little similarity between them. Indeed, the differences are such that to the student weaned on a study of the United States Constitution, the British Constitution is nearly incomprehensible. Even to the student of British politics it is not well understood. Nonetheless, the differences should not be emphasized to the exclusion of certain common features. Both Constitutions are strong ones in that they reflect and reinforce their respective political cultures.

The United States Constitution is considered by Americans to embody the principles of a higher law, to constitute "in fact imperfect man's most perfect rendering of what Blackstone saluted as 'the eternal immutable laws of good and evil, to which the creator himself in all his dispensations conforms: and which he has enabled human reason to discover, so far as they are necessary for the conduct of human actions.'"[2] As the embodiment of a higher law, it thus not only needs to be distinguished from ordinary law but also needs to be protected from the passing whims of politicians—hence the introduction of extraoradinary procedures for its amendment.

By contrast, the British Constitution is admired by Britons for reflecting

59

TABLE 4.1
American and British Constitutions

Characteristics	Constitutions	
	United States	United Kingdom
Form of expression	Written	Part written but un-codified
Date and manner of formulation	1787 by a constitutional convention	No one date of formulation; no precise manner of formulation
Means of formal amendment	By two-thirds majorities in both Houses of Congress and by ratification of three-quarters of the states, or by conventions	No extraordinary provisions for amendment
Location of its provisions	The written document (judicial decisions, custom usage, works of authority)	Statute law, common law, conventions, works of authority
Bodies responsible for interpretation of its provisions	The judiciary primarily (can be overridden by constitutional amendment)	The judiciary (statute and common law), scholars and politicians (conventions)
Main provisions	Document as "supreme law," judicial review, separation and overlap of powers, federal system, bill of rights, republican form of government	Parliamentary sovereignty, "rule of law," unitary system, parliamentary government under a constitutional monarchy
Public promulgation of its provisions (in textbooks, etc.)	Extensive	Infrequent

the wisdom of past generations, as the product of experience—in short, a constitution that stipulates what should be on the basis of what has proved to work rather than on abstract first principles. The empirical orientation to change that underpins such a constitution also favors flexibility in amendment: as conditions change, so some amendment may be necessary. Formal extraordinary procedures for its amendment have not been found necessary.

The differences in political culture have thus produced somewhat different constitutions, but the attachment to them is similar in the two countries. Also, as we shall see, there are certain similarities in sources and in the means of interpretation.

FORMS OF EXPRESSION

New nations from the eighteenth century onward have found it both necessary and useful to codify their constitutions. At the time that the Founding
Fathers promulgated the United States Constitution in Philadelphia, a written constitution was exceptional. Today it is the norm. Having lacked the
opportunity to create a new constitutional framework afresh from first principles, Britain now stands out as one of the few nations lacking such a
document.

The absence of a written constitution similar to that of the United States
and other nations has led to the British Constitution being described as
unwritten, but such a description is misleading. As we shall see, various
elements of the Constitution find expression in formal, written enactments.
What distinguishes the British Constitution from others is not that it is
unwritten, but rather that it is part-written and uncodified. The lack of
codification is of especial importance. It makes it difficult to identify clearly
and authoritatively what constitute the provisions of the Constitution. There
are certain principles that are clearly at the heart of the Constitution, parliamentary sovereignty being the prime example, but there are many provisions, be they expressed through statute law or the writings of constitutional
experts, that are of constitutional significance but on which there is no clear
agreement that they form part of the British Constitution. It is this lack of
codified certainty that makes a study of it so fraught with difficulty.

SOURCES

Because one cannot have recourse to one simple authoritative document to
discover the provisions of the Constitution, one has instead to research four
separate sources: statute law, common law, conventions, and works of authority. Such sources are also relevant in analyses of the United States
Constitution. Congress may pass measures of constitutional significance, for
example, certain stipulations of electoral law or the War Powers Act. Provisions of the Constitution are developed and molded by judicial decisions. In
seeking to interpret the Constitution, the courts may have recourse to works
by constitutional experts. The difference between the two countries is that in
Britain such sources are primary sources, and in the United States, the
primary source is the written document.

Of the four sources, statute law is perhaps the best understood and
nowadays, the most extensive. It provides the main source for the part-
written element of the Constitution. It comprises acts of Parliament and
subordinate legislation made under the authority of the parent act. Many
acts of Parliament that have been passed clearly merit the title of constitutional law. Acts that define the powers of the various state organs (for exam-

ple, the 1911 and 1949 Parliament Acts) and acts that define the relationship between Crown and Parliament (notably the Bill of Rights of 1689), between the component elements of the nation (the Act of Union with Scotland of 1706, for example), between the United Kingdom and the European Communities (the 1972 European Communities Act), and between the state and the individual (as with the Habeas Corpus Act of 1679 or the Administration of Justice Act of 1960) clearly constitute important provisions of the Constitution. They are published in authoritative, written form and, as acts of Parliament, are interpreted by the courts. This is the most important of the four sources both in quantitative and qualitative terms. It has increasingly displaced common law as the most extensive form of law in Britain and it is the most definitive of the four. It takes precedence over any conflicting common law and is superior to the conventions of the Constitution and to works of authority. Its precedence derives from the concept of parliamentary sovereignty.

Common law constitutes the law and customs of ancient lineage that have been upheld as law by the courts in cases decided before them. Once a court has upheld a provision as being part of common law it creates a precedent to be followed by other courts. In past centuries, when few statutes were enacted, common law constituted the main body of English law; today, it has been largely but not wholly displaced by statute law. Certain principles derived from common law remain fundamental to the Constitution, and these include the principle of parliamentary sovereignty.

Under the heading of common law comes also prerogative powers—the powers and privileges recognized by common law as belonging to the monarch. Although many prerogative powers have been displaced by statute, many matters at the heart of government are still determined under the authority of the prerogative. These include the appointment of ministers, the making of treaties, and power of pardon, the dispensing of honors, and the declaration of war. By convention, such powers are normally exercised formally by the monarch on the advice of ministers (the ministers, in practice, take the decisions). There is no formal requirement that Parliament assent to such decisions. This is in stark contrast to the position in the United States, where Congress alone has the formal power to declare war and the Senate's consent is necessary for the ratification of treaties and the appointment of federal public officers. (In practice, the differences are not that great: "presidential wars" have been waged without a congressional declaration of war, while in Britain a government taking military action abroad will seek the consent of Parliament.) In 1972, the Treaty of Accession to the European Communities was signed under prerogative powers. In 1982, a naval task force was despatched to the Falkland Islands under the same authority. Although diminishing in number, prerogative powers clearly remain of great importance.

Generally included under the generic heading of common law is the judicial interpretation of statute law. Unlike those in the United States, British courts have no power to hold a measure unconstitutional. They are limited to the interpretation of provisions of acts of Parliament. Even in exercising their power of interpretation, they are limited by rules of interpretation and by precedent. (The exception is the House of Lords, the highest domestic court of appeal, which is not now bound by its previous decisions.) Nonetheless, judges retain the power to distinguish cases and by their interpretation they can develop a substantial body of case law. In interpreting acts of Parliament, they assume Parliament to have meant what, on the face of it, the words of an act appear to mean. Unlike the United States Supreme Court, which can delve deep into the deliberations of the Founding Fathers to try to elucidate what was meant by a particular provision of the Constitution, British courts are not permitted to look at the proceedings of Parliament in order to determine what Parliament really meant.

The third and least tangible source of the Constitution is that of convention. Conventions of the Constitution are most aptly described as rules that are considered binding by and upon those who are responsible for making the Constitution work, but rules that are not enforced by the courts or by the presiding officers in either house of Parliament.[3] They derive their strength from the realization that not to abide by them would make for an unworkable constitution. They are, so to speak, the oil in the formal machinery of the Constitution. They help fill the gap between the constitutional formality and the political reality. For example, ministers are responsible formally to the monarch. Because of the political changes wrought in the nineteenth century, they are by convention responsible now also to Parliament. By convention, the government of the day resigns or requests a dissolution if a motion of no confidence is carried against it in the House of Commons. By convention, the monarch gives the Royal Assent to all legislative measures approved by Parliament. The last time a monarch refused assent was during the reign of Queen Anne (1702–1714). Queen Victoria in the nineteenth century contemplated refusing her assent to a measure but wiser counsels prevailed.

No formal, authoritative documents set forth these rules, and they find no embodiment in statute law. The courts may recognize them, but the courts have no power to enforce them. They are complied with because of the recognition of what would happen if they were not complied with. For the Queen to refuse her assent to a measure passed by the two Houses of Parliament would draw her into the realms of political controversy, hence jeopardizing the claim of the monarch to be "above politics." A government that sought to remain in office after losing a vote of confidence in the House of Commons would find its position politically untenable: it would lack the political authority to govern. For ministers to ignore Parliament completely would prove equally untenable.

Some conventions may be described as being stronger than others. Some on occasion are breached, while others are adhered to without exception. On three occasions in this century, the convention of collective ministerial responsibility has been suspended temporarily by the prime minister of the day. In contrast, no government has sought to remain in office after losing a parliamentary vote of confidence. The point at which a useful and necessary practice is accorded the status of a constitutional convention is not clear. Once a practice has become well established in terms of the relationship within or between different organs of the state, finding recognition in works of authority and by those involved in its operation, then it may be said to have reached the status of a convention. At any one time, though, there are a number of relationships that may be said to be in a constitutional haze. Is it a convention of the Constitution that the government of the day must consult with interested bodies before formulating a legislative measure for presentation to Parliament? A noted constitutional lawyer, Sir Ivor Jennings, once argued that it was.[4] Prime Minister Harold Wilson appeared to give some credence to this view in 1966 when he said in the House of Commons that it was the *duty* of the government to consult with the Trades Union Congress and the Confederation of British Industry.[5] Few other authorities have supported Jennings' assertion and it has not found acceptance by most practitioners of government. It is usual for governments to engage in such consultation, but it is not yet a convention of the Constitution that they do so.

The fourth and final source of the Constitution is that of works of authority. These have persuasive authority only. What constitutes a "work of authority" is rarely defined. Various early works are accorded particular standing by virtue of the absence of statutes or other written sources covering a particular area. The statements of their writers are presumed to be evidence of judicial decisions that have been lost and are therefore accepted if not contrary to reason.[6] Among the most important early sources are Fitzherbert's *Abridgment* (1516) and Coke's *Institutes of the Law of England* (1628–1644). More recent works have been called in aid on those occasions when jurists and others have sought to delineate features of the contemporary Constitution; this has been the case especially in determining the existence or otherwise of conventions. Such conventions are prescribed neither by statute nor by judicial interpretation, so one must study instead scholarly interpretations of political behavior and practice. Especially important authoritative works in the nineteenth century were those by John Austin and A. V. Dicey. Important names in the twentieth century have included Sir Ivor Jennings, Sir Kenneth Wheare, O. Hood Phillips, and E. C. S. Wade.[7]

Given the disparate sources of the Constitution and the fact that important relationships within and between organs of the state are not laid down in any one formal or binding document, it is not surprising that one must have recourse to books by constitutional scholars to discover the extent and nature of those relationships. Works of authority tend to be consulted more frequently in the field of constitutional law than in any other branch of English law.

MEANS OF AMENDMENT

Given the disparate primary sources of the Constitution and the difficulty in determining where the Constitution begins and ends, it is perhaps not surprising that there are no extraordinary procedures for its amendment. Statute and common law of constitutional significance are subject to amendment by the same process as that employed for other legislative enactments. Conventions can be modified by changes in behavior or by reinterpretations of the significance of certain behavior. Works of authority can be rewritten or subjected to different interpretations in the same way as can other texts.

Much the same can be said about constitutionally significant statute law, judicial decisions, and works of authority in the United States. Even the provisions of the formal document, the United States Constitution, may be amended by judicial decisions and custom usage. The difference between the two countries is that the formal wording of the United States Constitution can be amended only by an extraordinary process, i.e., one that goes beyond the provisions employed for amending the ordinary law. (Because of the extraordinary procedures necessary for amendment, the provisions of the Constitution are sometimes referred to as "entrenched.") No such formal amending procedures exist in Britain, where there is no formal document.

INTERPRETATION

As may be surmised from the foregoing, there is no single body endowed with the responsibility for interpreting the provisions of the Constitution. As in the United States, statute and common law are subject to judicial interpretation, but there is no power of judicial review, at least not as the term is understood in the United States. The courts cannot declare a legislative measure or an executive action contrary to the provisions of the Constitution.

The courts can influence and to some extent mold certain provisions through their interpretation of statute and common law. Indeed, their use of common law has been of especial importance in outlining and protecting certain rights of the individual. However, at the end of the day, they are subject to the wishes of Parliament. Judicial interpretation of statute law can be overridden by a new act of Parliament. By virtue of the concept of parliamentary sovereignty, the act would be definitive. The judges serve to enforce and interpret such acts: they cannot strike down an act.

Identification and interpretation of conventions has little to do with the courts. Conventions arise as a result of changes in the relationships within and between different organs of the state. Their delineation rests with scholars, and their enforcement rests with those at whom they are aimed. As with conventions, they are beyond the purview of the courts.

The Constitution, in short, is subject to interpretation by different bodies, the most prominent being politicians, judges, and scholars. The same can be said of the United States Constitution, but in Britain there is no body that stands in a position analogous to that of the United States Supreme Court. It is an important difference, reflecting the differences in political culture. The Lockean basis of constitutional interpretation in the United States—a higher law cognizable by independent, rational magistrates operating free of outside interests[8]—finds no parallel in Britain.

MAIN PROVISIONS

The central provisions of the Constitution are listed in Table 4.1: parliamentary sovereignty, the rule of law, a unitary (as opposed to a federal) system, and what I have termed parliamentary government under a constitutional monarchy. Although there is some dispute as to whether it should remain so, the preeminent provision is that of parliamentary sovereignty. In the nineteenth century, the great constitutional lawyer A. V. Dicey identified it as being one of the two main pillars of the Constitution, the other being that of the rule of law.[9] Dicey's work has had a major and lasting impact. Despite subsequent criticisms, the two pillars identified by Dicey still stand. While some critics have considered them weak and unnecessary pillars, supporting a crumbling edifice, they remain crucial to an understanding of the British Constitution.

The most succinct definition of parliamentary sovereignty was offered by Dicey. Parliamentary sovereignty, he wrote, meant that Parliament had "the right to make or unmake any law whatever; and, further, that no person or body is recognized by the law of England as having a right to override or set aside the legislation of Parliament."[10] An act passed by Parliament would be enforced by the courts, the courts recognizing no body other than Parliament as having authority to override such an act. Parliament itself could substitute an act for an earlier one. One of the precepts derived from the principle is that Parliament is not bound by its predecessors. Once Parliament has passed an act, it becomes the law of the land. It is not open to challenge before the courts on the grounds of being unconstitutional.

Although Dicey claimed more ancient lineage for it, the principle of parliamentary sovereignty became established as a judicial rule in consequence of the Glorious Revolution of 1688 and subsequent Bill of Rights, which established the relationship between the Crown and Parliament (see

Chapter 3). It was the product of an alliance between Parliament and lawyers and of the intimidation of judges by the House of Commons. Assertion of the principle served to do away with the monarch's previously claimed powers to suspend or dispense with acts of Parliament and it served to deny judges the power to strike down measures. It came to occupy a unique place in constitutional law. The principle finds no expression in statute or any other formal enactment. It exists in common law but enjoys a special status beyond that enjoyed by other principles of common law. Its underpinnings are not only legal but also political and historical. It is now too late to challenge the principle. Judicial obedience to it constitutes what H. W. R. Wade referred to as "the ultimate political fact upon which the whole system of legislation hangs."[11] No statute can confer the power of parliamentary sovereignty, for that would be to confer the very power being acted upon. It is therefore considered to be unique. As Hood Phillips states, "It may indeed be called the one fundamental law of the British Constitution."[12]

The second pillar identified by Dicey was that of "the rule of law." Identifying what is meant by the term is extremely difficult. Few students of the constitution would deny the importance of the tenet. Dicey himself argued that it comprised "at least three distinct though kindred conceptions": "that no man is punishable or can be lawfully made to suffer in body or goods except for a distinct breach of law established in the ordinary legal manner before the ordinary courts of the land"; that "no man is above the law [and] every man, whatever be his rank or condition, is subject to the ordinary law of the realm and amenable to the jurisdiction of the ordinary tribunals"; and that "the general principles of the constitution [are] the result of judicial decisions determining the rights of private persons in particular cases brought before the courts." These three conceptions have been subject to various criticisms: that many of the discretionary powers are vested in officials and public bodies, that many officials and bodies have powers and immunities that the ordinary citizen does not have, and that certain rights have been modified by or enacted in statute. Further it is not clear why Dicey's third conception should be considered "kindred" to the other two. Some students of the Constitution find Dicey's analysis useful, and others tend to be dismissive. The important point for our purposes is that there is no agreed definition.

The rule of law, then, stands as a central element of the British Constitution, but no one is sure precisely what it means. There is some common ground in that it is assumed to imply certain substantive and procedural rights, government must be subject to the law, and the judiciary must be independent. The problem is one of determining what those rights are, how they are to be protected, and how the independence of the judiciary is to be maintained.

There is a further problem. The concept of the rule of law is not logically compatible with that of parliamentary sovereignty. Parliament could if it so wished confer arbitrary powers upon government. It could fetter the independence of the judiciary. It could limit or remove altogether certain rights presumed to exist at common law. The rule of law, in short, could be threatened or even dispensed with by parliamentary enactment. Dicey himself recognized this problem and sought to resolve it. He argued, in essence, that the rule of law prevented government from exercising arbitrary powers. If government wanted such powers, it could obtain them only through Parliament (Parliament itself has never sought to exercise executive powers) and the granting of them could take place only after deliberation and approval by the triumvirate of monarch, Lords, and Commons.[13]

Such an argument serves to explain potential impediments to a government intent on acquiring arbitrary powers. It does not deny the truth of the assertion that Parliament could, if it wished, confer such powers upon government. Indeed, many observers would argue that given the growth of cabinet government, the potential for government to seek and receive such powers is significantly greater now than was the case at the time when Dicey was writing. For many critics of the existing Constitution, parliamentary sovereignty no longer constitutes an encouragement to the rule of law but rather exists as an impediment to its attainment. So long as parliamentary sovereignty remains "the one fundamental law" of the Constitution, there is no way in which substantive rights can be entrenched and put beyond the reach of Parliament.

The third feature of the Constitution that I have listed—that the United Kingdom is a unitary state—is a less difficult one to comprehend. The United States is a federal nation. The power vested in the federal government is that delegated in the United States Constitution: all other powers not delegated rest with the states or the people. In the United Kingdom, no powers are reserved to national or regional bodies. If they were, Parliament would not be omnicompetent. Parliament exercises legal sovereignty. It can confer certain powers and responsibilities upon regional and local authorities, and it can also remove those powers.

The unitary nation is that of the United Kingdom of Great Britain and Northern Ireland. Wales was integrated with England in 1536 by act of Parliament (the Laws in Wales Act), and Scotland and England were incorporated in 1707 by the Treaty of Union and by the Act of Union with Scotland. Ireland entered into legislative union in 1801. Following an armed uprising, the emergence of the Irish Free State was recognized in 1922 and given the status of a self-governing dominion. (The Irish Constitution of 1937 declared the country to be a sovereign independent state, a position recognized by the Westminster Parliament in 1949.) Excluded from the Irish Free State were the northern six counties of Ireland, forming part of the traditional region of Ulster. The Protestant majority in Ulster wished to remain part of the United Kingdom, and the province of Northern Ireland has so remained.

The fourth element of the constitution is one that I have described as a parliamentary government under a constitutional monarchy. It is this element that is especially important in terms of the current relationships among the different organs of the state and the one in which conventions of the Constitution are predominant. It constitutes an assembly of different relationships and powers, the product of traditional institutions being adapted to meet changing circumstances. The developments producing this form of government were sketched in Chapter 3. The results, as we have seen, were parliamentary government in the sense of government *through* Parliament rather than government *by* Parliament, with a largely ceremonial head of state. The essentials of this form of government may be adumbrated as follows.

In the relationship among government, Parliament, and the monarch, the government dominates. Although lacking formal powers, the cabinet is recognized by convention as being at the heart of government. It is responsible for the final determination of policy to be submitted to Parliament, for the supreme control of the national executive in accordance with the policy prescribed by Parliament, and for the continuous coordination and delimitation of the interests of the several departments of state.[14] It is presided over by the prime minister. The prime minister is appointed by the monarch. By convention, the monarch summons the leader of the party with a majority of seats in the House of Commons. (In the event of a party having no overall majority, the monarch summons whoever he or she believes may be able to form an administration.) The prime minister then selects the members of his or her cabinet and other government ministers and submits their names to the monarch who, by convention, does not deny the prime minister's choice. By convention, ministers are drawn from Parliament and, again by convention, predominantly from the elected house, the House of Commons. Although the government is no longer chosen by the Commons, it nonetheless is elected through the House of Commons: there is no separate election of the executive. There is a separation and overlap of powers between the government and the House of Commons in Britain but no equivalent separation of personnel. Government ministers are drawn from, and remain within, Parliament.

Formally, ministers are responsible to the monarch. By convention, they are responsible for their policies and actions to Parliament. Ministers are responsible to Parliament through the convention of individual ministerial responsibility which assigns to them control of their departments, for which they are answerable to Parliament. The cabinet is similarly responsible to Parliament through the convention of collective ministerial responsibility. This convention, one scholar writes, "implies that all cabinet ministers assume responsibility for cabinet decisions and actions taken to implement those decisions."[15] It also has begotten two other conventions. It is a corollary of collective responsibility that any minister who disagrees publicly with a cabinet decision should resign and that a government defeat in the House of Commons on a vote of confidence necessitates either the resignation of the government or a request for a dissolution (there is no convention as to which of these alternatives the government should select). Party cohesion ensures that the cabinet usually enjoys a parliamentary majority, but political parties remain unknown to the Constitution.

The cabinet approves government bills to be presented to Parliament. (In drawing up measures, it is aided primarily by its officials—that is, civil servants—and will consult normally with interested bodies: such consultation, though, enjoys no formal recognition in constitutional terms.) Within Parliament, the most important house is the Commons. The House is expected to submit bills to sustained scrutiny and debate before giving its assent to them (or not giving its assent to them, but the influence of party usually precludes such an outcome). Formally, the House is free to pass or reject bills as it wishes. The House of Lords is more constrained (see Chapter 3); it was forced to accept a restricted role under the terms of the 1911 and 1949 Parliament Acts. Under the provisions of the 1911 Act (a measure to which the Lords acquiesced under threat of being swamped with a mass of new Liberal pro-reform peers), the House could delay passage of nonmoney bills for only two successive sessions, such bills being enacted if passed by the Commons again in the succeeding session. Money bills, those certified as such by the Speaker of the House of Commons, were to receive the Royal Assent one month after leaving the Commons, whether assented to by the House of Lords or not. The only significant power of veto retained was that over bills to prolong the life of a Parliament. (The delaying power over nonmoney bills was reduced by a further session under the terms of the 1949 Parliament Act, itself passed under the provisions of the 1911 Act.) In practice, it is rare for the Lords to reject government measures, and there is a gentleman's agreement among the parties in the House that a bill promised in a government's election manifesto should be given an unopposed Second Reading (see Chapter 11).

Once a bill has received the assent of both Houses it then goes to the monarch for the Royal Assent. By convention, this assent is always forthcoming. As already mentioned, not since Queen Anne's reign has a monarch refused assent. Queen Victoria contemplated such refusal but was persuaded otherwise. By convention, the Queen exercises her powers on the advice of her ministers. In certain extreme circumstances, Her Majesty may find herself in a position in which she is called on to use her discretion in making a political decision. Such cases are rare, though the Queen would probably prefer them to be nonexistent. The strength and the value of the contemporary monarchy derives from being above and avoiding political decisions.

The moment a bill receives the Royal Assent it becomes an act of Parliament. It is then enforced and upheld by the agencies of the state. It is binding and, by virtue of the doctrine of parliamentary sovereignty, cannot be challenged by the courts, nor can it be overridden by any other authority. The development of a form of representative democracy in the nineteenth century led Dicey to distinguish between legal sovereignty, which continued to reside with the triumvirate of the monarch, Lords, and Commons, and political sovereignty, which he deemed to rest with the electorate. This somewhat clumsy distinction has a certain utility. The electorate may have the power to choose the members of the House of Commons but the will of the electorate is not something formally recognized by the courts. The courts recognize and will enforce only acts of Parliament.

Under the provisions of the 1911 Parliament Act, the maximum life of a Parliament is five years. (Previously, the period was seven years.) Within that period, the prime minister is free to recommend to the monarch a dissolution—in effect, to call a general election. Unlike the United States, Britain has no fixed-term elections at a national level. The ability of a prime minister effectively to call a general election has been regarded by some writers as the most important weapon in ensuring parliamentary support. The prime minister can threaten to recommend a dissolution if he or she does not receive the necessary support to get a measure through. Such a threat may constitute a bluff in that the prime minister would have more to lose if an election was called than would most MPs (the PM could lose office: most seats are safe seats and so most MPs could expect to be reelected), but nonetheless it has proved a potent influence in determining parliamentary behavior. It would be exceptional, albeit not unknown, for MPs of the government party to vote against their own side on a vote of confidence. No government in the twentieth century has lost a vote of confidence as a result of dissent by its own supporters[16]—hence the dominance of government.

In summary, then, the fourth element of the Constitution—parliamentary government under a constitutional monarchy—may be seen to comprise different relationships and powers. These relationships and powers are the product of traditional institutions being adapted to meet changing circumstances and are prescribed by a variety of measures of statute and common law and by convention. The working of the various relationships within the framework established by law and convention is made possible by the operation of bodies not formally recognized by the Constitution, namely political parties. To understand contemporary British politics, one has to understand the constitutional framework. As we shall see, to understand British politics fully one has also to go beyond that framework.

CONCLUSION

The shifting and complex web of relationships and powers that forms the British Constitution is not an easily discernible one. There are some powers and relationships that recognizably fall within the rubric of the Constitution. Others are less easy to classify. Sometimes a feature of the Constitution is discerned as such only at the time when it has just ceased to have much relevance. Walter Bagehot's *The English Constitution,* published in 1867, constituted a classic description of a Constitution that had not previously been so well sketched, yet a Constitution that was to undergo significant modifications as a result of the passage that very same year of the Second Reform Act. Bagehot's work continued to be regarded as an authoritative work long after the Constitution had undergone fundamental change.

Grasping the essentials of the Constitution at any given moment is clearly a demanding and confusing task. It is confusing even to those charged with its interpretation and to those who seek to make it work. To the student of the subject, the British Constitution appears complex, confusing, ill defined, and in many respects amorphous. Such a reaction is both natural and understandable: the Constitution does exhibit those very characteristics.

At the heart of the difficulty of delineating clearly the essential features of the Constitution is its ever-changing nature. Constitutional norms serve to influence and mold political behavior. Conversely, political behavior helps influence the contours of the Constitution. As we have seen, such changes are made possible by the assimilating influence of conventions. "The conventions of the constitution," as Professor LeMay observed, "have meaning only when they are looked at against a background of continuous political change. It is very difficult to say with certainty what they were at any particular moment. Above all, they cannot be understood 'with the politics left out.'"[17]

The Constitution has proved adaptable to changing political conditions. In recent years, however, its relevance has been questioned. The patchwork quilt of powers and relationships stipulated by the Constitution has been criticized for being neither useful nor relevant in the political environment of the 1970s and 1980s. There is, as we shall see, pressure from many influential sources for the Constitution not only to be further amended but also to be radically altered. In some cases there are calls for a new constitutional settlement. It is this pressure for change and its implications that subsequent chapters will explore.

NOTES

1. O. Hood Phillips, *Constitutional and Administrative Law,* 6th ed. (Sweet & Maxwell, 1978), p. 5.

2. C. Rossiter, prefatory note to E. S. Corwin, *The 'Higher Law' Background of American Constitutional Law* (Cornell University Press, 1979 ed.), p. vi.

3. See G. Marshall and G. Moodie, *Some Problems of the Constitution,* 4th rev. ed. (Hutchinson, 1967), p. 26.

4. I. Jennings, *The Law and the Constitution,* 5th ed. (University of London Press, 1959), p. 102.

5. A. H. Hanson and M. Walles, *Governing Britain,* rev. ed. (Fontana, 1975), p. 156.

6. Hood Phillips, p. 25.

7. P. Norton, *The Constitution in Flux* (Martin Robertson, 1982), p. 9.

8. See L. Hartz, *The Liberal Tradition in America* (Harcourt, Brace and World, 1955), p. 9.

9. A. V. Dicey, *An Introduction to the Study of the Law of the Constitution,* first published 1885; 10th ed. (Macmillan, 1959).

10. Ibid., pp. 39–40.

11. H. W. R. Wade, "The basis of legal sovereignty," *Common Law Journal,* 1955, quoted by E. C. S. Wade in his introduction to the 10th edition of Dicey, p. lvi.

12. Hood Phillips, p. 46.

13. Norton, pp. 16–17.

14. As listed by *The Report of the Machinery of Government Committee* (Her Majesty's Stationery Office, 1918).

15. S. A. de Smith, *Constitutional and Administrative Law* (Penguin, 1971), p. 176.

16. The government of Neville Chamberlain effectively fell in 1940 because of dissent by its own backbenchers, though it retained a majority in the parliamentary vote that took place. The government, in effect, got the message without having to be defeated formally.

17. G. LeMay, *The Victorian Constitution* (Duckworth, 1979), p. 21.

The Electoral System

Fair and Workable?

IN THE UNITED STATES, citizens are presented with the opportunity to go to the polls at frequent and fixed intervals to elect at national, state, and local levels a host of legislators, executive heads, councilpersons, officials, and even, in some states, judges. It has been estimated that there are approximately 1 million elective offices to be filled. In any given year there may be 120,000 or 130,000 elections held, most of them for local school boards.[1] Before polling day, the citizen is faced with a lengthy election campaign: there are primary campaigns, the primary elections, the general election campaign, and the general election itself. The presidential election campaign lasts for nearly a year; with all the preplanning, advance publicity, and fund raising it lasts for much longer. Given the short interval between elections, campaigns for the United States House of Representatives are virtually continuous. Once in the polling booth, the voter is faced with a daunting array of candidates: given the number of offices to be filled and the number of people seeking to fill them, the number of names may be a three-figure one. Voting and its subsequent tabulation is much eased by the use of voting machines. Choosing between Republican and Democratic candidates is not always an easy task, and ticket splitting is a well-recognized phenomenon. Such characteristics of United States elections are well known. They have little in common with those of British elections.

In the United Kingdom, a citizen may have the opportunity to vote in a national election only once every five years. That election is for the House of Commons and the House of Commons alone. The members of the House of Lords are not elected: they serve by virtue of birth or, for life peers, by appointment for life. There is no separate election of the executive: the leader of the party with a majority of seats in the House of Commons is invited to form a government. (The choice of party leaders is a matter for the parties themselves.) The date of an election is not known until a few weeks before the event, when the prime minister recommends a dissolution of Parliament to the Queen. Although there is much anticipatory planning, the election campaign proper extends over approximately three weeks. There are no primaries: candidate selection is an internal matter for the parties. As we shall see, there are also significant differences in registration procedures. The campaign is fought on a national, and party, basis. Funding and organization in the constituencies as well as nationally is undertaken by the established parties, not by individual candidates or campaign organizations created by the candidates. The amount of money spent on electioneering during this period is strictly limited by law. On polling day, the elector is faced with a small ballot slip on which are printed the names usually of only three or four candidates. (Six or more candidates standing in any one constituency would be unusual.) The voter places his or her cross besides the name of one of them. With each elector having only one vote to cast for only one candidate there is no such thing as ticket splitting. At the close of polling, the votes are collected in one central area in each constituency and counted by hand. The process of counting is a proficient one and a sufficient number of results are usually announced within a few hours of the close of the polls to know which party has won the election. If the party in office has lost, the prime minister goes to Buckingham Palace to tender his or her resignation. The leader of the party newly returned with a majority of seats is then summoned. The new cabinet and other ministerial appointments are announced within a matter of days, sometimes within a matter of hours. Within a month of an election being called, Britain may find itself with a new government.

An elector in Britain has more opportunity to vote in local elections than in national ones. These are fixed terms and the elector has the chance to vote for members of councils at district and county (or metropolitan) levels and sometimes at parish level as well. However, only council members (councillors) are elected; no executive officers are subject to election. Councils choose their own chairmen and the chief administrative officials are appointed professionals. There is no election of any local official, be it police chief, register of wills, city auditor, or judge. The one similarity between local elections in Britain and the United States is the turnout: it is very low, in some instances as low as 10% of eligible electors.

The essential characteristics of national elections in the United States

TABLE 5.1
United States and United Kingdom National Elections

Characteristics	United States	United Kingdom
Bodies elected	President and Vice President United States Senate United States House of Representatives	House of Commons
Constituencies	President: national Senate: state House: districts	Single-member constituencies (650)
Terms of office	President: 4 years (two-term maximum) Senator: 6 years (one-third elected every 2 years) Representative: 2 years (no limits of seeking reelection)	Maximum of 5 years (no limit to MPs seeking reelection)
Eligibility for candidature	President: citizen, aged 35 years or over, 14 years resident in US Senator: aged 30 years or over, 9 years a citizen, inhabitant of state Representative: aged 25 years or over, 7 years a citizen, inhabitant of state	Citizen aged 21 years or over (certain exceptions)
Fixed-term or irregular elections	Fixed-term	Irregular (but must not go beyond 5-year intervals)
Mode of election	Plurality vote for Senate and House, popular vote and electoral college for president	Plurality vote
Date of election determined by	Provisions of United States Constitution	Recommendation of prime minister to monarch (within limits of 1911 Parliament Act and subject to certain qualifications)
Franchise	Citizens aged 18 and over (certain exceptions)	Citizens aged 18 and over (certain exceptions)

TABLE 5.1 *(continued)*

Characteristics	United States	United Kingdom
Registration procedures	Generally required to register in person at stipulated times and places (certain state exceptions)	Head of household required by law to complete annual registration form, submitted by mail
Turnout at elections	Less than 60% post-1968 (40% or less in mid-term elections)	Regularly over 70%

and Britain are contrasted in Table 5.1. Let us consider in a little more detail some of the main features of British elections (in other words, election of the House of Commons) before proceeding to a consideration of the current controversy surrounding the electoral system.

THE ELECTORAL STRUCTURE

Electors

As we have seen (Chapter 3), the franchise was variously extended in the nineteenth century. The basis on which the vote was given was that of property. Not until 1918 was universal manhood suffrage introduced on the basis of (six months') residence. In the same year, women aged 30 and over, if already local government electors or married to such electors, were given a vote in general elections. The vote was extended to all women aged 21 and over in 1928. It was extended to 18- to 20-year-olds in 1969. The various extensions of the franchise during the course of the century, much more radical in numerical terms than the various extensions of the previous century,[2] and the growth in population have resulted in the electorate growing from one of 6,730,935 in 1900 to one of 42,703,019 in 1983.[3] The 1949 Representation of the People Act effectively brought to final fruition the principle of "one person, one vote." The only people excluded from the franchise are peers (they have their own House), imprisoned criminals, those of unsound mind, people convicted of certain election offences, and aliens.

In order to exercise one's right to vote it is necessary to be on the electoral register, which is compiled annually. Each year every household receives an electoral registration form. The head of the household is required by law to complete it and to list all those who are resident in the dwelling on October 10 of that year and are eligible for inclusion, including those who will attain the age of 18 years during the period that the new register comes into effect. These forms are returned by mail to the Registration Officer for the Constituency. The register then compiled is open for inspection once compiled, which takes effect the following February, and is in force for one year. Electors who move to another constituency during the course of the year are entitled to apply to vote by post in the constituency in which they are registered.

Compared with registration practice in most American states, the British method is both simple and effective. Given that people die, sometimes fail to complete the registration forms correctly, or move without applying for a postal vote, the electoral register is never 100% accurate. However, it has been estimated that it is 93% accurate when published, declining to 85% accuracy on the last day of validity.[4] In registration there is no procedure analogous to the American practice of registering as a Republican, Democrat, or Independent: given the absence of primary elections in Britain, there is no logical reason why one should.

Constituencies

The United Kingdom is divided into single-member constituencies. There are currently 650, though the number can and does vary. From 1974 until 1983 there were 635, and at one time earlier in this century there were over 700.

The drawing of boundaries is the responsibility of bodies known as boundary commissions: there is a commission each for England, Scotland, Wales, and Northern Ireland. Each commission is chaired by the Speaker of the House of Commons (a nonparty figure) and each has a judge as deputy chairman. Assistant commissioners, usually lawyers, are appointed to supervize local inquiries, and the staff of the commissions includes the country's main officials dealing with population and geographic surveys.

In redrawing boundaries the commissions are guided by rules laid down by act of Parliament. They are supposed to ensure that constituencies are as equal as possible in size of their electorates. However, they are permitted to deviate from this if special geographic considerations (for example, the size, shape, and accessibility of a constituency) appear to render such a deviation desirable. Other rules further complicate the position. The commissioners are enjoined not to cross local authority boundaries in creating parliamentary constituencies. They also have to work within the context of regional disparities. To compensate for the absence of its own national assembly, Scotland has a greater number of constituencies allocated to it than its population strictly allows, and the same exception applies to Wales. Hence, the electoral quota (the national electorate divided by the number of seats) is greater in England than in Scotland or Wales.

Under existing legislation, the commissioners are required to review electoral boundaries every 10–15 years. (It used to be at more frequent intervals, but this was found to be too disruptive.) Before making their recommendations, the commissioners consider submissions from interested bodies, primarily the local political parties. If a proposed change has the support of the local parties, it is usual for the commissioners to accept it. Once they have completed their work, their recommendations are presented to a government minister, the home secretary, who is then required to lay them before the House of Commons for approval. They are rarely free of criticism, and in 1969 the Labour home secretary advised his supporters in the House to vote against the commission's recommendations, which they did. As a result, the 1970 general election was not fought on the basis of the new boundaries recommended by the boundary commissioners. The recommendations were implemented in the new Parliament. The next review by the commission was completed in 1982 and challenged in the courts by the Labour party. It contended that the commissioners had acted outside the terms of the act by giving undue weight to some of the criteria for determining boundaries as against others. (There were some notable disparities in constituency sizes.) The courts determined that the commissioners had exercised properly the wide discretion given them by Parliament and rejected the case. The commission's recommendations were subsequently approved by Parliament and the 1983 general election was fought on the new boundaries.

A combination of population shifts (about three-quarters of a million people move house every year in Britain), the disparity among constituency electorates recommended by the commissioners in favor of other criteria (maintaining local government boundaries and the like), the lapse of time between reviews, and the disparity in the number of seats allocated to the different countries in the United Kingdom has meant that there are often marked differences among the sizes of electorates. In 1979, the electoral quota for English constituencies was a little under 70,000.[5] The constituency of Bromsgrove and Redditch (constituencies are given names, not numbers) had an electorate of 104,375, while Newcastle-upon-Tyne Central had an electoral register of but 23,678. (The smallest electorate was in Scotland— Glasgow Central, with 19,826 electors.) Even after the redrawing of boundaries in 1983, there were still some significant disparities. Of the seats, 5% deviated from the electoral quota by ±20% (though this was down from the 39% of seats that had deviated by that much on the 1982 register.) The Isle of Wight, an English constituency, had an electorate of 94,768, while the Scottish constituency of the Western Isles, difficult to enlarge for geographic reasons, had but 22,901 electors.[6]

Campaigns

Election campaigns are short, sharp, and dominated by the political parties. In British elections, unlike those in America, the personalities of candidates (except for national leaders) and their personal wealth play but a marginal role. The campaign is fought in practice on a national level between the two main parties, the candidates and the local campaigns serving to reinforce the national campaigns of their leaders. Candidates are selected locally by the parties, and the parties provide the finance and the organization for the campaign. Election expenses are limited by statute and have been since 1883. Expenditure is permitted only where authorized by a candidate, a candidate's election agent, or a person authorized in writing by the agent. The maximum permitted expenditure is calculated on the basis of a fixed sum plus a limited amount based on the number of electors:[7] in an average-sized English county constituency in 1983, the ceiling was approximately £4,700 (just over $7,000). There are certain types of expenditure that are illegal (for example, paying an elector to exhibit an election poster or paying for voters to be taken to and from the polling booths), and separate committees to promote a candidate are not permitted. Even with the modest expenditure that is permitted, most candidates fail to spend the maximum allowed. Some devices for keeping costs low are employed and these can, where required, provide up to an extra 20% of expenditure:[8] a popular ploy is to purchase stationery in advance and then resell it cheaply to the candidate as second-hand stock. Few candidates, though, are prepared to run too many risks for fear of having their elections challenged and declared void: expenses have to be declared and opponents keep a wary eye open for any infringements of election law. Two other constraints also operate: the parties have difficulty raising sufficient money to fight campaigns (national and local appeals are common when an election is in the offing) and there is little evidence that increased expenditure in local campaigns necessarily helps win elections.[9]

Each candidate is permitted one postage-free mailing of one piece of election literature. Other literature is distributed by the unpaid party activists. The main item of literature is the candidate's election address. This will usually incorporate a summary of the main points of the party's national election manifesto. The candidate will spend most of the campaign making speeches throughout the constituency, not infrequently at thinly attended meetings, and canvassing door to door where possible. He or she will be aided by volunteers who do doorstep canvassing to try to determine where supporters live: on election day they will keep a running tab on who has voted in order to ensure that support is maximized.

The main focus of the campaign is a national one. The party leaders will make regular and well-publicized appearances throughout the country, ensuring that the national press and television reporters follow in their wake as well as holding daily press conferences.[10] The national party organizations increasingly make use also of press and poster advertising. As long as expenditure cannot be said to apply in support of specific candidates, national party campaigns do not fall foul of the election finance restrictions. In the 1979 election the Labour and Conservative national party organizations are estimated to have each spent a little over 1 million pounds on the campaign, roughly the same amount expended in total by their candidates in the local campaigns. The largest single item of expenditure was advertising.[11] The parties enjoyed also the benefit of free but limited television time. Paid political advertising on television is not allowed: each party is allocated a set number of 10-minute party political broadcasts that are transmitted on all television channels. The allocation of the number of broadcasts to the parties is a somewhat contentious one. The broadcasts themselves are often regarded by voters as the least appetizing part of election campaigns.[12]

The basis of the parties' appeal to the country is the election manifestos that they issue. In recent elections, these have become increasingly lengthy and specific documents, detailing the intended policies and measures to be pursued by a party if returned to office. They constitute a topic of some controversy. It has been argued that very few electors actually read them and that many of the commitments made do not enjoy widespread support among voters, even among those voting for the parties that issued them.[13] They are also viewed by some observers as hostages for the future, parties in office being perceived as often doing the reverse of what was promised in their manifestos.[14] In practice, they constitute something of a guide to interested bodies and provide a framework for the main items of legislation introduced by an incoming government in the first session or two of a new Parliament: most manifesto promises are usually implemented.[15] A more relevant criticism is that manifesto promises may not address themselves to the country's real problems. Some would argue that, by virtue of the manner of their compilation and their utilization as a means of furthering the adversary relationship between the parties, manifestos add to those problems rather than offering solutions.[16]

Candidates

Any citizen aged 21 years or over is eligible to be a candidate for election to the House of Commons. There are certain limited exceptions. Precluded from serving in the House of Commons are those who are disqualified from voting, as well as policemen, civil servants, judges, members of the boards of nationalized industries, undischarged bankrupts, members of the armed services, and clergy of the Churches of England, Scotland, Ireland, and the Roman Catholic Church. The exclusion of public servants has an acceptable rationale to reinforce it; they are free to resign their positions should they wish to stand for election. The exclusion of certain clergy is less easy to justify (a relic of the time when religious disputes were at the heart of national affairs), as is the exclusion of 18- to 20-year-olds: when the voting age was lowered in 1969, the age of eligibility for candidature was not.[17] To be a candidate one has to obtain the signature of 10 electors in the constituency and submit a deposit of £150 (approximately $225), returnable in the event of receiving one-eighth of the votes cast. In Britain, unlike the United States, there are no residence requirements: hence, parties enjoy a wider range of choice in the selection of candidates.

In practice, candidates are party candidates. As a result of an innovation introduced in 1969, this is now more formally recognized: candidates are permitted to include their party designation on the ballot paper. It is generally assumed that an individual candidate has little influence on voting behavior: party is the decisive factor, though the candidate can have some impact. In the 1979 and 1983 elections there were examples of locally popular candidates holding their marginal seats against the national swing.[18] Indeed, in the marginal constituency of Ipswich, the Labour MP was elected on both occasions despite the national swing in favor of the Conservatives. Such instances remain rare, and party remains the primary and almost exclusive influence.

Virtually all constituencies (the exceptions are in Northern Ireland) are contested by Conservative and Labour candidates. In the general elections of the 1970s, the Liberal party regularly contested more than 500 seats (indeed, over 600 in October 1974), and in the 1983 election the Social Democratic/Liberal Alliance fielded candidates in all 633 seats in Great Britain. These are the only parties to each obtain several million votes in general elections. They are also the only ones to be successful in recent years in winning seats in England.

In Scotland, there is the challenge of the Scottish National Party. It won 11 seats in October 1974 but only 2 in 1979 and 1983, despite fighting all Scottish seats. In Wales, there is Plaid Cymru (the party of Wales), which won 3 seats in 1974 and 2 in 1979 and 1983. In Northern Ireland, the dominant force is that of the Ulster Unionists, though divided now into different parties: in 1983 Unionists of different hues won 15 of the 17 seats in the province. The 1979 and 1983 elections also witnessed an increase in the number of candidates fielded by minor parties, to whom the £150 deposit (first set in 1918) no longer serves as the bar to nonserious candidates that was intended. The Ecology party fielded 109 candidates in 1983 (up from 53 in 1979), the right-wing National Front 60 candidates (though down from its 1979 peak of 303 candidates), the British National party (a breakaway movement from the National Front) 54 candidates, and the Communist party 35 candidates. All the candidates of these parties lost their deposits, as did a few scattered independents and other candidates standing under rather esoteric banners. (In 1983, for example, there was a Justice for Divorced Fathers

TABLE 5.2
General Election Results, 1945–1983

General Election (Winning party in capital letters)	Votes Cast*		Seats Won*	
July 1945				
LABOUR	11,995,152	(47.8%)	393	(61.4%)
Conservative	9,988,306	(39.8%)	213	(33.3%)
Liberal	2,248,226	(9.0%)	12	(1.9%)
Others	854,294	(2.8%)	22	(3.4%)
Turnout: 72.7%	25,085,978	(99.4%)	640	(100.0%)
February 1950				
LABOUR	13,266,592	(64.1%)	315	(50.4%)
Conservative	12,502,567	(43.5%)	298	(47.7%)
Liberal	2,621,548	(9.1%)	9	(1.4%)
Others	381,964	(1.3%)	3	(0.5%)
Turnout: 84.0%	28,772,671	(100.0%)	625	(100.0%)
October 1951				
CONSERVATIVE	13,717,538	(48.0%)	321	(51.4%)
Labour	13,948,605	(48.8%)	295	(47.2%)
Liberal	730,556	(2.5%)	6	(1.0%)
Others	198,969	(0.7%)	3	(0.5%)
Turnout: 82.5%	28,595,668	(100.0%)	625	(100.1%)
May 1955				
CONSERVATIVE	13,286,569	(49.7%)	344	(54.6%)
Labour	12,404,970	(46.4%)	277	(44.0%)
Liberal	722,405	(2.7%)	6	(0.9%)
Others	346,554	(1.2%)	3	(0.5%)
Turnout: 76.7%	26,760,498	(100.0%)	630	(100.0%)
October 1959				
CONSERVATIVE	13,749,830	(49.4%)	365	(57.9%)
Labour	12,215,538	(43.8%)	258	(40.9%)
Liberal	1,638,571	(5.9%)	6	(0.9%)
Others	142,670	(0.8%)	1	(0.2%)
Turnout: 78.8%	27,859,241	(99.9%)	630	(99.9%)
October 1964				
LABOUR	12,205,814	(44.1%)	317	(50.3%)
Conservative	12,001,396	(43.4%)	304	(48.2%)
Liberal	3,092,878	(11.2%)	9	(1.4%)
Others	347,905	(1.3%)	0	(0.0%)
Turnout: 77.1%	27,655,374	(100.0%)	630	(99.9%)
March 1966				
LABOUR	13,064,951	(47.9%)	363	(57.6%)
Conservative	11,418,433	(41.9%)	253	(40.2%)
Liberal	2,327,533	(8.5%)	12	(1.9%)
Others	422,226	(1.2%)	2	(0.3%)
Turnout: 75.8%	27,263,606	(99.5%)	630	(100.0%)

(continued)

TABLE 5.2 (*continued*)

General Election (Winning party in capital letters)	Votes Cast*		Seats Won*	
June 1970				
CONSERVATIVE	13,145,123	(46.4%)	330	(52.4%)
Labour	12,179,341	(43.0%)	287	(45.6%)
Liberal	2,117,035	(7.5%)	6	(0.9%)
Others	903,299	(3.2%)	7	(1.1%)
Turnout: 72.0%	28,344,798	(100.1%)	630	(100.0%)
February 1974				
LABOUR	11,639,243	(37.1%)	301	(47.4%)
Conservative	11,868,906	(37.9%)	297	(46.8%)
Liberal	6,063,470	(19.3%)	14	(2.2%)
Others (Great Britain)	1,044,061	(3.4%)	11	(1.7%)
Others (Northern Ireland)†	717,986	(2.3%)	12	(1.9%)
Turnout: 78.7%	31,333,226	(100.0%)	635	(100.0%)
October 1974				
LABOUR	11,457,079	(39.2%)	319	(50.2%)
Conservative	10,464,817	(35.8%)	277	(43.6%)
Liberal	5,346,754	(18.3%)	13	(2.0%)
Scottish National Party	839,617	(2.9%)	11	(1.7%)
Plaid Cymru	166,321	(0.6%)	3	(0.5%)
Others (Great Britain)	212,496	(0.8%)	0	(0.0%)
Others (Northern Ireland)†	702,094	(2.4%)	12	(1.9%)
Turnout: 72.8%	29,189,178	(100.0%)	635	(99.9%)
May 1979				
CONSERVATIVE	13,697,690	(43.9%)	339	(53.4%)
Labour	11,532,148	(36.9%)	269	(42.4%)
Liberal	4,313,811	(13.8%)	11	(1.7%)
Scottish National Party	504,259	(1.6%)	2	(0.3%)
Plaid Cymru	132,544	(0.4%)	2	(0.3%)
Others (Great Britain)	343,674	(1.2%)	0	(0.0%)
Others (Northern Ireland)†	695,889	(2.2%)	12	(1.9%)
Turnout: 76.0%	31,220,010	(100.0%)	635	(100.0%)
June 1983				
CONSERVATIVE	13,012,602	(42.4%)	397	(61.1%)
Labour	8,457,124	(27.6%)	209	(32.1%)
SDP/Liberal Alliance	7,780,577	(25.4%)	23	(3.5%)
Scottish National Party	331,975	(1.1%)	2	(0.3%)
Plaid Cymru	125,309	(0.4%)	2	(0.3%)
Others (Great Britain)	198,834	(0.6%)	0	(0.0%)
Others (Northern Ireland)	764,474	(2.5%)	17	(2.6%)
Turnout: 72.7%	30,670,895	(100.0%)	650	(99.9%)

*Figures do not always add to 100% due to rounding.
†Prior to 1974, Ulster Unionists were affiliated to the Conservative party. They thereafter sat as a separate parliamentary party.

candidate, one representing Freddie's Alternative Medicine party, and another standing for Law and Order in Gotham City—a label derived from the old Batman comic book series!) Their main impact was to lengthen the ballot paper.[19] In 1959, there was a total of 1,536 candidates, an average of 2.4 per seat. In 1983, there were 2,579 candidates—an average of 4 per seat.

Candidate Selection

The candidates of the main parties are selected locally, though the national party in each case retains some veto power. In Britain, unlike the United States, there are no primary elections and the selection of a candidate is in practice usually in the hands of a small group of party activists. Given that most seats are safe seats for one party or another, this selection is usually tantamount to election. Within the Conservative party, aspiring candidates have to be on a candidates list maintained by the party's national headquarters. (A local party may choose someone not on the list, but it must obtain approval from the national party for its choice.) A local Conservative association seeking a candidate will invite applicants, and in a safe Conservative seat, several hundred aspiring candidates can be expected to put their names forward. The association will then appoint a selection committee, usually comprising representatives from its different branches and associated groups such as the Young Conservatives. This committee will sift through the applications and then recommend three or more names to the executive council, the main decision-making body of the association. The council may then recommend one name for approval to a general meeting of the association, or it may put forward more than one name and leave it to the general meeting to decide.

The researches of both Austin Ranney and Michael Rush have found that, despite the political importance of choosing a candidate, the political views of applicants are not important considerations in the selection process.[20] Selection committees have tended to be influenced by an applicant's knowledge of the constituency, his or her stature and delivery of speech, and whether there are the makings of a good "constituency member" (one who will represent diligently the interests of constituents) or, in some cases, of a national figure. On occasions, more esoteric considerations may apply, as I can testify, having served on a selection committee. "Can't we interview him? He has a nice name" was one comment made during the selection deliberations. (The response: a polite "no.") Other influences can include, in some areas, religion and quite often age and sex: local parties are reluctant to adopt women candidates (the folklore being that women voters dislike voting for them) and anyone aged under 30 or over 50 years. There is also a tendency to prefer married men (single men over 30 are considered somewhat suspect), and wives are often asked to appear before selection committees. Because wives are looked on as surrogates for their husbands while the latter are at Westminster, their attitudes to constituency work and their appearance are considered important. In the selection I was involved in, one prominent candidate—a nationally known figure—suffered from the poor impression his wife gave to some of the selectors. Arrogant or pretentious wives can sometimes kill the political ambitions of their husbands.

Although the Labour candidates selected are increasingly similar in background to Conservative candidates, the selection procedure in the Labour Party is not quite the same. A local Labour party will seek a candidate by inviting nominations. Nominations may be made by local ward committees, party groups such as the women's section, and by affiliated organizations, principally affiliated trade unions. (An aspiring candidate can approach such groups to solicit a nomination.) Once nominations are received, the executive committee, responsible for the day-to-day running of the party, will draw up a short list of candidates for interview. The final choice is made by the governing body, the General Management Committee, comprising representatives from the different ward committees and affiliated organizations. The candidate then requires the endorsement of the party's National Executive Committee.

In 1980, the Labour party conference approved the principle of mandatory reselection of sitting Labour MPs. What this meant was that sitting MPs should no longer be reselected automatically by local parties just before a general election was held. Instead, a full selection procedure was to be gone through during the lifetime of a Parliament, thus allowing other aspiring candidates to be considered. It was a contentious issue and was generally seen as an attempt by the party's left wing to try to remove some Labour members of whom they disapproved. In practice, the number of members denied reselection was small (only seven by the time the 1983 general election was called), but the issue served to highlight the more overt emphasis placed by Labour activists on a candidate's political stance than was the case on the Conservative side. In the Conservative party, there is no procedure for mandatory reselection.

In the Liberal party, selection is by the local party also, with the national party maintaining an approved list of candidates. However, national approval has tended in the past to be given without much discussion, in large part because the number of aspirants for candidatures has not been great: the party has often had to adopt whoever was willing to stand. The number of aspiring candidates increased in the 1970s, but so too did the number of seats fought. In many cases during 1974, candidate selection took place just before the election campaign got under way.[21]

Within the Social Democratic party (SDP), candidate selection is made through the area parties. These are organized usually on a multiconstituency basis and are responsible for organizing and choosing candidates for constituencies within their areas. Unless the task is delegated to local (constituency) groups, candidates are chosen by a postal ballot of all members of the area party. Candidates must be on the party's national list of approved candidates and require the endorsement of one of the party's regional committees to get on that list.[22]

When the Alliance between the Liberals and the Social Democrats was formed in 1981 a formula was devised for allocating constituencies between the two parties. Negotiating the allocation encountered problems (some entrenched Liberal candidates were unwilling to step down in favor of SDP candidates) but, once achieved, the local party responsible for fielding a candidate made its choice and that candidate was then endorsed by the other party. There were no joint selection procedures. There was numerical parity in the distribution of seats (though not necessarily in the distribution of seats considered winnable),[23] and in the 1983 election, each party fielded more than 300 candidates. Only in two seats (one in Liverpool, one in London), where there was some feuding between the two Alliance partners, were Liberal and SDP candidates to be found contesting the same seats.

The candidates selected by the parties tend on the whole to be middle-aged, male, and white. Female and nonwhite candidates are exceptional. The successful candidates more than the unsuccessful ones tend to be middle-aged, university-educated (as well as public school-educated, in the case of Conservatives), and drawn from the ranks of business and the professions.[24] In postwar years there has been a tendency for MPs to be even more middle-class than they were hitherto.[25] Past years, according to some analysts, have witnessed the emergence of a more professional member of Parliament.

Elections

In each of the 650 single-member constituencies, the method of election employed is the plurality or "first-past-the-post" method. What this means is that the candidate receiving more votes than any other candidate is declared elected. It is the same method as that employed in Senate and House elections in the United States. Examples of constituency results from the 1983 general election are given in Table 5.3.

In practice, most seats are considered to be safe seats for one or other of the two main parties—that is, the winning candidate has been returned with a majority that represents 10% or more of the votes cast. In the safest seats, the majority may constitute as much as 40% or 50% of the votes cast. The constituency of Blaenau Gwent (Table 5.3) serves as a good example. Turnover in seats is relatively modest. Fewer than 5% of seats changed hands in the 1970 general election. Even in 1983, with the challenge of the Social Democrat/Liberal Alliance and a major redistribution of constituency boundaries, fewer than 16% of the seats changed hands among the various competing parties.

TABLE 5.3
Selected Constituency Results, 1983

Surrey East

Electorate: 58,485

Sir G. Howe (Conservative)	27,272	(62.9%)
Mrs. S. Liddell (Liberal/Alliance)	11,836	(27.3%)
H. Pincott (Labour)	4,249	(9.8%)
Conservative majority	15,436	(35.6%)

Total vote: 43,357
Turnout: 74.1%

A safe Conservative seat in the South of England, represented by Sir Geoffrey Howe, the current foreign secretary.

Leicester South

Electorate: 73,573

D. Spencer (Conservative)	21,424	(40.3%)
J. Marshall (Labour)	21,417	(40.3%)
R. Renold (Liberal/Alliance)	9,410	(17.7%)
C. Davis (Ecology)	495	(0.9%)
C. Pickard (British National Party)	280	(0.5%)
D. P. Roberts (Workers Party for a Workers State)	161	(0.3%)
Conservative majority	7	(0.0%)

Total vote: 53,187
Turnout: 72.3%

A Conservative gain (the seat had been represented in the previous Parliament by the Labour candidate), this result was the closest in the 1983 election.

Blaenau Gwent

Electorate: 55,948

M. Foot (Labour)	30,113	(70.1%)
G. Atkinson (Liberal/Alliance)	6,408	(14.9%)
T. Morgan (Conservative)	4,816	(11.2%)
S. Morgan (Plaid Cymru)	1,624	(3.8%)
Labour majority	23,705	(55.2%)

Total vote: 42,961
Turnout: 76.8%

A Welsh seat (formerly known as Ebbw Vale), this is the safest Labour seat in Britain, represented by Michael Foot, leader of the Labour party 1980–1983.

TABLE 5.4
Parliamentary Majorities, 1945–1979

Parliament	Party Returned to Office	Overall Majority*
1945–1950	Labour	146
1950–1951	Labour	5
1951–1955	Conservative	17
1955–1959	Conservative	60
1959–1964	Conservative	100
1964–1966	Labour	4
1966–1970	Labour	98
1970–1974	Conservative	30
1974	Labour	−33
1974–1979	Labour	3
1979–1983	Conservative	43
1983–	Conservative	144

*Overall majority following general election. The Speaker is included in the party of which he was previously a member. A negative number indicates that a minority government was returned to office.

The results from the 650 constituencies, as already mentioned, determine which party will form the government. In all but one of the elections since 1945, one party has won an absolute majority of the seats and the leader of that party has formed a government. The Labour party achieved an overall majority in five elections, on two occasions by slim margins, and formed the government following the February 1974 election, in which it had more seats than any other party but not an absolute majority (see Table 5.4). The Conservatives have won overall majorities, by clear margins, in six elections since 1945, including the most recent.

VOTING BEHAVIOR

Three generalizations can be drawn about voting behavior in the four general elections held in the period from 1950 to 1959:

1. There was a high turnout of electors;
2. Of those who voted, virtually all voted for either the Conservative or Labour parties;
3. The most significant predictor of party voting was class.

The first two generalizations are borne out by the data in Table 5.2. More than three-quarters of those on the electoral register turned out on each occasion to cast their vote and, of those who did so, more than 90% voted usually for either the Conservative or Labour candidate. In the 1950 election, turnout reached 84%. In the 1951 election, almost 97% of those who voted cast their ballots for one or other of the two main parties.

The third generalization is drawn from survey data. Gallup Poll data showed that in these four elections, 79% or more of upper-middle-class voters and 69% or more of middle-class voters cast their votes for the Conservative party, while more than 50% of working-class and very poor voters voted for the Labour party.[26] Class clearly was not an exclusive predictor nor was the relationship between class and party symmetrical: the middle class was more Conservative than the working class was Labour. One-third of working-class voters regularly voted Conservative.[27] Nonetheless, class remained the most important predictor of how an elector might vote.

In the 1960s and since, these generalizations have lost some of their force. Between 1964 and 1983, turnout in general elections failed to reach 80%, falling below 73% in 1970, October 1974, and 1983. More notably, there was a relative desertion by voters of the two main parties. In the two elections of 1974, 75% of those who voted cast their ballots for one or other of the main parties. In 1983 the figure was 70%.

The class–party nexus also began to wane. The survey by Butler and Stokes detected a weakening of the class alignment among younger voters in the 1960s.[28] Further analysis of their data and of additional data for the period from 1970 to 1975 showed that, though the vote for the two main parties had declined in the 1960s, major party identification had not: in other words, electors—whatever they may have done in the polling booths—continued to express a sense of affiliation with one of the two main parties. However, partisan identification declined abruptly in 1974, though the decline was relative: many "very strong" identifiers switched to being "fairly strong" identifiers.[29] The authors speculated that this partisan dealignment reflected a continuing erosion of the class–party tie. By October 1974, barely half of the electorate identified (let alone voted) with their "natural" class party.

The relative decline in the importance of class is borne out by a survey of voters in the 1983 election (Table 5.5). Support for the SDP/Liberal Alliance was drawn evenly from different social classes. The Labour party failed to achieve even half the votes of working-class and unemployed voters. The gap between its share of the manual and nonmanual votes was only 21%, compared with 27% in 1979 and 40% in 1959.[30] The Conservatives made no significant inroads among their traditional class supporters, though attracting the votes of almost one in three of trade unionists. (Most trade unions are affiliated to the Labour party.) Although social class continues to structure party choice, it is no longer as reliable a predictor as it was in the 1950s and 1960s.

What other variables, independent of class, can be identified as being

TABLE 5.5
Vote by Social Class, 1983

Party	Professional and Managerial (AB)	Office and Clerical (C1)	Skilled Manual (C2)	Semiskilled and Unskilled Manual (D)	Trade Unionists	Unemployed
Conservative	62%	55%	39%	29%	32%	30%
Labour	12%	21%	35%	44%	39%	45%
SDP/Liberal	27%	24%	27%	28%	28%	26%

SOURCE: Gallup Poll, undertaken for BBC, on June 8 and 9, 1983. Published in *The Guardian*, June 13, 1983. Copyright 1983 The Guardian. Reprinted by permission.

correlated to voting behavior? Age, religion, gender, region, population density, and home ownership are among the most significant to have been identified. Some of these have become more pronounced as a result of the weakening of the class–party relationship; others are of declining significance.

Age and gender are among those variables of declining significance. In the 1983 general election, the older age groups were marginally more Conservative than the younger ones, but the difference was small. Among those aged over 65 years, 48% voted Conservative (a 15% lead over the proportion voting Labour), whereas among those aged 18 to 22 years, 41% voted Conservative (a 12% lead over Labour voters). Conservative support among the over-65s was lower than in 1979, indeed dropping by more than the national average. This decline could support the generational cohort theory developed by Butler and Stokes: that is, that it is not age as such that influences voting behavior but the period at which one becomes politically aware. Thus, the over-65s in 1983 were the generation of the 1930s and of the Second World War (see Chapter 3). As one analyst puts it, "Some of the Labour loyalty induced in their formative years will have lasted until today."[31]

As a predictor of voting behavior, though, age is of marginal utility, and so too is gender. Traditionally, women have been somewhat more likely than men to vote Conservative. In most postwar elections, more men have voted Labour than have voted Conservative, whereas more women have voted Conservative than have voted Labour. However, the bias was a slight one. According to the Gallup Poll, it disappeared in the 1983 election, the Conservatives drawing more support from men than from women (46% to 43%),[32] thus replicating similar developments in the United States and Scandinavia during the 1970s. However, according to a Market and Opinion Research International (MORI) poll, the Conservatives continued to draw more support from female than from male voters (Table 5.6). The disparity in

TABLE 5.6
Party Support by Gender, 1974–1979, General Elections

	October 1974		1979		1983	
	Men	Women	Men	Women	Men	Women
Conservative	32%	39%	43%	47%	42%	46%
Labour	43%	38%	40%	35%	31%	26%
Liberal	18%	20%	13%	15%	—	—
Liberal/SDP	—	—	—	—	25%	27%

SOURCE: MORI poll, *New Statesman*, June 17, 1983. Copyright 1983 the New Statesman. Reprinted by permission.

the data highlights the marginal significance now of gender as a predictor of voting behavior.

Religion is another variable of limited importance. It was significant in the nineteenth century but declined rapidly in the twentieth, as class became more important. Butler and Stokes found the relationship between religion and party of declining relevance with each generation. However, in some areas where religious loyalties remain strong, such loyalties can still alter the pattern of class voting. An obvious example is Northern Ireland (see Chapter 9), though mainland examples can be found in certain cities, notably Glasgow. In such cities there is a sizable Irish Catholic vote, and this swells the Labour vote in elections.[33] Elsewhere, the impact of religion is small, though those who are not members of the Church of England are less likely than others in their class to support the Conservatives.[34] The marginality of religion in influencing voting behavior is reflected in the fact that it did not figure in analyses published in the wake of the 1983 election.

More significant predictors, especially in recent elections, have been location and home ownership. Increasingly, Labour and Conservative support has become polarized between North and South and between urban and rural areas. It is also becoming polarized between those who own and those who rent their houses. The Conservative party, in terms of its voting support, has always been the party of England and, indeed, of a particular part of England.[35] That concentration has become marked in recent elections. In a good postwar election year, the Conservatives would normally expect to pick up a respectable number of seats in Northern England and to some extent in Scotland. This is no longer the case. The party's regional strength has become more pronounced. Mrs. Thatcher carried her party to victory in 1979 largely on the votes of the electorate in the southern half of England, below a line drawn from the River Severn to the Wash (see Map 5.1). The swing to the Conservatives in the election was highest in the southern half of the country (and in Wales), lowest in the northern parts of the country and in Scotland. Compared with the 1955 election, the party had 20 fewer seats in the North and 14 fewer in Scotland; conversely, it had 34 more in the South and the Midlands and 5 more in Wales.[36] This concentration became even more pronounced in 1983. In the southern half of the country, the Labour party won only three seats outside of Greater London and was largely displaced as the main challenger to the Conservatives by the Liberal/SDP Alliance (see Table 5.7). The Labour vote declined least in Scotland, while the Conservative vote declined most in the Northwest of England. The wide margin between support for the Conservatives in the South of England and Labour in the North and Scotland is shown in Table 5.7 and in Map 5.1. Scotland and the North of England is more working-class than the South of England, but this is not sufficient to explain the disparity. A MORI poll conducted in 1981 found that among skilled workers in the North of England, Labour had a 32% lead over the Conservatives. Among the same group in the South, the Labour lead was only 6%.[37]

Not only is the North–South divide becoming more pronounced in terms of Labour–Conservative polarization, so too is the divide between urban and rural areas. Conservative support in the larger cities has been declining for more than 25 years. In the 1983 election, the party won less than half the number of seats it had won in the larger cities in 1959, the last election when it was returned with a three-figure majority. In some cities, the decline in support has been dramatic. In 1959 in the three cities of Glasgow, Liverpool, and Manchester, the Conservatives won a total of 15 seats. In the same three cities in 1983, they won 1. There are now no Conservative-held seats in Glasgow or Liverpool. Conversely, the rural areas have moved further away from Labour. In 1983, the swing away from Labour in rural and mixed areas was twice what it was in urban areas: not one rural constituency in the South of England was won by Labour.

These changes have been attributed to changing economic patterns. "The peripheral areas of Britain," write two analysts, "with their higher unemployment, and the declining inner parts of conurbations, have become steadily more Labour; while the expanding, more prosperous areas have become more Conservative."[38] Prosperity would also appear relevant to the increasing importance of home ownership. In 1983, the Labour vote held up well among those who rented their homes from the local authorities (Table 5.7). Among those who owned their own homes the party trailed third behind the Conservatives and the Liberal/SDP Alliance. Working-class home-owners were more likely to vote Conservative than working-class council-house tenants. The problem for the Labour party is that the latter category is declining in size: more workers are buying their own homes.

Increasingly, then, the Conservative party is becoming a party that draws its support predominantly from the South of England, from the rural and suburban constituencies, and from home-owners. Labour, in contrast, is becoming a party confined to the North of England, Scotland, and the urban

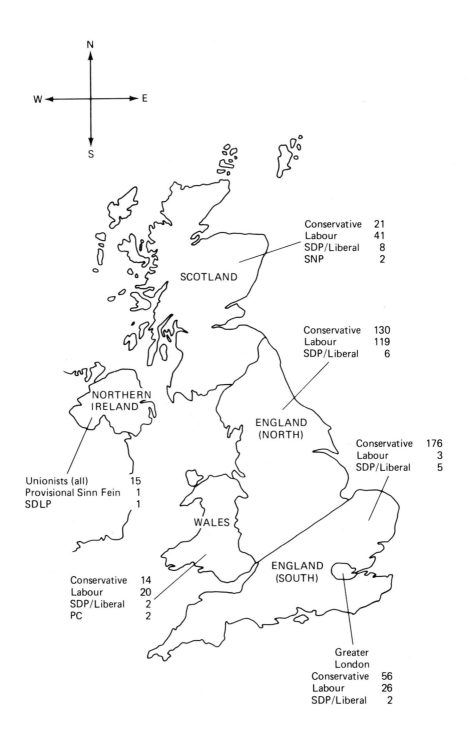

N

W ← → E

S

SCOTLAND

Conservative 21
Labour 41
SDP/Liberal 8
SNP 2

Conservative 130
Labour 119
SDP/Liberal 6

NORTHERN
IRELAND

ENGLAND
(NORTH)

Conservative 176
Labour 3
SDP/Liberal 5

Unionists (all) 15
Provisional Sinn Fein 1
SDLP 1

WALES

ENGLAND
(SOUTH)

Conservative 14
Labour 20
SDP/Liberal 2
PC 2

Greater
London
Conservative 56
Labour 26
SDP/Liberal 2

TABLE 5.7
Party Support by Location and Home Ownership, 1983

	Location		Home Ownership	
	South	Scotland/ North	Occupier- Owned	Council- Owned
Conservative	42%	32%	47%	19%
Labour	26%	42%	25%	57%
Liberal/SDP	32%	26%	28%	24%

SOURCE: Gallup poll, undertaken for BBC, on June 8 and 9, 1983. *The Guardian*, June 13, 1983. Copyright 1983 the Guardian. Reprinted by permission.

areas, especially the inner cities. As for the Liberal/SDP Alliance, it appears to draw its support fairly evenly from the different classes (Table 5.5), from different parts of the country (though marginally more from the South than from the North and Scotland), and from owner-occupiers as well as council-house tenants (Table 5.7). Anyone seeking to find a reliable predictor of Alliance voting would be hard pressed to find one.

Are there any other correlations to be drawn? Education remains important, independent of class. Voters with above the minimum of education are more likely than those who have only a minimum of education to vote Conservative. Where the British equivalents of Continental peasants (crofters, lumbermen, isolated agriculturalists) are gathered, there is a tendency for voters to deviate from overall patterns of class voting, a tendency in Scotland and Wales favoring the Liberals (and, in 1983, the SDP) as well as the Nationalist parties. The presence of nonwhite voters in certain urban constituencies may cause further deviations from the class pattern, but the evidence on this is mixed.[39] Issue voting, which one might expect to have increased in significance given the decline in class voting, appears to remain extremely limited. The images that the parties convey are important,[40] more so than their stance on specific issues. In the 1983 election, more electors thought the Conservatives had the better policies than actually voted for the party. The most important issue was considered by electors to be that of unemployment, an issue on which more preferred the Labour position to that of the Conservatives. Against this, the Conservatives were preferred by

MAP 5.1 General election results by region for 1983. (*Note:* South of England comprises Avon, Bedfordshire, Berkshire, Buckinghamshire, Cambridgeshire, Cornwall, Devon, Dorset, Sussex, Essex, Gloucestershire, Hampshire, Hertfordshire, Isle of Wight, Kent, Norfolk, Northamptonshire, Oxfordshire, Somerset, Suffolk, Surrey, and Wiltshire.

far greater margins on the issues of defense and prices.[41] Negative voting was also a significant feature of the election, 59% of all voters disliking the other party (or parties) more than they liked their own.[42] There is little evidence to suggest voters voting for a particular party because of its stand on a particular issue.

THE CURRENT DEBATE

Electoral changes and their relationship to the political parties have been the subject of much recent analysis and debate. A review of this debate is more appropriate following a consideration of the political parties in Britain and hence is covered in the following chapter. Here I propose to confine my discussion to the contemporary debate surrounding the electoral system as an electoral system. By the middle of the twentieth century, Britain had developed an electoral system the basic characteristics of which have been delineated above: single-member constituencies, first-past-the-post election to determine the winner in each, and each adult citizen having the right to cast a vote. That system was both perceived and expected to perform three related functions: through election to the House of Commons it was expected to produce a government;[43] through a purportedly democratic franchise and mode of election, it was expected to confer legitimacy upon the government to govern, subject to the approval of Parliament; and, through facilitating a choice between parties propounding specific programs, it was expected to influence public policy, the party in government carrying through the promises embodied in its election manifesto. In the 1950s such expectations were assumed to have been met. Governments were returned with overall majorities. There were few complaints about the mode of election. Governments appeared to carry out their promises. The electoral system appeared to form an intrinsic part of a stable polity.

In the 1970s, and especially in the wake of the two general elections of 1974, the extent to which the electoral system was capable of fulfilling such functions became a matter of controversy. In the February 1974 election, no party was returned to office with an overall majority of seats. In the election of October of the same year, the Labour party achieved an overall majority of only three seats: as a consequence of by-election losses and defections, it lost its majority in April 1976, and by the end of the Parliament was in a minority by 17 seats.[44] The Conservative party achieved a swing of 5.2% in its favor in the May 1979 election, being returned with a majority of 43 seats. In previous decades a similar swing would have produced a much higher majority. Shifts in the distribution of party support within the country were, according to one important study, likely to increase the likelihood of "hung" Parliaments, no one party being returned with an overall majority.[45] The ability of the electoral system to produce a government in the way previously expected of it was thus called into question. Furthermore, the system also came under attack as being unfair—hence undermining consent by calling into doubt the legitimacy of both the mode of election and the government produced by it—and for facilitating the adversary relationship between the parties, a relationship that significantly influenced public policy, but did so in a manner harmful to the interests of the country. The effects of this adversary relationship on public policy in terms of both continuity and substance was considered to threaten rather than enhance the effectiveness of government.

The accusation that the electoral system is an unfair one is not new. It has been advanced for some time by both the Liberal party and the Electoral Reform Society. It gained ground as a result of the election results of the 1970s and the development of the adversary politics thesis. The first-past-the-post plurality method of election in single-member constituencies, it was argued, did not allow realization of the principle of "one person, one vote, one value." Each adult citizen may have one vote but each vote was not of equal value. The disparity in the size of constituency electorates meant that a vote cast in a constituency with a small electorate such as Glasgow Central was worth more than one cast in, say, Bromsgrove and Redditch. Furthermore, the extensive number of safe seats meant that many electors cast "wasted" votes. What was the point of voting Conservative in a constituency such as Blaenau Gwent, for example, where the Labour candidate had a majority in excess of 20,000 at the previous election? An elector consistently voting Conservative in the constituency would never contribute towards the election of an MP.

The two most central criticisms, though, have been directed at the aggregate effects of such a method of election. Given the difference in the spread of support between the parties, it is possible for one party to get more votes than its opponent party but receive fewer seats. For example, party A could win two marginal seats by the barest of margins while party B won one seat with an overwhelming majority; the aggregate vote for party B in the three seats could well exceed that of party A, but party A has won twice as many seats. (A similar spread of support among states in the United States presidential elections may result in a president obtaining a majority in the electoral college without obtaining a majority of the popular vote.) On two occasions in postwar elections, such a situation actually occurred. In the 1951 general election, the Conservatives won a majority of seats but the Labour party won more votes (see Table 5.2). In the February 1974 election, the position was reversed, the Conservatives winning more votes nationally than Labour but Labour winning more seats. In terms of forming a government, it is the number of seats that count: the Conservatives formed the government in 1951, the Labour party in 1974.

The other major and related criticism, the one emphasized most often, is that the plurality system of voting works against national third parties. Those who benefit most from such a system are the two largest parties and those with regionally concentrated support. This is as true in the United States as it is in Britain. In presidential elections, a third-party candidate with concentrated support, such as George Wallace in 1968, can carry some states and hence win some electoral college votes. A candidate with support that is broad but not deep, such as John Anderson in 1980, can amass several million votes but carry no state at all. The system favors the Republican and Democratic parties. Similarly in Britain, a party can win several thousand votes in each constituency yet not come out top of the poll in any; in consequence, it amasses a large popular vote but no seats in Parliament. This is almost the position in which the Liberal party has found itself in recent elections (see Table 5.2). In 1979, for example, it won in excess of 4 million votes yet topped the poll in only 11 seats, less than 2% of the total. This phenomenon is even more marked in the case of the SDP/Liberal Alliance: in 1983 it achieved more than a quarter of the votes cast in the general election, yet won only 3.5% of the seats in Parliament. The largest party, by contrast, can top the poll in most constituencies with, say, 40% of the poll, the remaining votes split among the other party candidates (see the example of Leicester South in Table 5.3), thus achieving a majority of seats without receiving an absolute majority of the votes cast. Indeed, at no election since 1935 has a party obtained more than 50% of the votes cast, yet at only one election since that time has a government been returned without a majority of seats. In the election of October 1974, the Labour party obtained a bare majority of seats for fewer than 40% of the votes cast. Not surprisingly, the Liberal and Social Democratic parties are in the vanguard in arguing for a reform of the electoral system to eliminate such anomalies. The Conservative and Labour parties, by contrast, retain a preference for the existing system.

The other more recent criticisms of the electoral system has derived from the characterization of the existing political system as an adversary one. The "adversary politics" thesis was developed following the 1974 elections by a number of academics, led by S. E. Finer.[46] The essence of their argument was that the electoral system encouraged a polarized contest between two parties for the winner-take-all spoils of a general election. One party would be returned to office with an overall majority and implement its manifesto program, a program neither known nor supported by most electors and one drawn up on the basis more of party dogma than of a dispassionate and well-informed analysis of Britain's problems. The other party would then win at a subsequent election, enter office and largely undo the work of its predecessor, implementing instead its own program. Given that the two parties were perceived as representing different poles of the political spectrum, government policy would lurch from being right of the political center under one administration to being left of center under another. The results, in short, were unrepresentative governments—pursuing policies more politically extreme than those favored by the more centrist electorate—and policy discontinuity. Policy discontinuity frustrated industrialists and investors who wished to engage in forward planning: they could not anticipate stability in government programs. Adversary politics and changes in government may make for "exciting politics," but they produced "low-credibility Government strategies, whichever party is in power."[47]

Indeed, the conditions created by the electoral system were seen as being the heart of Britain's current problems. In order to win an election, a party would make extravagant promises, doing so in order to outbid the other party. In office, it would find it could no longer raise the resources to meet those promises. It therefore had to change tack, further adding to confusion in governmental policy-making. However, it also had to act in a way that would not jeopardize its chance of winning the next election. Hence it was reluctant to take the unpopular measures deemed by some to be necessary to tackle Britain's long-term problems. The result, in short, was a vicious circle.[48]

The solution, or at least a partial one, to the problem was perceived by these critics as the introduction of a new electoral system, one that introduced a method of proportional representation. Proportional representation (PR), it was argued, would be fairer than the existing electoral system, ensuring that a party received the share of parliamentary seats equivalent to its national vote. Furthermore, giving existing voting behavior, it would deprive any one party of an overall majority of seats. To form a government with an overall parliamentary majority would thus necessitate a coalition. This would likely involve one of the main parties having "to co-operate with a party or parties taking a more central stance," hence leading to greater moderation in policy.[49] Given that such a coalition would enjoy the support of more than 50% of electors and that the turnover of seats under PR is small (Professor Finer estimated that a swing of 1% would result in the loss of only six seats), it would most likely remain in office for the foreseeable future and hence be in a position to ensure a degree of policy continuity. The overall effect of PR would thus be to put an end to the worst features of adversary politics and its unfortunate consequences.

Of the systems of proportional representation, the one favored by the Liberal Party and the Electoral Reform Society is the single transferable vote (STV) system. It is the method of election currently employed in the Republic of Ireland, in Tasmania, and in Malta and for elections to the Australian Senate. Under STV there are multimember constituencies, with each elector able to indicate a preference on the ballot paper, putting the number 1 beside the name of the candidate most preferred, number 2 against the name of the elector's second choice, and so on. A quota is established by the formula of dividing the number of valid ballots cast by the number of seats, plus one; to the resulting figure, one is added. Thus in a five-member constituency in which 120,000 ballots are cast, the formula would be

$$\frac{120,000}{5 + 1} + 1.$$

Hence the quota (the number of ballots required to elect one member) would be 20,001. Any candidate receiving this number of votes is declared elected. The second preferences of any of the candidate's surplus votes, plus those of the candidate at the bottom of the poll, are then redistributed, and so on until the necessary number of candidates reach the quota.

The other main system that has been advocated is the additional member system, similar to that employed in West Germany. Under this system, single-member constituencies would be retained with the first-past-the post method of election retained in each—in other words, the same as at present. However, there would be additional seats allocated to parties on a regional basis, a minimum of 5% of the vote in any area of allocation being necessary to obtain any additional seats. Additional seats would go proportionately to the parties on the basis of the proportion of votes received in the region. Under a scheme proposed by the Hansard Society for Parliamentary Government, there would be 480 single-member constituencies and 160 seats allocated on a regional basis.[50] Proponents of this system and of STV argue that the effect would be a representative House of Commons, the proportion of seats going to parties being the same as the proportion of the votes won in the election.

Support for a new electoral system has developed since the mid-1970s, encompassing academics and politicians. The Conservative and Labour parties have witnessed the creation of bodies within their own ranks favoring such reform.[51] The Liberal party has an important ally in its partner, the Social Democratic party: both are strongly committed to electoral reform. Various attempts were made in the 1974–1979 Parliament to introduce PR throughout the United Kingdom for elections to the European Parliament and for elections to the proposed assemblies in Scotland and Wales. The attempts failed, but they helped keep the issue of electoral reform on the agenda of political debate. The outcome of the 1983 election added a further spur to the reform movement.

Despite this pressure for reform, the existing system retains its support-ers. A majority of both the Conservative and Labour parliamentary parties prefer the first-past-the-post method of election. One keen defender is the present prime minister, Mrs. Thatcher. The arguments deployed against the reformers' case are varied. The essential line of argument is that a reformed electoral system could constitute a greater threat to the maintenance of political authority than any defects of the existing system. The STV system, it is argued, could threaten the essential link between an elector and his MP given that it would necessitate in rural areas constituencies of massive size. Given the reformers' argument that PR would enhance the likelihood of coalition government, consent could be undermined if government was to result from post-election bargaining between parties; by a small center party holding the balance of power and hence wielding undue influence over government policy; and by the alienation of voters who support a party excluded on a long-term basis from becoming a partner in coalition.[52] Such rebuttals are based on accepting the assumptions made by PR advocates about the likely consequences of electoral reform. Some observers have drawn attention to the fact that such assumptions themselves rest on flimsy foundations. The reformers argue their case on the assumption that voting behavior experienced under the current mode of election would most likely continue under a new mode: this is, as Geoffrey Alderman has pointed out, a most unlikely hypothesis.[53] Arguments that PR works well in countries such as West Germany are countered by pointing to the experience of Italy, where turnover in governments is rapid and a significant fraction of the population vote for a party that is consistently excluded from government. Given the different political cultures that exist, seeking to anticipate what would happen in Britain on the basis of experience abroad is an undertaking of limited usefulness.

The adversary politics thesis developed by the reformers has also been variously challenged. There are two mutually exclusive arguments deployed against it. One line of argument accepts the notion of an adversary relationship between the parties but considers this a beneficial rather than a harmful process. It offers a clear choice to the electorate and it results in one party with a mandate from the people getting on with the job of governing. If the electorate disapproves of the policies or their outcomes, it has the opportunity to replace the government at the next election. There may be some discontinuity in policy occasioned by governments of different political persuasions pursuing different paths, but that is the price—an acceptable price—one has to pay for the advantages offered by the existing system. Proportional representation, it is feared, would facilitate a blurring of the choice before the electorate and prevent a party being returned with a mandate clearly approved by the people.

Such a line of argument is pursued especially by the two largest parties. It is in their own interests to do so: each wants to pursue its own policies, which it believes to be in the best interests of the country, without having those policies tempered or abandoned because of the need to enter into alliance with another party. For a brief period of one year, 1977–1978, the Labour government of James Callaghan entered into a Pact with the Liberal parliamentary party: in return for voting support in the House of Commons (necessary to maintain its majority), the government modified certain policies of its own and introduced certain measures favored by the Liberals.[54]

The experience was not one much enjoyed by the Labour party, certain sections of which were extremely hostile to the arrangement. Both the Conservative and Labour parties appeared to draw the conclusion that it was an experience to be avoided, not one to be encouraged.

The other argument deployed against the adversary politics thesis calls into doubt the relevance of the notion itself. The rhetoric of adversary politics, it is argued, hides a more consensual substance. In terms of government legislation, empirical research has indicated that a consensual model is indeed more applicable.[55] In this view, parties are seen as being not quite as central to formulation of public policy as both reformers and the politicians themselves believe. The external demands on government are such that it can often act only as arbiter between competing demands and respond, under guidance from civil servants, to international events and trends over which it has no direct influence. Whichever party is in power makes some but not a great deal of difference. Elections may help produce the personnel at the apex of government but they tell us little about likely public policy.

The electoral system, in summary, has again become a subject of political debate. In terms of the political system, it can be said to provide the means by which a government is chosen but, despite the results of the 1983 general election, the extent to which it will continue to be capable of providing a government (at least in the way it has previously done) remains under question. It operates on the principle of "one person, one vote," but there is now some dispute as to its legitimacy and that of the government it produces on the grounds that the principle of "one person, one vote, one value" has not been fully realized. And there is debate and notable disagreement about the consequences that elections not only do have but should have for public policy. The debate is very much a current one. It revolves around arguments for and against a reform of the electoral system. Whether Britain will witness electoral reform in the next decade or so rests on the outcome of that debate. The 1983 general election result fueled rather than ended the controversy.

NOTES

1. M. J. C. Vile, *Politics in the USA* (Hutchinson, 1976 ed.), p. 91.

2. See G. Alderman, *British Elections: Myth and Reality* (Batsford, 1978), pp. 9–22.

3. "The General Election 1983," *Politics Today* (12), July 11, 1983, p. 233.

4. Alderman, p. 45.

5. A. Ranney, "British General Elections: An Introduction" in H. Penniman (ed.), *Britain at the Polls, 1979* (American Enterprise Institute, 1981), p. 5, shows the average size of English constituencies to be just under 90,000. This figure is misleading since it refers to the average population of each constituency, not the number of electors.

6. *The BBC/ITN Guide to the New Parliamentary Constituencies* (Parliamentary Research Services, 1983).

7. The figure is £1,750 plus 1½p per elector in borough constituencies and £1,750 plus 2p per elector in county constituencies. In the 1979 election, Conservative candidates on average spent £2,190 on their campaigns, Labour candidates £1,897, and Liberal candidates £725.

8. M. Pinto-Duschinsky, *British Political Finance 1830–1980* (American Enterprise Institute, 1981), p. 249.

9. See A. P. Hill, "The Effect of Party Organisation: Election Expenses and the 1970 Election," *Political Studies,* 22, 1974, pp. 215–17.

10. See D. Butler and D. Kavanagh, *The British General Election of 1979* (Macmillan, 1980).

11. M. Pinto-Duschinsky, "Financing the British General Election of 1979," in H. R. Penniman (ed.), *Britain at the Polls, 1979,* pp. 215–27.

12. See M. Pilsworth, "Balanced Broadcasting" in Butler and Kavanagh, p. 229.

13. See S. E. Finer, *The Changing British Party System, 1945–1979* (American Enterprise Institute, 1980), pp. 125–26.

14. Alderman, pp. 25–27.

15. See D. Kavanagh, "The Politics of Manifestos," *Parliamentary Affairs,* 34 (1), 1981, pp. 13–14.

16. For a thorough discussion, see Kavanagh, "The Politics of Manifestos," pp. 7–27.

17. See P. Norton, "The Qualifying Age for Candidature in British Elections," *Public Law,* Spring 1980, pp. 55–73.

18. See Butler and Kavanagh, pp. 293–94.

19. Ibid., p. 284.

20. See M. Rush, *The Selection of Parliamentary Candidates* (Nelson, 1969); A. Ranney, *Pathways to Parliament* (Macmillan, 1965).

21. D. Kavanagh, "Organisation and Power in the Liberal Party" in V. Bogdanor (ed.), *Liberal Party Politics* (Oxford University Press, 1983), p. 130.

22. *SDP Newsletter,* No. 3, 1981.

23. J. Curtice and M. Steed, "Turning Dreams Into Reality," *Parliamentary Affairs,* 36 (2), Spring 1983, pp. 166–82.

24. Butler and Kavanagh, pp. 284–87.

25. See C. Mellors, *The British MP* (Saxon House, 1978).

26. The Gallup Poll, "Voting Behaviour in Britain, 1945–1974" in R. Rose (ed.), *Studies in British Politics,* 3rd ed. (Macmillan, 1976), p. 206.

27. For various theories to explain the phenomenon of working-class Conservative voting, see P. Norton and A. Aughey, *Conservatives and Conservatism* (Temple Smith, 1981), Ch. 4.

28. D. Butler and D. Stokes, *Political Changes in Britain* (2nd ed.), (Macmillan, 1974), p. 414.

29. I. Crewe, B. Sarlvik and J. Alt, "Partisan De-alignment in Britain, 1964–1974," *British Journal of Political Science,* 7 (2), April 1977, pp. 182–83.

30. I. Crewe, "The disturbing truth behind Labour's rout," *The Guardian,* June 13, 1983.

31. Ibid.

32. Ibid.

33. R. Rose, *The Problem of Party Government* (Penguin, 1976), p. 43.

34. Ibid., p. 44.

35. See Norton and Aughey, p. 186.

36. J. Curtice and M. Steed, "An analysis of the voting," in Butler and Kavanagh, appendix 2, p. 402. See also "General Election Results by Region" in D. Butler and A. Sloman, *British Political Facts 1900–1979*, 5th ed. (Macmillan, 1980), pp. 212–13.

37. D. Lipsey, "Is the North-South divide a great British myth?" *Sunday Times*, September 13, 1981, p. 13.

38. Curtice and Steed, "An analysis of the voting," p. 402.

39. See Rose, *The Problem of Party Government*, pp. 34–49 for a summary of these relationships. See also S. E. Finer, *The Changing British Party System 1945–1979* (American Enterprise Institute, 1980), pp. 55–58.

40. See Butler and Stokes, Ch. 19.

41. I. Crewe, "How Labour was trounced all round," *The Guardian*, June 14, 1983.

42. Ibid.

43. That is, the political apex of government as formed by ministers. See the comments of A. King, "What do elections decide?" in H. Penniman (ed.), *Democracy at the Polls* (American Enterprise Institute, 1980), pp. 295–96.

44. P. Norton, "The Changing Face of the British House of Commons in the 1970s," *Legislative Studies Quarterly*, V (3), 1980, Table 2, p. 337.

45. J. Curtice and M. Steed, "Electoral Choice and the Production of Government: The Changing Operation of the Electoral System in the United Kingdom since 1955," *British Journal of Political Science*, 12 (2), 1982, pp. 249–98.

46. S. E. Finer (ed.), *Adversary Politics and Electoral Reform* (Wigram, 1975). See also S. A. Walkland, "Whither the Commons?" in S. A. Walkland and M. Ryle (eds.), *The Commons Today* (Fontana, 1981); D. Coombes, *Representative Government and Economic Power* (Heinemann, 1982); and P. Norton, *The Constitution in Flux* (Martin Robertson, 1982), pp. 232–34.

47. M. Shanks, *Planning and Politics* (Political and Economic Planning, 1977), p. 92.

48. Note the observations of P. Jay, "Englanditis" in R. E. Tyrell, Jr., *The Future that Doesn't Work* (Doubleday, 1977), p. 181. See also S. Brittan, *The Economic Consequences of Democracy* (Temple Smith, 1977).

49. Finer, *Adversary Politics*, pp. 30–31.

50. *The Report of the Hansard Society Commission on Electoral Reform* (Hansard, 1976).

51. See Norton, *The Constitution in Flux*, p. 230.

52. See ibid., p. 240.

53. Alderman, p. 39.

54. See A. Michie and S. Hoggart, *The Pact* (Quartet, 1978).

55. I. Burton and G. Drewry, *Legislation and Public Policy* (Macmillan, 1981); R. Rose, *Do Parties Make a Difference?* (Macmillan, 1980).

Political Parties
A Two or a Multiparty System?

IN THE UNITED STATES, political parties serve to provide some measure of choice among candidates at election time. They do little else. American politics remain characterized by faction rather than by party.[1] Consensus on basic values,[2] federalism, and the separation of powers has served to mold political parties that are basically nonprogrammatic and decentralized, and that operate within a political system structured in such a way as to favor stalemate or compromise. Political parties are not geared to presenting a coherent program to the electorate. The parties are too decentralized, the elections too tiered, to be conducive to such an approach. Even if parties were so geared, the political structure would militate against carrying a coherent program into effect: a party would need to be cohesive and to capture the White House and would need to achieve the return of a majority of its supporters in both houses as well as overcoming internal procedural constraints within Congress. The occasions when these constraints have been overcome, as during the New Deal era, are notable for their rarity— and their brevity. It has proved impossible to sustain strong party government. In their writings, American political scientists often give little priority to a discussion of the importance of political parties. When parties are mentioned, it is not unusual for their minimalist role to be mentioned. When they are considered as programmatic bodies having an influence on the shaping and implementation of public policy, it is usually in order to lament their absence from that role.[3]

Britain lacks those features that have facilitated a weak party system within the United States. A unitary and parliamentary form of government has favored the development of centralized and cohesive parties, parties geared to offering a programmatic choice to the electors and to carrying out that program once the all-or-nothing spoils of a general election have been gained. The executive dominance of the House of Commons ensures legislative approval of the party program: the doctrine of parliamentary sovereignty puts its implementation beyond the challenge of the courts. It is, in short, the very model of a strong party government. It is a model that for years was much admired. It was admired by many American scholars because of its apparent ability to ensure the realization of social reform.[4] It was contrasted with the brokered politics of the United States.

To stress the differences of the two systems is both important and necessary. However, it runs the risk of obscuring some important similarities. American parties may be weak and British parties strong by comparison, but both the United States and Britain are notable examples of two-party systems. In elections in the United States, electoral contests are dominated by Republicans and Democrats. Elections in Britain have usually been dominated by the Conservative and Labour parties. There are also *some* similarities between the parties themselves. The Republican party in the United States and the Conservative party in Britain are, in broad terms, right-of-center parties that tend to attract support from similar constituencies, notably the middle class. The Democratic party and the British Labour party are left-of-center parties that tend to appeal to working-class voters. (In the 1960s, Labour party leader Harold Wilson was reputed to have wanted to model himself on John Kennedy and his party on the Democratic party.) These are broad generalizations and should not be pursued too far. Nonetheless, they are relevant and it is instructive to note the apparent empathy between a Republican president, Ronald Reagan, and a Conservative prime minister, Mrs. Thatcher, in the 1980s. Furthermore, parties in both countries have in recent years witnessed similar but not identical falls in support and partisan identification among electors. The analyses of this decline in support also display similarities. This decline in support and the debate surrounding it I shall explore later.

It is important first to consider the growth and the nature of the two main political parties in Britain. In their origins and growth, they are distinctly British and can be understood only within the context of British history and the political culture.

THE PARTIES IN BRITAIN

The first principle of party, according to Edmund Burke in the eighteenth century, was "to put men who hold their opinions into such a condition as may enable them to carry their common plans into execution." At the time that he was writing, that "condition" meant gaining the confidence of the king. With the widening of the franchise in the nineteenth century, it came instead to depend on the confidence of the electors. As bodies that seek electoral success in order to form the government, political parties may be said to have developed in Britain following the Reform Act of 1832; as bodies seeking that success in order to fulfil a particular program—a stage arguably never reached by American parties—they are more especially the product of the Reform Act of 1867.

The need for electoral support after 1832 and the difficulty of establishing direct personal contact with the enlarged electorate encouraged the development of embryonic political *organization*: political clubs were formed, election funds were established, registration societies—to ensure that supporters were registered to vote—were brought into being, and in some parts of the country (notably Lancashire) constituency associations were formed. Nonetheless, as we have seen (Chapter 3), the differences between pre-. and post-1832 days were not as marked as some might have supposed: the aristocracy remained politically eminent, voting was still by open ballot, and corrupt practices were still common. All this was to change as a result of the Reform Act of 1867 and the reforming measures of the next 18 years. The electorate was now of such a size (2.5 million: see Chapter 3) and of such a nature that highly organized parties became necessary both for facilitating contact and for aggregating the interests of voters through some form of party platform. Bribery and other corrupt practices, as well as the open ballot, were formally done away with by statute, though the size of the electorate alone did much to remove bribery as an effective weapon of influence. Organized corruption, as Richard Crossman observed, was gradually replaced by party organization,[5] and the two main parties of the day, to employ Maurice Duverger's terminology, were developed from cadres into mass-membership parties. The Liberal party created the National Liberal Federation to widen its appeal to the newly enfranchised voter. The Conservative party created the Conservative National Union in 1867 and Conservative Central Office in 1870, the latter to provide professional support to the voluntary wing of the party. Highly organized, mass-membership political parties became a feature of British political life.

In the latter half of the nineteenth century, the two dominant parties were the Conservatives and the Liberals.[6] Both adhered to a hierarchical conception of party structure and both had parliamentary parties that pre-dated the creation of the extraparliamentary parties. The voluntary organizations were created primarily to mobilize support for the parliamentary leaders: they were not expected to formulate policies or to give instructions. The conventions of the Constitution also facilitated this form of "top down" leadership within the parties. Although both parties began to appeal to the country on the basis of particular platforms, the notion of "the manifesto" was not well developed. The party leaders were expected to make an appeal to the country and, if elected, were expected to proceed with the task of governing.

Such approaches were to be modified in the twentieth century. One important influence was the development of the Labour party. It was created to achieve the return to Parliament of representatives of the working classes and it adhered to the concept of intraparty democracy. Implementation of the party's election manifesto became the touchstone by which party activists could determine if party leaders were adhering to the party's program. The party's internal norms were not altogether compatible with those of the Constitution. The party favored the election of party leaders, which in government would mean the members of the cabinet. The Constitution conferred such power on the prime minister. Under the leadership of Ramsay MacDonald, the first Labour prime minister, this conflict was resolved largely in favor of the Constitution. Nonetheless, tension between a "top down" form of political leadership, in which the party defers to the guidance given by its leaders, and a "bottom up" form, in which leaders are bound by decisions taken by party members, has been a recurrent feature of Labour party politics. As we shall see, it remains a central feature of the contemporary Labour party.

The Labour party displaced the Liberal party as one of the two main parties in Britain in the 1920s. In 1922, it was recognized as the main Opposition party in Parliament. The interwar years, between 1918 and 1939, were years of Conservative dominance. Since the Second World War the two parties have been more evenly matched: Labour has been in government for 17 of the 38 years since 1945, and the Conservatives for 21 years. The parties are similar in that they have developed national organizations and cohesive parliamentary parties with complex infrastructures,[7] and at election time, they issue detailed and specific manifestos. Both, not surprisingly, favor the existing party duopoly in British politics. In other respects, as we shall see, the two differ significantly. In the 1970s and 1980s, both have come under challenge from other parties: in the 1970s notably from nationalist parties and in the 1980s from the newly formed Social Democratic party in alliance with the Liberal party. The Social Democratic party was established in 1981 with the aim of "breaking the mold" of British politics.

The Conservative Party

Although British Conservatism can be traced back several centuries, indeed to Hooker in the sixteenth century, the emergence of a political party with the name Conservative took place in the fourth decade of the nineteenth century. The name Conservative was first used by an anonymous writer in 1830, and the term was in common usage by 1832. The party set up an election fund in 1835.[8] It was the successor to the Tory party, the party of the land-owning gentry, which had largely disintegrated under the leadership of the Duke of Wellington in the 1820s. It inherited both the base of Tory support and the party's central tenets. Foremost among these was a belief in the organic nature of society. Society was seen as a historical product, a thing of slow and natural growth, an organic entity with unity and character. Concomitantly, the party inherited from the philosophy of Edmund Burke a belief in gradual change: society was evolutionary, not static. Change, though, had to be evolutionary, not revolutionary. It had to improve, not destroy. Change had to take place without doing violence to the existing fabric of society. The party was committed to the defense of existing and worthwhile institutions: it stood for the defense of Constitution, Crown, and Church. If there was to be reform it should be to save the Constitution, not to subvert it. It was a corrolary of such beliefs that the party adhered to an ordered society, one in which law, order, and authority were upheld. It stood for the defense of property. Private property, as Burke contended, was a bulwark against tyranny: without private property, the over-powerful state could not be resisted. One could identify the party as adhering also to limited but not necessarily weak government. Government was perceived as having but a limited role to play in society, primarily that of the defense of the realm, but if strong government was on occasion necessary to maintain the King's government, then so be it. In short, then, a party standing basically for the existing order of things but prepared to admit of the need for occasional change, change not for change's sake but change in order to preserve.

The party's base of support was initially a restricted one. It was essentially a party of the landed interest. It had no national appeal and for the middle years of the century was very much the "out" party in politics. It was transformed into a national party by Benjamin Disraeli. He had to devise an appeal that made the party relevant to the problems of the day. This he did: to the corpus of Conservative beliefs he added adherence to the notion of One Nation—that is, One Nation at Home and One Nation Abroad. Domestically, this meant that the party would not divide the nation in the interests of one class but would look after the interests of all classes. The party would balance social forces and establish common goals. Internationally, it meant the development and maintenance of Empire. This identified the party with the achievements of the nation; it provided an inspiring theme to unite in patriotic harmony all Englishmen, if not all Britons. As part of the theme of One Nation, Disraeli was to demonstrate concern for the welfare of the people—much of the social reform legislation of the latter half of the century was Conservative-inspired[9]—while stressing the imperative of maintaining institutions and social stability. Coupled with this national appeal was the development of the party as a mass-membership organization, one that ensured that the party's message reached the new electors. By the time of Disraeli's death in 1881, the Conservative party had laid claim to be a national party, a party of responsibility and government. For the last quarter of the century and for much of the twentieth, the party was to dominate British politics.

As the party developed to acquire its national status, so it acquired new support. It obtained the support of a substantial fraction of working-class voters, in large part because industrialists and mill owners—the employers of the workers—were associated with the Liberal party. Today, approximately one-third of working-class voters cast their ballots for the Conservative party, comprising about half of the party's electoral strength. It acquired defectors from the ranks of the Liberals, notably the Liberal Unionists toward the end of the nineteenth century. The influx of Liberals tended to move it more in the direction of a capitalist party, supporting the making of money by individual enterprise rather than looking down on it as a slightly degrading pursuit. By the twentieth century, the Conservative party was a cohesive party but one that constituted a coalescence of different strands of thought.

Within British Conservatism, there are two main strands: the Tory and the Whig, each of which may be further subdivided.[10] The Tory strand of thought places emphasis on social discipline, on authority, on continuity, and on ensuring that change does not do violence to the essential fabric of society; it tends to adhere strongly to the Disraelian concept of One Nation. The Whig strain is more concerned with future goals and places emphasis on the creation of wealth and the most efficient form of economic organization. It is thus more concerned with economics; the Tory strain is more concerned with morals. Within the party, there is the potential for tension between continuity and change, between those favoring change in more radical or rapid form and those favoring moderation, and between the Tory emphasis on social unity and the neoliberal element within Whig thought that stresses creative tension and competitive struggle. On occasion, such tension has been realized: in the 1840s and again in the first decade of the twentieth century on the issue of tariff reform (the liberal strain within the party favoring free trade, the Tory element favoring the erection of tariff barriers to protect British industry), and in the 1970s and 1980s on the issue of economic policy, to which we shall return shortly. Such occasions, though, are the exceptions rather than the rule. Cohesiveness is a distinguishing feature of the party.

The cohesiveness of the party may be attributed largely to the fact that, unlike the Labour party, it is a party of tendencies rather than one of factions[11]—that is, it lacks permanent factions organized in order to promote a specific set of beliefs. Rather, it comprises a set of differing but not mutually exclusive strands of thought that are not aligned in consistent opposition to one another. On some issues, there may be dissent within the party but the composition of the dissenting body within the party changes from issue to issue, almost like a chemical reaction. One may be a Tory on one issue, something of a Whig on another. The distinction between Whig and Tory is not so clearly and starkly drawn as to permit a permanent divide. Within each Conservative there is a Tory element and a Whig element, though one element may tend to be more dominant at certain times and on certain issues. In consequence, a party member may disagree with the party on one issue but agree with it on other issues. This is in marked contrast to the Labour party, in which there is a factional divide: someone on a particular wing of the party on one issue is likely to be on that wing across the whole gamut of current political issues. There is in essence a mutually exclusive struggle between left and right.

The Conservative party traditionally has been led by leaders drawn more from the Tory than the Whig strain within the party. The postwar leaders—Winston Churchill (1940–1955), Sir Anthony Eden (1955–1957), Harold Macmillan (1957–1963), and Sir Alec Douglas-Home (1963–1965)—were men essentially in the Tory paternalist mold, more concerned with social harmony and order than with the intricacies of economic management. In the 1960s the party's fortunes took a turn for the worse. The economy began to falter, and the party suffered a bitter, public battle for the party leadership in 1963 and seemed unable to offer a young and dynamic leadership to match that which the Labour party was providing. Macmillan had married into the family of the Duke of Devonshire and was often photographed on the Scottish moors shooting grouse. Sir Alec Douglas-Home was able to assume the office of prime minister only after renouncing his title as the 14th Earl of Home. (The prime minister, by convention, must sit in the Commons, not the House of Lords.) The Party seemed to be out of touch with the tenor of the times, and in 1964 it lost the general election.

In July 1965, Douglas-Home resigned the party leadership. Previously the leader had not been elected but had been allowed to "emerge" following private consultations within the party hierarchy. Following the struggle for the leadership in 1963, rules for the election of the leader were adopted in 1964 and first employed in 1965. The electorate was that of the parliamentary party and the MPs chose as leader Edward Heath in preference to former Chancellor of the Exchequer Reginald Maudling. Maudling was in the traditional Tory mold, though lacking the aristocratic background of previous leaders. Heath was seen by his supporters as a neoliberal and as capable of challenging the Labour party under the leadership of Harold Wilson. Both Heath and Wilson came from relatively humble origins, they were of similar age, and both stressed the need for economic efficiency.

The first four years of Heath's leadership were inauspicious ones. The party lost badly the general election of 1966, and Heath proved no match to Wilson in parliamentary debates. However, as economic conditions worsened in the late 1960s, the unpopularity of the Labour Government increased. In the 1970 general election, Heath dominated the Conservative campaign, pursuing a rigorous schedule and doggedly putting across his message. When the party won the election, the credit for victory was given to Heath, and he dominated the party for the next four years.

In the first two years of government, Heath pursued an essentially neoliberal policy, eschewing a prices-and-incomes policy and preferring the operation of the free market to intervention by government. The aim was to force British industry to be more efficient. This goal provided part of the motivation also for British membership in the European Communities, which Heath achieved in 1972 (see Chapter 9). However, the government's economic policy failed to stem the rise in inflation. Unemployment also began to rise, more than three-quarters of a million people being out of work in 1971. Against this background of rising unemployment and inflation the Heath government in 1972 embarked on a number of policy changes, dubbed "U-turns" by critics. Public money was made available to aid regional development and to assist ailing companies. An attempt was made to reach voluntary agreement with unions and employers on a prices-and-incomes policy. When that failed, a statutory policy was introduced, beginning with a 90-day freeze on pay and prices. [12]

The government's economic policy encountered opposition from the trades unions. The National Union of Mineworkers introduced an overtime ban in pursuit of a pay claim and then announced plans for a national strike. When negotiations with the Government broke down, Mr. Heath in February 1974 called a general election, ostensibly to be fought on the issue of "Who Governs? The Government or the Miners?" In practice, other issues intervened during the campaign, and despite winning more votes than the Labour party, the Conservatives won fewer seats. Mr. Heath sought to arrange an alliance with the small parliamentary Liberal party in order to stay in office. He failed, and Mr. Wilson was summoned to Buckingham Palace and asked to form a government.

The loss of the election and his U-turns in office much reduced Mr. Heath's popularity within the party. He was heavily criticized by the growing neoliberal wing within the party. A number of Conservatives began to argue for a vigorous neoliberal policy, allowing the forces of a free-market economy to prevail, with government merely providing the conditions in which that economy could flourish. The means of achieving this was through control of the money supply, and the name of American monetarist economist Milton Friedman began to be much quoted. When the Conservatives lost the general election of October 1974, pressure for Heath to resign as party leader built up, and early in 1975 he was persuaded to offer himself for reelection, an event for which there was no precedent. His main challenger in the election was Mrs. Margaret Thatcher, who had served in his government as education minister. She espoused the rhetoric of the neoliberal wing of the party and offered the party a new style of leadership. In the first ballot, she won 130 votes to Mr. Heath's 119. (A third candidate received 16 votes.) Mr. Heath then withdrew from the contest. Under the election rules, a second ballot could be held in which new challengers could come forward. A number did, but proved unsuccessful against Mrs. Thatcher's growing support: she received 146 votes and her nearest rival (William Whitelaw), 79 votes. For the first time in its history, the Conservative party had elected a female leader, one who was more clearly identified with the neoliberal wing of the party than any previous leader.

Mrs. Thatcher led the party in Opposition until 1979, when the minority Labour government was defeated on a vote of confidence in the House of Commons. A general election ensued. Labour unpopularity following a period of strikes by public employees helped the Conservatives to victory, and Mrs. Thatcher entered 10 Downing Street as Britain's first female prime minister. Under her leadership, the government pursued a policy of controlling the money supply, reducing direct taxation, and keeping public expenditure within stipulated limits. The government soon encountered difficulties. Techniques for controlling the money supply proved inadequate for the purpose. Attempts to reduce planned public spending generated political opposition from within the party (and, indeed, from some members of the cabinet) as well as from political opponents. Mrs. Thatcher failed to persuade her own government to accept more stringent measures. Subsidies to nationalized industries were continued. Despite maintaining neoliberal rhetoric, the government ceased to pursue a rigorous neoliberal economic policy.

Within two years of entering office, the government was trailing in the opinion polls, bitterly divided internally between those who supported the government's restrictionist economic policy and those who opposed it (known as the "Wets," a term of abuse used by the Prime Minister),[13] and had failed to produce the economic fruits that might produce a change in its fortunes. These conditions were to change in 1982. The government's response to the Argentinian invasion of the Falkland Islands—despatching a naval task force to expel the invaders—restored it to popular favor. Following the successful recapture of the islands, the Conservative lead in the opinion polls held until the 1983 General Election, sustained by some change in economic indicators (inflation and interest rates both fell) and by disarray within the Labour party. The Falklands campaign also served to provide a boost to the Prime Minister's popularity: the campaign transposed her from a very poorly rated prime minister to a very highly rated one in the perception of electors (the proportion of electors satisfied with her leadership prior to the campaign was less than 30%: after the campaign, it was nearly 60%).[14] In the 1983 general election, the Conservative party was able to offer the image of a relatively united party that had pursued with determination harsh but necessary policies at home and had stood up for Britain's interests abroad. In its election manifesto, it stressed the need to maintain the existing economic policy (see Table 6.1), committing itself to controlling the money supply and public expenditure, reducing taxation, and returning

TABLE 6.1
Manifesto Promises, 1983

Issue	Conservative	Labour	Alliance
Economy	Control of public spending, borrowing and money supply; main priority remains to reduce inflation.	"Massive" rise in public spending; annual "national economic assessment" agreed by the Trades Union Congress and government on how to distribute national income.	Increased government borrowing (by £3 billion) to reduce unemployment plus various job-creation programs.
Defense	Keep independent nuclear deterrent. Deployment of Cruise missiles in Britain.	Cancellation of Trident program. Support for immediate nuclear freeze. Non-nuclear defense policy to be carried through in lifetime of next Parliament.	Cancellation of Trident. Deployment of Cruise dependent on arms talks and stance of allies.
European Communities	Britain to remain a member, but attempt to shift spending priorities.	Withdraw from EC within the lifetime of the next Parliament.	Britain to remain a member.

Industry	Further denationalization, including British Telecom, Rolls Royce, and British Airways.	Assets privatized under Conservatives to be returned to public ownership. "Significant public stake" in various industries such as electronics. Five-year national plan to rebuild industry through a national planning council and Department of Economic and Industrial Planning.	No nationalization or denationalization. Industrial credit scheme to help modernize private industry.
Trade Unions	Union members given right to hold secret ballots at least every five years to elect leaders. Legal immunities to call strike removed if no prior approval through secret ballot.	Repeal of Conservative Employment Acts. Unions to assist in "national economic assessment" (see above).	Secret ballots for electing national officers and for strike action if demanded by 10% of those involved. Pay and prices commission to monitor pay settlements.
Taxation	Lower rates of income tax. Improvements in allowances. Encouragement of greater share ownership.	Increases in personal tax allowances. Wealth tax to catch "the richest 100,000."	Increase in child benefit and unemployment and sickness benefit. Supplementary benefit for long-term unemployed.

some nationalized industries to private ownership. It also stressed the need for Britain to retain an independent nuclear deterrent. In the election, a Gallup survey found that 50% of electors thought that the Conservatives had "the best policies" (compared with 25% for Labour and 24% for the SDP/ Liberal Alliance). The results of the election surprised few observers: the Conservative party won 397 seats, giving it an overall parliamentary majority of 144. Mrs. Thatcher became the first Conservative prime minister in the twentieth century to lead her party in two successive election victories.[15]

Party Organization.   In terms of its internal organization, the Party is hierarchical. The party brings to bear for its own organization the principles it seeks to apply in society. Weight is given to seniority and experience as well as to the wisdom of past generations. The fount of all policy is the party leader. The party's annual conference as well as other organs of the party (see Figure 6.1) serve in an advisory role only. At the end of the day, the leader determines the policy of the party and the contents of the election manifesto. Although the leader is now elected, other leading party officials, including the party chairman and the parliamentary spokesmen when in Opposition, are appointed by the leader. While some writers have sought to apply a monarchial or a Hobbesian model of leadership to the party, a traditional family model may be more appropriate, emphasizing as it does the mutual dependence and trust that exists between leaders and led within the party.[16] Each needs the other. As long as the leader appears likely to lead the party to electoral success, the party defers to that leader. If the party looks doomed to electoral defeat, the position of the leader becomes vulnerable. Mrs. Thatcher was in a vulnerable position in 1981 but ceased to be in 1982.

Like other parties, the Conservative party recruits dues-paying members. (In Britain, one cannot register as Conservative or Labour: one has to make the conscious effort, independent of voter registration, to join a party.) Unlike the Labour party, the Conservative party has no indirect dues-paying membership through affiliated organizations. Instead, it recruits individuals directly as members. Although there are no definitive figures available, it is believed to have a membership of about 1.5 million. Members are organized in constituency associations, based on the parliamentary constituencies. Each local association is responsible for various fund-raising activities, recruiting new members, and organizing election campaigns, both at the parliamentary and local government levels. About half of the associations employ full-time agents, paid executive officers responsible for the efficient running of the organization.[17]

Of the political parties, the Conservative is the best financed. Its income derives from three sources: business donations, individual donations, and

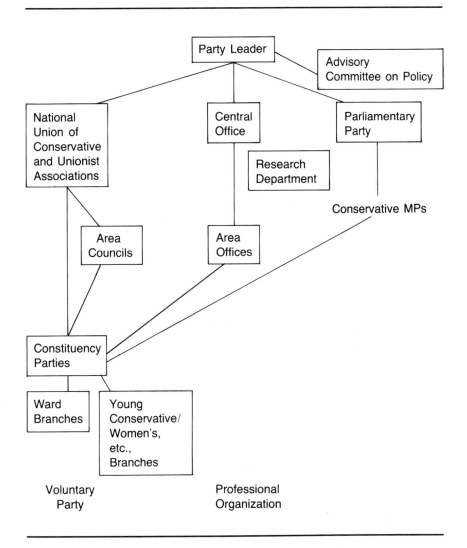

FIGURE 6.1 Conservative Party Organization. *Note:* (1) The Advisory Committee on Policy provides advice on policy, working usually through policy groups composed of MPs and outside experts. (2) The Research Department undertakes research for the party, publishes research briefs and pamphlets, assists in drawing up the manifesto, and services the Advisory Committee on Policy and parliamentary party committees. This department was previously independent of Central Office but is now under its roof both organizationally and physically.

constituency associations. A little over half of the national party's income comes from institutions such as companies, banks, and partnerships. The party is seen as the one most sympathetic to the interests of business, and a number of firms give the party a proportion of their profits each year. However, the proportion of its income coming from this source is declining. (Prior to 1974, this proportion constituted well in excess of 60% of income.) Income from constituency associations is becoming more important. In the 1950s and early 1960s a little over 10% of the party's income came from local parties; in the period from 1967 to 1974, the proportion increased to nearly 20%; and since 1974, it has exceeded 20%. Each local association is given a quota (a stipulated amount) that it is expected to contribute each year to national party funds. Some associations give more than the quota and a number give less. Roughly 15% of income derives from individual donations: the proportion has not changed much over past decades. The total income from these three sources is now usually in excess of 2 to 3 million pounds ($3.5 to $4.5 million), though that will increase substantially in election years when the party makes a special appeal for funds. In 1979–1980, for example, the party had an income of £5,292,000.[18] Outside of election years this income is spent on routine administration, paying salaries, and maintaining the services that the central party provides to local associations. In election years the party usually manages to outspend its opponent parties: in the 1983 election, for example, it is believed to have spent about £5 million ($6.5 million), compared with £2.5 million ($3.75 million) spent by Labour, £1 million($1.5 million) spent by the Social Democratic party, and £500,000 ($750,000) by the Liberal party.

Approximately twice as much money is raised by the local parties as is raised by the party centrally. Most money comes from fund-raising events: individual subscriptions constitute but a small proportion of the income.[19] As with the party nationally, most of the income is spent on routine management, primarily paying the agent's salary. Local appeals will normally be made to provide money to fight election campaigns. Parties are constrained by the election finance limits (see Chapter 5), though in practice few local parties have funds that would allow them to exceed the limitations even if they wished to.

In common with its main competitor, the party has had difficulty in recent years in raising funds sufficient to meet all its organizational commitments. The party has maintained a sizable staff in a large, expensive headquarters close to the Houses of Parliament, and in recent years streamlining of the professional organization has taken place. Costs have increased more rapidly than has income. In 1982 the party was hampered by a number of firms, hit by the recession, cutting back on their donations to party funds.[20] With an election in the offing, the party fell back on local parties and launched a campaign to raise an extra £1 million.

The Labour Party

The Labour party is best described as a coalition of disparate interests. It was formed, in effect, on February 27, 1900, at a conference comprising representatives of the socialist Independent Labour party (the ILP), the marxist Social Democratic Federation (the SDF), the Fabian Society (which believed in socialism by gradual means), and 65 trade unions. It called for "establishing a distinct Labour Group in Parliament, who shall have their own whips and agree upon policy, which must embrace a readiness to cooperate with any party which for the time being may be engaged in promoting legislation in the direct interest of labour, and be equally ready to associate themselves with any party in opposing measures having an opposite tendency." The conference refused to accept an SDF motion linking it with socialism and the class war, and the SDF withdrew subsequently from the movement. An executive committee, the Labour Representation Committee, was set up, consisting of representatives from the different organizations, the trade union representatives being in the majority. There was thus witnessed, in Carl Brand's words, "an alliance between socialism and trade unionism"; he added, "It was done in characteristically British fashion: with scant regard for theory, the best tool possible under the circumstances was fashioned. In spite of the fact that for two decades the drive had come from the socialists, they did not insist upon their name or programme."[21] In the general election of 1906, 29 Labour MPs were elected and the Labour Representation Committee thereupon changed its name to that of the Labour party. The Labour party had established itself on the British political scene.

The next major event in the party's history was the adoption of a new constitution in 1918. There was a strong socialist element within the party, notably represented by the ILP, and the First World War had appeared to make socialist principles more relevant than they had been hitherto. It has also been argued that adopting a socialist program served a functional purpose in differentiating the party from the Liberals.[22] In any event, the party adopted what has been termed a Socialist Commitment and, in clause four of its new constitution, committed itself to the common ownership of the means of production. (The words "distribution and exchange" were added in 1928.) At its subsequent conference it adopted a program, *Labour and the New Social Order*, incorporating four principles: the enforcement of a national minimum (in effect, a commitment to full employment and a national minimum wage); the democratic control of industry, essentially through public ownership; a revolution in national finance (financing of social services through greater taxation of high incomes); and surplus wealth for the common good, using the balance of the nation's wealth to expand opportunities in education and culture. The program was to form the basis of party policy for over 30 years.[23] At the same time, however, the party amended its own procedures in a way that weakened the socialist element within its ranks: the trade unions, on whom the party depended for financial support, were given greater influence through the decision to elect members of the party's national executive committee at the party conference, where the unions dominated; and the ILP was weakened by the decision to allow individuals to join the Labour party direct. Previously, membership was indirect, through membership of affiliated organizations, and the ILP had been the main recruiting agent for political activists. Socialists within the party were to become increasingly wary of the attitude adopted toward the party's program by those who dominated the party leadership.

At the 1918 General Election, 63 Labour MPs were returned. In 1922 the number rose to 142, making the party the second largest in the House of Commons. In the 1923 general election, the Conservatives lost their overall majority and Labour, with Liberal acquiescence, formed a short-lived minority government under the leadership of Ramsay MacDonald. Given the political constraints, the government achieved little—its main domestic success was the passage of a Housing Bill—and lasted less than 10 months. A second minority Labour government was formed following the 1929 general election. Its domestic program was largely crippled either by the Liberals in the Commons or the Conservatives in the Lords. In response to the Depression, it sought international loans, but these were dependent on financial cutbacks at home. The cabinet was divided on the issue and MacDonald tendered the government's resignation, subsequently accepting the King's invitation to form a coalition, or "National," government incorporating Conservative and Liberal MPs. The new government, though led by MacDonald, was dominated by the Conservatives. Within the Labour party, MacDonald's action was seen as a betrayal of the party's cause and only a handful of Labour MPs followed him into the new government. The majority of the parliamentary party, along with the trade unions, disavowed his action and he and his supporters were subsequently expelled from the party. The National government, with MacDonald and his supporters standing as National Labour candidates, won a landslide victory in a quickly called general election. The Labour party was returned with only 52 MPs and, though the number increased to 154 in the 1935 general election, spent the 1930s in a political wilderness.

The Second World War, as we have seen (Chapter 3), had a significant impact on the fortunes and the appeal of the party. There had been a shift in popular attitudes, conducive to some form of social welfare program, and the party had proved itself a responsible partner of government in the wartime coalition. In 1945 it was returned with a large overall majority. In office, it implemented its election manifesto "Let Us Face the Future," bringing into public ownership various public utilities and introducing a comprehensive social security system and national health service. Much of its program was soon implemented, perhaps too soon. By the end of the Parliament, the party had begun to lose its impetus and there were growing doubts as to the direction in which it should be going. In the general election of 1950 it was returned with a bare overall majority, and in the general election called the following year, it lost that majority altogether (despite receiving more votes than any other party), the Conservatives being returned to office.

The 1950s proved to be a period of bitter dispute within the party. The left wing within the party continued to press for greater control of the economy and the taking into public ownership of important industries: it remained committed to clause four of the party's constitution. Revisionists within the party, led by Anthony Crosland, argued that public ownership was no longer necessary because of the absence of large-scale unemployment and primary poverty.[24] Rather, they argued, one should accept the mixed economy and seek instead the goal of equality—equality of opportunity, especially in the sphere of education. Such a goal was possible in an affluent managerial society. Public ownership was seen as largely irrelevant. The dispute between the two sides culminated at the turn of the decade, when the then party leader, Hugh Gaitskell, sought to remove clause four from the constitution. The major unions swung against him and he was defeated at the party's 1960 Conference. He then turned his attention to the issue of the British nuclear deterrent, opposing vigorously attempts to commit the party to a policy of unilateral nuclear disarmament, and in so doing instigating another serious internal party dispute.

Conservative unpopularity in the early 1960s and the election of Harold Wilson as party leader in 1963 following the sudden death of Gaitskell helped restore a sense of unity to the Labour party as it sensed electoral victory. The party was returned to office in 1964. However, its periods of office from 1964 to 1970 and later from 1974 to 1979 were not successful ones. The attempt at a national plan in the first Wilson Government was effectively stillborn, and both periods of government witnessed generally orthodox attempts to respond to economic crises.[25] The period of Labour government from 1974 onward, in particular, appeared to lack any clear direction, being pushed in different directions by international pressures and the domestic problems associated with trying to stay in office while lacking an overall parliamentary majority. The period witnessed a growing tension within the party between those who adhered to a gradual approach to the achievement of socialist goals, recognizing the constraints imposed by prevailing conditions, and those on the left who pressed for more immediate action and the taking into public ownership of key industries such as the banks. This tension effectively emerged onto the political stage as open and violent political warfare following the election defeat of 1979. It was not only to take the form of a policy dispute but also to be fought largely and ostensibly on the question of the party's constitution.

The left within the Labour party argued that the social democratic con-

sensus policies of the 1950s had been tried and had failed. What was needed
was a socialist economic policy, one not seriously tried before by a Labour
government. The left sought to increase its influence within the Party by
arguing for (a) the election of the party leader by a wider franchise than the
parliamentary Labour party (the left was much stronger within constituency
parties than it was in the parliamentary party); (b) the compulsory reselection of MPs—that is, for MPs to be subject to a full reselection process by
local parties during the lifetime of a Parliament rather than the usual process
of automatic readoption when an election was called; and (c) the vesting of
the responsibility for writing the election manifesto in the party's National
Executive Committee (the NEC), where the left was strong, rather than
jointly by the NEC and the parliamentary leadership. At the party's 1980
conference, the left was successful in achieving two of these three objectives:
the widening of the franchise for electing the leader, and for MPs to be
subject to compulsory reselection procedures. At a special conference in
January 1981, the party adopted a formula for the election of the leader by an
electoral college, the trade unions to have 40% of the votes, constituency
parties 30%, and the parliamentary Labour party 30%.[26] This new method
was employed for the first time in 1983 following the resignation of Michael
Foot.

For a number of politicians on the right of the party, already bitterly
opposed to the party's policy to withdraw from the European Communities,
the changes in the party's constitutional arrangements constituted the final
straw. They responded by creating the Council for Social Democracy and
then, in March 1981, broke away from the party completely, forming their
own party: the Social Democratic party. Others in sympathy with their views
remained within the Labour party to fight the battle there.

In terms of the ensuing dispute within the party, it would probably be
fair to summarize the position as one in which the party's socialist wing won
the policy war but lost the organizational battles. Compulsory reselection
had a limited effect on sitting MPs (only seven were denied reselection), and
at the party conference in 1982, the Party's right wing gained a majority on
the party's National Executive Committee. It was also successful in persuading the conference to vote for immediate action to be taken against a left-
wing group within the party, the Militant Tendency, which a party report
earlier in the year had found to be "a party within the party," with its own
organization and program contrary to the party's constitution. In January
1983, the NEC voted to expel from the party five leading members of the
Tendency. Earlier, in 1981, the left had been unsuccessful, albeit narrowly,
in seeking to get their leading figure, Tony Benn, elected to the deputy
leadership of the party.

While these disputes were being waged, attracting considerable press
publicity in the process, the policy groups in the party (subcommittees of the

NEC) were busy working on policy recommendations for inclusion in the party's program. In June 1982, the party published a policy document, *Labour Programme 1982*, which was approved at the party conference in the autumn, and followed this up with another, *The New Hope for Britain*, in March 1983. The latter document formed the basis of the party's election manifesto (see Table 6.1). Apart from a sharp rise in public spending (it estimated a £10 billion increase in expenditure in the first year of a Labour government), a wealth tax, a "national economic assessment" (in essence, annual discussions between government and the Trades Union Congress on how to distribute the national income), and a greater public stake in leading industries—measures acceptable to most sections of the party—this document included commitments not supported by the party's right wing. These included, notably, withdrawal from the European Communities and a non-nuclear defense policy, the latter implicitly but not overtly constituting a commitment to unilateral nuclear disarmament. Despite right-wing misgivings over the program, it was agreed on as the party's election manifesto after less than one hour's discussion at the beginning of the 1983 election campaign.

In the 1983 election, the party was not in a strong position. Its internal disputes had attracted much unfavorable publicity. More important, the Falklands campaign in 1982 dramatically eroded its support. Although initially supporting the sending of a task force, the party appeared to equivocate once fighting seemed imminent, and a number of prominent party figures led by Tony Benn voiced their opposition to the whole venture. The party proved unable to overcome the lead in the polls that the Conservatives achieved in the wake of the British victory in the islands. It entered the election campaign as the party standing second in the opinion polls. Rather than improving its position, it lost support throughout the campaign. It was thrown on the defensive by the Conservatives, who attacked the Labour manifesto as "extremist" (it was compared in election broadcasts and newspaper advertisements to the Communist party manifesto), and suffered badly from some of its own leading figures publicly dissenting from parts of the party program. Both Denis Healey and former leader James Callaghan spoke against unilateral nuclear disarmament. It also suffered from poor campaign management, the Conservatives adopting techniques realized to good effect in American election campaigns. The Labour party chairman was subsequently to admit that his party ran "a rag, tag and bobtail" campaign. The result was largely to favor the SDP/Liberal Alliance. In the last two weeks of the campaign, Labour support began to hemorrhage and newspapers began to speculate as to which party would come second in the contest.

On election day, the party suffered a major setback in votes, though somewhat less of a setback in seats. Its concentrated support ensured that it won 209 seats, but it received only 28% of the votes cast (compared with 37% in 1979), marginally ahead of the percentage gained by the Alliance. It was the party's worst result, in terms of the percentage of votes cast, since 1918.

Party Organization.   The basic structure of the party is given in Figure 6.2. Formally, the Party stresses the concept of intraparty democracy. In the Labour party, unlike the Conservative party, the leader is not the fount of Party policy. The body formally responsible for determining the Party program is the party conference, which meets each year in the autumn. Under the party's constitution, a proposal that receives two-thirds or more of the votes cast at conference is adopted as part of the program. Between conferences, the body responsible for party organization and policy discussion is the party's National Executive Committee, which will normally bring policy documents forward for approval by the Conference.

Complicating the picture, however, is the fact that the party's program is not the same as its election manifesto. Under the party's constitution, the NEC in conjunction with the leaders of the parliamentary party decide which items of the program are to be included in the manifesto. In 1983, the program and the manifesto were synonomous, but in practice, this has not always been the case. In 1979, for example, the party leader, James Callaghan, was criticized within the party for effectively blocking inclusion of the commitment to abolish the House of Lords. Furthermore, when it comes to implementing the party's program, some latitude is given to the parliamentary leadership, which is expected to give effect to the party's principles "as far as may be practicable." In office, Labour ministers have sometimes found it not "practicable" to implement party commitments, and on occasion the policy of a Labour government has not been congruent with that of the Labour party. Some of the foreign policy of the Labour government in the late 1960s, for instance, failed to gain approval at the party conference.

At party conferences, voting is based on an organization's membership, not on the individual votes of those present. Thus the trade unions, with large affiliated memberships, cast the most votes. In the 1950s the so-called bloc votes of the unions used to be cast regularly in support of the party's right-wing leadership. In the 1960s, the leadership of some major trade unions changed and they became less predictable in their conference behavior. In the 1980s, they have supported the moves against the Militant Tendency (union leaders are reputedly dismayed by the internal wranglings of the party) while supporting the policy documents, such as *Labour's Programme 1982*, brought forward for conference approval. The influence of the trade unions is reflected in the Party's commitment to repeal Conservative trade union legislation.

Labour conferences differ markedly from Conservative conferences. The latter are purely advisory (and often criticized as stage-managed affairs),

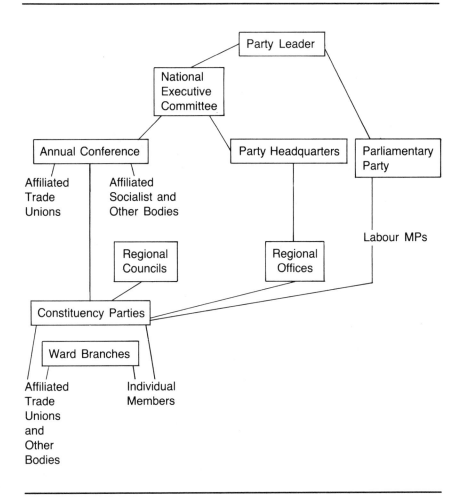

FIGURE 6.2   Labour Party Organization.

votes are cast by those attending in an individual capacity, and votes are extremely rare. Labour conferences are lively, often unpredictable gatherings, with ballots being frequent.[27] There are also significant differences between the parties in terms of membership. The Conservative party, as we have seen, recruits members directly. The Labour party, by contrast, has a large indirect membership in addition to a small direct membership. The indirect membership derives from trade unions and other organizations affiliated with the party. Members of unions pay, as part of their annual subscription, a "political levy" (unless they formally opt out of doing so) and thus become affiliated members of the Party. This affilliated membership provides the party with much of its income as well as a large paper membership: it has over 5 million affiliated members. In contrast, the number of direct members is small. One source estimated that in 1978 it was as low as 250,000, of which only about one-quarter were active party workers.[28] Part of the explanation for this may lie in the dependence for support on the affiliated groups, though it would not explain an apparent decline in membership over recent years.

For its income, the party nationally is heavily dependent on the trade unions. During the 1970s, it had an annual income of between £1 and £2 million ($1.5 to $3 million), of which approximately 90% came from the trade unions. The constituency Labour parties contributed only 8%.[29] The unions contribute a similar proportion of the party's election funds. In 1982, an additional £2 million ($3 million) was made available by the trade unions to help the Party fight the next election. (The unions also provided the capital expenditure for the new headquarters the party now occupies south of the Thames.) Most of the income, as with the Conservatives, is spent on routine management. However, the party has had problems in raising income sufficient to meet its costs, and at the 1982 conference the party treasurer reported that a deficit of more than £1 million had been carried forward from 1981 to 1982.

Income raised by constituency parties varies considerably. It was estimated in 1973 that the average party raised just under £2,000,[30] over half of which came from fund-raising schemes (social events and, most productive of all, lotteries) and individual subscriptions. Donations and grants from trade unions and other affiliated bodies accounted for less than 20% of the income. In practice, in some constituencies the income from union sources is more substantial. Unions can sponsor parliamentary candidates, which means essentially the candidate has the backing of the union and the union contributes a certain sum toward the local party's expenses.[31] As with the Conservatives, most local income is spent on such routine functions as maintaining a local office. However, a greater proportion of funds tend to be allocated to fighting local elections than is the case on the Conservative side. The limited income of local parties also restricts the employment of full-time agents. There are now fewer than 100 local parties with full-time agents.

The Liberal Party

The Liberal party had a relatively short history as a major political party, spanning less than 60 years. Succeeding the Whigs in the 1860s, it was a major force on the British political scene until the 1920s, when it went into rapid decline. Like the other parties, it was a coalition of interests. The main tenets of Gladstonian Liberalism in the nineteenth century were free trade, home rule for Ireland, economy wherever possible, and social reform where necessary. Within the party there was a radical wing, placing more emphasis on social reform, as well as an imperialist wing.[32] Returned to government in 1906, the party enacted a number of social reforms but proceeded on the basis of no coherent program and was divided on a number of important issues. The second decade of the century proved a disastrous one. The party was beset by such problems as division in Ireland, the suffragettes, and the First World War.[33] It was also rent asunder by a rift between Asquith, the party leader until 1916, and Lloyd George, who successfully displaced him. The rift was never really healed successfully. The party's internal problems and its declining electoral appeal were to reduce its parliamentary numbers. In 1918, the Election was won by a coalition consisting of Lloyd George Liberals and the Conservatives. The Conservatives were the dominant partner, though Lloyd George remained as premier. In 1922, Conservative MPs brought the coalition to an end. In the ensuing general election, 62 National Liberal and 54 Liberal MPs were returned. The position improved temporarily in 1923 and 159 Liberal MPs were returned. In 1924 the number returned was only 40. In subsequent elections the number returned was 59 (1929), 33 (1931, 41 Liberal National MPs also being returned),[34] and 20 (1935). In the general elections between 1945 and 1979, the number of Liberal MPs elected varied from 6 to 14.[35] The only occasion in postwar years when it came close to government was during the period of the Liberal–Labour (known as the Lib-Lab Pact) from 1977 to 1978, when it achieved some concessions and the opportunity to consult in return for sustaining the minority Labour government in office.[36]

Its fortunes appeared to improve in 1981, when it entered into an alliance with the newly formed Social Democratic party. By the autumn, the two partners were ahead of the other parties in the polls, and at the Liberal conference, the party leader, David Steel, told delegates to go "and prepare for government." In 1982, particularly following the Falklands campaign, such statements appeared overly ambitious, as the Alliance slipped back in the opinion polls (SDP support declining more than Liberal). However, the party won a notable by-election victory early in 1983 in the London constituency of Bermondsey and, with its allocation of seats with the Alliance finalized (see Chapter 5), looked forward to a significant increase in support in the general election. In the campaign, the Alliance issued an agreed manifesto (see Table 6.1) and each partner supported the other. The only distinction was in campaign funding, with each party maintaining control of its own expenditure. The party is estimated to have spent £500,000, as against £1 million spent by the SDP.

Of the votes cast in the election, the Alliance partners captured 26%— nearly 8 million—compared with the 14% (4 million) won by the Liberals in 1979. However, electoral support was not reflected in the number of seats. The Liberals won 17 seats, an increase of only 6 on the number won in 1979. The Social Democrats, with their support more evenly spread, did far worse, with only 6 seats.

Party Organization.   In organization, the Liberal party is not dissimilar to the Conservative party. It has a professional organization, the Liberal Party Organization, that is the equivalent to Conservative Central Office. Its voluntary organization is based on constituency associations. There are regional councils and at the apex, a Council comprising representatives drawn from the various sections of the party. A smaller number of representatives are appointed to a National Executive Committee, which has responsibility for directing the work of the party. There is an annual conference, the Liberal Assembly, with representatives from the local parties and regional and national bodies of the party, as well as Liberal MPs, peers, and candidates. According to the party constitution, the Assembly decides Party policy. However, decisions are not binding on Liberal MPs.[37] There is a standing committee to link MPs with the party organization, and this committee has played an increasing role in the writing of the party manifesto, previously the preserve of the party leader.

The party leader was elected by the Liberal parliamentary party until 1976, when the party agreed to widen the electorate to encompass the whole party. Candidates had to be Liberal MPs (and had to be nominated by MPs), but party members in each constituency were given a vote, weighted according to a formula based on how much support the Liberals had achieved in the constituency at the previous election. (In 1981 this was changed to the more simple formula of "one member, one vote.") The new method was employed for the first time in 1976 and resulted in the election of David Steel, who has held the position since. Elected to Parliament in 1965 at the age of 26, he has proved an electoral asset to the party. In the 1983 election campaign, 35% of electors thought he would make the best prime minister and only 2% thought he would make the worst.[38]

Like the Conservatives, the Liberal party has only individual, as opposed to affiliated, members. In 1973, it was estimated that the average size of a Liberal constituency party was 300 members, giving it a national total of a little under 200,000 members. In income, the Liberal Party Organization in the 1970s received approximately £100,000 a year (the figure varied significantly from year to year). Michael Pinto-Duschinsky, in a study of party finance, has estimated that about 35% of this income derived from constituency quotas and other sums collected in small amounts from rank-and-file supporters, about 35% in medium and large donations from individuals, and about 30% from companies.[39] The relatively modest income of the party has meant that it maintains only a small professional staff. Funds are raised separately for election campaigns and are not included in the foregoing figures. The average income of local parties was estimated in 1973 as being just under £1,000. (It was much higher the following year, an election year.) A significant proportion of local income is spent on local election campaigns. The proportion used for paying salaries is low, largely because only a handful of local parties can afford the services of a professional agent: in 1979, the party had only 15 full-time agents. In running elections, Liberal campaigns at local level tend to be notable for being labor- rather than capital-intensive.

The Social Democratic Party

The Social Democratic party was formed in March 1981 when a number of Labour politicians broke away from the Labour party. The new party was led by four former Labour cabinet ministers, dubbed by newspapers as "the Gang of Four": Roy Jenkins, Shirley Williams, Dr. David Owen, and William Rodgers. The latter two were already in the House of Commons. The other two, both former MPs, were to return later in by-elections. The party was created with the ostensible aim of "breaking the mold" of British politics.[40] It wanted to get away from the adversary relationships that had characterized British politics, favoring instead consensus government that would represent the center ground of British politics. It favored decentralization, equality, electoral reform, a pay-and-prices policy, and especially membership in the European Communities.

The new party attracted support both within the House of Commons and within the country. By the end of 1981, a total of 27 Labour MPs and 1 Conservative had defected to join it. It attracted over 70,000 members and by December, its support in the Gallup Poll exceeded that of any other party. It formed an Alliance with the Liberal Party, and Alliance candidates began to score some notable victories in by-elections: Croydon North-West in October, Crosby in November (won by Mrs. Williams), and Glasgow, Hillhead the following March (won by Mr. Jenkins). Within a year of its formation, it posed a threat to the two main traditional parties.

During 1982, it began to develop its internal organization and to formulate policies. It also witnessed a decline in support. The former may provide a partial explanation for the latter. As the party committed itself to specific policies and as it selected a leader with a distinctive leadership style and appeal, so it began to shed its "catch-all" appeal. A contest for the party leadership and a dispute with the Liberals over the allocation of Alliance candidatures produced some loss of support.[41] The Falklands campaign also served to rob it of much-needed publicity. The Party failed to maintain the momentum it had built up in 1981: it failed to top the poll in any of the seven by-elections held between April and December 1982. Indeed, it actually lost a seat when a maverick SDP MP insisted on resigning and fighting a by-election. Held in the midst of the Falklands campaign, the election was won by the Conservative candidate. The party's membership declined—from 78,000 in April to 62,000 in June—and by the end of the year its support among electors, according to the Gallup Poll, was down to 10.5%.

The election year of 1983 was one of mixed fortunes for the SDP. An Alliance candidate, a Liberal, won the Bermondsey by-election but in the

Darlington by-election, in which the Alliance candidate (a Social Democrat) started out as clear favorite to win, the party finished third in the poll. The poor result generated tension between some Liberal and SDP supporters. However, unity was restored for the general election campaign. The SDP leader, Roy Jenkins, was appointed prime minister-designate in the event of an Alliance victory.

In the election campaign, the Alliance began as a clear third party in the opinion polls. During the first two weeks of the campaign it appeared to make little headway. Attacks on the government and on the failure of the Labour party to provide credible policies or leaders did not make the dent in Labour (and Conservative) support that party leaders expected. Halfway through the campaign, Liberal and SDP leaders met to discuss progress and to give impetus to the campaign. At the same time, Alliance standing in the polls began to improve and in the remaining two weeks of the campaign, started to close the gap with the Labour party. By election day, polls differed as to whether the Alliance enjoyed more support than the Labour party.

The election results I have mentioned already. Despite 26% of voters opting for Alliance candidates, the Alliance won only 23 seats and of these only 6 were SDP candidates. All except 5 of the SDP MPs seeking reelection lost their seats. Among those defeated were Mrs. Williams and William Rodgers. The Party won only one seat from another party: Ross, Cromarty and Skye in the north of Scotland. In the new House of Commons, the Party had the unusual distinction of one-third of its members (Dr. Owen, a former foreign secretary, and Mr. Jenkins, a former chancellor of the Exchequer and home secretary) having held most of the major offices of state. The party now ranked fifth in the House in numbers—after the Conservative, Labour, Liberal, and Ulster Unionist parties. In the old House, it had ranked third.

Party Organization.   In the SDP, unlike the other parties, the basic unit of organization is that of the area party. This covers or can cover a number of parliamentary constituencies. Some area parties encompass only one constituency, while others encompass five or more. Area parties are responsible for selecting, by postal ballot of members, candidates for parliamentary elections, though this task can be delegated to local groups. The area parties fulfill tasks normally carried out by the constituency associations in other parties, though they lack the help of professional agents. It was announced at the end of 1982 that the party did not plan to employ full-time election agents, primarily on grounds of cost.

There is no formal regional structure within the party, though a group of area parties can establish a regional committee, subject to the approval of the national committee. Each area party elects a number of representatives to the Council for Social Democracy. This is the party's national policy-making body, though there is provision for a postal ballot of all members on a major policy should the Council or the party's national committee initiate such a move. The national committee is responsible for the organization of the SDP outside Parliament and comprises representatives from the Council, MPs, local councillors and peers, and nationally elected members. (Of eight members elected by a national ballot of members, four must be men and four women.) Social Democratic MPs are expected to have regard for the party's policy but are not bound by decisions of any party organ.

The party has a leader and a president. Following a ballot of party members at the beginning of 1982, it was agreed to elect the leader on the basis of "one member, one vote." An election by postal ballot was held in June in which there were two candidates: Roy Jenkins and Dr. Owen. Mr. Jenkins won by 26,256 votes to 20,864. In a ballot for president (responsible for chairing the Council and the national committee), Mrs. Williams emerged an easy victor. In the wake of the 1983 general election result, Mr. Jenkins resigned as party leader. Dr. Owen was elected, unopposed, to replace him.

There is little published material on SDP finances. It appears heavily dependent on members' subscriptions, paid directly to the national party. Its decline in membership in 1982 placed a strain on party finances, limiting both its employment of professional staff and its plans for election campaigns. Nonetheless, it managed to raise twice as much money to fight the 1983 campaign as did its Liberal partner.

Other Parties

The remaining significant political parties within the United Kingdom, or parts of it, may be briefly identified. Prior to the 1960s, the nationalist parties in Scotland and Wales had not proved to be politically important. Their main achievement had been "simply to survive."[42] In the 1960s they began to have some electoral success: the Plaid Cymru (Party of Wales) won a seat at a by-election in 1966, and the Scottish National Party won one in 1967. Their achievements were to be greatest in the 1970s. Favoring independence for Scotland, though being prepared to accept an elected national assembly as a step on that path, the Scottish National party was able to exploit dissatisfaction with Westminster government and to make use of an issue that became salient during this period: North Sea oil. It argued that the oil was Scottish oil and that revenue from it could make an independent Scottish government viable. In the February 1974 election it won 7 seats. In the October 1974 election it won 11 and came second in 35 out of 41 Labour-held seats. In Wales, the Plaid argued more for self-government than for independence and was able to play on the fears of the indigenous Welsh population, which felt its heritage to be threatened by English encroachment. In the 1974 elections it won 2 seats in February (out of a total of 36

Welsh seats) and 3 in October. Responding to the nationalist threat, especially in Scotland, the Labour government introduced a scheme for elected assemblies in the two countries, which was subsequently put to the peoples of Scotland and Wales in referendums. The Welsh referendum resulted in an overwhelming vote against the government's proposals. In Scotland 1,230,000 people voted for the scheme and 1,153,000 voted against it. Under the rules laid down by Parliament, the "yes" vote was not sufficiently large for the scheme to be implemented (see Chapter 9). The referendum results and apparent decline of interest in devolution took much of the wind out of the sails of the nationalist parties. In both the 1979 and 1983 general elections, the Scottish National Party won 2 seats, as did Plaid Cymru.

In Northern Ireland, the main party is the Unionist party, standing for the maintenance of the Union with Britain. Originally a united party and one tied to the British Conservative Party, it dissociated itself (though in organizational terms not totally) from the Conservative party following the 1972 imposition of direct rule in the province. It also divided within itself, the two main Unionist parties today being the Official Unionists, holding 11 of the province's 17 seats at Westminster, and the Democratic Unionist party, led by fundamentalist protestant clergyman Ian Paisley, which holds 3 seats. The Official Unionists tend to be more middle-class and Anglican and Methodist, whereas the Democratic Unionists appeal more to working-class Protestants and are more heavily Presbyterian. There is also a predominantly Catholic party within the province, the Social Democratic and Labour Party (the SDLP), which won 1 seat in the 1983 General Election. The Alliance party (not connected with the British SDP/Liberal Alliance) seeks to bridge the divide between the two communities: it has never won a parliamentary seat and won only 8% of the votes in the province in 1983. Sinn Fein, the political wing of the Provisional IRA (see Chapter 9), contested seats in the 1983 election, capturing 1 seat and gaining 13.4% of the votes in the province. The elected Sinn Fein Member refused to take his seat in the House of Commons.

Other British parties that might be mentioned include the National Front and the Communist party. Founded in 1967, the National Front is a right wing neofascist party that attracts support largely on the basis of opposition to immigration by black and other nonwhite people. It has proved something of a disruptive influence, having more success in staging demonstrations and having skirmishes with opposing groups than in the electoral arena. In the 1979 election it contested more than 300 constituencies, losing its deposit in all of them and obtaining but 0.6% of the votes cast nationally. Following a split within its ranks, it contested only 60 seats in 1983, again losing its deposit in all of them and picking up but 0.1% of the vote nationally. The breakaway British National party contested 53 seats and suffered a similar fate: its candidates garnered a total of 14,321 votes (less than

0.1% of the poll) among them. The British Communist party, formed in 1921, has had little significant impact in electoral terms. One Communist MP was elected in 1924, one was elected in 1935 and two were elected in 1945. Since then, the party has achieved no parliamentary representation and has not really come close to doing so. In the 1983 election it contested 35 seats and lost its deposit in every one: its total vote was 11,596, well under 0.1% of the total poll. It has had greater influence at times within certain intellectual circles, notably in the 1930s, and in the trade union movement. A significant fraction of trade union officials are believed to be party members. In 1977, for example, 6 members on the 27-strong executive of the National Union of Mineworkers were Communists. According to a study by Robert Taylor, the party has also succeeded in recent years in dominating one section of the Amalgamated Union of Engineering Workers (AUEW) union.[43]

Other minor parties include the Ecology party, the Workers Revolutionary party, and the Socialist party of Great Britain as well as a variety of fringe groups.[44] Candidates contesting the 1983 election included a host standing under esoteric and largely individual banners. I mentioned one or two in the previous chapter. (Others, for the record, include the Fancy Dress Party, the Loony Monster Party, the Southport Back in Lancashire Party, and a candidate representing "Jesus and his Cross.")[45] Such candidates represent no recognizably organized parties, despite some of their labels, and have little appreciable electoral impact. In the 1983 general election, the total vote for candidates in Great Britain standing under minor party labels (that is, other than Conservative, Labour, Alliance, Plaid Cymru, and Scottish National) was 191,432, in itself a not insignificant figure but representing only 0.6% of the poll.

PARTIES AND THEIR SUPPORT

The Current Debate

The past decade has witnessed significant changes not only in the stance of the political parties but also in their electoral appeal. Critics of the two-party duopoly have contended that decline in support for the two parties reflects dissatisfaction not only with the parties themselves but also with the two-party system that has characterized postwar British politics. Critics *of* the two party system have argued for constitutional as well as political change, the former to facilitate the latter. Critics *within* the two parties have pressed for political change. Supporters of the two parties and the system within which they operate oppose change and tend to discount the emphasis given by critics to recent electoral developments.

In this section, I propose to consider briefly the decline in party support and then the different analyses and prescriptions that have been proffered. In so doing, I propose to draw out certain parallels with the United States, where a similar but not identical decline in party support has been observed, one that has been subject to similar analyses. What has differed, though, have been the prescriptions.

Decline

The decline in party support has been discerned in voting behavior, partisan identification, and party membership. In the past decade, fewer electors than before have voted for the Conservative and Labour parties, fewer have identified with them, and fewer have joined them as members.

The decline in voting support for the two parties has been sketched in the preceding chapter. Ever since the peak of two-party support reached in the 1950s, electors increasingly deserted the two parties, voting either for other parties or not voting at all. In the 1983 general election, more than one-quarter of those on the electoral register stayed at home. (In 1950, the proportion was less than one-fifth.) Of those who did vote, the proportion voting for either the Conservative or Labour parties was 70%. (In 1950 it was more than 98%.) Given the coverage of the preceding chapter, the point need not be belabored here.

A decline in party identification was detected in the period from 1970 to 1974 by the analysis of Ivor Crewe and his colleagues.[46] This decline was relative, the most significant component being the decline in the number of "very strong" identifiers (Figure 6.3). This partisan dealignment continued after 1974, particularly among Labour voters. Between 1964 and 1974, the number of Labour identifiers declined by 5% (from 43% to 38% of electors), not in itself an obviously dramatic decline. What is important, though, is that by 1979 the electorate, for the first time since the survey was begun in 1963, contained more Conservative than Labour identifiers (40% to 38%) and that within Labour identifiers, the proportion of "very strong" identifiers declined significantly: from 50% in 1966 to 27% in 1979.[47] In 1979, only 1 in 10 electors was a "very strong" Labour partisan. In 1966, the proportion had been more than 1 in 5.

Figures for a decline in party membership are less well chronicled, in large part because no definitive membership figures are available. However, what data are available suggest that both the Conservative and Labour parties have been losing members since the 1950s. The Conservative party, as I have already noted, probably has a membership of about 1.5 million, in itself not a poor figure but much less than its peak membership of nearly 3 million in 1953.[48] The Labour party achieved a peak in its individual membership at about the same time, with a membership on paper of just over 1 million in

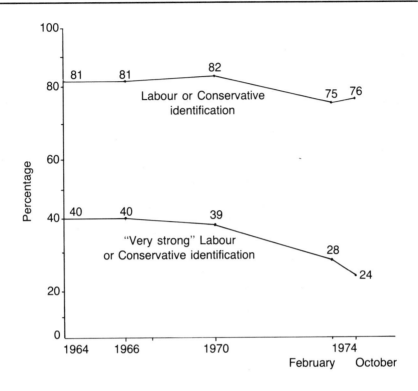

FIGURE 6.3   Labour and Conservative Partisanship, 1964–1974. (*Source: I. Crewe et al., "Partisan Dealignment in Britain 1964–1974," British Journal of Political Science, 1977, Figure 4, p. 143.* Copyright 1977 the British Journal of Political Science. Reprinted by permission.)

1952, and since then has witnessed a steady decline. "On the published figures," one analyst states, "the party has on average been losing more than 11,000 members per year, and the true loss of membership may well be much higher than this."[49]

On all three indicators—voting behavior, partisan identification, and party membership—the two parties have witnessed a decline in support in recent years. How specific is this decline in Britain? Are similar trends discernible in the United States? The answer to this last question must be a qualified "yes." Given the absence of a system of party membership in the United States comparable to that in Britain, a strict comparison of changes in party membership cannot be made. However, the United States has witnessed a decline in support for Republican and Democratic parties in both votes cast and partisan identification.

The number of Americans turning out to vote Republican and Democrat at presidential elections since 1960 has shown a steady decline. This has taken the form less of voting for third *parties* (though independent candidates siphoned off a considerable fraction of the vote in the elections of 1968 and 1980) than of staying at home. This is borne out by the comparative data in Table 6.2. In Britain, citizens not wishing to support the Conservative or Labour party either stay at home *or* vote for third parties, while in the United States, citizens not wishing to vote Republican or Democrat tend to stay at home. The net effect in both countries is the same. Of the adult citizens in the United States and Britain, fewer than before are now turning out and voting for the traditional two main parties.

Identification with the Republican and Democratic parties in the United States has also declined. There has been a decline both in the number identifying with one or other of the parties and in the number identifying themselves as "strong" Republicans or Democrats (see Figure 6.4). The

TABLE 6.2
Turnout and Two-Party Voting, United States and United Kingdom, 1959–1983

United States Presidential Elections			United Kingdom General Elections		
Year	Percentage Turnout	Of those voting, percentage voting Republican or Democrat	Year	Percentage Turnout	Of those voting, percentage voting Conservative or Labour
			1959	78.8	93.2
1960	63.8	99.3			
1964	62.1	99.6	1964	77.1	87.5
			1966	75.8	89.8
1968	61.0	86.1			
			1970	72.0	89.4
1972	55.7	98.2			
			1974 February	78.7	75.0
			1974 October	72.8	75.0
1976	54.3	98.1			
			1979	76.0	80.8
1980	54.0	91.8			
			1983	72.7	70.0

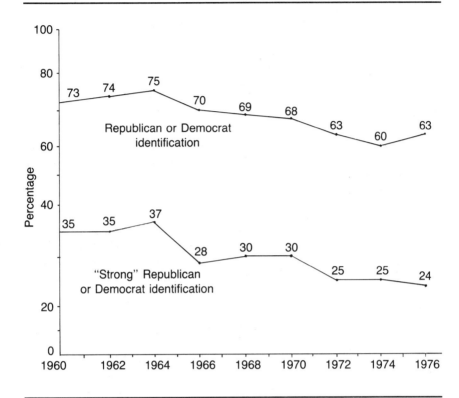

FIGURE 6.4 Democratic and Republican Partisanship, 1960–1976. (*Source: University of Michigan survey data, as reported in J. Kirkpatrick, "Changing Patterns of Electoral Competition" in A. King (ed.), The New American Political System [American Enterprise Institute, 1978], p. 270.* Copyright 1978 the American Enterprise Institute. Reprinted by permission.)

difference between the United States and Britain is that in Britain, the level of identification remains much higher, and between 1964 and 1974, the significant decline was in the number of "very strong" identifiers. Furthermore, the decline in identification in the United States did not affect the position of the two parties relative to one another: the Democrats maintained a clear lead over the Republicans.[50] In Britain, as we have seen, the number of Labour identifiers had by 1979 slipped from being more numerous to less numerous than Conservative identifiers.

It is thus possible to generalize that the two main parties in Britain and those in the United States have witnessed a significant decline in support in both votes and identification. Two caveats need to be entered. One is that these are generalizations and, as can be seen from the foregoing data, need to be treated with caution if one seeks to develop transatlantic similarities. The second is that in both countries, the two main parties still retain significant support, both in votes and partisanship. In Britain, there is a serious third-party challenge but it remains that: a *third-party* challenge. Of those who vote, the majority cast their ballots for the traditional two main parties.

Analyses

Given this relative decline in support for the two main parties in Britain, what analyses have been offered to explain it? The four main ones can be subsumed under the headings of class, issue, consensual, and structural dealignment.

Class.   The decline in the class–party nexus I covered briefly in Chapter 5. The studies of both Butler and Stokes and of Crewe and his colleagues detected this decline,[51] attributing it in part to a decline in class attachment. Unlike Butler and Stokes, Crewe found that this development was not confined to a particular generation of voters: the willingness to provide a subjective class identity fell away in all the generational cohorts that he studied.[52] The weakening of the class alignment cannot in itself be seen as causing significant changes in electoral behavior, but it helped facilitate them. Butler and Stokes comment: "An electorate which saw politics less in class terms could respond to other issues and events."[53] More transient influences came to have greater impact. The consequence was greater volatility in electoral behavior and an eroding of the traditional class support on which the parties could previously depend. The decline in the class–party relationship was sketched in the previous chapter: as I recorded there, by October 1974 barely half of the electorate identified, let alone voted, with their "natural" class party.

The importance of the decline in the class–party nexus, however, should not be overstated.[54] The decline is relative. Social class continues to structure party choice, more so than any of the other variables touched upon in Chapter 5. That remained the case in the 1983 general election.[55] Furthermore, of other variables that have increased in significance in structuring party choice, that of home ownership is generally considered to be a corollary of class. Nor does the decline in the importance of class and the erosion of the class–party nexus necessarily explain the *decline* in support for the two parties. Other analyses need to be considered as well.

Issue.   The second analysis points us in the direction of some of "the issues and events" to which electors could respond given the weakening of class identity. This analysis suggests that the 1960s and 1970s witnessed new issues coming onto the political agenda to which the established political parties could not provide a structured and cohesive response. Most notable among such issues have been those of British membership in the European Communities and a prices-and-incomes policy.[56] Neither issue was one on which the traditional stance of the parties provided a uniform response, and both parties divided, sometimes bitterly, on both issues.[57] A related but not identical analysis is provided by Crewe and his colleagues. According to their study, the decline in support for the Labour party in the 1970s was the product of a growing divergence between the traditional policies of the Labour party and the views of Labour supporters. In their stance on such issues as nationalization, Labour voters were moving further away from the stance taken by the party. "What was already an ideological split in the 1960s," writes Crewe, "had turned into an ideological chasm by 1979."[58] Decline in Conservative support in 1974, by contrast, was attributed to a reaction to more immediate events.[59] In 1979, the stance of the Conservative party on important issues was not diverging dramatically from that of its supporters.[60]

Such an analysis is useful but has its limitations. While the parties may not have been able to provide an internally unified response to new issues on the political agenda, there is little evidence that their stance on these particular issues generated a loss of support, at least not directly. (How the parties handled the issues, particularly of prices-and-incomes policy, while in government may have affected perceptions of their competence in office.) Crewe's explanation of Labour's loss of support is plausible but his analysis does not necessarily help us understand the loss of Conservative support in 1983. Although the Conservatives won a landslide in seats, their share of the poll compared with that in 1979 was down. In 1983, 42% of those who voted cast their votes for Conservative candidates, yet according to a Gallup Poll taken at the time of the election, 50% of electors thought that the Conservatives had "the best policies."[61] A partial explanation for this discrepancy may lie in the fact that the decline in the class–party nexus was not so great as to completely rob the Labour party of some of its traditional class-based support. That, though, still does not help explain a *decline* in Conservative support.

Consensual.   The third analysis is that which contends that the decline in party support is attributable to the consensus politics of the 1950s and 1960s, when the two parties appeared to converge and pursue similar policies. This was the era of the social democratic consensus, or what Samuel Beer termed the "Collectivist" era.[62] Increasingly, especially as the 1970s progressed, socialists within the Labour party and neoliberal Conservatives argued that the policies pursued in the 1950s and 1960s had failed to solve Britain's fundamental problems. More radical policies were needed, policies that offered a clear choice to the electorate: on the Labour side this entailed more socialist measures (extension of public ownership, greater control of the national economy, import controls), while on the Conservative side it entailed pursuit of a free-market economy. As we have seen, pressure built up within both parties, resulting in a shift of policies in the 1970s and early 1980s.

Opponents of this analysis contend that it is pursuit of more radical policies that is responsible for the decline in Labour support. Certainly, survey data have shown the unpopularity of Labour policies put forward in both the 1979 and 1983 elections.[63] Against this, those on the left within the Labour party have argued that what counts is performance in office. If a Labour government was to pursue successfully socialist policies, then those policies could become electorally popular. One analyst writes, "If centrist policies fail, as they have done for the most part during Labour's tenure in office, no amount of moderation will bring electoral success."[64] The problem for this argument, of course, is that in order for left-wing policies to be pursued successfully, the Labour party has first of all to achieve electoral success. How is that success to be achieved if the policies advocated are not electorally acceptable? As for the Conservative neoliberals, they would argue that their stance has been proved successful in electoral terms in both the 1979 and 1983 elections. Against this can be set the fact that the Conservative party witnessed a decline in electoral support in 1983 and that there was more negative voting than positive voting—that is, more voters were voting against the Labour party than were voting for the Conservative party.[65] Social Democrats would contend that the vote for the Liberal/SDP Alliance was indicative of the support for consensus politics and a vote against the arguments advanced by both the Labour left and the neoliberals of the Conservative party.

Structural Dealignment.   The final analysis is that which contends that the decline in support for the two main parties is the product of the two-party *system* in Britain. The two parties dominate the national political agenda, taking positions that are not congruent with the wishes of most electors. Aided by the electoral system, they fight for the all-or-nothing spoils of a general election, and in so doing compete vigorously with one another in an adversary relationship. Once in office, a party reverses the policies of its predecessor and pursues wildly different policies, policies it often subsequently must modify or abandon when other pressures are brought to bear (economic resources often not being sufficient to match extravagant election promises). In short, Britain has a dysfunctional two-party system.[66] This party system cannot be separated from the workings of the electoral system, and thus it is not surprising that the prescription advanced by critics of the electoral and the two-party system is the same: reform of the electoral system. Indeed, the critics are usually the same people, notably academics, such as S. E. Finer and S. A. Walkland, and politicians, such as the leaders of the Social Democratic party.[67] Reform of the electoral system, they argue, would allow for political change. Under a system of proportional representation, no one party would be able to achieve an overall parliamentary majority. This would necessitate some form of center-coalition government, allowing for a return to the consensus politics that electors seek.

The problem with this argument, as Nevil Johnson has observed, is that a decline in support for one or both of the two main parties does not of itself demonstrate a decline in support for the two-party system.[68] Britain may be witnessing a transitional stage in which the Social Democratic party displaces the Labour party as the second of two major parties in Britain. There are no objective data to suggest that electors wish to dispense with what supporters view as the fruits of a two-party system—that is, a clear choice between parties and a party government with an overall majority. In the 1983 general election, only one in four of electors who voted cast their ballots for a party (or alliance of parties) that advocated consensus politics and a reform of the electoral system.

Do these analyses have any parallels in the United States? Again, the answer is a qualified "yes." While a strict transatlantic class comparison is not possible, there has been in the United States a relative decline in the alignment between parties and certain social groups. The Democrats in the 1970s, compared with the 1950s, lost much of their support among Southern whites while improving their position among blacks and upper-status northern Protestants.[69] The Republican party, by contrast, lost some of the support it enjoyed among middle- and lower-status white Northern Protestants, while increasing its support among high-status Southerners.[70] These changes in support did not affect the relative position of the parties. Any realignment that took place was in the base of their support. This realignment appeared to continue in the 1980 election, when Republican support, compared with 1976, improved among Southerners, while Democratic support declined among all the groups that made up the old New Deal coalition. The support that the Democratic candidate lost among the college-educated, young, female, Protestant, higher-status, and nonsouthern voters went not to the Republican but to the independent candidate, John Anderson.[71] Thus, in both the United States and Britain, social groups no longer provide the predictable party support that they once did. However, as in Britain, this weakening relationship in the United States does not in itself explain a decline in party support.

In the 1960s, the United States witnessed also the emergence of issues that were not congruent with the traditional stances taken by the parties. Most notable among these issues were the Vietnam war, civil rights, public order, and trust in government.[72] Given the political significance of these issues—generating reactions hardly comparable to the (relatively) minor expressions of dissent on such issues as membership in the European Communities in Britain—this analysis seems far more plausible than does its equivalent analysis in Britain. As for the remaining analyses, the consensus or rather anticonsensus argument seems to find expression primarily on one side of the political spectrum: the Republican right. Although in a sense currently being tested in government (as with neoliberal Conservatism in Britain), it is subject to similar objections as its equivalent analysis in Britain: Americans in 1980 voted not for the Republican candidate because he sought an end to consensus politics but because he was not Jimmy Carter.[73] Only about one in four adult Americans actually went to the polling booths on November 4 and cast their votes for Ronald Reagan.

The equivalent to the structural analysis is interesting because it provides the converse explanation to that offered in Britain. In Britain, criticism of the two-party system stems from the success of the system in allowing one party to govern and to ensure passage of its program. In the United States, the two-party system is attacked for failing to provide that success. The reasons for this are to be found in the opening passage of this chapter. The constraints of the political structure are such that a party system has failed to overcome them. Political parties have not been able to acquire sufficient strength to bridge the gap created by the Founding Fathers between Congress and the White House. The rare occasions when they have come closest to transcending this institutional divide, as during the period of the New Deal and the Congress of 1964–1966, have been held up as experiences to be admired and emulated. Not surprisingly, given this different analysis, prescriptions for change in the United States differ significantly from those in Britain.

Prescriptions

For many members of both the Conservative and Labour parties, the electoral changes of recent years are not such as to require fundamental political or constitutional change. The parties may not be able to draw to the same extent as before on their traditional class support. However, the response to this is to emphasize the need to get the party message across to the electorate. The Conservatives consider that they succeeded in doing so in the general elections of 1979 and 1983 and that pursuit of the policies embodied in the party's manifesto will bring further success. They see little need for significant changes in policy or in the constitutional framework that has facilitated their return to government. Those within the Labour party who adhere to the program embodied in the 1983 manifesto similarly reject such changes. For them, defeat in the general election was the result of poor communications and, according to some, of the failure of a number of party leaders to advocate the party's manifesto program.[74] To change an electoral system that allowed the party to win 32% of the seats in the House of Commons in an election that brought them 28% of the votes is also, for many, an unattractive prospect. Insofar as change is advocated, it is in respect of better communication and a more united leadership and not in policies or constitutional structures.

For some critics within both parties, the changes of recent years do necessitate reform. For the "Wets" within the Conservative party, a significant shift in economic policy is required if the Conservative party is to maintain its appeal as a party of "One Nation" and to avoid economic and social tragedy. When economic conditions worsened in 1980 and 1981, the "Wets" gained ground within the party and the period was one of serious and bitter internal divisions.[75] The critics were relegated to a minor position as a result of the Falklands campaign and the Prime Minister's use of her power of appointment and dismissal to isolate them within government. Leading critics, such as Sir Ian Gilmour and Norman St. John-Stevas, were dismissed from the cabinet. Another, James Prior, was given the demanding and isolated post of Northern Ireland secretary. Despite these developments and the Conservative victory in the general election of 1983, the Party's "Wets" maintain their criticism of government economic policy[76] and seek a shift back to a more traditional Tory approach.

Within the Labour party, there has been pressure for the party to abandon a number of its more radical policies. In the wake of the 1983 general election defeat, a number of leading members of the party pressed for a revision of the party's program. Roy Hattersley, a contender for the party leadership in 1983, argued that the party should abandon its commitment to withdraw from the European Communities.[77] Another contender for the leadership in 1983, Peter Shore, asserted that the party's non-nuclear defense policy was "fatally flawed."[78] One trade union leader called for the party to reexamine its manifesto.[79] Change is thus sought but it is change in policy within the Labour party. More fundamental political change, in the form of new parties or constitutional reform, is not being advocated.

For such change one has to look primarily though not exclusively beyond the two main parties.[80] Liberals and Social Democrats urge both a political realignment within Britain and constitutional change. A realignment, they contend, is both necessary and desirable. What is envisaged is a realignment of the political center, allowing a center party or parties to emerge and return to the consensus politics that proved successful in past decades. Political polarization, they argue, has proved divisive and bad for government.[81] The creation of the Social Democratic party in 1981 and its subsequent alliance with the Liberal party was intended to provide one medium through which this realignment could take place. The standing of the new party in the opinion polls in 1981 and, more recently, its success in conjunction with the Liberals in capturing more than a quarter of the votes cast in the 1983 general election are taken as indications of its popular appeal. Social Democrats contend that, if it were not for the vagaries of the electoral system, they would have received even more votes, and there is some empirical justification for this assertion. A Gallup Poll at the time of the election found that many potential Alliance supporters voted for another party because they believed that an Alliance vote would be "wasted."[82]

Social Democrats and Liberals draw attention also to the disparity that exists between the number of votes they did receive in 1982 and the number of seats they won. What is needed in order to permit a political realignment is a reform of the electoral reform. A system of proportional representation would both be fair and allow center parties to play a part in government. This argument I have touched upon above, and it was dealt with in some detail in the preceding chapter: there is no need to repeat the argument here. Reformers believe that electoral reform would help break the mold of the two-party system. The success of the SDP/Liberal Alliance has helped weaken the grip of the two main parties, but a new electoral system is necessary if the workings and consequences of the two-party system are to be permanently done away with. The problem with achieving such reform is that it is opposed by the Conservative and Labour parties. Both favor the existing system, which works more to their advantage than would a system of proportional representation. Neither is keen to support a new system that would benefit political opponents. For that reason, electoral reform is an unlikely prospect in Britain in the near future.

Pressure for electoral reform in Britain stems in part from the consequences of a strong two-party system. In the United States, pressure for change comes, as I have mentioned, from the failings of the two-party system. There is little pressure for a system of proportional representation, in large part paradoxically because of the hegemony of the Republican and Democratic parties in electoral contests. There are no significant national third parties. What demands there are for change are designed to strengthen parties in the political system, to allow them to achieve the implementation of a promised program. In 1963, James MacGregor Burns put forward six proposals of political reform designed to make this possible. His proposals included the organizational merging of the presidential and congressional wings of each party, the building of grass-roots memberships, and the financing of the parties on a mass, popular and systematic basis.[83] He did not recommend significant constitutional changes, "partly because it is so difficult."[84] More recently, Charles Hardin has argued for a constitutional reformulation that would allow the United States to experience party government. Party government, he declared, "provides the best hope that our government will be able to meet its problems."[85] Among his proposals for constitutional change were the election of the president, senators, and representatives on the same day for four-year terms, the abolition of the vice-presidency, the designation of the runner-up in the presidential election as leader of the opposition (and as having a seat in the House of Representatives), and provision for congressmen to serve in other offices in government. Hardin further asserts that "all parts of the present Constitution in conflict with the foregoing proposals should be repealed or modified to conform to them."[86]

In pressing for such change, Professor Hardin is in a vocal minority. Nonetheless, his argument is instructive. It illustrates the differences between the arguments for constitutional change in the United States and in Britain, at least those derived from experiences of the political parties in the respective electoral system. Both countries in recent years have witnessed significant and similar changes in support for established political parties. The analyses of these changes have, in some respects, been similar. Yet the analysis underpinning the prescription of constitutional change derives in one country from strong two-party government and in the other from weak two-party government. Hence, the constitutional changes advocated in Britain differ dramatically from those put forward in the United States.

NOTES

1. See C. O. Jones, "Can our Parties Survive our Politics?" in N. J. Ornstein (ed.), *The Role of the Legislature in Western Democracies* (American Enterprise Institute, 1981) pp. 20–23.

2. See L. Hartz, *The Liberal Tradition in America* (Harcourt, Brace and World, 1955).

3. As, e.g., J. M. Burns, *The Deadlock of Democracy* (Prentice-Hall International, 1963). See also above, Ch. 2.

4. L. D. Epstein, "What happened to the British Party Model?" *American Political Science Review,* 74 (1), 1980, pp. 9–22.

5. R. H. S. Crossman, "Introduction" to Walter Bagehot, *The English Constitution* (Fontana, ed., 1963), p. 39.

6. See J. Vincent, *The Formation of the British Liberal Party 1857–68* (Penguin, 1972).

7. P. Norton, "The Organisation of Parliamentary Parties" in S. A. Walkland (ed.), *The House of Commons in the Twentieth Century* (Oxford University Press, 1979), pp. 7–68.

8. R. Blake, *The Conservative Party from Peel to Churchill* (Eyre and Spottiswoode, 1970), p. 2.

9. See C. E. Bellairs, *Conservative Social and Industrial Reform* (Conservative Political Centre, rev. ed. 1977).

10. P. Norton and A. Aughey, *Conservatives and Conservatism* (Temple Smith, 1981), Ch. 2.

11. See R. Rose, "Parties, Factions and Tendencies in British Politics," *Political Studies,* 12, 1964, pp. 33–46.

12. See P. Norton, *Conservative Dissidents* (Temple Smith, 1978), Ch. 4.

13. The epithet *Wet* has different meanings and uncertain origins. In the present context, it derives from the habit of Mrs. Thatcher's annotating papers with the word when she wished to indicate that a particular proposal or comment was indecisive, bland, and poorly argued.

14. *The Economist,* May 21, 1983.

15. Stanley Baldwin led the party in the 1931 and 1935 general elections in which the Conservatives won overall majorities but that government was officially designated a "National" one and Baldwin was not prime minister.

16. See Norton and Aughey, pp. 241–43.

17. See ibid., pp. 211–13.

18. M. Pinto-Duschinsky, *British Political Finance 1830–1980* (American Enterprise Institute, 1981), p. 138. This paragraph is based largely on this work.

19. Ibid.

20. *Guardian,* August 2, 1982.

21. C. F. Brand, *The British Labour Party* (Stanford University Press, 1965); see also F. Williams, *Fifty Years March* (Oldham, no date), Part 1.

22. S. H. Beer, *Modern British Politics,* rev. ed. (Faber, 1969).

23. H. Pelling, *A Short History of the Labour Party,* 5th ed. (Macmillan,1976), p. 44.

24. See especially A. Crosland, *The Future of Socialism* (Jonathan Cape, 1956).

25. On the first period of Labour government, see W. Beckerman (ed.), *The Labour Government's Economic Record 1964–70* (Duckworth, 1972).

26. On the internal battle within the Labour Party see, for example, D. Kogan and M. Kogan, *The Battle for the Labour Party* (Fontana, 1982).

27. See F. W. S. Craig, *Conservative and Labour Conference Decisions 1945–81* (Parliamentary Research Services, 1982).

28. P. Whiteley, "The Decline of Labour's Local Party Membership and Electoral Base, 1945–79" in D. Kavanagh (ed.), *The Politics of the Labour Party* (George Allen and Unwin, 1982), p. 115.

29. Pinto-Duschinsky, p. 170.

30. *Report of the Committee on Financial Aid to Political Parties* (Her Majesty's Stationery Office, 1976), p. 178. The average income in 1974, an election year, was £3,486.

31. See Pinto-Duschinsky, pp. 159–60.

32. P. Rowland, *The Last Liberal Governments* (Macmillan, 1969), p. 34.

33. See T. Wilson, *The Downfall of the Liberal Party 1914–1935* (Fontana, 1968), p. 20.

34. The Liberal National MPs became allied with and were eventually absorbed into the Conservative Party.

35. On the Liberal Parliamentary Party, see P. Norton, "The Liberal Party in Parliament" in V. Bogdanor (ed.),*Liberal Party Politics* (Oxford University Press, 1983).

36. See A. Michie and S. Hoggart, *The Pact* (Quartet, 1978).

37. See D. Kavanagh, "Organisation and Power in the Liberal Party" in V. Bogdanor (ed.), *Liberal Party Politics,* p. 125.

38. *The Guardian,* June 14, 1983. The percentage thinking Mrs. Thatcher would make the best prime minister was higher (46%), but so too was the proportion thinking she would make the worst (25%). No fewer than 63% thought Michael Foot, the then Labour leader, would make the worst PM, and only 13% thought he would make the best.

39. Pinto-Duschinsky, p. 200.

40. See I. Bradley, *Breaking the Mould?* (Martin Robertson, 1981); and P. Zentner, *Social Democracy in Britain* (John Martin, 1982).

41. See *The Sunday Times,* February 7, 1982.

42. H. M. Drucker and G. Brown, *The Politics of Nationalism and Devolution* (Longman, 1980), p. 167.

43. R. Taylor, *The Fifth Estate* (Pan Books, 1980), p. 325.

44. See F. W. S. Craig, *Minor Parties at British Parliamentary Elections 1885–1974* (Macmillan, 1975).

45. The most complex label, probably incomprehensible to anyone not closely familiar with the subtleties of British politics, was that of the candidate standing for "Tactically Vote Conservative Annihilate Bennites Livingstoneites"! The fate of some of the minor candidates can be seen in the example of Leicester South in Table 5.3.

46. I. Crewe, B. Sarlvik, and J. Alt, "Partisan Dealignment in Britain 1964–1974," *British Journal of Political Science,* 7 (2), 1977, pp. 129–190.

47. I. Crewe, "The Labour Party and the Electorate" in D. Kavanagh (ed.), *The Politics of the Labour Party,* pp. 15–17.

48. Norton and Aughey, p. 213.

49. Whiteley, p. 111. For a rather different analysis, however, see P. Seyd and L. Minkin, "The Labour Party and its members," *New Society,* September 20, 1979, pp. 613–15.

50. J. Kirkpatrick, "Changing Patterns of Electoral Competition" in A. King (ed.), *The New American Political System* (American Enterprise Institute, 1978), p. 270.

51. D. Butler and D. Stokes, *Political Change in Britain* (2nd ed.) (Macmillan, 1974), pp. 411–14.

52. Crewe et al., p. 176.

53. Butler and Stokes, p. 414.

54. See especially M. N. Franklin and A. Mughan, "The Decline of Class Voting in Britain: Problems of Analysis and Interpretation," *American Political Science Review,* 72 (2), June 1978, pp. 523–24.

55. I. Crewe, "The disturbing truth behind Labour's rout," *The Guardian,* June 13, 1983.

56. P. Dunleavy, "Voting and the Electorate" in H. Drucker et al. (eds.), *Developments in British Politics* (Macmillan, 1983), p. 43.

57. For the depth of divisions within the two parties in Parliament, see P. Norton, *Dissension in the House of Commons 1945–74* (Macmillan, 1975), passim.

58. I. Crewe, "The Labour Party and the Electorate," p. 37.

59. Crewe et al., p. 187.

60. I. Crewe, "The Labour Party and the Electorate," p. 28.

61. *The Guardian,* June 14, 1983.

62. S. H. Beer, *Modern British Politics,* rev. ed. (Faber, 1969).

63. Crewe, "The Labour Party and the Electorate"; Crewe, "How Labour was trounced all round," *The Guardian,* June 14, 1983.

64. Whiteley, p. 132.

65. Crewe, "The disturbing truth behind Labour's rout."

66. See S. E. Finer, *The Changing British Party System 1945–1979* (American Enterprise Institute, 1980).

67. See S. E. Finer, *Adversary Politics and Electoral Reform* (Wigram, 1975); S. A. Walkland, "Whither the Commons," in S. A. Walkland and M. Ryle (eds.), *The Commons Today* (Fontana, 1981), Ch. 12; D. Owen, *Face the Future* (Oxford University Press, 1981).

68. N. Johnson, book review, *The Times Higher Education Supplement,* July 22, 1983.

69. N. H. Nie, S. Verba, and J. R. Petrocik, *The Changing American Voter* (Harvard University Press, 1976), p. 239. •

70. Ibid.

71. W. Schneider, "The November 4 Vote for President: What Did it Mean?" in A. Ranney (ed.), *The American Elections of 1980* (American Enterprise Institute, 1981), p. 255.

72. R. E. Dawson, *Public Opinion and Contemporary Disarray* (Harper & Row, 1973).

73. A survey undertaken for *Time* magazine in January 1981 asked respondents if the Reagan victory was a mandate for more conservative policies or mostly a rejection of President Carter and his policies. Of the respondents, 63% replied that it was a rejection of President Carter and his policies (*Time,* February 2, 1981). Only 24% considered that it was a mandate for more conservative policies.

74. See, e.g., *Tribune,* June 10, 1983.

75. See Martin Burch, "Mrs. Thatcher's Approach to Leadership in Government." Paper presented at the annual conference of the Political Studies Association of the United Kingdom, Newcastle-Upon-Tyne, April 1983.

76. See, for example, Sir Ian Gilmour's most recent work, *Britain Can Work* (Martin Robertson, 1983).

77. *Morning Star,* June 13, 1983, quoted in *Politics Today* (12), July 11, 1983, p. 229.

78. *The Times,* August 2, 1983.

79. Bill Sirs, general secretary of the steelworkers union, quoted in *The Daily Telegraph,* June 16, 1983.

80. Support for electoral reform is not confined to the SDP and Liberal party. A significant minority of Conservative MPs support reform as do a handful of Labour MPs: see above, Chapter 5.

81. See Owen, *Face the Future.* Also, see previous mention in text.

82. Of electors who considered voting for the SDP/Liberal Alliance, 31% decided not to on the grounds that it was "obvious that Alliance could not win." *The Guardian,* June 14, 1983.

83. J. M. Burns, *The Deadlock of Democracy* (Prentice-Hall, 1963), pp. 327–30.

84. Ibid., p. 330.

85. C. M. Hardin, *Presidential Power and Accountability: Towards a New Constitution* (University of Chicago Press, 1974), p. 139.

86. Ibid. p. 185.

7

Interest Groups
Pluralist or Corporatist?

INTEREST GROUPS have commonly been defined as bodies that seek to influence government in the allocation of resources without themselves seeking to assume responsibility for government. This definition is usually employed to distinguish such groups from political parties, which do seek, through electoral success, to form the government. The distinction, though not watertight, is nonetheless a useful one.

Interest groups have been variously subdivided for analytic purposes. The two most common categories employed are those of sectional interest groups and promotional groups. The former, as the name implies, are formed to defend and pursue the interests of specific sections of the community, sections usually defined on an economic basis. (Indeed, to emphasize the point, some writers distinguish between economic or producer groups and promotional groups.) Promotional groups exist to promote particular causes, causes that may draw their support from disparate individuals and that are not based on economic divisions within society. There are a number of recognizable interest groups that fall somewhere between the two categories (for example, the Automobile Association) and others that do not obviously fall into either category.

Sectional interest groups are usually permanent bodies formed for a purpose other than that primarily of influencing government. Most are created to provide services of one form or another to their members: for example, negotiating on their behalf; providing legal, social, and insurance facilities; offering advice and information; and providing a forum in which matters of common interest can be discussed and policy determined. Such groups are numerous. Obvious examples would be trade unions (of which there are nearly 500—for instance, the National Union of Mineworkers, the Association of University Teachers, the Transport and General Workers Union), the Law Society, the National Farmers Union, the Royal College of Nursing, the Police Federation, the British Medical Association, and various employers' associations. Membership in such bodies is normally exclusive and actual membership is often close to the potential membership. In some instances, membership in a professional body is a requirement for pursuing a particular vocation. Many of the bodies named have their counterparts in the United States: the AFL-CIO, for example, is the rough equivalent of the Trades Union Congress in Britain (see below), and the American Medical Association the equivalent of the British Medical Association.

Whereas sectional groups seek to promote the interests, normally the economic interests, of their membership, promotional groups seek to promote a cause or causes that are not usually of direct economic benefit to their members. The motivation for joining a sectional group is economic, and for joining a promotional group, often moral or ideological. Promotional groups may seek to promote and defend the interests of particular categories of individuals within society (for example, the Child Poverty Action Group, Shelter, Age Concern, the National Council for One-Parent Families), of particular rights (the National Council for Civil Liberties), or of shared beliefs (the Lord's Day Observance Society). Some seek to achieve a specific objective, one often embodied in their title (for example, the Abortion Law Reform Society, the Campaign for Homosexual Equality). A number are essentially defensive groups, formed to counter the campaigns mounted by reform movements: for example, the Society for the Protection of the Unborn Child (SPUC) was formed to oppose the proabortion lobby, and the British Field Sports Society was created to defend hunting against the activities of the League Against Cruel Sports. A number of such groups, by their nature, are little concerned with public policy and rarely engage in political activity. The Royal Society for the Protection of Birds, for example, will have little reason to make demands of government. Others, by contrast, often exist for the purpose of pursuing a public campaign to achieve a modification of public policy and the enactment of legislation.

Interest-group activity and the study of it has been more apparent in the United States than it has in Britain. This is largely explicable in terms of the different political systems. The United States has been characterized as enjoying a "multiple access" system. A group can seek to influence a particular department or bureau. If that fails, it can lobby the White House. It can lobby Congress. The separation-of-powers and the relative weakness of political parties—in essence, depriving Representatives of a protective party shield to hide behind—make Representatives worthwhile targets for group pressure. Such pressure is applied continuously on Capitol Hill. Well in excess of 5,000 lobbyists are retained by groups of one sort or another to lobby congressmen. If pressure in Washington fails, a group can always turn to the congressman's district to try to rouse support there. Rallies may be organized. A mass mailing to Congress may be instigated. Not surprisingly, such visible activity and its apparent effect have been the subject of serious study and much academic debate. The United States has been the breeding ground of group and pluralist theory.

In terms of group activity and the study of it, the position in the United Kingdom has been somewhat different. For groups seeking to influence government decisions, the focus of activity is the executive: that is, the ministers and officials occupying the government departments. As we shall see, for sectional groups such contact is often institutionalized. Attempts to lobby Parliament or to maintain regular contact on a scale analogous to that maintained on Capitol Hill are notable for their rarity. Many groups maintain friendly contact with members of Parliament, but few sectional groups mount or would even know how to mount an effective lobby. What lobbying does take place is conducted usually by the promotional groups. Lobbying of the House of Commons is a sign of failure, an admission that attempts to influence ministers and their officials have failed. It is often an unprofitable exercise: failure to influence ministers is likely to be replicated in a house dominated by those same ministers. The number of professional parliamentary lobbyists can be numbered on the fingers of two hands. Interest group activity, certainly that of the well-entrenched sectional interest groups, is thus not as visible as it is in the United States. Only relatively recently has it begun to attract significant academic attention. A pioneering article by W. J. M. Mackenzie in 1955 was later followed by other studies.[1] Only in the past 20 years has group activity become an important topic of study in British political science: even then it has often been much overshadowed by the study of more conventional topics.

The relative lack of visibility of group activity and the attention accorded it by students of politics should nonetheless not be misconstrued. Lack of attention accorded such activity is explained by the difficulty of studying it. Group activity in Britain is difficult to study because it is not conducted as obviously and as openly as it is in the United States. And the lack of such obvious public conduct may be indicative of group influence, not weakness. Only if groups fail to influence ministers or officials do they need to go public and to concentrate on Parliament and the media. For much of the postwar period, in which group pressure increased, goverment was able to satisfy the wants of those groups making demands of it as well as of consumers: there was little need for the more influential sectional groups to mount campaigns. In recent years, with governments having to pursue redistributive rather than distributive policies, important groups have become far more visible in their attempts to influence government. And as group activity has become more visible, the role played by particular groups in the political arena has become a topic of controversy, both academic and political.

GROUP TYPES

Sectional Interest Groups

Sectional groups in one form or another have existed for many years. Some can be identified as existing in the fifteenth and sixteenth centuries—for example, various merchant guilds. The earliest, according to R. M. Punnett, was the fourteenth-century Convention of Royal Burghs in Scotland.[2] There was considerable group activity in the nineteenth century, but the phenomenon of a large and diverse body of permanent, well-organized sectional groups making demands of government is a relatively recent one, largely associated with the growth of government activity, especially in the years after the Second World War. "This surely was inevitable," wrote Robert McKenzie. "Once it had been largely agreed by all parties that the governments (national and local) should collect and spend over a third of the national income, tremendous pressures were bound to be brought to bear to influence the distribution of the burdens and benefits of public spending on this scale."[3] Those pressures were channelled through and articulated by the sectional interest groups. Groups needed government in order to ensure that their members got the share of the economic cake that they desired. Conversely, government needed the groups. It needed them for advice, for information, and for cooperation. The relationship became one of mutual dependence.

As government extended its activities into the economic and social life of the nation, and especially as it began to utilize Keynsian techniques of economic management, so it came to depend on information on which it could base both particular as well as macroeconomic policies. Such information could often be supplied only by the sectional interest groups. The groups were also in a position to offer advice. The nearer the actual membership of a group came to its potential membership (all lawyers are members of the Law Society, for example; 85% of full-time farmers are members of the National Farmers Union of England and Wales), the closer the group came to enjoying a monopoly of the expertise and understanding peculiar to that section of society. "If doctors are powerful," writes one observer, "it is not just because of their characteristics as a pressure group but because of their functional monopoly of expertise."[4] Government also became dependent on such groups for cooperation in the implementation of policies. If groups are ill-disposed toward a government proposal that affects them, they have the sanction of withdrawing their support in the carrying-out of that proposal. A policy of noncooperation may cause grave and sometimes insurmountable difficulties for government. In 1949, for example, steel producers refused to cooperate with government in the nationalization of the industry. Their actions seriously weakened the ability of the new public corporation to achieve adequate control over the policy and operations of the publicly owned companies.[5] The 1971 Industrial Relations Act failed largely because of the refusal of trade unions both to register under its provisions and to recognize the National Industrial Relations Court it created. The act was subsequently repealed. Such instances of noncooperation are rare, a sign not of group weakness but of political strength. Anticipation of opposition from affected groups will frequently induce government to refrain from pursuing a particular policy or, more likely, to seek some modification acceptable to the groups concerned.

The growing interdependence of government and groups led some observers to view sectional groups as central to policy-making. The ideological gap between the parties was perceived as having narrowed, government acting primarily as arbiter between competing group demands, seeking to meet the demands of groups while meeting the expectations of consumers. It was seen as the age of what Beer referred to as the "new group politics." Whereas the electoral contest between parties may appear to emphasize an adversary relationship, the relationship between government and groups was perceived as a consensual one. In order to proceed with a given policy, government and the affected groups had to reach some measure of accord: one had to influence the other. In the formulation of public policy, government and groups could be seen increasingly as being inseparable.

As the relationship between government and sectional groups developed, various models were formulated and applied by political scientists in order to further understanding of that relationship. The three most important are the pluralist, the rational action, and the corporatist. These I shall discuss in looking at the current debate. As a preliminary to study of that debate, two important features of sectional groups and of their relationship with government need to be drawn out. One is the diversity of the groups themselves, and the other is the extent of the institutionalization of their relationship with government.

Diversity.   There are at least several thousand bodies in Britain that constitute sectional interest groups. It is common to look at such groups under the three sectoral headings of business, labor, and agriculture. Although the business and labor sectors have "peak," or umbrella, organizations, they are notable for the number of groups that exist within them.

The groups within the labor sector comprise primarily trade unions. As already mentioned, there are nearly 500 of these. Some are extremely small and specialized, while others are large and not confined to a particular industry or trade. An example of the former is the Cloth Pressers' Society, with 30 members. The largest union is the Transport and General Workers Union (the TGWU), with a membership in 1980 of 2,086,281. In 1977, the eight largest unions had among them a total membership of 6,214,000, accounting for just under half of the total membership of trade unions. Within the union movement, the older unions representing manual workers have suffered a decline in membership, and those representing white-collar workers (scientists, teachers, technicians, and other professional employees) have grown rapidly in recent years. Between 1948 and 1974, union membership among manual workers declined by 6.8%, whereas membership among white-collar workers increased by 104.7%. In 1974, white-collar unions had a total membership of 3.5 million.[6] In 1974, just under 50% of the total labor force in the United Kingdom belonged to a trade union.

The income of each union comes primarily from membership subscriptions and from interest on invested capital. (Union pension funds are among the major investors in Britain.) Annual subscriptions vary from union to union, ranging from a few pounds a year (the average income per member for unions in 1970 was just over £5, or $6.50) to £20 or £30 a year. In 1982, for example, academics in the Association of University Teachers in Hull paid a subscription of £33.60 (approximately $50). In return, unions provide a variety of services to members—for example, insurance schemes, benevolent funds, discounts on purchases at certain stores, help with house purchases, strike funds, wage negotiations with employers, and the compiling and publishing of information useful to members. More than two-thirds of union expenditure is on working expenses (paying the salaries of full-time officials, rent, and running of headquarters), and most of the remaining one-third is spent on providing various benefits to members.

The "peak" organization for trade unions is the Trades Union Congress (TUC). In 1981 there were 109 unions affiliated to it. Although a majority of trade unions are not affiliated, it is a far more inclusive body in terms of the large and important unions than is its equivalent in the United States, the AFL-CIO (the American Federation of Labor-Congress of Industrial Organizations). A number of the largest unions in the United States, such as the Teamsters Union, are not affiliated to the American body. In Britain, all the largest unions are in the TUC. Indeed, the 109 affiliated unions between them represent more than 95% of all trade unionists.

The TUC serves to coordinate the activities of its members and to represent them in dealings with government, of which more later. It has a number of specialist departments on topics such as employment, economic matters, social matters, and education; these departments research and compile data and help various specialist committees of the TUC formulate policy. It provides a service of trade union education and it provides, as we shall see, members to serve on various advisory and quasigovernmental bodies.

It has an executive body, the General Council, which until 1983 comprised 41 members elected from 18 industrial groupings, such as the railways and mining. This was changed in 1983 following pressure from white-collar unions that considered themselves underrepresented on the council. In 1983, the method of representation was changed so that any union with a membership in excess of 100,000 had at least one place on the council, with additional places allocated on a sliding scale (unions with a membership of 1 to 1.5 million, for example, are entitled to four seats). The net effect of this change has been to increase the representation of white-collar unions on the council and reduce the number representing the old manual unions.

Three important points can be made about trade unions, pertinent to this study. First of all, they are largely decentralized. The TUC conference represents at best a federal body. Individual unions are largely autonomous and often have difficulty in asserting their wishes over local branches. Most industrial stoppages, for example, are unofficial, that is, taking place without the official sanction of the union. (Since the relevant statistics on strikes began to be collected in 1960, unofficial strikes have accounted for more than 90% of strikes.) However, in terms of the number of strikes and days lost through such stoppages, Britain is not unusual in international comparison.[7] It is in the remaining two features that unions are unusual by comparison with many other countries. Politically, the trade unions have a close relationship with the Labour party, much closer than is the case between any union and party in the United States or in most other European countries.[8] As we have seen (Chapter 6), the trade unions were the largest sponsoring element when the Labour Party was formed and continue to be its main provider in both income and affiliated membership. This relationship may in part help explain the third feature. Although unions may and do seek to influence government policy on such issues as employment and the economy, union militancy and strikes are used to pursue wage claims rather than political ends. Overtly political strikes or "days of action" are rare; unions rather look to the Labour party to achieve their political goals. However, when in government, Labour leaders are not always able or willing to implement policies favored by the trade unions. Relations between unions and Labour governments vary considerably: at times they are antagonistic (as, for example, in the late 1960s when a Labour government sought to introduce legislation to reform trade unions), and at other times close (as during the Labour government of 1974–1979 when a "social contract" was negotiated, the government introducing various measures favored by unions in return for moderate wage claims). The general relationship between groups and the government qua government will be considered later.

In the business sector, sectional groups are equally if not more diverse. A report in 1972 identified 865 functioning associations claiming to represent employers. Although there is a well-known peak body for firms in industry, the Confederation of British Industry, it is far from all-encompassing. Write two analysts: "There is . . . a large and complex system of associations which look after the interests of individual industries or, in some cases, the interests of manufacturers of particular products, and many large firms deal directly with government."[9] Finance and the retail sector have their own structures and arrangements with government that are separate from those of the industry sector. "The City," the name given to the interests and institutions that inhabit the square mile of the City of London (Bank of England, the Stock Exchange, the Discount Market, the London Bankers' Clearing House, the commodity markets, insurance companies, and the like), is essentially a separate interest with its own structures and concerns, the latter not always compatible with those of business organizations. There are chambers of commerce throughout the country, though they tend to be most active and effective at regional and local levels than on a national scale. In 1967 an attempt was made to create a peak organization for the retail trade with the formation of the Retail Consortium, a loose confederation of the Multiple Shops Federation, the National Chamber of Trade, the Retail Distributors' Association, and the Cooperative Union. Only gradually is it beginning to establish itself as an influential body in its relations with government.[10] In addition, there is a host of trade associations, important ones being bodies such as the Society of Motor Manufacturers.

This gives one some flavor of the diversity of business organizations. The most important body, that which receives most academic and media attention, is the Confederation of British Industry (the CBI). It was formed in 1965 as a result of the amalgamation of the Federation of British Industries (known, confusingly to Americans, as the FBI), the British Employers' Confederation, and the National Association of British Manufacturers. It sought to bring together the resources of the amalgamated bodies in order to form a more efficient servicing body and a more effective representative of industry's needs in discussions with government. Indeed, its two primary functions are not dissimilar to those of unions: it provides various services to its members and it seeks to represent them in negotiations with government departments and with government generally. It provides advice and assistance on industrial problems, it provides information on such things as technical translation services and conditions in foreign countries, it produces its own economic reports, and, in practice, it provides a medium through which firms and associations can make new and useful contacts. It seeks to act as a spokeman for the needs of industry, not only through making representations directly to government and through appointing representatives to various advisory bodies, but also now through its own annual conference, a recent innovation. (The TUC, by contrast, has been holding annual conferences since the last century.) A survey by Grant and Marsh found that the smaller firms in the CBI joined particularly because of the services it offered, whereas the larger industrial giants tended to join because of its position as a lobbying body on behalf of industry.[11]

The membership of the Confederation comprises predominantly industrial companies, with manufacturing industry being notably to the fore. In 1975, its membership included 10,112 industrial companies, 488 commercial companies, 163 employers' organizations and trade associations, 34 commercial associations, and 15 public-sector bodies.[12] Of its industrial company membership, 40% were firms with fewer than 50 employees and 31% were companies with between 51 and 200 employees. These small firms, however, constitute a minority of small firms in Britain (the Smaller Businesses Association, a body created to represent such companies, claims 20,000 firms as members), whereas half of the top 1,000 companies and three-quarters of the top 100 companies are members.[13] More than half the CBI's income comes from the large companies with more than 1,000 employees each (subscriptions now being based on a company's salary bill and its United Kingdom turnover), and more than three-quarters comes from the industrial companies.[14] In 1975, it had an income of £2.4 million ($3.6 million approximately), used primarily to finance its staff (about 400 strong), headquarters, and various services to members.

The main body within the CBI is its council, a large body comprising up to 400 members nominated by the trade associations, CBI Regional Councils, and the CBI General Purposes Committee. The council meets several times a year but most of the work is conducted through a variety of committees, particularly the formulation of policy on industrial and economic questions. Within the council, the two most prominent and influential figures are the president, usually an industrialist drawn from one of the major companies, and the director-general, the full-time chief executive, usually drawn from a senior position in industry.

Politically, the CBI has no formal link with any political party but is closely associated with the Conservative party and tends to be sympathetic to its policies. In 1981, when the director-general of the CBI, Sir Terence Beckett, made some critical comments about Conservative government policy, a number of firms withdrew or suspended their membership. Although the CBI itself makes no contribution to Conservative party funds, a number of its members are contributors to party funds and, as we have seen (Chapter 6), a significant proportion of Conservative party income nationally derives from business donations.

Although not an inclusive peak organization, the CBI nonetheless is more extensive than any similar body in the United States. Similarly, in the agriculture sector, the National Farmers Union of England and Wales (NFU) is the predominant body; in the United States, there are more obviously competing bodies in the form of the Farmers' Union, the National Grange, and the American Farm Bureau Federation. Of full-time farmers in England and Wales, the NFU claims to represent 85%. (There are separate NFUs in Scotland and Northern Ireland.) It is by no means the only body seeking to represent farming interests. The Farmers' Union of Wales, for example, is now recognized by the Ministry of Agriculture as a representative body for

the purposes of discussions on the annual farm price review. There are also
bodies representing more specialized interests within the broad sector of
agriculture, such as dairy producers.

Like its union and business counterparts, the NFU seeks to provide
various services to members (notably advice and information), as well as
representing the interests of members in discussions with government. Unlike the two other sectors, the agriculture sector is covered primarily by one
government department, the Ministry of Agriculture, Fisheries and Food,
and so the relationship with government is more concentrated and, in many
respects, more structured and discreet than is the case with the TUC and the
CBI. The ministry and the NFU discuss on a regular basis the annual review
undertaken of farm prices and the union is represented on a host of advisory
bodies.

Rather like the CBI, the union has a large national council, with the
most influential members being the president and the general secretary.
Below national level, the main unit of organization is the county branch, an
often active and well-organized body, particularly in the large agricultural
counties. Although farmers are traditionally strong supporters of the Conservative party, the union nationally as well as at county level tends to adopt a
strict political neutrality, though this is essentially of postwar origin. Before
1945 (the union was founded in 1908), it was more closely associated with the
Conservative party, despite formal assertions of nonpartisanship.[15]

Institutionalization.   As its responsibilities expanded, government came to
have greater need of what groups could offer and the groups, in turn, looked
to government for the satisfaction of their demands. This relationship often
necessitated frequent contact and increasingly became institutionalized.
Groups were asked not only for advice on an informal or nonroutine basis,
they became drawn into the processes of government by being invited to
appoint representatives to serve on advisory bodies, tribunals, and committees of different sorts. This in itself is not a recent phenomenon. The National Health Insurance Act of 1924 provided for the functional representation of specific interests, such as the medical profession, on various committees appointed to administer the system of social insurance. Analogous
provisions had appeared in the Trade Board acts of 1909 and 1918.[16] By the
late 1950s, more than 100 advisory bodies existed under statutory provision.
Recent years have witnessed the growth of bodies that comprise representatives of the peak organizations of the CBI and the TUC as well as representatives of the government. These last represent the institutional embodiment
of a form of tripartite relationship among government, employers, and
unions that we shall explore shortly. Examples of such bodies are the National Economic Development Council (the NEDC, known as "Neddy"),
created in 1961 to provide a forum in which representatives of the three

could meet to discuss the economy; the Manpower Services Commission, to promote training and job creation schemes; the Health and Safety Commission, to help regulate and supervise safety and health at work; and the Arbitration and Conciliation Service (known as ACAS), to help resolve industrial disputes.[17] At the same time, the various bodies at a lower level, to consider more specialized topics and to bring together representatives of the various core (as opposed to peak) groups, continued to proliferate. Between 1974 and 1978, for example, 11 new governmental bodies were created in the sector covered by the Department of the Environment: these included an advisory group on commercial property development and an advisory board of constructions experts.[18] A report on such bodies in 1978 identified more than 1,560 advisory bodies and nearly 500 similar bodies with executive powers (to issue regulations, dispense funds, and carry out similar functions), such as the Manpower Services Commission.[19] The Scottish Office alone had in excess of 60 advisory bodies, ranging from the Scottish Industrial Development Advisory Board to the Scottish Food Hygiene Council. Methods of appointment to these disparate bodies vary. In some cases statutory requirements exist to include representatives of particular groups, and in other cases the power is vested with the relevant minister, who may appoint people in a representative capacity (on behalf of a group) or in an individual capacity (drawn from but not officially representing a particular group). What is significant for our purposes is the number of such bodies and the extent to which they are manned by, and indeed would be unable to function without, members of affected interest groups.

It is important to remember that such bodies constitute the formal, institutional embodiment of the close relationship between groups and government. Over and above these, there is regular contact between groups and government departments through formal and informal meetings, sometimes through formal or informal social gatherings. A luncheon hosted by a minister for a visiting foreign dignitary or businessman, for example, may be attended by leading representatives of certain groups. Both the director-general of the CBI and the general-secretary of the TUC may be invited to such occasions hosted by the prime minister in Downing Street. At the level of regular contact, the National Farmers Union and the Ministry of Agriculture follow fairly well-established procedures each year in discussing the annual price review. Throughout the year the two are in constant touch with one another, "almost hourly contact," according to one study.[20] There is similar contact between other departments and groups within their sphere of responsibility.

What emerges from even this brief review of the institutionalization of group-departmental relationships is its range and diversity, the existence of which should not be surprising. Groups, as we have seen, are remarkably diverse, with peak organizations being at best federal or confederal bodies. Government departments are not dissimilar in diversity. Each department will usually be divided into a number of usually functional units. A given unit will have contact with the relevant outside group. Few departments if any lack such divisions and none has the luxury of being able to negotiate with one inclusive outside group. Senior government ministers may on occasion consult with representatives of the TUC and the CBI, but most government policy is formulated, or more often adjusted, at a much lower level, often at the subdepartment level. The relevant outside groups will discuss a proposal with the relevant unit within a department. If agreement is reached, the proposal is then "sold" to the department itself before, if necessary, being put forward for approval at a higher level. Only major policy decisions percolate up to the cabinet for discussion and approval. Most policy is made at departmental and subdepartmental levels. There are functional and legal, as well as cultural, reasons encouraging this practice. The range and extent of government policy-making is such that the cabinet is able to deal with only a fraction of it. Formally, legal powers are vested in individual ministers (not the cabinet), and for a proposal to be authoritative and enacted, it is often sufficient for a minister to give it formal approval. Furthermore, the political culture favors consensus. Disputes are neither sought or encouraged. It is to the advantage of both group and civil servants (with whom most contact tends to take place) to avoid dissent. Each needs the other and disputes could jeopardize their relationship as well as pass the problem on for others to resolve. A desire to decide the issue for themselves impels civil servants and the groups to seek agreement. One of the characteristics of the British policy style, according to Jordan and Richardson, is that of "bureaucratic accommodation."[21] Such accommodation ensures that the relationships involved are not much in the public gaze, which instead tends to be fixed on the more public tripartite relationship among government, employers, and unions.

A combination of this diversity and institutionalization has important implications for the nature of policy-making in Britain, for it favors incrementalism. Policy is rarely subject to major surgery but, through this disparate, established relationship of groups and departments, is subjected rather to minor or at least not fundamental change. Conversely, it creates problems for any government seeking to impose a comprehensive new policy on both its own departments and affected groups. Departments or their various units often become so closely associated with the groups with which they deal that they tend to represent the interests of the groups to the government, rather than (or in addition to) representing the interests of government to the groups. This, sometimes referred to as a form of "clientelism," results in departments speaking on behalf of different interests and often competing among themselves where those interests are not compatible. Thus, a government determined on cuts in public expenditure has the task of imposing cuts upon departments that are keen to resist them and come up with plausible arguments for their own exemption, arguments that have the backing of the department's clientele groups. For example, cuts in the defense budget are likely to be resisted by officials, sometimes the minister (if persuaded by department officials) as well as by the armed services and the various industries that help manufacture and maintain military hardware and equipment. Cuts, it is argued, would jeopardize the nation's defenses. Similarly, cuts in other departments would be resisted on analogous grounds, ministers competing to defend their own departmental budgets. For government to impose a comprehensive policy, it must persuade a variety of what have been aptly termed policy communities to agree to that policy. While a party manifesto might provide a government with its plan of action, achieving that plan is a task for which neither the manifesto nor control of a party majority in the House of Commons may be sufficient.

Promotional Groups

Promotional groups generally lack the political clout enjoyed by sectional interest groups. They rarely have a monopoly of information and expertise, certainly not information and expertise that is needed by government. A feature of promotional groups is that normally anyone sympathetic to their aims is welcome to join them. There is no exclusive membership. Their potential membership, technically, constitutes the adult population. They have few if any sanctions that they can employ against government if it proves unresponsive to their overtures. In short, they are without the attributes enjoyed by the sectional interest groups in achieving leverage in their relationship with government. Not being dependent on promotional groups for advice, information, or cooperation, departments will not usually maintain regular or institutionalized contact with them. Indeed, given the causes promoted by some groups, a government may be keen to keep some of them at arm's length. To achieve their goals, promotional groups will often find themselves compelled to seek support outside the corridors of government departments.

Failure to influence ministers or their officials will result usually in the groups turning their attention to Parliament, either directly or indirectly. Direct contact with MPs will take the form of letters or pamphlets sent to all MPs or, in the case of better-organized groups, to MPs likely to be sympathetic to their cause and through lobbying of members by group supporters. Sympathetic MPs, some of whom may hold office in the groups (quite often as honorary vice-presidents), may arrange for delegations from a group to meet with other MPs or even a minister. All such contact, though, is less systematic, less professional, and less obvious than in the United States. It takes place on a smaller scale, and the use of professional lobbyists is virtually unknown. It often attracts little publicity.

Indirectly, groups will seek to influence MPs through mass demonstrations, marches, public meetings, and press releases. Similar activities will often be pursued by sectional groups in instances when they have failed to achieve their goals through contact with ministers and officials. In the absence of extremely large numbers or violence, attracting publicity by such means can be an uphill struggle.

Through persuading MPs of the justice of their case, promotional groups seek some parliamentary action—a parliamentary question or a debate for example—in the hope that it will arouse parliamentary interest in the subject and, if persistent and widespread, will influence government to act. On some issues, government action may not even be needed. A private member's bill on an issue about which the government would prefer not to take a stand (for instance, a moral issue that cuts across party lines) may make it to the statute book with government acquiescence rather than support. Indeed, even when it has sympathy for a particular cause, a government may prefer to leave the matter for determination by private member's legislation, thus avoiding responsibility for the measure and any public resentment that may result from its passage. This reticence was a feature of the period from 1964–1970, when several major measures of social reform were enacted as private members' bills.[22]

The success of groups vary considerably. Some enjoy the respect and sympathy of the public, MPs, and ministers (especially those of charitable status, e.g., the Royal National Institute for the Blind). Some have proved effective because of the dedication of their supporters, albeit limited in numbers, in mounting campaigns and lining up a number of committed MPs. The Lord's Day Observance Society, for example, has been especially able in obstructing attempts to reform the Sunday trading and entertainment laws.[23] Such obstruction can prove effective despite popular support for reform. Conversely, some groups have proved effective in persuading MPs of the need for change despite popular resistance to reform. This was notable in the case of a number of so-called conscience issues in the 1960s: for instance, abolition of the death penalty for murder.

Other groups have not proved so successful. Some groups fail or have limited impact because their cause arouses little popular interest (for example, the Temperance Alliance); because they are viewed as politically suspect bodies by certain parties (Conservatives and some Liberals look on the National Council for Civil Liberties as a front organization for the Labour party); because they pursue a cause unpopular at both the mass and elite levels (for example, EXIT, favoring voluntary euthanasia); because they pursue contentious issues that arouse strong feelings across party lines, often encountering well-organized opposition groups; because they make financial demands that government is unable or unwilling to meet; because they make demands that run counter to those made by well-placed sectional interest groups (on legal matters, for example, the National Council for Civil Liberties against the Law Society); or because for one reason or another they are not taken too seriously (the National Viewers' and Listeners' Association, concerned with moral standards in broadcasting, tends to fall into this category). In most such cases, MPs and ministers will tend to prefer to leave well alone.

Many of the features of British promotional groups, and indeed the causes pursued, are not dissimilar to those of American promotional groups. Both have benefited from the development of television, allowing them to have more visual impact through many of their public demonstrations and lobbies. British groups, though, are arguably more limited than their American counterparts by virtue of the strength of party. On an issue about which a party stance is taken, an MP can hide behind his party's position in responding to group pressure. It is an effective shield. Promotional groups present no significant threat to a sitting MP. They stand no chance of persuading electors to vote the MP out at the next election: party label will normally determine whether the MP stays or goes. Groups will have no leverage through campaign donations: donations go to parties and, as we have seen, campaign expenditure is limited and strictly controlled. Contributions from promotional groups would be considered impolitic. Occasionally, issues will become important as divisive issues within parties—for example, capital punishment in the Conservative party or abortion in the Labour party—but rarely will they impinge upon an MP's chosen behavior or his or her continuance as a party candidate. Even where they do, it is not because of group activity. A good constituency MP who remains loyal to party will have little difficulty in ignoring any or all promotional groups that he or she chooses to ignore. Indeed, many MPs are so tired of the mass of material sent them by promotional groups that it is filed automatically in the wastepaper basket.

This is not to argue that MPs do not align themselves with or are not persuaded by promotional groups. Many are associated with such groups and not infrequently serve as very active advocates of their cause. The point is that MPs are in a much stronger position than are congressmen to resist pressure from groups with which they are not in sympathy. MPs do not need such groups and rarely if ever could groups even remotely be considered a threat to their political survival. Congressional victims of the Moral Majority or of the National Rifle Association would probably concede that a similar point could not be made by an MP's counterpart in the United States.

GROUPS AND MODELS

The Current Debate

The activity of interest groups in the political process in Britain is clearly significant. In order to further understanding of this activity, a number of models have been constructed. The most important of these are, as I have mentioned, the pluralist, the rational action, and the corporatist. These three models are not necessarily mutually exclusive, but they help direct our attention and deepen our understanding of particular aspects of group behavior in the political process.

The Pluralist Model

The basic framework of this model is that there is a consensus on the nature of the political system, on "the rules of the game," and that the role of government is to act as independent arbiter among the competing demands of groups. Within the political process, the essential element is the group, and the political system is characterized by individuals having the opportunity to join groups, doing so, and then, through those groups, enjoying access to government. Pluralists emphasize the extent and range of groups, their access to government, and the competition between them.[24] There is presumed to be something of a balance among groups, no one group enjoying supremacy, and the balance and institutionalized relationship between groups and government provides for both stability in the political system and incremental policy-making.

As with all models, the pluralist one constitutes an ideal. However, it is the model to which both American and British experiences have been seen to provide a reasonably close fit. The importance of groups in Britain has been emphasized by a number of writers,[25] and from our brief survey of sectional and promotional groups one can discern substantial empirical evidence to support a pluralist analysis. Clearly there is a wide range of interest groups, and the relationship between sectional groups and government is regular and institutionalized. A large proportion of the population are members of groups (over 12 million are members of trade unions, for example, and nearly 4 million are members of Christian churches), and there are groups with mutually countervailing goals. The TUC, for example, is often assumed to provide a balance to the CBI. In most spheres, the government could be characterized as serving as arbiter. Incrementalism is a predominant feature of policy-making. Thus, pluralism would seem an adequate description of policy-making in Britain.

The pluralist model, however, is a far from perfect fit and a number of weighty objections have been leveled against it. Marxists would dispute the role of government, conceiving it as a subjective rather than a neutral actor.[26] For groups, there are problems with pluralist analysis in terms of their membership, their internal organization, and their impact on government. Although many people in Britain are members of groups, a great many are not. Only about half the workforce, for example, belong to trade unions. Furthermore, group membership and more especially group activity is much more notably a feature of the middle class than it is of the working class. A study of planning decisions, for example, found that those who participated were generally middle-class, having both the time and the knowledge to be involved; the poor and the inarticulate tend not to be heard.[27] The exception of this generalization is that of the trade unions, but consideration of union membership and activity leads on to the next criticism, one not confined to the unions.

Many groups, as Reginald Harrison has pointed out, lack developed democratic structures and extensive member participation.[28] Practices within groups vary but the number with extensive consultative procedures designed to inform group representatives of members' opinions does not appear extensive. Given the extent to which groups maintain contact with government, it would be time-consuming and expensive to consult members about every matter on which they as groups are asked to offer advice. Furthermore, as Grant and Marsh have observed, given the absence of the equivalent of "parties" in groups, "it is difficult to operate an electoral system within a group."[29]

For many groups the formal decision-making body is a national committee or council, which is elected annually and may meet intermittently or regularly, policy being formulated by committees, as is the case with both the TUC and the CBI. The disapprobation of members in response to an unpopular decision taken by the national body is often post hoc—that is, removing those responsible after the event, though anticipation of such a response can influence the representatives in their negotiations with government. In the case of other groups there may not even be procedures for election and consultation. The Automobile Association, for example, claims to speak on behalf of motorists yet has no developed procedures for consulting its members.

In policy impact, pluralist theory is criticized for emphasizing a balance among competing groups. While few pluralists would contend that there is perfect balance among groups, the concept of some measure of balance is central to their thesis. There are presumed to be potential countervailing groups to existing ones, the potential groups to be realized by the activities of the existing ones. The creation of the CBI as a counterweight to the TUC, for example, would be stressed. Yet, from the preceding study, one can glean material that throws doubt on the thesis. Obviously, the concept of balance is difficult to apply in any comparison between sectional and promotional groups: the latter are clearly the weaker brethren. Within sectional interest groups, some have far more extensive wealth and resources than others and are more needed by government. They thus tend to wield disproportionate influence in their relations with government. Insofar as it represents one coherent interest, for instance, the City of London is a powerful body that has few obvious and comparable countervailing groups.

Recognition of some imbalance in internal relationships has led some pluralists to develop the concept of elite pluralism, which accepts the importance of group leaderships but considers them acceptable as long as there are multiple and competing elites. Elite theorists, such as C. Wright Mills in the United States, have contended that there is no such competition between elites. Members of elites share common backgrounds and values and so there is one over-arching elite with the power to shape the agenda of political debate.[30] This thesis has been subjected to a number of significant and, to my mind, persuasive critiques[31] but nonetheless it serves to sensitize one to the importance of non-decision-making, of the consensus within which negotiations are conducted.

Finally, pluralist theory has been criticized on the grounds that it fails to acknowledge the impact of political parties and of elections in policy-making. Political parties help provide a framework for government action, a government being elected with the intention of implementing a particular manifesto. Although Richard Rose in his study of political parties found that the particular party in office did not make a great difference in terms of various economic indicators, he nonetheless contended that parties did make *some* difference: the fact that one party was in office, rather than another, was important.[32] A party in office adopts a particular approach, it adheres to a particular program, and it may adopt a specific style of government. Clearly, a Labour government under Michael Foot or its new leader, Neil Kinnock, would behave very differently from the present Conservative government under Mrs. Thatcher. In any study of public policy, political parties cannot be left out of consideration.

Rational Action Model

The rational action model, deriving in large part from the work of Mancur Olson,[33] interprets group strength as a function of the members' reasons for joining. It may thus serve to explain some disparities among groups. This model contends that people join a group only if a rational calculation of costs and benefits shows that their personal welfare would be improved by becoming a group member.

Groups that are all-encompassing—that is, are able to negotiate benefits intended only for their members—are in a strong position to recruit members. These groups include professional bodies in which membership is necessary to remain and progress in a given profession—for example, the British Medical Association and the Law Society. They are well-organized and powerful bodies, enjoying influence in relation both to their members and to government.

Groups that are not all-encompassing, on the other hand, that negotiate benefits to be enjoyed by members and nonmembers alike (for example, wage rises), are in a weaker position to recruit members. These include most promotional groups; generally, what they can offer to their members exclusively is advice and information. Such groups tend to be weak and are often poorly organized.

The model is helpful in understanding the "pluralist stagnation" argument advanced by Samuel Beer and others. The absence of all-encompassing groups militates against the ability of government and groups to formulate and impose policies in the public interest. The range of groups, pursuing the interests of members who have joined to benefit their own and not the public interest, results in a lack of agreement, each group recognizing that by itself it cannot produce the end desired by government for the public good. One group's accepting the need for moderation in wage demands, for example, will have little effect if all other groups do not follow suit. The consequence, according to Beer's analysis (see Chapter 3), is pluralist stagnation.

This model tends to draw attention to inequalities among groups and hence is not strictly compatible with the pluralist model. Like pluralism, however, it has been subject to a number of important criticisms. For example, it fails to offer an explanation for the existence of well-organized and influential promotional interest groups. The welfare of a promotional group member may not benefit from membership but the moral or ideological stance of the group moves some people to commit both their time and their money to a particular cause. The Campaign for Nuclear Disarmament, to take a contemporary example, has become an important "cause" group in recent years in Britain, yet few of those who go on marches and demonstrations would claim to be doing so for their own welfare (rather, justification tends to be expressed in terms of the welfare of others). Similarly, a well-organized environmental conservation group, Greenpeace, has attracted much useful publicity, yet many of its members risk personal injury in their attempts to prevent the slaughter of animals. Nor does this model explain extensive membership of sectional groups that negotiate benefits that can be enjoyed by nonmembers. The study of the CBI by Grant and Marsh, for example, found that many members, particularly a number of large and medium-sized firms, were aware that nonmembers could receive some of the benefits (such as research reports) they received as members and that, as members, they did not receive value for money.[34] Many firms had not even attempted to do a costs–benefit analysis of membership.

The model thus has its uses, though one of its important contributions to a study of groups lies in its failure to provide a comprehensive explanation— that is, it points attention to the need for more extensive studies of why people join groups. The rationality model provides but a partial explanation.

The Corporatist Model

The final and probably most contentious model is the corporatist. Corporatism has been subject to varying definitions but basically it entails a system in which government directs the activities of industry, which remains predominantly in private hands, through the representatives of a limited number of singular, compulsory, noncompetitive, hierarchically ordered, and functionally differentiated interest groups.[35] *Societal* corporatism exists where government tends to be but one participant in a complex of negotiations with such groups. Where government is dominant in the relationship, there exists a form of *state* corporatism.[36]

The first and most obvious point to be made about corporatism is that, on the foregoing definition, it does not exist in Britain. The various peak organizations, primarily the CBI and the TUC, do not conform to the conditions stipulated for the interest groups. Nonetheless, corporatist trends have been identified in Britain in the tripartite relations among government, employers, and trade unions. Tripartism, taken to its logical conclusion, would be a relationship in which, as Mr. Heath put it, all three "share fully . . . the benefits and obligations of running the country."[37] In practice, the relationship has taken two forms. There is the co-option of the representatives of the TUC and the CBI onto bodies concerned with administration and resolving disputes (as in the case of Advisory, Conciliation, and Arbitration Service [ACAS]) and onto those concerned with discussing economic policy, notably the National Economic Development Council. During the 1960s and 1970s, there was also a greater recognition of the informal negotiations among government, employers, and unions, often conducted at prime-ministerial level. Labour Prime Minister Harold Wilson was keen to consult with the TUC and CBI and, as already seen (Chapter 6), Conservative Prime Minister Edward Heath sought to arrange a voluntary prices-and-pay policy with both bodies in 1972. The conduct of industry and the economy was seen as coming more under the direction of this tripartite influence, excluding other groups and creating a quasi-corporatist arrangement. This relationship was seen by critics to reach a peak under the Labour government of 1974–1979. In 1976, Chancellor of the Exchequer Denis Healey made a 3% reduction in income tax, conditional on the acceptance of pay restraint by trade unions. The government also negotiated with the TUC a "social contract" that, as already mentioned, entailed the government's introducing various measures (on employment law, for example) favored by the unions in return for which the unions moderated wage demands.

Many writers on corporatism are divided on its merits. Some see it as a threat to existing representative institutions, decisions being taken by un-elected bodies rather than by the citizens' elected representatives.[38] Adherents to a free-market economy regard corporatism as a direct threat and are vigorous in their condemnation of it. The present Conservative government under Mrs. Thatcher, for example, clearly rejects tripartism as an acceptable form of policy making; trade unions are conscious of effectively being left out in the cold as far as government policy-making is concerned (so much so that in 1983 there was discussion within the TUC as to whether or not it should withdraw from the NEDC in protest). In contrast, some economists and political scientists consider that some form of tripartism, or a more full-blooded form of corporatism, would offer the best way of dealing with Britain's economic problems.[39] Corporatism would allow government to persuade or induce groups to give up the pursuit of narrow goals in favor of the national interest. Marxists provide a somewhat different interpretation, seeing corporatism as a device used to defend capitalism and, according to some Marxist analyses, to incorporate the working class into a system dominated by business interests.[40]

Parallel but not coterminous with the debate on the merits of the concept is the debate as to whether Britain is experiencing a form of tripartism, or even quasi-corporatism, and is moving ineluctably toward a corporate state. From our earlier review and the foregoing comments, it is difficult to argue that Britain is characterized by a form of tripartism among government, TUC, and CBI, let alone experiencing a drift toward corporatism. The TUC and CBI, as we have seen, are not all-encompassing organizations and do not enjoy strong control over their members. As noted already, a number of firms left the CBI in 1981 following remarks by the director-general that were critical of the Conservative government. The "social contract" between the Labour government and the TUC effectively collapsed following a series of disruptive strikes by public sector unions in the winter of 1978–1979. Furthermore, periods of pure tripartite relations are difficult to discern. Much of the relationship has been bipartite rather than tripartite. The example given above of Chancellor Healey's budget, for example, was an instance of such a relationship. On other occasions, negotiations are effectively multilateral, going beyond the TUC and CBI. The Labour government of 1974–1979, for example, had in effect to negotiate with the TUC, the International Monetary Fund, the CBI, the City of London, and, to some extent, the House of Commons (though here, *negotiation* would be the wrong word), where it lacked an overall majority. This experience helps point to the fact that, though they are peak organizations, the CBI and TUC are not the only peak organizations and are certainly not by themselves sufficient to encompass those bodies on which government is dependent in order to achieve fulfilment of its economic aims. The present Conservative government, as already recorded, has eschewed tripartism. Although one might discern corporatist trends in the formation of various bodies such as the NEDC since 1962, there is little substantial material to lead to the conclusion that Britain is moving inevitably in the direction of a corporate state.

NOTES

1. W. J. M. Mackenzie, "Pressure Groups in British Government," *British Journal of Sociology*, 6 (2), 1955, pp. 133–48. Subsequent studies included S. E. Finer, *Anonymous Empire* (Pall Mall Press, 1958); J. D. Stewart, *British Pressure Groups* (Oxford University Press, 1958); the seminal work of Samuel H. Beer, *Modern British Politics* (Faber, 1965); A. M. Potter, *Organised Groups in British Politics* (Faber, 1961).

2. R. M. Punnett, *British Government and Politics* (Heinemann, 1970 ed.), p. 134.

3. R. T. McKenzie, "Parties, Pressure Groups and the British Political Process," *Political Quarterly*, 29 (1), 1958.

4. R. Klein, "Policy making in the National Health Service," *Political Studies*, 22 (1), 1974, p. 6.

5. S. H. Beer, *Modern British Politics*, rev. ed. (Faber, 1969), p. 326.

6. D. Butler and A. Sloman, *British Political Facts 1900–1979*, 5th ed. (Macmillan, 1980), p. 337.

7. In 1970–1974, for example, the average annual number of disputes per 100,000 employees was 11.5 in the United Kingdom, compared with 16.4 in France, 24.1 in Italy, 43.9 in Australia, 6.0 in Japan, 5.9 in the United States, and 1.9 in Sweden.

8. See C. Crouch, "The Peculiar Relationship: The Party and the Unions" in D. Kavanagh (ed.), *The Politics of the Labour Party* (George Allen & Unwin, 1982), pp. 175–77.

9. W. Grant and D. Marsh, *The CBI* (Hodder & Stoughton, 1977), p. 55.

10. Ibid., pp. 61–8.

11. Ibid., pp. 44–50.

12. Ibid., p. 35.

13. Ibid., p. 34.

14. Ibid., pp. 36–7.

15. P. Self and H. Storing, "The Farmer and the State" in R. Kimber and J. J. Richardson (eds.), *Pressure Groups in Britain* (Dent, 1974), pp. 58–59.

16. Beer, 1969, p. 78.

17. See *Report on Non-Departmental Public Bodies*, Cmnd. 7797 (Her Majesty's Stationery Office, 1980), pp. 38–47.

18. J. J. Richardson and A. G. Jordan, *Governing Under Pressure* (Martin Robertson, 1979), p. 61.

19. *Report on Non-Departmental Public Bodies*, p. 5.

20. G. K. Wilson, *Special Interests and Policy Making* (Wiley, 1977), quoted in Richardson and Jordan, p. 114.

21. A. G. Jordan and J. Richardson, "The British Policy Style or the Logic of Negotiation?" in J. Richardson (ed.), *Policy Styles in Western Europe* (George Allen & Unwin, 1982), p. 81.

22. See P. G. Richards, *Parliament and Conscience* (George Allen & Unwin, 1970).

23. See J. Parker, *Father of the House* (Routledge and Kegan Paul, 1982), Ch. 23.

24. The main works on pluralism are American, most notably those of Dahl and Truman. See especially R. A. Dahl, *A Preface to Democratic Theory* (Chicago University Press, 1956) and *Who Governs?* (Yale University Press, 1961). See also D. Truman, *The Governmental Process* (Knopf, 1962).

25. See especially Richardson and Jordan.

26. See, e.g., R. Miliband, *The State in Capitalist Society* (Quartet, 1973).

27. M. Fagence, *Citizen Participation in Planning* (Pergamon, 1977).

28. R. J. Harrison, *Pluralism and Corporatism* (George Allen & Unwin, 1980), Ch. 5.

29. Grant and Marsh, *The CBI*, p. 87.

30. C. Wright Mills, *The Power Elite* (Oxford University Press, 1956). See also W. L. Guttsman, *The British Political Elite* (MacGibbon & Kee, 1963).

31. See, e.g., A. M. Rose, *The Power Structure* (Oxford University Press, 1967), and T. R. Dye, *Who's Running America?* 2nd ed. (Prentice-Hall, 1979).

32. R. Rose, *Do Parties Make a Difference?* (Macmillan, 1980). See also the summary by A. King, "What do elections decide?" in H. Penniman (ed.), *Democracy at the Polls* (American Enterprise Institute, 1980), pp. 304–8.

33. M. Olson, *The Logic of Collective Action* (Schocken Books, 1968). See also by the same author, *The Rise and Decline of Nations* (Yale University Press, 1982).

34. Grant and Marsh, pp. 50–52.

35. See A. Cawson, "Pluralism, corporatism and the role of the State," *Government and Opposition,* Spring 1978, p. 197.

36. The distinction between societal and state corporatism is drawn by P. C. Schmitter, "Still the Century of Corporatism?," *The Review of Politics,* 36 (1), 1974, pp. 85–131. See also R. Pahl and J. Winkler, "The Coming Corporatism," *New Society,* October 10, 1974.

37. Edward Heath, quoted in Richardson and Jordan, p. 50.

38. See P. Norton, *The Constitution in Flux* (Martin Robertson, 1982), pp. 275, 179, 282.

39. See the summary of the Weberian approach in A. Cox "Corporatism and the Corporate State in Britain" in L. Robins (ed.), *Topics in British Politics* (Politics Association, 1982), p. 128.

40. Ibid., p. 129.

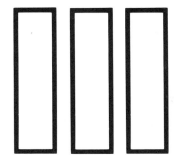

Governmental Decision-Making

The Executive
Government at the Center

THE FORMAL PROCESS of determining public policy in Britain is dominated by the executive. Once the executive has agreed on a measure, the assent of Parliament can usually be assured. Parliament is essentially a policy-ratifying rather than a policy-making body.[1] Once the measure is enacted in legislative form, it will be enforced by the courts: it cannot be struck down on grounds of being contrary to the provisions of the constitution. In the United States, by contrast, the executive enjoys no such dominance.[2] The president cannot proceed on the basis that any proposals he makes can be assured the assent of Congress. Once enacted, legislative measures can be and occasionally are struck down by the courts as contrary to the provisions of the Constitution. The American political system has been described as a "multiple access" one. It may also be characterized as a "multiple check" system. A proposal emanating from one branch of government can be checked—that is, negated—by another. Congress has negating powers that it is prepared to and not infrequently does use; Parliament has negating powers that it can but hardly ever does use. The executive in Britain can make assumptions about legislative support that few American presidents would dare to make.

Viewed in terms of the Constitution and the relationships governed by conventions, the policy-making process in Britain may appear clear and effective. An executive is formed and proceeds to implement a party program with the support of a parliamentary majority. That has been a popular perception, in Britain itself as well as elsewhere. In practice, the process has

175

proved to be neither clear nor altogether effective. I have considered already some of the problems associated with party and the implications of attempting to enact a party program. Chapter 7 covered the major constraints imposed by group pressures. An executive has to work within the complex political framework generated by public expectations, group pressures, party expectations, limited resources and a changing international environment, some or all of which on any given issue may be mutually exclusive. What is acceptable to the TUC at home may not be acceptable to the International Monetary Fund abroad. What is popular with the electorate (for example, trade union reform) may be strongly resisted by affected groups. The executive has to operate in an increasingly confused environment, one in which fulfilling the role of juggler may sometimes or often be substituted for that of leadership. Advocates of pluralist theory, as we have seen (Chapter 7), emphasize the role of arbiter assumed by government. Few would deny that the executive operates within an increasingly complex political milieu.

THE STRUCTURE

It is not only the environment external to the executive that is complex and not always (if ever) harmonious. The same may be said of the executive itself. It comprises an entangled web of bodies, powers, and relationships that, in

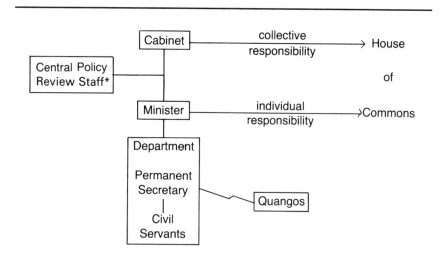

FIGURE 8.1　The Executive in Britain. (*In effect until 1983, when it was wound up.)

practice, are not easy to discern and that confuse any attempt to delineate clearly how policy is formulated and where power lies within government. At the apex of government stands the cabinet, and below that the individual government departments headed by ministers and manned by civil servants. But even within the Cabinet there exist a complex infrastructure and sometimes shifting relationships. As government has grown, it not only has become more complex but also has experienced problems of political accountability. The civil service has grown. At the edges of government, nondepartmental public bodies have burgeoned. For the cabinet, maintaining control of the government body itself has become an awesome task.

In terms of the structure of the executive and the lines of responsibility to Parliament, the formal position is outlined in Figure 8.1. For the purposes of analysis, it is necessary to identify the essential features of the different elements of the executive. The main elements may be subsumed under the headings of the cabinet, ministers, departments, civil servants, and nondepartmental public bodies, known popularly as "quangos." The powers, structure, and composition of each element and the relationships among them have become increasingly a matter of some controversy.

The Cabinet

The cabinet stands at the pinnacle of government. It comprises nowadays between 20 and 25 members (see Table 8.1), constituting the ministerial heads of the main government departments as well as a number of ministers with nondepartmental responsibilities (for example, the chancellor of the Duchy of Lancaster). By convention its members are drawn from Parliament—there have been a few exceptions—and, again by convention, predominantly from the House of Commons. A minimum of two peers, but rarely more than three or four, are appointed to the Cabinet. The members are chosen by the prime minister (PM), who enjoys the power of both appointment and dismissal. In choosing a cabinet, a PM will normally seek to incorporate senior colleagues with support on the backbenches as well as taking into account other factors: for example, the need to include representatives of different opinions within the party, the political and administrative capabilities of colleagues, the desire to reward loyal supporters, as well as certain geographical considerations (for instance, the secretary of state for Scotland will be expected to sit for a Scottish constituency). Once appointed, cabinet ministers are in a somewhat stronger position politically than are their American counterparts. They remain within Parliament and many will enjoy significant parliamentary support. For a PM, dismissal of a minister with powerful support on the backbenches or possibly within the party in the country could create more problems than it would solve. Aside from some celebrated exceptions, PMs have rarely proved "good butchers," a quality that Clement Attlee deemed necessary for any occupant of the office. The

PM's powers are exercised more often in the reshuffling of cabinet posts than in dismissing holders of those posts.

The cabinet, as we have seen (Chapter 4), is deemed to be responsible for the final determination of policy to be submitted to Parliament as well as for control of the national executive and the coordination and delimitation of the interests of the various departments of state. In the nineteenth century, it was not a very efficient body: it often had little to do, discussions were frequently leaked by waiters (it met for dinner at the home of one of its members), members sometimes slept during meetings, and there was no agenda. In the twentieth century, as the demands on the cabinet have grown, it has developed a complex infrastructure in order to fulfil its tasks. A cabinet secretariat was created in 1916, responsible for circulating agenda, papers, and minutes as well as monitoring the implementation of cabinet decisions. The period since 1945 has been notable for the spread of cabinet committees. They are formed from the ministers relevant to the area covered by the committee as well as some ministers free of departmental responsibilities. The committees' creation, membership, and chairmanship is determined by the prime minister. They are serviced by the cabinet secretariat, which, among other things, provides briefing papers for the chairmen. The committees are shrouded in secrecy. Neither their existence nor their membership is officially supposed to be revealed, though Prime Minister Mrs. Thatcher did break with tradition in 1979 to admit their existence.[3] The committees comprise a number of standing committees, designated by letters of the alphabet (E committee, for example, designates the economic strategy committee) and others created on an ad-hoc basis to cover particular problems. Mrs. Thatcher announced that she had established four standing committees: economic strategy, defense and overseas policy, home and social affairs, and legislation, the first two being under her chairmanship. Although she did not reveal the number of subcommittees, they are believed to be numerous. (There were about 100 subcommittees during Harold Wilson's premiership.) Decisions emanating from the committees have the same authority as full cabinet decisions, and since 1967, disputes within committees can be referred to the full Cabinet only with the approval of the committee chairman. When important issues are under discussion it is usual for the designated members to attend, though on other occasions senior ministers can and do replace themselves with their junior ministers.[4] Richard Crossman, subsequently a cabinet minister himself, took the view that the committees detracted from the power of the cabinet,[5] though the more general view is that they serve as a useful complement to cabinet, lightening its workload, clarifying issues for it, and allowing it to concentrate on the more central and general matters of government.[6]

The full cabinet usually meets each week, on Thursday morning, in the Cabinet Room at 10 Downing Street. In addition to the cabinet ministers, meetings are attended by the government chief whip: he is the minister responsible for ensuring the support of the parliamentary party in parliamentary votes and acts as a channel of communication between the cabinet and its parliamentary supporters. He advises on likely parliamentary reaction to proposed measures. The cabinet secretary, one of the two most

TABLE 8.1
The Cabinet, August 1983

Prime Minister, First Lord of the Treasury, and Minister for the Civil Service—the Rt. Hon. Margaret Thatcher, M.P.

Lord President of the Council and Leader of the House of Lords—The Rt. Hon. Viscount Whitelaw, C.H., M.C.

Lord Chancellor—The Rt. Hon. The Lord Hailsham of St. Marylebone, C.H.

Secretary of State for Foreign and Commonwealth Affairs—The Rt. Hon. Sir Geoffrey Howe, Q.C., M.P.

Secretary of State for the Home Department—The Rt. Hon. Leon Brittan, Q.C., M.P.

Chancellor of the Exchequer—The Rt. Hon. Nigel Lawson, M.P.

Secretary of State for Education and Science—The Rt. Hon. Sir Keith Joseph, Bt., M.P.

Secretary of State for Northern Ireland—The Rt. Hon. James Prior, M.P.

Secretary of State for Energy—The Rt. Hon. Peter Walker, M.B.E., M.P.

Secretary of State for Defense—The Rt. Hon. Michael Heseltine, M.P.

Secretary of State for Scotland—The Rt. Hon. George Younger, T.D., M.P.

Secretary of State for Wales—The Rt. Hon. Nicholas Edwards, M.P.

Secretary of State for the Environment—The Rt. Hon. Patrick Jenkin, M.P.

Lord Privy Seal and Leader of the House of Commons—The Rt. Hon. John Biffen, M.P.

Secretary of State for Social Services—The Rt. Hon. Norman Fowler, M.P.

Secretary of State for Employment—The Rt. Hon. Norman Tebbit, M.P.

Secretary of State for Trade and Industry—The Rt. Hon. Cecil Parkinson, M.P.

Chancellor of the Duchy of Lancaster—The Rt. Hon. The Lord Cockfield

Secretary of State for Transport—The Rt. Hon. Tom King, M.P.

Minister of Agriculture, Fisheries and Food—The Rt. Hon. Michael Jopling, M.P.

Chief Secretary to the Treasury—The Rt. Hon. Peter Rees, Q.C., M.P.

powerful civil servants in Britain, attends and sits on the prime minister's right. Meetings usually last for one to three hours, with additional meetings on Tuesdays and sometimes other days as necessary. Each meeting is chaired by the PM, who decides the agenda and sums up the discussions: votes are rarely taken, practice varying from PM to PM. Some PMs will sum up concisely the points made in a discussion and reach a consensus on the issue; others will sum up in a matter that favors one particular approach, be it a minority view or otherwise. The minutes of the meeting are drawn up by the cabinet secretariat, which also follows through on them to ensure their implementation. It is not unknown for cabinet minutes to record decisions that the PM felt should have been taken, even when they were not.

The relationship between the PM and the cabinet is a matter of some dispute. Formally, the PM is deemed to be *primus inter pares* (first among equals) in the cabinet. Some observers have argued that the premier is very much more than that.[7] The powers of appointment and dismissal, the ability to decide cabinet agenda and sum up discussion, control of the civil service, and the power of patronage—all combined with the position of party leader coalesce to create a politically dominant figure. The PM may take decisions unilaterally or in conjunction with a few senior colleagues. The cabinet may be asked to ratify such decisions or not even be told of them. At times of crisis, a small body of senior ministers under the PM may be formed to direct government action, as for instance at the time of the Suez crisis in 1956 or the Falklands crisis in 1982. The cabinet is not usually informed of the contents of the budget until shortly before its presentation to the House of Commons, and a number of members of Mrs. Thatcher's cabinet have been critical of the Prime Minister's careful avoidance of cabinet discussions of government economic policy. It has been argued by some that since 1945, Britain has begun to witness a form of prime ministerial government. Others have responded that the PM is constrained by the need to maintain cabinet support, by limited time and resources (there is no formal prime minister's department), and by the broad spectrum of government responsibilities.[8] The main task of a PM, according to some analyses, is as much one of coordination as it is of dictating matters to the cabinet.[9]

In policy-making, the main influence of the PM is probably realized through the selection of ministers. As Maurice Kogan has observed, the authority to appoint, transfer, or dismiss enables the PM to allocate values and thus change or confirm an individual minister's policies.[10] In cabinet meetings, policy decisions may result from a prearranged strategy of the premier and a few senior colleagues. Certainly, the discussions themselves are often not the product of rational deliberation, members weighing the advantages and disadvantages of the range of options possible. Rather, ministers will frequently pursue or not pursue a particular line on the grounds of personal friendship, departmental defense, personal or political animosity, or lack of interest because it is someone else's subject.[11] Decisions may also be affected by the absence of some ministers.

The cabinet is the central forum for the resolution of disputes between departments, particularly in the allocation of public expenditure. Ministers will usually defend their particular department, often supported on a reciprocal basis by ministers representing other spending departments. Much will depend on the personalities involved, not least that of the PM. Some PMs will tend to involve themselves in a wide range of items being brought forward by ministers, while others will content themselves with concentrating on central issues of the economy and foreign affairs, leaving other departmental ministers to get on with their jobs unhindered. The process by which a cabinet determines policy will thus vary from PM to PM and, depending on changing political circumstance, may vary during the tenure of office of one PM. The cabinet remains the forum for the resolution of most major issues of public policy, but a number of those issues may effectively be resolved elsewhere, either in cabinet committee or by a meeting of senior ministers. Less central issues will usually not reach the cabinet at all.

No formal powers are vested in the cabinet: it exists and operates by convention. The most important convention, one that in part governs its behavior as well as its relationship to Parliament, is that of collective responsibility. The convention developed during the eighteenth and nineteenth century and prescribes that members of the cabinet accept responsibility collectively for decisions made by it. Ministers may argue in cabinet but once a decision has been made they are required to support that decision publicly. Any minister failing to support a cabinet decision in public once it had been announced would be expected to resign: failure to do so would result in the PM's requesting that minister's resignation.

The convention is deemed also to dictate the necessity for secrecy to attach to cabinet discussions. The authority of the cabinet and of particular ministers could be undermined if cabinet disputes were made public. Ministers publicly defending decisions with which they are known to have disagreed in cabinet would weaken the cabinet in trying to ensure implementation of those decisions. A minister's authority and influence could be undermined if it was known that he was implementing a policy against which he had fought in cabinet. Nonetheless, recent years have witnessed a weakening of this aspect of the convention, with ministers engaging in semipublic and, for all intents and purposes, public leaks and disagreements, with some ex-ministers recording cabinet discussions in their memoirs.[12] On two occasions in the Labour government of 1974–1979, the convention was actually suspended in order to allow ministers to vote against government policy in the House of Commons. Although the convention remains extant, it is becoming a difficult one for PMs to enforce. Both occasions concerned the issue of British membership in the European Communities, on which cabinet members were bitterly divided. To avoid the possibility of resignations or the cabinet falling apart, the PM (Harold Wilson in 1975, James Callaghan in 1977) decided to suspend the convention.

One other condition dictated by the convention of collective responsibility continues to be followed. A government defeat in the House of Commons on the motion "that this House has no confidence in Her Majesty's Government" necessitates the government's resigning or requesting a dissolution. On March 28, 1979, when the minority Labour government was defeated on a vote of confidence, the PM immediately went to Buckingham Palace to request a dissolution. This requirement stipulated by the convention is one of the few about which it remains possible to generalize with any degree of confidence.

The cabinet remains at the heart of British government, but its behavior and decision-making are forcing many old assumptions to be revised. Increasing demands made of government make it difficult for cabinet to contain an exclusive decision-making capacity, having to call in aid the use of committees, and disagreements generated by its inability to raise resources necessary to maintain policy commitments are of such a nature as to have started spilling over into the arena of public debate.

Ministers

When a PM forms an administration, he or she is called on to select not only the senior ministers to head the various departments of state, as well as senior ministers without portfolio, but also a host of junior ministers. In addition to a ministerial head, usually of secretary of state rank, each department will have normally one and sometimes more ministers of state and one or more undersecretaries of state. The PM also appoints a chief whip and 12 or 13 other whips in the Commons as well as a chief whip and 6 other whips in the House of Lords. In total, a little over 100 ministerial appointments are now made (see Table 8.2). Despite the demands made of government, the increase in the number of ministers during the course of the century has been a modest one.[13]

Of the ministers appointed, the most important are, as one would expect, those appointed to head the various departments (see Table 8.1). The significance of junior ministers tends to vary. In past decades, many parliamentary undersecretaries had little to do and often were regarded as constituting something of an insignificant life form within the departments. To some extent, that remains the case today for a number of undersecretaries, known in Whitehall circles under the acronym PUSS (parliamentary undersecretaries of state). The influence of junior ministers within Departments will tend to depend on the ministerial head. There is a growing tendency for ministers to assign greater responsibility for certain functions to their ministers of state and undersecretaries; sending junior ministers to attend cabinet committees allows the junior ministers to gain some knowledge of the workings of the higher echelons of government. Nonetheless, disputes between junior ministers and the chief civil servant, the permanent secretary, in a

TABLE 8.2
Number of Government Ministers, July 1982

Rank	House of Commons	House of Lords	Total
Cabinet ministers (excluding PM)	18	3	21
Ministers of state*	23	5	28
Law officers†	3	1	4
Undersecretaries of state	29	3	32
Whips (including chief whips)	14	7	21
Total	87	19	106

*Includes Financial Secretary to the Treasury.
†Attorney-General, Solicitor General, Lord Advocate, and Solicitor-General for Scotland.
N.B.: Three nonpolitical Household appointments (officers of the Royal Household, traditionally listed as part of the government) excluded.

department can be resolved only by the ministerial head, and there remains a tendency for interested bodies to try to influence the senior minister even on matters delegated to junior ministers.

The heads of departments have tended to become even more important decision-makers than they were hitherto. Indeed, there is a case for arguing that, far from having prime ministerial or cabinet government in Britain, one has a form of ministerial government. As demands on government have increased, only the most important matters have percolated up to the cabinet for resolution. Most important decisions affecting a department will be taken by the minister. The relationship between a minister and the House of Commons and between the minister and his or her department is governed by the convention of individual ministerial responsibility. The convention is important not only for determining who is responsible to whom (civil servants to minister, minister to Parliament), but also for determining who is responsible for what. The cabinet as a body has no legal powers. Powers are vested in ministers. When government takes on new responsibilities by statute, powers to fulfill those responsibilities are granted to a minister. "The Secretary of State shall have power to . . ." will appear in the statute, not "The Cabinet shall have power to . . . ." According to Nevil Johnson, "the enduring effect of the doctrine of ministerial responsibility has been over the past century or so that powers have been vested in ministers and on a relentlessly increasing scale."[14]

Ministers, then, are very much at the heart of the governmental process. Major issues will be resolved in cabinet as will the battle for departmental budgets. Other issues will usually but not always be resolved at departmental level. Two former education ministers, Edward Boyle and

Anthony Crosland, both asserted that "the individual Minister of Education rather than the Cabinet is the focal point of political initiatives and decisions in Education."[15] Crosland himself took only two matters concerning education policy to the cabinet. Nonetheless, ministers operate within the context of a number of significant constraints. Because of parliamentary, constituency, and various public duties, the time they have to devote to the job is limited. They are largely dependent on their departments for advice. They have few independent channels for obtaining advice and information: a number of ministers in recent years, especially Labour ministers, have appointed political advisers, but the practice has become neither widespread nor very effective. Ministers have little time to get to know the department before moving on to another post. Few ministers serve in the same post for the lifetime of a Parliament. Since 1944, the average tenure of office of each minister of education has been a little under two years. Turnover in junior ministers is sometimes even more rapid. Furthermore, and perhaps most importantly, the number of decisions that a minister is now called on to make is such that many have to be delegated to officials to make in the minister's name. Even matters that do come before a minister for a personal decision may be heavily weighted by the advice of officials and by the manner in which the issue is brought to the minister's attention. Such decisions have also to be taken within the context of increasingly limited resources. The minister has to battle with treasury ministers to try to get what share of the government cake he can. Given economic cutbacks, it is rarely likely to be enough to meet a department's self-perceived needs.

Departments

Ministers are appointed to head departments. The way those departments are structured and the responsibilities vested in them can affect the nature of policy-making. If departments are small and are allocated responsibility for very specific subjects, particularly those subjects that have been the responsibility of government for many decades, there is a problem of achieving coordination on matters that touch on the responsibilities of different departments and that may recently have come onto the political agenda. Interdepartmental coordination has tended to be dominated by officials rather than ministers and hence it has been viewed as reinforcing the influence of the civil service. Attempts to solve the problem of divided responsibilities by creating large departments may help improve the quality of decision-making, the issue being dealt with more efficiently within one department, but may also generate difficulties in trying to keep the departments under ministerial control. In Britain, these difficulties have been realized as a result of various restructurings of the different departments.

The number of major departments has fluctuated during the course of the twentieth century. Sir Richard Clarke listed 18 as being in existence in 1914, 23 in 1935, 30 in 1951, 27 in 1964, 18 in 1973, and 21 in 1974.[16] There are currently 19 main functional departments, plus 2 with no major functions (Table 8.3). Following his return to office as prime minister in 1951, Winston Churchill attempted to achieve some greater degree of coordination through the appointment of a number of departmental "overlords," ministers with responsibility for a broad range of departments. The experiment was not successful, in part because a number of the overlords were, indeed, Lords and hence were sitting in the Upper House away from the scrutiny of MPs. Since then, there has been a tendency instead to amalgamate departments. In 1964, the Defense Department was expanded to encompass the three service departments, and in 1968, the Foreign Office and the Commonwealth Office were merged to form the Foreign and Commonwealth Office. Following the return of a Conservative government under Mr. Heath in 1970, two so-called "super departments" were created. The Department of Trade and Industry (DTI) encompassed the former Board of Trade and the Ministries of Technology and Power. The Department of the Environment incorporated the former Ministries of Housing and Local Government, Transport, and Public Buildings and Works. The government made a conscious effort to improve the machinery of government. The amalgamations were designed to reduce the need for interdepartmental compromise, to enable a single strategy to be pursued within one department, to create the capacity to manage larger resource-consuming programs, and to allow more direct indentification to the public of ministers responsible for defined functions.[17] These intentions were not to be wholly fulfilled. Because of the oil crisis of 1973–1974, Mr. Heath sliced off part of the DTI to form the Department of Energy. In any event, there had been problems in maintaining ministerial control of the DTI. Under the subsequent Labour government, the concept of "super ministries" did not find such strong support. Transport was reinstated as a separate department and the DTI was broken up into the Departments of Trade, Industry, and Prices and Consumers Affairs. When Mrs. Thatcher came into office in 1979, Prices and Consumer Affairs was put back under the Department of Trade and the Departments of Trade and Industry subsequently merged again.

Of remaining departments, a number have remained largely unchanged in terms of title and responsibilities throughout the century. Others have lost some of their functions to other or newly created departments. The Welsh Office, created in 1964, and the Northern Ireland Office, created in 1972, took over responsibilities previously vested in the Home Office, for example. Such changes may serve certain purposes, such as improved coordination or more clearly defined responsibility for a particular subject, but may also be costly in resources and manpower, especially where there is a frequent change in a ministry's status and responsibilities. They also can lead to confusion as well as competition, certain groups demanding the recogni-

TABLE 8.3
Government Departments
The Principal Government Departments Headed by Ministers in 1983*

Department	Responsibilities
Agriculture, Fisheries and Food	Agriculture, horticulture, fishing, food
Defense	Defense policy, control and administration of armed services
Education and Science	Education, fostering development of civil science
Employment	Manpower policy, unemployment benefits
Energy	Energy, government relations with nationalized industries, Atomic Energy Authority
Environment	Wide range of responsibilities covering the physical environment, including housing, construction, land use, regional planning, new towns, countryside, and local government structure and finance
Foreign and Commonwealth Office	International relations; protecting British interests overseas; certain administrative responsibilities in dependent territories
Health and Social Security	Administration of National Health Service (in England); social services; certain aspects of public health
Home Office	Covers domestic functions not assigned to other departments; includes administration of justice, police, immigration, public morals and safety, broadcasting policy, and prisons
Law Officers' Department	Law officers are chief legal advisers to the government; appear on behalf of the Crown in major court cases; Attorney-General has ultimate responsibility for enforcement of criminal law
Lord Advocate's Department	Equivalent in Scotland to the Law Officers' Department in England
Lord Chancellor's Department	Assists Lord Chancellor in the administration of the courts and the law
Management and Personnel Office	Responsible for civil service management (minister in charge is the prime minister)
Northern Ireland Office	Exercises executive powers in Northern Ireland on behalf of United Kingdom government: encompasses agriculture, commerce, education, community

TABLE 8.3 (*continued*)

Department	Responsibilities
	relations, finance, environment, health and social services, housing, and manpower
Privy Council Office	Minor functions (e.g., for arranging making of Royal Proclamations); primarily office occupied by minister with responsibility for government's legislative program in House of Commons
Scottish Office	Governmental functions in Scotland, including agriculture, education, economic planning, Home and Health, and development
Trade and Industry	National and regional industrial policy, aerospace policy, overseas trade policy, information technology
Transport	General transport policy, railways, ports, freight movements, road safety, inland waterways
Treasury	Economic strategy, public expenditure, fiscal policy, foreign currency reserves, international monetary policy
Welch Office	Within Wales, agriculture (jointly with Ministry of Agriculture), primary and secondary education, town and country planning, water, roads, tourism, new towns, forestry, urban grants
Chancellor of Duchy of Lancaster	Administration of royal estate of Duchy of Lancaster; primarily occupied by minister with no specific portfolio

*There are a number of other bodies classed officially as departments but not headed directly by a minister. These include the Cabinet Office (under the Cabinet Secretary), responsible to the cabinet as a whole; the Board of Customs and Excise (parliamentary responsibility for which is exercised by Treasury ministers); and the Board of Inland Revenue.

tion of having their area of interest being made the responsibility of a separate department, headed preferably by a minister of cabinet rank. Given the differences in the size and responsibilities of departments, only broad generalizations can be made about their internal structures. Each department, as mentioned in Chapter 7, is normally divided up into functional units. The hierarchical structure in each department is basically as shown in Figure 8.2. Each functional unit, the division, is headed by a civil servant of assistant undersecretary of state rank. Above the units are deputy undersecretaries,

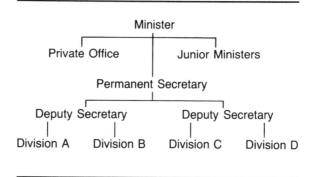

FIGURE 8.2   Department Structure.

and above them, the civil servant responsible for the running of the department, the permanent undersecretary of state (known as the permanent secretary). He (rarely she) is in effect the chief executive officer of the department and answers directly to the minister.

Figure 8.3 shows the organization within a relatively small department, the Department of Employment, chosen in order to provide a manageable and not too complex diagram. For the larger departments, the figure would have to be expanded a great many times to encompass all the functional units. In the Department of Health and Social Security, for example, there are at least 37 functional units, and in the Foreign Office there are more than 50. The Scottish Office, with responsibility for matters covered in England by separate departments, actually has bodies titled Department of Agriculture, Home and Health Department, and Education Department. Little point would be served in reproducing organizational charts for each government department. The foregoing is sufficient to indicate the basic structure of each department and, of equal importance, the diversity and extent of that structure. In terms of public policy-making, it may not just be the personnel of departments that is important, but also the structures and responsibilities of the departments themselves.

Civil Service

Ministers stand at the political apex of government. They head departments that are staffed by a body of permanent public employees, known collectively as the civil service. Currently, the number of civil servants is a little under 700,000. (The figure does not include employees of nationalized industries or local government, or members of the judiciary or the armed forces.) They serve to provide ministers with advice and information, to execute their decisions, and to administer the business of government. The

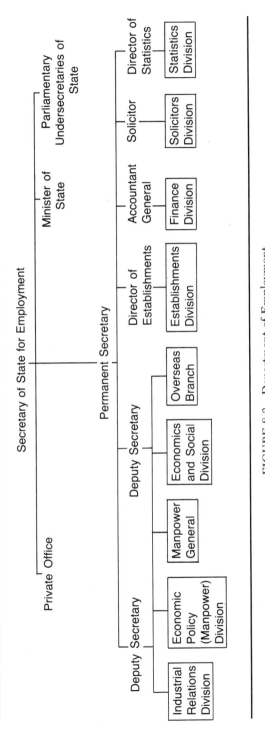

FIGURE 8.3 Department of Employment.

relationship between them and ministers is governed by the convention of individual ministerial responsibility. The minister is answerable to Parliament for his or her department and alone is formally responsible for that department and its activities. The civil service head of each department is, as just mentioned, the permanent secretary. He is answerable to the minister for the administration of officials within the department and serves usually as the minister's principal adviser. The convention of ministerial responsibility provides a cloak of anonymity to departmental activities. The advice a minister receives from officials and the manner of its formulation and presentation is kept from public gaze. Knowledge of what goes on in a department, certainly at the higher levels, may be made available only by the minister or by officials acting on his or her behalf.

Most civil servants carry out the routine tasks of government, administering various government programs and everyday matters for which government has responsibility. The largest departments are those of Defense and of Health and Social Security. The civil servants involved in advising ministers are comparatively few, comprising essentially the 3,000 or so of permanent secretary, deputy secretary, assistant secretary, senior principal, and principal rank (i.e., the most senior ranks within the service). They advise ministers, prepare briefs for them and ensure that their decisions are carried out. Officials take great care to study parties' election manifestos, and an incoming government will find the civil service ready with advice on how to implement its program. According to Bruce Headey, civil servants prefer ministers who are capable of taking decisions, of winning cabinet battles, and of defending their departments from parliamentary criticism.[18] Ministers, for their part, look for officials who will provide them with a range of options from which to choose, expert advice, and the loyal implementation of ministerial objectives and policies.

As a rule, civil servants behave as their political masters expect them to behave. A number of former prime ministers and ministers have praised officials for their loyalty and their ability. Nonetheless, various criticisms of the civil service have been heard. One concerns the recruitment and training of civil servants. Although selected by open, competitive examination, those recruited to the senior ranks of the service have been and are predominantly public-school- and Oxford-educated applicants, despite attempts to widen the intake.[19] Recruitment also tends to favor generalists over specialists; that is, there has been a tendency to select graduates in the arts and humanities rather than those in the pure or applied sciences. The presence of generalists has been a point of some contention, some observers considering it to be responsible in large measure for poor advice to ministers and poor appreciation of new developments in science and technology. Once an applicant is in the service, most training is on-the-job training. Senior civil servants are geared to assisting ministers in the formulation and implementation of policy; they have little training as managers, even though they have extensive responsibilities for personnel and finance.[20] Other criticisms are directed at the relationship between ministers and civil servants. There is a school of thought tending toward the view that Britain has, if anything, not a cabinet or ministerial form of government, but rather a form of rule by civil servants.[21]

The argument advanced by this school of thought is that civil servants are able to exert undue influence over decisions nominally taken by ministers. The body of civil servants is able to exert such influence because of its permanence, size, expertise, coordination, anonymity, and control of information as well as, to a large extent, the ministers' timetables. Furthermore, so it is argued, this influence has grown in recent years, not only because of the increase in the number of decisions needing to be made by ministers (the greater the number, the less time a minister has to devote to each one), but also because of Britain's membership in the European Communities and the uneven implementation of the Report of the Fulton Committee (of which more below). Civil servants' influence in the 1970s was also enhanced, according to Tony Benn, by their access to the Central Policy Review Staff, which existed until 1983, officials using it as a vehicle for getting their views injected into cabinet committees.

Civil servants effectively enjoy tenure in their appointments and once recruited to the service, tend to make a career of it. More than 80% of permanent secretaries have spent more than 25 years in the service.[22] While ministers will come and go, their senior officials remain in place. Ministers will look to their permanent secretaries for knowledge of how their departments work. They will look to their officials for briefing documents and advice on the merits and demerits of available options. They will look to their private offices to control the flow of paperwork that reaches their desks. Officials, if so inclined, may seek to influence a minister's decision by the content of the papers they submit to him or her, or by the manner of presentation of such papers. By submitting papers at the last minute and forcing a speedy decision, or by inserting the relevant documents in a mass of paperwork in the minister's file in order that their significance may not be obvious, officials may get the response they favor. Similarly, ministers may have little time to give to important decisions because of the schedule prepared for them by their private offices.

If decisions that are reached run counter to those preferred by the senior civil servants within a department, various techniques are still available to them to try to delay or negate those decisions. They may reach their counterparts in other ministries to persuade them to brief the other ministers against their own minister's decision, they may try internal delaying tactics (including nonimplementation, in the hope that the minister will neither notice nor raise the matter again), they may try to inject their views into cabinet discussion, or they may try to stall until a new minister takes over. "Oh, in another year or so he won't be minister here anyway" is a phrase that has been heard from the lips of some civil servants in unguarded moments, including in the hearing of this writer. A new administration provides even greater scope for officials to refight old battles. By tradition, incoming ministers do not see the papers of their predecessors. This provides senior civil servants with almost a clean ministerial canvass on which to try their persuasive brushwork.

Many of these techniques will be familiar to anyone with experience of bureaucratic machinery. In recent years, civil-service influence has been enhanced by other developments. Membership in the European Communities (EC) has been identified as being one of the most important. Not only has it entailed greater demands on ministerial time in attending meetings of the Council of Ministers, but most of the matters discussed are based on extensive preliminary work done at official level both within the EC itself and between EC officials and civil servants in the member states. Officials, it has been argued, have benefited also from the implementation of the Report of the Fulton Committee, published in 1968. The report argued for a more specialized, more open, and better-trained civil service and made various recommendations to achieve that. It recommended also the provision of independent policy advice to ministers through the appointment of political advisers and the creation of policy units within each department. In effect, the civil service achieved the implementation of those elements of the report that strengthened their position. For example, a recommendation that civil servants should constitute a majority on service selection boards was readily accepted, as was a proposal for the committee that advises the prime minister on senior appointments within the civil service to include a number of senior officials (the committee now includes no one else). In contrast, policy units never saw the light of day, and civil servants effectively worked around rather than with those political advisers who were appointed.[23]

A combination of these factors has helped to produce an influential breed of senior civil servants, sharing a common background and experience and meeting together regularly for lunch and other social occasions. Insofar as they consciously exert influence over ministerial decisions, they do so not in pursuit of a particular party bias but rather in furtherance of what they perceive to be some "national interest," seeking to steer ministers toward what one permanent secretary referred to as "the common ground."[24] That common ground is geared to a longer-term perspective than the more short-term perspective usually taken by ministers. It is a somewhat amorphous concept but one that tends to favor incremental change carried out within the context of departmental norms and that appears to militate against proposals that might limit civil service influence or undermine the status of individual departments. The dividing line between the perceived national interest and departmental interest is not always a clearly perceptible one.

Against the arguments adduced in support of the contention that civil servants exert undue influence in policy-making must be set some countervailing points. Officials are guided by ethics that lead them to carry out a minister's wishes and, as we have mentioned, they prefer a minister who is capable of taking decisions to one who is not. Nor do they constitute a monolithic entity. Civil servants differ in their approaches, both in style and in substance. The ethos of a particular department may differ from that of another (the Environment Department has a reputation for being a fairly open one, for example, and the Home Office one of excessive secrecy), and the perception of the national interest may differ from one department to another.

In the relationship between ministers and civil servants, a determined minister capable of winning cabinet battles and defending his or her department in the House of Commons will normally enjoy mastery of that department. Even so, that mastery will extend primarily to the important issues drawn to the minister's attention or to the specific policy goals which he or she has set. Other matters, of necessity, will be dealt with at lower levels. On occasion, a forceful minister may run into conflict with his or her officials (Barbara Castle at the Ministry of Transport, for example, and Tony Benn at the Department of Energy), in which case prime ministerial support may be necessary for a minister to prevail (and such support is not always forthcoming). Less forceful, less energetic, or less intelligent ministers may be content to be guided by the papers and recommendations put before them by their officials. Joel Barnett records one occasion when a senior cabinet minister attended a cabinet committee and "studiously read out one line from his brief: 'I agree with the Chief Secretary.'"[25] (Unfortunately for the minister's officials, the Chief Secretary to the Treasury had taken the line opposite to what they had expected.) In the days before he became a minister, Ian Gilmour estimated that "only about one Minister in three runs his Department."[26] When queried about this estimate after he had served as a cabinet minister, he replied that "on reflection, I think it was probably an overestimate."[27]

Quangos

The term *quango* is used to denote what in American terminology would be referred to as an off-line governmental agency (for example, the Environmental Protection Agency). It is supposed to be the acronym for quasi-autonomous non-governmental organizations, though it has confusingly been assumed to denote quasi-autonomous national government organizations. An official enquiry into quangos concluded that the term was inappropriate, preferring instead to refer to nondepartmental public bodies.[28] The latter is a more accurate description of the bodies concerned. They comprise various public bodies set up either by administrative act or specifically by statute in order to carry out various executive actions or to operate in an advisory capacity on a particular subject. Although they may be associated with a particular department (for example, the University Grants Committee with the Department of Education), they do not form an official part of that department and are not under the day-to-day control of a minister or permanent secretary.

Advisory bodies are usually formed to provide government with advice that it cannot obtain from within its own ranks. Such bodies will normally comprise representatives or appointees of interested groups (see Chapter 7). Bodies with executive powers are often formed in order to facilitate an arm's-length relationship between government and a particular concern. For example, the government provides the main source of finance to universities in the United Kingdom. In order to obtain advice on the distribution of its annual grant, the University Grants Committee (UGC) was set up in 1919. Although the government determines the total amount of the grant, one report states, "as a matter of policy it always accepts the U.G.C.'s recommendations on its distribution, so that in practice it is the U.G.C. who are the arbiters in this respect, and the arrangements achieve the effect if not the form of an arm's length relationship."[29] Such an arrangement allows government to avoid the appearance of interfering with the academic freedom of universities. In 1981–1982, when the government took a more direct role in indicating general priorities to the UGC in the allocation of a reduced grant, it encountered much criticism from the academic community.

A number of nondepartmental public bodies are long-standing and are not confined to the twentieth century.[30] The number has shown a considerable increase in this century, especially after the Second World War and again after 1968. The Report of the Fulton Committee on the Civil Service (1968) recommended the creation of accountable units of management within departments and raised the possibility of separating, or "hiving off," autonomous units from departments. Although admitting that such hiving off would raise parliamentary and constitutional issues, it commented, "We see no reason to believe that the dividing line between activities for which Ministers are directly responsible, and those for which they are not, is necessarily drawn in the right place today." Among those activities that they thought could be hived off were the work of the Royal Mint, air traffic control, and parts of the social services. The concept of hiving off found favor with the Labour government and fitted in well with the managerial revolution that the incoming Conservative government of Mr. Heath sought to achieve. Mr. Heath formed a team of businessmen and financiers to identify those units of management that could be separated from ministerial line control. The justification for this was provided by Mr. Heath: "what we said," he recalled, "was that quite large areas of government really appear to be things which could be run in a businesslike way and they're not so politically delicate that the Secretary of State or a Minister has got to be worrying about them all the time."[31] The emphasis was to be on managerial efficiency rather than political accountability. Mr. Heath's business team proposed various elements of government departments to be hived off. Said Mr. Heath, "This we did in a number of different ways and I think it has been very successful."[32]

The hiving-off process was continued under the Labour government of 1974–1979. Among the more important creations were those of the Manpower Services Commission, the Health and Safety Commission, and the Advisory, Conciliation, and Arbitration Service (see Chapter 7). In 1980, the report on nondepartmental public bodies, conducted by Sir Leo Pliatzky, identified the existence of over 2,000 such bodies. It identified 489 executive bodies ("between them these carry out a wide range of operational or regulatory functions, various scientific and cultural activities, and some commercial or semi-commercial activities") and 1,561 advisory bodies. The report recorded that the executive bodies in 1978 were the channel for expenditure on capital and current account of nearly £5,800 million (about $8,700 million) and had staff of around 217,000. In addition, departments spent about £24 million ($36 million) in their sponsoring capacity for those bodies.[33] Of the expenditure by the executive bodies, 87% of the total was spent by 20 bodies. Top of the league were the Regional Water Authorities, the Manpower Services Commission, the New Town Development Corporations, and the Housing Corporation. Other large spenders, each with an expenditure of over £200 million ($300 million) were the Research Councils, the Atomic Energy Authority, the National Enterprise Board, and the 24 Industrial Training Boards.[34] The University Grants Committee, formally an advisory rather than an executive body, had responsibility for allocating a grant of £775 million (about $1160 million).

Support for quangos and the policy of "hiving off" came to an end with the return of a Conservative government under Mrs. Thatcher in 1979. Such bodies were viewed as contributing to the development of a corporate state. One Conservative MP even saw them as contributing to the development of a British Soviet society: "The *apparatchiks* of that Soviet society would be the new generation of warlords—the quangurus—controlling not only the commanding heights of the economy, but the way of life of the people, and the complex structure of a directed educational system and state propoganda machine."[35] The government took the view that there were too many quangos, that they constituted too heavy a drain on the public purse, that they were not sufficiently accountable to Parliament, and that in the case of some with quasi-judicial functions, they were a threat to the rule of law. As a government committed to a free-market economy, it was keen to reduce the number of interventionist and unaccountable quangos, especially those with significant expenditure powers.

The government initiated a process of abolishing quangos wherever possible. In January 1982, the Prime Minister listed a total of 441 nondepartmental public bodies that had been abolished since 1979 and 109 more scheduled for abolition or reduction before April 1984.[36] She also reported that certain nationalized industries' boards were affected by the selling off to the private sector of certain nationalized bodies. (Nationalized industries were not included in the Pliatzky study.) It was estimated that what Mr. Holland referred to as "the Quango cull" would result in the saving of £57.5 million (about $86 million) in a full year, and about £600 million ($900 million) annually if the effects of denationalization of various industries were taken into account.[37] As for quangos that were not abolished, it was decided that ministers would be responsible for those coming under their department's sponsorship and that they would have the duty to ensure that the quangos were run effectively and efficiently. In this way, quangos would come within the scope of parliamentary scrutiny, including that of the new select committees.

Although nondepartmental public bodies remain a significant feature of government—Mrs. Thatcher has made clear in the House of Commons that those doing valuable and necessary work will be retained and that others would be created if it could be shown that a nondepartmental body was necessary to perform a particular function—the attitude of government to the hiving off of manageable units of departments has changed significantly. It is no longer seen as a desirable feature of a managerial revolution in government, but rather as a development to be kept under strict scrutiny. Nonetheless, the operation and expenditure of such bodies, such as the Manpower Services Commission, continue to have a significant impact on government and public policy.

Central Policy Review Staff

Finally, for the record, it is important to record the activities and influence of the Central Policy Review Staff (CPRS), formed by Edward Heath shortly after taking office in 1970. Conscious of the difficulties facing government in seeking to take a broad look at existing policies and to generate policy initiatives covering several departments, Mr. Heath formed the CPRS in order to provide such a reflective facility.

Known popularly as the "Think Tank," the CPRS had a membership usually of between 15 and 20, half of the members being civil servants drawn from the main departments and the rest being drawn from the universities, industry, and international organizations. It had two primary functions.[38] One was to review government overall strategy in applying its program. Every six months the cabinet spent a day discussing a strategy paper produced by the CPRS. Meetings with junior ministers were also organized. The second function was to undertake research into particular projects, to consider the options available, and to evaluate government policy. In the first seven or eight years of its existence the CPRS undertook about 40 such studies. About half of its time was taken up with these studies and most of the rest with collective briefings for ministers. Members of the CPRS met weekly on Mondays, though each of the various studies was usually undertaken by a small group of two or three members.

Initially, the body was regarded with suspicion by the departments, by the Treasury, and by the cabinet office.[39] Nonetheless, it appeared to have some influence during the period of the Heath administration. Its chairman, Lord Rothschild, was a highly capable and independent figure with direct access to the prime minister, and he managed to bring together a group of very capable individuals.[40] The group probably influenced government policy on a number of issues, notably energy and methods of combating inflation.[41] After that, its impact within the government machine waned. Lord Rothschild was succeeded by someone drawn from within the civil service (Sir Kenneth Berrill), and the CPRS reputedly came more under the influence of officials. The Labour government returned in 1974 appeared less keen on the idea than Mr. Heath had been, and a separate political policy unit, manned by political appointees, was created in 10 Downing Street to provide the prime minister with more party-oriented advice on short-term policy. Neither Mr. Wilson nor Mr. Callaghan were as keen as Mr. Heath had been on strategy reviews, and the status of the CPRS declined further under Mrs. Thatcher's premiership. By 1983, its main functions were those of monitoring cabinet papers and putting in briefing papers for cabinet and cabinet committees. Mrs. Thatcher herself appeared to make little use of it, turning instead to her own policy advisers within Downing Street. Shortly after the 1983 general election, she announced that it was to be wound up.

CURRENT DEBATE

For anyone seeking to identify the genesis of a policy that emerges from the executive, the task is a formidable one. Once in office, a government has a program that it proposes to implement. The extent to which the various proposals contained in that program are actually carried out in legislative or other form will be influenced strongly by civil-service advice, by the reaction of affected groups, and by extraneous events, such as the discovery of North Sea oil, a Middle East crisis, or a downturn in world economic conditions. The form that a proposal takes will be affected by the process by which it is considered and applied. How officials interpret and apply a policy may not coincide precisely with the intentions of those responsible for its initiation. How a nondepartmental public body responds to a government policy may not be in line with government expectations. The response of groups and individuals affected by a policy may be vastly different from that which the government expected. Such reactions may in turn influence and modify government policy. Over and above its original program, government will be faced with numerous demands and the task of continuing the day-to-day business of governing, of administering inherited programs and commitments, of maintaining essential services, and of engaging in diplomatic relations with other governments. The level at which and manner in which such matters are dealt with in government will vary from issue to issue and from government to government, as well as over time. As society has become more specialized, as government has accepted greater responsibility for the control and allocation of a large part of the national wealth, and as more and more demands have been made of it, government has developed a complex infrastructure. The elements of that have been identified above and in the identification process, the complexities of government emerged. Government does not operate in a vacuum. It has had to exist within and respond to an increasingly confused environment. And the government that responds to that environment is itself a complex web of bodies, powers, and relationships. For the political scientist seeking to explain governmental policy-making, a case-study approach may prove the most useful.

The complexity of government has proved part of the problem for those who have sought to identify government itself as being chiefly or partially responsible for Britain's poor economic performance in recent years. There is a perception that government policy and the manner in which and body by whom it is formulated have not served the nation as well as they might: hence a need for reform. But which element of government should be changed? And how? Does the problem lie with the civil service? With the cabinet? Or with the whole structure and mass of relationships that go to form the British government?

Since 1960, various attempts have been made by government to improve decision-making in a way that would enable it more efficiently and effectively to raise and allocate resources and, in some instances, to maintain or increase consent for its activities. In the 1960s, government went in for a form of economic planning and introduced the Public Expenditure Survey exercise. Previously, each item involving public expenditure had been judged on its merits and not considered in terms of the government's overall priorities or of the long-term consequences. The "forward look" form of quinquennial planning introduced by Selwyn Lloyd as chancellor of the exchequer was designed to rectify this state of affairs. Under the new exercise, each department costed the items on which government money was spent, doing so at current prices, and then entered into negotiation with the Treasury at official—i.e., civil-service—level in order to agree on the figures and the effect of existing policy commitments over the coming years. The figures so agreed on were then assembled and submitted to the Public Expenditure Survey Committee (PESC), a high-level committee of civil servants under Treasury chairmanship. The committee next presented a report to ministers showing where existing policies would lead in terms of public expenditure at constant prices over a period of five years. The report was then considered by ministers and decisions were taken on issues affecting the amounts to be spent by each department, on each public expenditure program, and on the total figure. The final figures required cabinet approval, and the cabinet was the forum for resolving disputes between ministers.

The PESC system had the attraction of helping establish relative priorities and of helping ministers to see where present policies would lead. Ministers could weigh the demands of the policies against the resources needed to fulfill them. However, the system did not prove to be the panacea that had been hoped for. It tended to favor incremental change (because priorities and commitments were established on a rolling five-year basis, immediate changes could be wrought only at the margin), and cabinet battles tended to result in conceding more to departments than had been recommended. It was also only as good as the projected figures on which it was based.[42] In the Labour government returned in 1964, the exercise was undermined by exaggerated growth rates postulated by the new (and short-lived) Department of Economic Affairs,[43] and in the 1970s, it was largely vitiated by the effects of high inflation rates. By 1974–1975, actual expenditure exceeded planned expenditure by £5,000 million ($7,500 million). To try to deal with this problem, the Government introduced cash limits in 1976. Today, the government makes an estimate of the likely rate of inflation and then translates spending plans into "cash" terms, each department being allocated the amount of money it can actually spend. Although not fulfilling initial expectations, the PESC exercise remains useful for providing a framework in which priorities may be established.

Other attempts since 1960 to reform government have included, as we have seen, the hiving off from departments of manageable units of account and a limited attempt to create a more open and specialized civil service. From a somewhat different perspective, the period also witnessed attempts, eventually successful, to join the European Communities (see Chapter 10). Mr. Heath's government, apart from trying initially to improve industrial efficiency by limiting government intervention in the economy, undertook various reforms of the governmental machine. Apart from the policy of hiving off elements of departments that could be separated from ministerial line control, there was the creation of the "super departments" and also of the Central Policy Review Staff. In addition, a system of Program Analysis and Review (PAR) was instituted. This was designed to provide for an independent body of analysts to review particular programs within a department and to ensure that the best means were being employed to achieve the desired end. In practice, the PAR exercise comprised officials as well as outsiders and soon came under Treasury control. Because of the demands it made on limited resources, it could be employed only very selectively. Departments tried to use such surveys to lay claim to extra resources, in effect negating the purpose of the exercise. In November 1979, PAR was phased out.[44]

By the end of the 1970s, it was apparent that many of the reforms of government of the past decade or so had either failed or, at best, had only modest success relative to what was expected of them. Britain's economic condition remained a parlous one and there was apparent growing dissatisfaction with government. Part of the debate as to what should be done continued to revolve around the structure and operation of government (as opposed to the particular policies pursued by individual governments), and various proposals for further change were advanced. However, the problem remained that there was no agreement as to the causes of apparent malfunctioning on the part of government. Hence, there was and is no agreement as to what should be done.

Of the criticisms leveled at the structure and operation of government, a number have been of government as a whole, while others have been directed at specific elements of government. At the level of government qua government, one criticism has been that the political culture has encouraged a government characterized by political inertia, geared toward problem avoidance rather than problem-solving.[45] Policy-making has tended to be a process of minimizing conflict between competing groups (see Chapter 7): hence the failure of the Heath reforms of the early 1970s that were based on an attempt at problem-solving. Another has been the identification of the problem of "overload." According to Anthony King, government has become overloaded because the range of problems it is expected to deal with has expanded and its capacity to deal with problems, even many of the ones it had before, has decreased. Writes King, "It is not the increase in the number of problems alone that matters, or the reduction in capacity. It is the two coming together."[46] Both these approaches are explanatory rather than prescriptive.

Of criticisms leveled at specific components of or relationships within government, the civil service has continued to be a focus of attention. The preference for the generalist and for the socially privileged strata from which civil servants are drawn continues to draw criticism, as do civil servants' manner of operation and their relationship with ministers. Their background and lack of training has been considered by some to be a factor in formulating inadequate policies to deal with Britain's problems, civil servants lacking the technical and managerial skills necessary to identify the nation's current problems and to formulate an adequate response to them. The secrecy in which they operate, guarded by the convention of ministerial responsibility and the Official Secrets Act, creates also a problem of consent and accountability. Civil servants operate behind a screen of anonymity, working on documents that often are classified, from "Restricted" to "Top Secret."[47] An anonymous body of powerful bureaucrats, believed to enjoy a degree of mastery over their nominal masters, is not considered conducive to public confidence in and support for government. Secrecy in government, according to Tony Benn, works only in the interests of weak ministers and strong civil servants, "both of whom prefer to keep the public in the dark."[48] Neither wishes to be found out.

Other problems identified have included the degree of political power vested in the prime minister. As we have seen, the existence of a form of prime ministerial government has been identified by some writers. The concentration of power in the hands of the PM, according to Mr. Benn, has gone too far "and amounts to a system of personal rule in the very heart of our parliamentary democracy."[49] It denies a sense of responsibility to electors. The public, Parliament, and even the cabinet are presented on occasion with decisions that they cannot change. Ignoring such bodies could lead to seeking change through other than parliamentary means. As a result, parliamentary democracy could be undermined.[50] Another criticism leveled has been that there has been a concentration of power, not so much in the hands of the prime minister, but in government in Whitehall. Such concentration, it is argued, makes for poor decision-making in that government is too large and too remote from the areas for which it is making decisions, and its remoteness from the people affected lessens support for the political system.[51] Citizens have difficulty identifying with a government that is geographically somewhat distant (in United Kingdom terms) and that, especially at the civil-service level, is rather faceless and secretive. As we have seen, criticism has been directed also at the machinery of government and the spread of quangos, the latter in particular generating problems of accountability.

Given the problems identified with government, it is not surprising that the prescriptions proffered differ. The main changes that have been recommended may be considered under four headings:

1. Changing the relationship within the political apex of government;
2. Changing the machinery of government;
3. Changing the relationship between ministers and civil servants;
4. Changing the civil service, in both composition and procedures.

Changing the Relationship within the Political Apex of Government. This recommendation concerns primarily limiting the powers of the prime minister. In order to dissipate the concentration of powers in the PM's hands and in order to make him or her more accountable, Mr. Benn, among others, has recommended that, in the case of a Labour government, members of the cabinet should be elected by the parliamentary Labour party and not selected by the PM. He has also argued that prime ministerial power would and should be reduced by an extension of the select committee system in the House of Commons, by abolishing the House of Lords (hence removing the premier's power of recommending life peerages), by making major public appointments subject to confirmation by the House of Commons, by withdrawal from the European Communities, and by the enactment of a free-dom-of-information act, thus stripping away much of the secrecy surrounding the operations of the premier and the civil service.[52] "Strong leadership there must be," wrote Mr. Benn, "but it must be open, collective, and accountable, and must learn to exercise its necessary powers by persuasion and, above all, through the development of a constitutional premiership."[53]

It is an argument that has not enjoyed universal support. A number of the reforms advocated by Mr. Benn, it has been pointed out, would not necessarily produce the result he desires. Few of these reforms would strike directly at the heart of the prime minister's powers.[54] One that would—election of the cabinet by members of the parliamentary Labour party—has been variously criticized, not surprisingly by a number of former PMs. As Clement Attlee contended, election could result in some very able people being excluded because they were not popular. "I don't believe in that at all. You must have confidence in the man in charge. If he hasn't got that confidence, he's not fit to be Prime Minister."[55] Furthermore, as we have mentioned, the premise of Mr. Benn's argument does not enjoy universal assent. Various writers have challenged the supposed existence of prime ministerial government, drawing attention instead to the serious constraints under which the PM operates.[56]

Changing the Machinery of Government.   Attempts in this direction, as we have seen, have taken various forms. In the early 1970s, the emphasis was on a rationalization of government departments as well as the hiving off of various departmental activities to the burgeoning quangos. By the latter half of the decade, the attraction of "super departments" had worn off and, with the return of a Conservative government in 1979, the approach toward nondepartmental public bodies was put into reverse.

As the decade progressed, pressure began to mount for a devolved form of government. It had been the intention of the creation of the "super departments" that they would not only contribute to efficiency in policy-making but would also strengthen the link between government and the individual by identifying clear ministerial responsibility for particular functions.[57] That intention was not fully realized. It was increasingly argued during the decade that the intention could be realized if certain functions of government were to be devolved to elected assemblies in Scotland and Wales, as well as to regional assemblies in England. The argument concerning devolution we shall discuss in more detail shortly (Chapter 9). For the moment, it is important to record that an attempt to introduce elected assemblies in Scotland and Wales was made in the 1974–1979 Parliament by the Labour government of James Callaghan, but it failed in the face of parliamentary opposition and the results of referendums in the two countries.

Although interest in devolution appeared to wane in the wake of the referendum results in 1979, it has again emerged as an issue on the political agenda. A number of politicians favor not only devolution but a more extensive form of devolution than that proposed by Mr. Callaghan's government. The Liberal party for some time has favored a form of federal government, and the new Social Democratic party is committed strongly to the decentralization of government.[58] Devolution, it is argued, would not only increase government effectiveness, decision-makers being able to act with a greater knowledge of and concern for local conditions, but also increase consent for government. It would allow decisions to rest with the people, not with the state.

Critics of devolution have argued that it would most likely add another burdensome layer to government, would be expensive (thus adding to the costs of industry and the taxpayer), and could result in a greater degree of economic disparity among the regions. It would create problems in trying to ensure an equitable distribution of national resources.[59] There would also be potential for friction between national and regional governments. There is no evidence that there is overwhelming support for devolution (witness the result of the 1979 referendum), and the problems associated with implementing such a reform suggest it may prove to be an unlikely prospect.

Changing the Relationship between Ministers and Civil Servants. This proposal is concerned primarily with attempts to ensure that the reality matches the formality, with ministers being able to enjoy control of their own departments. The two main changes recommended to achieve this are for ministers to have alternative sources of advice to those of their officials, and for them to have power to dismiss their permanent secretaries. For alternative advice, as we have seen, there has been the innovation of ministers appointing political advisers. Various Labour politicians have also advocated the creation of advisory bodies similar to the French *cabinets*.[60] Some former Labour ministers have also indicated that they would prefer to have had more control over the appointment, transfer, or dismissal of their permanent secretaries, a power that rests with the PM. To achieve the removal of a permanent secretary, a minister needs the support of the PM, and when it has been sought it has not always been forthcoming. The need for such changes has been variously argued by Mr. Benn and a number of his supporters. "We need to ensure that ministers are able to secure compliance with the policies that they were elected to implement," he has written. "Proposals to this end have been widely discussed and would certainly involve making the most senior officials in each department more responsible to the ministers whom they serve."[61]

Various arguments have been deployed against such proposals. Giving ministers hire-and-fire power over permanent secretaries would raise the potential for senior officials to become more partisan in their orientation, ministers selecting those most in tune with their own views. There are also a number of practical problems. Ministers have not proved overly enthusiastic in the appointment of political advisers (a number of Labour ministers in the 1970s apparently viewed political advisers with suspicion, regarding them as possible party "spies") and the civil service has proved adept in working around such appointees. Finally, it is unlikely that the PM would readily give up the power of appointment and transfer of senior officials.

Changing the Civil Service in Terms of Composition and Procedures. As we have seen, the civil service has been criticized for comprising Oxford-educated generalists. Since the late 1950s, various critics have attacked the inherent attitude of effortless superiority displayed by senior civil servants, confident in their ability to deal with the nation's problems but lacking any real knowledge of the changing world and its problems. These criticisms were sufficient to prompt the first Labour government of Harold Wilson to establish the Fulton Committee, which reported in 1968. As we have seen, its recommendations were designed to achieve a more open, specialized, and trained civil service but with its intentions being largely vitiated by the skilled machinations of the civil service.[62] "The real difficulty," as one member of a committee set up to implement the Fulton proposals put it, "is that you are trying to solve a problem with people who are themselves part of the problem."[63] The civil service continues to favor Oxford-educated generalists, selection committees tending to favor candidates molded in their own image. Various calls have been made for the intentions of the Fulton Committee to be realized.[64] The problem remains one of how to achieve that in the face of inherent civil-service reluctance.

The other main reform advocated is to open up the civil service by ridding it of the shroud of secrecy in which it buries itself. Various attempts have been made to introduce a freedom-of-information bill similar to that enacted in such other countries as the United States, Sweden, Denmark, and Norway. The Fulton Committee asserted that "the public interest would be better served if there were a greater amount of openness."[65] More openness on the part of the civil service, it is argued, would most likely improve decision-making, decision-makers being more careful and responsive knowing that the reasons for their decisions would be subject to public scrutiny, and would remove much public suspicion of civil-service activity. Keeping material hidden unnecessarily from public gaze does nothing to increase public confidence in government.

So far, attempts to achieve passage of a freedom-of-information bill have been unsuccessful. A private member's bill introduced in 1980 by a Liberal MP failed, and a bill introduced by the government in 1979 to reform the Officials Secrets Act was withdrawn.[66] More success in reducing civil-service anonymity and secretiveness has been achieved by the new select committees in the House of Commons, though officials appearing before them still remain protected by the doctrine of ministerial responsibility.

Defenders of the existing system argue that more openness would undermine the convention of ministerial responsibility, would inhibit officials in tendering advice to ministers, and would cost too much to implement. Proponents point out that the first two consequences need not necessarily flow from the release of official documents and that the third argument does not necessarily detract from the merits of the case for more openness.[67] It could be argued that it would not cost too much for officials to give up responding to queries with a noncommittal answer and to spend less time imprinting papers with the designation of "Restricted."

As can be seen, the prescriptions to improve governmental decision-making differ. To some extent, the focuses of the prescriptions differ. They are derived from different approaches to constitutional change. Their chances of success differ. Although seeking to affect the relationship between government and citizens or at least to affect the perception of government by citizens, the reforms are all directed to the structure, machinery, and procedures of government. There are, as we have seen, reforms proposed that are external to the government yet would have a significant impact on its composition and behavior: most notable among these is the proposal for a new electoral system (see Chapter 5).

One further change recommended does not involve tangible structural or procedural change. Various analyses have suggested that government is malfunctional because of rising expectations and an inability of government now to meet those expectations (see Chapter 3). What is needed, according to some, is not a change in government but rather a change in expectations. There is some suggestion that there may have been a lowering of expectations.[68] If the problem of overloaded government is to be tackled, lowered expectations may prove a desirable development. As Anthony King concluded his essay on the subject, "Academic political scientists have traditionally been concerned to improve the performance of government. Perhaps over the next few years they should be more concerned with how the number of tasks that government has come to be expected to perform can be reduced."[69]

SUMMARY

The executive in Britain can be seen to be heterogeneous. It comprises disparate elements, some of which may pursue courses not altogether compatible with others: their motivations, goals, and perceptions differ. At the pinnacle of the executive pyramid sits the cabinet. It comes into office with a manifesto that, to a greater or lesser extent, it seeks to carry out. It is dependent on the rest of the executive branch to translate its wishes into concrete legislative and administrative form and to carry them out. The executive generally is subject continuously to a barrage of demands (many of which are mutually exclusive), from groups, individuals, and foreign interests. It has to respond to unforeseen events. The demands made of it are greater than before. The resources available to respond to them have decreased. In order to try to improve government efficiency and to reduce public disquiet, various reforms of its structure and the internal relationships between its component parts have been tried or are currently on the agenda of public debate. Like the different elements of the executive, the reforms are somewhat disparate and subject to conflicting arguments. The formal structure sketched in Figure 8.1 helps give shape to one's understanding of the executive, but it is important to bear in mind that the distribution of executive power is not as clear nor as accountable as the formal picture prescribes, nor is it static. The executive is a medium of change but is itself subject to change. Pressure for change has been and remains a feature of contemporary debate.

NOTES

1. See P. Norton, *The Commons in Perspective* (Martin Robertson, 1981), Ch. 1.
2. Ibid., pp. 5–6.
3. *House of Commons Debates (Hansard),* Vol. 967, col. 179.
4. J. Barnett, *Inside the Treasury* (Andre Deutsch, 1982), p. 27.
5. R. H. S. Crossman, Introduction to W. Bagehot, *The English Constitution* (Fontana, 1963 ed.).
6. See, e.g., H. Wilson, *The Governance of Britain* (Sphere, 1977), pp. 86–88, and P. Gordon Walker, *The Cabinet* (Fontana edition, 1972), pp. 46–47.
7. See especially Crossman, as above, and T. Benn, "The Case for a Constitutional Premiership," *Parliamentary Affairs,* 33 (1), 1980, pp. 7–22, and H. Berkeley, *The Power of the Prime Minister* (Chilmark Press, 1968).
8. See, e.g., P. Gordon Walker, as above, as well as A. King (ed.), *The British Prime Minister* (Macmillan, 1969); G. W. Jones, "The Prime Minister's Powers," *Parliamentary Affairs,* 18, 1965, pp. 167–85; and A. H. Brown, "Prime Ministerial Power (Part II)," *Public Law,* 1968, pp. 96–118.
9. See G. W. Jones, "The Prime Minister's Aides," *Hull Papers in Politics No. 6* (Hull University Politics Department, 1980).
10. M. Kogan, *The Politics of Education* (Penguin, 1971), p. 35.
11. See especially R. Crossman, *The Diaries of a Cabinet Minister,* Vols. 1, 2, and particularly 3 (Hamish Hamilton/Jonathan Cape, 1975, 1976, 1977); and also, for Cabinet Committees, Barnett, p. 17.
12. See Crossman, *Diaries,* Barnett, and also B. Castle, *The Castle Diaries 1974–76* (Weidenfeld & Nicolson, 1980).

13. See D. Butler and A. Sloman, *British Political Facts 1900–1979,* 5th ed. (Macmillan, 1980), p. 78.

14. N. Johnson, *In Search of the Constitution* (Methuen ed. 1980), p. 84.

15. Kogan, p. 38.

16. Sir R. Clarke, "The Machinery of Government" in W. Thornhill (ed.), *The Modernization of British Government* (Pitman, 1975), p. 65.

17. P. Norton, *The Constitution in Flux* (Martin Robertson, 1982), p. 75.

18. B. Headey, "Cabinet Ministers and Senior Civil Servants: Mutual Requirements and Expectations" in V. Herman and J. Alt (eds.), *Cabinet Studies* (Macmillan, 1975), pp. 131–35.

19. See P. Kellner and Lord Crowther-Hunt, *The Civil Servants* (Macdonald Futura, 1980), pp. 119–23.

20. On this, see J. Garrett, *Managing the Civil Service* (Heinemann, 1980).

21. See Norton, *The Constitution in Flux,* pp. 82–83.

22. 1979 figures: Kellner and Crowther-Hunt, p. 103.

23. See Norton, *The Constitution in Flux,* pp. 86–87.

24. Sir A. Part, speaking on the Independent Television program, "World in Action," January 7, 1980.

25. Barnett, p. 17.

26. I. Gilmour, *The Body Politic,* rev. ed. (Hutchinson, 1971), p. 201.

27. Sir I. Gilmour M.P. to author, in conversation.

28. *Report on Non-Departmental Public Bodies,* Cmnd. 7797 (Her Majesty's Stationery Office, 1980), pp. 3–4.

29. Ibid., p. 27.

30. See P. Holland, M.P., *The Governance of Quangos* (Adam Smith Institute, 1981), pp. 10–12.

31. E. Heath and A. Barker, "Heath on Whitehall Reform," *Parliamentary Affairs,* 31 (4), 1978, p. 370.

32. Ibid.

33. *Report on Non-Departmental Public Bodies,* p. 1.

34. Ibid., pp. 14–15.

35. P. Holland M.P., *Quelling the Quango* (Conservative Political Centre, 1982), p. 21.

36. *House of Commons Debates,* Vol. 16, cols. 296–307 (Written Answers, January 26, 1982).

37. Holland, *Quelling the Quango,* p. 24.

38. See generally W. Plowden, "The British Central Policy Review Staff" in P. Baehr and B. Withrock (eds.), *Policy Analysis and Policy Innovation* (Sage, 1982), pp. 61–91.

39. B. Smith, *Policy Making in British Government* (Martin Robertson, 1976), p. 140.

40. See J. Fox, "The Brains Behind the Throne" in Herman and Alt, pp. 277–92.

41. See F. Stacey, *British Government 1966–1975* (Oxford University Press, 1975), p. 91.

42. See A. Maynard and A. Walker, "Cutting Public Spending," *New Society,* December 4, 1975, p. 529.

43. See H. Heclo and A. Wildavsky, *The Private Government of Public Money* (Macmillan, 1974), pp. 210–11.

44. See Norton, *The Constitution in Flux,* pp. 77–78.

45. See J. E. S. Hayward, *Political Inertia* (University of Hull, 1975). See also J. J. Richardson and A. G. Jordan, *Governing Under Pressure* (Martin Robertson, 1979).

46. A. King, "The Problem of Overload" in A. King (ed.), *Why Is Britain Becoming Harder to Govern?* (BBC, 1976), p. 25.

47. See D. Leigh, *The Frontiers of Secrecy* (Junction Books, 1980), pp. 39–42.

48. T. Benn, "Manifestos and Mandarins" in *Policy and Practice: The Experience of Government* (Royal Institute of Public Administration, 1980), p. 75.

49. Benn, "The Case for a Constitutional Premiership," p. 7.

50. Ibid.

51. See Norton, *The Constitution in Flux,* Ch. 9.

52. T. Benn, *Arguments for Democracy* (Penguin, 1982), pp. 39–41.

53. Ibid.

54. See Norton, *The Constitution in Flux,* Ch. 1.

55. Interview with F. Williams, in A. King (ed.), *The British Prime Minister* (Macmillan, 1969), p. 74.

56. See note 8.

57. See Norton, *The Constitution in Flux,* Ch. 3.

58. See *Draft Constitution of the Social Democratic Party* (SDP, 1981), p. 1; I. Bradley, *Breaking the Mould?* (Martin Robertson, 1981), pp. 130–34; and D. Owen, *Face the Future* (Oxford University Press, 1981), Ch. 2.

59. Norton, *The Constitution in Flux,* Ch. 3.

60. See "New style aides for Labour ministers," *Tribune,* July 10, 1981, p. 6.

61. Benn, *Arguments for Democracy,* p. 66.

62. See Lord Crowther-Hunt, "The Case for Civil Service Power," *The Listener,* January 13, 1977.

63. Quoted in B. Page and I. Hilton, "The 'reformers' who made sure nothing changed," *Daily Express,* April 6, 1977, p. 11.

64. See Kellner and Crowther-Hunt, *The Civil Servants,* Postscript.

65. *Report of the Committee on the Civil Service,* Cmnd. 3638 (Her Majesty's Stationery Office, 1968), para. 177.

66. Some critics argued that it would not improve upon the existing position, and the bill was withdrawn when it was realized that under its provisions a book that had recently identified spy Anthony Blunt would have been prohibited.

67. See Norton, *The Constitution in Flux,* Ch. 4.

68. See J. Alt, *The Politics of Economic Decline* (Cambridge University Press, 1979) and below, Ch. 15.

69. King, "The Problem of Overload," p. 29.

Subnational Government

Government below the Center

THE UNITED STATES enjoys, or at any rate labors under, three distinct tiers of government: national, state, and local. Because the nation is federal rather than unitary, Congress can legislate only on those matters enumerated or implied in the Constitution: all remaining powers are reserved to the states or to the people. The position in the United Kingdom is somewhat different: as a unitary nation, it lacks the equivalent of state governments. Although, as we shall see, attempts have been made to introduce an intermediate level of government in the form of national assemblies in Scotland and Wales and regional assemblies in England (and Northern Ireland for 50 years, had its own provincial Parliament), such assemblies would be able to exercise only those powers delegated to them by Parliament. This is the case with local government in Britain. Parliament enjoys legislative sovereignty and can both give and remove as it chooses delegated powers to subordinate units of government. Even in the case of the European Communities, the legislation that emanates from the Communities is applied by virtue of the provisions of the 1972 European Communities Act, an act that Parliament retains the power to amend or, should it so choose, to repeal.

Subnational government (see Map 9.1) within the United Kingdom can be discussed under two headings: actual and proposed (see Table 9.1). The first of these, existing subnational government, comprises local government,

209

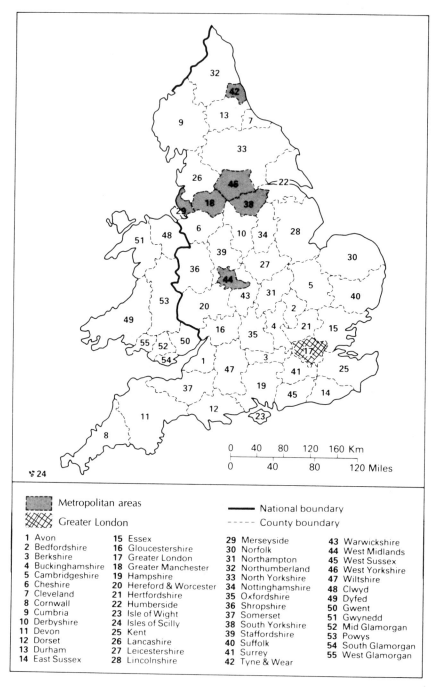

MAP 9.1 England and Wales: Metropolitan and non-metropolitan counties. (*Source: A. Alexander, The Politics of Local Government in the United Kingdom* [Longman, 1982]. *Copyright 1982 Alan Alexander. Reprinted by permission.*)

Legend for the map:

Metropolitan areas
Greater London
National boundary
County boundary

1 Avon
2 Bedfordshire
3 Berkshire
4 Buckinghamshire
5 Cambridgeshire
6 Cheshire
7 Cleveland
8 Cornwall
9 Cumbria
10 Derbyshire
11 Devon
12 Dorset
13 Durham
14 East Sussex
15 Essex
16 Gloucestershire
17 Greater London
18 Greater Manchester
19 Hampshire
20 Hereford & Worcester
21 Hertfordshire
22 Humberside
23 Isle of Wight
24 Isles of Scilly
25 Kent
26 Lancashire
27 Leicestershire
28 Lincolnshire
29 Merseyside
30 Norfolk
31 Northampton
32 Northumberland
33 North Yorkshire
34 Nottinghamshire
35 Oxfordshire
36 Shropshire
37 Somerset
38 South Yorkshire
39 Staffordshire
40 Suffolk
41 Surrey
42 Tyne & Wear
43 Warwickshire
44 West Midlands
45 West Sussex
46 West Yorkshire
47 Wiltshire
48 Clwyd
49 Dyfed
50 Gwent
51 Gwynedd
52 Mid Glamorgan
53 Powys
54 South Glamorgan
55 West Glamorgan

TABLE 9.1
Subnational Government in the United Kingdom

Level	Existing Governmental Bodies	Proposed Governmental Bodies
Territorial		
England	No specific English bodies	
Scotland	Scottish Office (United Kingdom government department)	Elected assembly with legislative/executive powers
Northern Ireland	Northern Ireland Office (United Kingdom government department)	Elected assembly with executive powers
	Elected Assembly (no executive powers)	
Wales	Welsh Office (United Kingdom government department)	Elected assembly with limited executive powers
Regional	Regional offices of government departments	Elected regional assemblies
	Disparate public bodies, e.g., regional water authorities, regional health authorities	
Local (counties and towns)	Elected councils	Some modification to existing structure

regional government, and administrative devolution in Scotland, Northern Ireland, and Wales. The only level of elected government below national level in Britain is local government. There is no government elected at an intermediate level, either at a regional level or for the whole of Scotland or Wales. However, though not elected, there are governmental bodies operating at these levels. The most important of these are the Scottish Office, the Northern Ireland Office, and, to a lesser extent, the Welsh Office, enjoying executive powers that for the rest of the United Kingdom are exercised in London. The carrying out of these powers by government departments is essentially a substitute for their exercise by elected bodies. Various proposals have been put forward for the creation of such bodies, in Scotland and Wales as well as in Northern Ireland. A measure to establish elected assemblies in Scotland and Wales was introduced in 1976 but failed for reasons to be explored shortly. Several schemes have been put forward for constitutional change in Northern Ireland, none of which has yet proved successful. Such proposals remain on the political agenda. Their importance is such that they deserve attention.

ACTUAL: LOCAL GOVERNMENT, REGIONAL GOVERNMENT, AND ADMINISTRATIVE DEVOLUTION

Local Government

For most of the twentieth century, local government in England and Wales was based on the system created by the Local Government Act of 1888. It created two main tiers of local authorities (Figure 9.1). First, there were county boroughs, exercising control over all local government services within their boundaries, and county councils, each exercising control over certain local government services within the county (though not over any county boroughs within the county). Second, and below the county councils, were noncounty boroughs, urban districts, and rural districts, all exercising limited functions. There was also a third tier of local government: small parish councils exercising very limited responsibilities.

As demands on government grew and the responsibilities of local government expanded, the structure of local government appeared increasingly less appropriate. Allowing county boroughs to exercise functions that seemed more suitable to a larger authority (for example, control of planning and roads) came in for criticism, while many noncounty boroughs exacerbated the problem by applying for county borough status. By the 1960s there was growing awareness of the need for some reform of the structure of local government. Local government in London was reformed during the decade, with the creation of the Greater London Council (GLC). Established under

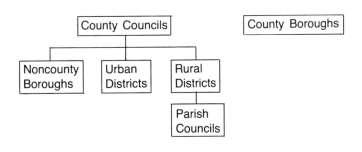

FIGURE 9.1   Local government structure pre-1972 (excluding Greater London).

the 1963 London Government Act, the GLC was vested with responsibility for planning, roads, traffic, overspill housing, and other needs affecting the whole of the Greater London area; responsibility for personal health services (except ambulances) and for most local authority housing was retained by 32 borough councils within the GLC area. Responsibility for education in the area covered by the old London County Council was vested in an Inner London Education Authority (ILEA). Reform of the remaining local government in England and Wales was effected under the Local Government Act of 1972. Local government in Scotland was reorganized under the Local Government (Scotland) Act of the following year.

Under the 1972 Act, a new two-tier system was introduced. A Royal Commission on Local Government in England, which reported in 1969, had recommended the creation of a single tier, with the creation of all-purpose local authorities. The government decided against this for fear that the new authorities would be too distant from the local communities: the need for more efficient authorities had to be tempered with the need to have some form of local government that to citizens would be recognizably "local." The result was the creation of 47 county councils, each with responsibility for education, transport, highways (except motorways and unclassified roads), planning, housing, personal social services, libraries, police, fire service, refuse disposal, and consumer protection. Below them (Figure 9.2) were created a second tier of more than 300 district councils, each with responsibility for town planning, environmental health, building and housing management, and various functions of registration and licensing. Also created were six separate metropolitan counties (West Midlands, Greater Manchester, West Yorkshire, South Yorkshire, Merseyside, and Tyne and Wear). The metropolitan counties were each vested with responsibility for the same functions as the other counties, with the exception of education, personal social services, and libraries. Below the metropolitan counties was created a

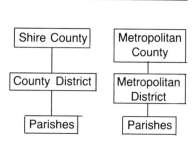

FIGURE 9.2   Local government structure post-1972 (excluding Greater London).

second tier of metropolitan districts (a total of 36) that, because of their size, were given control of education, personal social services, and libraries, as well as the other functions given to district councils. In addition, the metropolitan counties and districts were to share responsibilities for certain matters, principally parks, museums, and airports. Below the two tiers, provision for parish councils was also retained. In Scotland, the 1973 Act created a two-tier division between nine large regional councils and district councils. Because of the concentration of population in the western lowlands of Scotland, one region—Strathclyde—contains more than half of the country's population.

The aim of the reorganization was to create a more rational system of local government. Within the new bodies, the emphasis was on an efficient managerial approach. The chief permanent officials of the old borough councils were titled town clerks. The chief appointed officials of the new authorities were titled chief executives and the approach to administration adopted by many councils was that of corporate management. The chief executive was viewed as a coordinating head, advised and supported by a team of management officers. Councils continued to exercise their functions largely through committees, though with each council now having greater latitude than they had hitherto in deciding what committees they wished to establish. (Certain committees were and remain mandatory, principally police, education, and social services committees.) Especially popular was the creation of a policy committee, with responsibility for establishing priorities and monitoring resources and policy implementation. By the end of the decade, though, the corporate approach had not proved as worthwhile as many councils had hoped and a number reverted to the more traditional prereform approach, doing away with the concept of a chief executive and redrawing committee responsibilities based on established services rather than expenditure functions. One important point to note is the different approach to government administration adopted at local government level (committee-based, emphasis on professional administrators) and that adopted at national level (non-committee-based, emphasis on the generalist).

The relationship between national and local government is an important one, given the dependence of the latter on the former. Local authorities in Britain can exercise only those powers vested in them by law. They cannot exercise initiative in branching out into spheres of activity for which they have no specific statutory authority. If they were to do so, their actions could be challenged as being *ultra vires* (beyond the powers) and councillors could be made subject to a surcharge—that is, being made personally responsible for the extra cost incurred by their action. Local government is also heavily dependent on central government for its revenue. Each local authority obtains its revenue from three main sources: a central government grant, local rates (a tax on real estate, based on the value of the property), and income from services provided by the authority. Of these, the grant from central government (known as the rate support grant and fixed on the basis of a complex formula) is the largest and constitutes nearly 60% of what local government spends. About one-quarter of what is spent is derived from the rates. Local government expenditure is considerable: in the financial year 1979–1980 it amounted to £13,784 million, and in the following year it totalled £13,643 million, constituting more than one-quarter of the total public expenditure in Great Britain. The extent of the expenditure in recent years has been such as to be the subject of restrictions by national government. The present Conservative government in particular has attempted to limit local expenditure as part of its policy of limiting public expenditure. In 1981, the Environment secretary reduced the block grant to those authorities that had exceeded the government's expenditure targets. The 1982 Local Government Finance (No. 2) Act abolished supplementary rates in England and Wales (that is, additional rates levied after the rate for the year has already been decided) and gave the environment secretary power to make adjustments in the level of expenditure.[1] In August 1983, the government announced its intention to introduce legislation to give the minister power also to impose a maximum limit on the rates that could be levied by big spending authorities.[2]

Over and above the financial limitations imposed by central government, local authorities are also constrained to work within the confines of powers held and policies pursued by national government. Ministers have various statutory powers to make orders as well as to issue circulars to local authorities giving guidance on the implementation of government policy. The normal mode of conducting central-local government discussions is negotiation, though on occasions the government has found it necessary to enforce its wishes over the objections of local authorities, the number of occasions in recent years showing an increase rather than a reduction. Local authorities that are out of sympathy with government policy have sometimes sought to frustrate it by employing delaying tactics (as with a number of Conservative councils opposed to Labour government plans for the introduction of comprehensive education) or by overspending against government wishes (as with a number of Labour-controlled councils under the present Conservative administration). Although in the end the central government can impose its wishes, either through existing powers or through the passage of new legislation,[3] this type of obstruction can seriously frustrate its policies and its expenditure plans. In expenditure and employment (with 2.8 million employees), local government is an important element in the British polity and one not totally subservient in its behavior to government at the center.

National politics also impinge upon local government at election time. Local elections are held at fixed intervals, councillors serving for stipulated terms of office (though eligible for reelection). County councils are elected *en bloc* once every four years, as are metropolitan counties. Practice varies within the district councils, which under the 1972 Act were given power to opt for staggered elections or for *en bloc* elections. (Although county councillors are elected on the basis of single-member constituencies, district authorities have also the option of choosing single-member or multiple-member constituencies.) In metropolitan districts, one-third of the councillors are elected in each of the three years in which there is no metropolitan county election. Although elections are fought ostensibly on local issues, candidates at other than parish council level now usually stand under a party label, a tendency that increased in postwar years and was given added impetus by the reorganization of 1972. Large authorities are now such significant bodies of public expenditure and policy-making that the national parties cannot afford to ignore them. Party appears to be the most important variable influencing the voting behavior of those few electors who bother to cast a vote (turnout rarely reaches 40% of eligible voters; Table 9.2), with local elections being viewed as an annual opportunity to pass judgment on the incumbent national government. The governing party is expected to do this badly during the midterm of a government. When the Conservatives did surprisingly well in the 1982 Local Elections, achieving a net gain of 26 seats in England and Wales, this was hailed as a success for the government.[4]

Although elected on party labels and usually operating within coherent party groupings, with elected officers and whips, councillors behave differently depending on local circumstances. Given that the needs and demands of communities vary, local parties will temper their responses accordingly. The councillors themselves tend to be disproportionately male and drawn from nonmanual occupations. The likelihood is greater now than it was prior to the mid-1970s that they will have university educations. As two observers write, "The rise in the proportion of councillors with higher educational qualifications suggests that local-authority service is attracting its fair share of the best-educated sections of society—although a fall in the number of man-

TABLE 9.2
Turnout in Borough Council Elections, 1960–1972

Year	Percentage Turnout
1960	35.4
1961	40.6
1962	40.2
1963	41.3
1964	40.5 (77.1*)
1965	37.7
1966	35.6 (75.8*)
1967	40.3
1968	35.8
1969	35.6
1970	37.6 (72.0*)
1971	39.2
1972	36.7

*Figures in parentheses indicate turnout in United Kingdom general elections.
SOURCE: D. Butler and A. Sloman, *British Political Facts 1900–1979*, 5th ed. (Macmillan, 1980), p. 403. Copyright 1980 Macmillan. Reprinted by permission.

ual workers elected might make some voters feel that local authorities might be remote from them and so unresponsive in their needs."[5] One innovation introduced in 1972 to increase the attractiveness of local government service to able and economically active citizens (many councillors were retired persons) was the introduction of attendance allowances for councillors.[6] The introduction of such allowances may also have been encouraged by the desire to lessen the incentives for corruption, an occasional unfortunate feature of local government life not usually witnessed at a national level.[7] In order to consider cases of alleged maladministration, a number of local government ombudsmen (known as local commissioners) were established under the Local Government Act of 1974.

Once elected, councillors devote much time to casework and also tend to specialize in their committee work. Very few appear interested in helping formulate authority-wide policy.[8] What motivates individuals to seek election to local councils is not at all clear. Some appear to see it as a stepping stone to higher things (though only a very few will subsequently be selected as parliamentary candidates); some do it out of a desire to further the aims of their party; some do it out of a sense of civic responsibility (to be found also in the performance of a wide range of other local activities, such as serving on the local magistrates bench and doing voluntary social work); some do it to enhance their status in the community; and some do it for the simple reason that they were inveigled into standing by friends or local party activists. Some individuals contest local elections in order to do their bit for their party without ever expecting to be elected and then find themselves topping the poll. Because of the number of councillors to be elected and the level of public indifference toward local government, local parties sometimes have difficulty in recruiting candidates to contest elections. In some areas, it might be described as a seller's rather than a buyer's market.

Many local authorities, like their United States counterparts, are having difficulty in maintaining effective political authority because of the difficulties in raising resources to maintain their commitments. Councils are expected to provide local services and to do so efficiently. Rising costs and restricted grant allocations by central government force them into the position of having to choose between a reduction in the level and quality of services provided and an increase in the rates. Reduction in services undermines support among those affected. Substantial increases in rates may increase civic indifference. This, coming up on top of a general lack of knowledge about local government among citizens as well as a frequent lack of interest, puts local authorities on an unenviable footing within the community. The problem would appear to be acute in certain areas and among certain segments of the population. When Environment Secretary Michael Heseltine visited Liverpool in the wake of the summer riots there in 1981, he asked a group of disaffected young people if they had been in touch with their councillors. The reply from one of the youngsters was "What's a councillor?"[9] A survey of young people in the same area found them indifferent to politics.[10]

Attitudes toward local government are reflected in some of the current discussions on the subject. It remains a topic of political debate because of its structure and the current relationships between central government and certain local authorities. The reorganization of 1972 proved costly and did little to enhance consent for the system of government: there was little apparent increase in the awareness on the part of citizens of local authority responsibilities. As Anthony King put it, "things are not working out quite as expected."[11] Certain features of the reorganization generated resentment. Inhabitants of counties dismembered or abolished were often vehement in their vocal opposition to the changes. So too were former councillors and other citizens in the boroughs that were reduced to parish council status. Within some of the new counties, a number of boroughs resented and continue to resent the dominance of larger conurbations. Dissatisfaction with the new structure found expression in the Labour party manifesto in 1979, which committed the party to restoring to the larger district councils in England the responsibility for education, personal services, planning, and libraries. The party repeated the commitment in 1983.

What has attracted most attention in recent years has been the policy adopted by the Conservative government of Mrs. Thatcher toward local government. On entering office, the Government was keen to reform the system of levying rates. It was considered burdensome and unfair, the rates paid by a household having no direct relationship to the extent of the local services that the household utilized. However, after exploring various alternatives to the existing rating system,[12] the government decided that no fundamental change was possible.[13] Instead, the government found itself engaged in a battle with local authorities to keep their expenditure within government targets. Local government spending was one of the major features of public spending exceeding Government targets and, as mentioned already, various measures were introduced to constrain the heavily spending councils. The need to limit public spending was accorded priority over the commitment to the principle of local autonomy. By the end of 1983, the government had announced its intention to seek powers to place a ceiling on the rates levied by large over-spending councils (usually Labour-controlled), as well as to abolish the largest-spending authority, the Greater London Council, which was, under its Labour leader Ken Livingstone, a significant thorn in the flesh of Government. In 1983–1984, GLC spending exceeded grant-related expenditure (the amount government considered it should spend) by 81%. The government proposed to dispense with the Council by 1986 and distribute its functions among the London boroughs.

Local government as such has thus become an important issue of political debate. The government's plans to restrict rate rises and abolish the GLC encountered the opposition of the Labour party. Also, the move to introduce legislation to provide a rates ceiling precipitated opposition within Conservative ranks: the conservative-controlled Association of County Councils described it as a threat to local democracy.[14] Although local authorities retain considerable latitude in the exercise of their functions, their scope for action has been constrained (though not yet to the extent favored by the government) and their relationship with central government has become a more adversary and politically contentious one.

Regional Government

Within Britain—that is, excluding Northern Ireland—there are no directly elected governmental bodies between the local and the national level. There are, though, a number of governmental or quasi-governmental bodies that operate at a regional level. They are significant not only for being nonelected but also for being disparate and not integrated with one another. Nonetheless, they constitute a significant level of government in Britain.

Various factors have contributed to governmental functions being fulfilled at regional level. Among the more important pressures toward this are administrative convenience, the need to involve more local authorities, the desire to dissociate central government from certain decision-making activities, technical advantages, and pressure from groups and professional bodies seeking some degree of regional autonomy for their sphere of activity.[15] Various government departments now have regional offices with some degree of independent decision-making authority: these include the Department of the Environment and the Department of Trade and Industry. In the latter, each regional office has a regional director with the power to authorize grants to firms seeking assistance from government funds. (In certain regions, for example, the director can authorize a grant of up to £2 million—approximately $3.5 million.) In making such grants, the director is assisted by an industrial director, recruited from the private sector, and by nonstatutory advisory bodies known as regional industrial development boards.[16] In addition, government may adopt a regional policy that entails the distribution of aid on a regional basis. Thus, for example, it gives grants to industrial development associations, bodies set up on a cooperative basis by local authorities (sometimes in conjunction with employers' organizations, trade unions, and statutory agencies) to promote industrial expansion in their region. In 1979, central government gave grants of £750,000 ($1,250,000) to four such agencies.[17]

The two most extensive and structured quasi-governmental bodies operating at regional level are regional water authorities and regional health authorities, both established in the 1970s. The regional water authorities were created in order to produce benefits of scale (management of water resources had previously been on a local basis) and to improve operational and financial management. There are 10 water authorities with overall responsibility for every aspect of water usage in England and Wales. This incorporates the conservation, supply, and distribution of water; sewerage and sewage disposal; land drainage; water pollution control; and water-based recreation and amenity.[18] The authorities enjoy a significant amount of autonomy in their operations, in part because there is no single government department responsible for their activities and because there is no national government policy on water management. What control is exerted by government is essentially negative, through establishing capital expenditure ceilings for the industry as a whole as well as for individual authorities. The authorities themselves comprise representatives of local authorities from the region, who constitute the majority on each authority, and a number of members appointed by ministers for their knowledge and expertise in the subject. This composition has been criticized as being not truly representative of the public or based adequately on the criteria of management expertise, the need for political accountability militating against small management boards.[19] Income is derived from water rates charged to consumers; in 1979–1980, the authorities had a revenue of nearly £900 million (approximately $1,350 million).[20]

The regional health authorities were created under the Health Service Reorganization Act of 1973. They involved less fundamental change than was

MAP 9.2 Regional health authorities.

the case with water authorities since they replaced, though having somewhat different functions, existing regional bodies, the regional hospital boards. The main responsibility for the new authorities was the planning of health services, and 14 authorities were created (Map 9.2), the members of each being appointed by the secretary of state for health and social services. The members serve part-time and are not paid (except for the chairman, who receives a part-time salary), and the secretary of state consults with a variety of interested groups, including professional organizations, local authorities, and voluntary organizations, before making the appointments. Each authority is served by full-time officials headed by a regional team of officers (RTO). Under the 1973 Act, a second tier of 90 area health authorities was created (Figure 9.3). These had planning and management functions and below them existed the main operational units, the district management teams.[21]

In practice, the reorganization of the Health Service did not work out as it was intended. It proved to be costly; the Department of Health and Social Services acknowledged in 1977 that there had been an increase of 16,400 administrative and clerical staff as a result of the reorganization.[22] A study of the new regional authorities discovered that the members had little impact

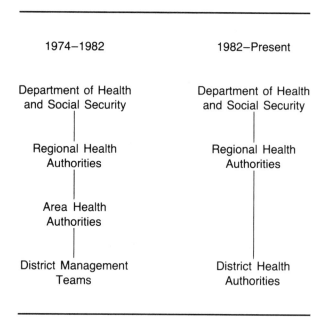

FIGURE 9.3   The structure of the National Health Service (England). Family Practitioner Committees and Community Health Councils are not included. (*Source: C. Ham, Health Policy in Britain [Macmillan, 1982]. Copyright 1982 Macmillan. Reprinted by permission.*)

on the work of the permanent officers. "Decision making is dominated by expert opinion," wrote two analysts.[23] The autonomy achieved by the regional and area authorities was such that they became almost beyond ministerial control.[24] A Royal Commission on the National Health Service was appointed and it reported in 1979, endorsing the view that there was one too many tiers of administration. In 1982, the area health authorities were abolished and district health authorities replaced the district management teams (Figure 9.3). Thus, within the structure of the National Health Service, the regional health authorities are the only bodies interposed between the Department of Health and Social Security nationally and the locally based district health authorities.

One final important point to be made about regional government is that not only is it disparate and unintegrated, but the various regional forms of government just identified themselves vary in size and authority. Part of the problem stems from the spatial disparity in population and resources and also from the absence of clearly acknowledged regions in England. The boundaries of regions vary, depending on which government department, public body, or political organization is responsible for defining them.[25] As the observant reader will have noted, there is an obvious disparity between regional water authorities in England (10) and regional health authorities (14). Map 9.1 shows the regional health authorities in England. (As can be seen, there are authorities covering Scotland, Wales, and Northern Ireland.) Other public bodies organized on a regional basis would not usually have a separate Mersey region nor divide the Southeast into Thames regions. The creation of Oxford and, to some extent, Wessex regions is not altogether common practice either. This lack of standardization provides not only for a muddled picture in any discussion of existing regional government, it also points to an important problem in any attempt to create a structured and elected tier of regional government in England. One would first of all have to determine the number of regions and their boundaries. The existing confusion adds to or rather helps reinforce an indistinct picture of public bodies operating at a level intermediate between central and local government.

Administrative Devolution

In England, the various functions of government are carried out by a number of functionally differentiated departments (agriculture, education, energy, and so on). In Scotland, those functions are vested in one single department. The same is true of Northern Ireland and, to a lesser extent, Wales. This concentration of functions in territorially defined departments has been given a number of labels, the most used and probably the most appropriate being administrative devolution. Instead of being governed by London-based departments, Scotland and Northern Ireland are in effect governed largely by single departments based in Edinburgh and Belfast, respectively.

The Scottish Office (SO) is a government department that has existed for some time. The first secretary for Scotland was appointed in 1885. However, not until 1939 did the department absorb many important functions affecting Scotland that had previously been carried out by other bodies. At the same time, the bulk of the department was moved from London to St. Andrew's House in Edinburgh.[26] Since then, the department has expanded and acquired new responsibilities. In the immediate postwar period it was given responsibility in Scotland for the National Health Service, assistance to agriculture, and town and country planning. More recently, it has acquired responsibility for economic planning.

The SO, as mentioned briefly in Chapter 8, is divided into functional units known as departments. There are currently five (see Table 9.3). At the political apex stands the secretary of state for Scotland, assisted by a minister of state (usually drawn from the House of Lords) and three parliamentary undersecretaries. Because the number of departments in the SO exceeds the number of junior ministers, one minister will often be given responsibility for more than one department. Below the ministers, at civil-service level, there is a management group made of department heads, with a secretariat and regular meetings. There is also a central services unit, in effect a sixth department, responsible for personnel and finance.

Despite this concentration of functions in one department and the attempt at coordination, the heads of each department retain considerable autonomy and, as two observers write, "departmental interaction resembles

TABLE 9.3
Scottish Office Departments

Department	Responsibilities
Agriculture and Fisheries for Scotland	Most agricultural and fisheries matters
Scottish Development	Planning, housing, roads, transport, local government
Scottish Economic Planning	Regional economic development, electricity, selective aid to industry, new towns, Scottish Development Agency
Scottish Education	Education outside the universities, social work services
Scottish Home and Health	Police, prisons, criminal justice, fire, National Health Service

SOURCE: M. Keating and A. Midwinter, *The Government of Scotland* (Mainstream Publishing, 1983). Copyright 1983 Mainstream Publishing. Reprinted by permission.

the independence of Whitehall ministers."[27] The individual departments in conjunction with outside interest groups would appear to form the policy communities within the SO. Which outside group raises an issue will normally determine which department will deal with it, and apparently groups rarely refer to the Scottish Office as such, talking instead of individual departments.[28] Once a policy has been agreed on by the SO, cabinet or cabinet committee discussion and agreement will often be influenced by the nature of the issue. Where a proposal falls clearly within the scope of the SO and affects Scotland solely, it will often be approved without any debate.[29] A proposal that has wider United Kingdom implications will be considered in the same way as proposals emanating from other government departments.

The picture that emerges is thus one of a government department that operates in a particular territory almost as a mini-government. It is a government department yet in many respects is more than a government department. The same is true of the Northern Ireland office. It is of more recent origin than is the SO. For the 50 years prior to 1972, Northern Ireland had its own parliament, granted it by the United Kingdom Parliament.[30] It was organized on the model of the United Kingdom government, with departments and ministers, and with members elected to it known as members of Parliament. For reasons to be discussed shortly, it was suspended in 1972 and replaced with direct rule from the United Kingdom government. This entailed the creation of the Northern Ireland Office. It was formed as a government department under a secretary of state and a number of junior ministers. Its civil service staff was drawn largely from the Northern Ireland civil service and the bulk of the department was based at Stormont, just outside Belfast, the home of the old Northern Ireland Parliament.

The department is similar to the SO in the scope of its responsibilities and the functional separation of its responsibilities into departments.[31] These departments encompass health and social services, finance, manpower services, environment, education, commerce, agriculture, and Northern Ireland Office responsibilities specific to the province. As with the SO the number of departments exceeds the number of junior ministers and so one minister may be given responsibility for more than one department. At the moment, the secretary of state is assisted by two ministers of state and two parliamentary undersecretaries. In addition, he has an executive committee, comprising these ministers and the civil-service heads of department. It serves as a coordinating committee and has been likened by one minister to a cabinet.[32]

The department is unlike the Scottish Office in that the ministers do not sit for seats in the province. Also, it is far less of a lobbying department for its territory in London. Rather, it is more concerned with the task of administration and with carrying out United Kingdom government policy in the province. Much of its time has been taken up with bringing the law in the province in line with that of the rest of the United Kingdom. For the secretary of state, the task is one of heading an administrative department while at the same time seeking a political solution to the problems peculiar to the province. It places him in a unique position.

When first introduced, direct rule in Northern Ireland was intended as a temporary expedient but has so far survived the various attempts to introduce new forms of government for the province. These will be discussed shortly. Under the provisions of the Northern Ireland Act of 1982 there now exists an elected assembly to which executive and legislative powers can be devolved on a rolling basis (see below), but so far no such powers have been transferred.

The Welsh Office constitutes something of a hybrid department. It is much smaller than the Scottish Office and the Northern Ireland Office—with a secretary of state, one minister of state, and one parliamentary under-secretary—and does not enjoy quite the same degree of autonomy. Nonetheless, it has multi-functional responsibilities. Within Wales, it has responsibility for health, primary and secondary education, town and country planning, housing, local government, new towns, roads, water, forestry, tourism, national parks, and historic buildings. It shares with the Ministry of Agriculture responsibility for agriculture in the principality. It also has a general duty to supervise the carrying out of government policy in Wales. Like its other territorial counterparts, it is based mainly in the territory itself, with its headquarters in Cardiff. It maintains only a small office in London.

To reiterate, the government of the United Kingdom fulfils various functions. In England, these are carried out by different, functionally based departments, whereas in Scotland, Northern Ireland, and, to a lesser extent, Wales they are carried out by single, territorially defined departments that operate largely as mini-governments. However, such an arrangement has not met with the overwhelming approval of the inhabitants of the territories concerned. Direct rule in Northern Ireland, as I have noted, was intended as a temporary expedient. In Scotland and Wales, government by non-elected and, despite their location, United Kingdom government departments has generated calls for change. In recent years, proposals for reform have been on the agenda of political debate.

PROPOSED: DEVOLUTION

Of reforms proposed in subnational government in recent years, the most prominent have been those for the devolution of executive and legislative powers to some form of elected assemblies in Scotland and Wales, and, in a somewhat different format, Northern Ireland. Various schemes have been proposed and received parliamentary approval but none has yet proved successful.

Devolution: Scotland and Wales

The proposal for devolving some executive and legislative powers to national assemblies in Scotland and Wales is not new. The Liberal party has advocated the somewhat more radical proposal of federalism for some time,[33] and the Scottish National party favors complete independence for Scotland, though prepared to accept some form of devolved government in the interim. Only in the past 10 to 15 years, however, has devolution become a significant issue of political debate.

Some form of home rule for Scotland and Wales has been advocated by the Scottish National (SNP) and Plaid Cymru (PC) parties, respectively, since their formation earlier this century, but the main achievement of the two parties prior to the 1960s was, as we have noted (Chapter 6), simply to survive. This situation was to change somewhat in the 1960s, with each party winning one seat at a by-election as well as making gains in local elections. The apparent growing strength of nationalist sentiment was sufficient to encourage the Labour government to establish a Royal Commission on the Constitution; announced in 1968, it was appointed in 1969 and reported in 1973. The nationalist parties had not done well in the 1970 general election, the SNP only winning one seat. Four years later, the picture had changed significantly: the Royal Commission had reported in favor of some form of devolved government and there had emerged what A. H. Birch has referred to as the "eruptive factor,"[34] North Sea oil. The SNP was able to play on the argument that the location of the off-shore oil fields meant that the oil was Scotland's as much as anyone's and that revenue from it would be sufficient to make a Scottish government viable. By playing on the expectation of a rising middle class in Scotland, whose expectations had been left unfulfilled by the Westminster government, the SNP began to make electoral inroads into the strength of both main parties. By playing on the cultural fears of the Welsh people, the PC also achieved a somewhat more limited impact in Wales.[35] In the February 1974 general election, the SNP won 7 of the 71 Scottish seats and the PC won 2 of the 36 Welsh seats. In the October general election, the SNP increased the number of seats won to 11 and the PC to 3. Of the SNP's 11 seats, 9 were won from the Conservatives but the party had come second in 35 out of 41 Labour-held seats. In the total number of votes received, it was the second largest party in Scotland.

The Labour government returned in 1974 saw the prospect of the SNP developing into the dominant political party in Scotland and in so doing ruining Labour's chances of winning future elections (both Scotland and Wales constitute important electoral bases for the party; see Chapter 5). In order to respond to the nationalist challenge, the government put forward proposals for a form of devolved government in both Scotland and Wales[36] and in 1976 introduced a Scotland and Wales bill. The bill provided for an elected assembly in each of the two countries, each with a fixed term of four years, with responsibility for country-wide concerns such as health, land-use, and tourism, though with Scotland having more devolved power than Wales. Neither assembly was to have powers of taxation; money was to be provided by means of a block grant voted by Parliament as well as through local authority taxation and borrowing by local authorities and public corporations.

The bill ran into serious parliamentary opposition. The Conservative Opposition did not like the provisions and decided to vote against it. Many Labour members also found it unpalatable. A number were opposed to devolution, seeing it as a step on the road to eventual independence. Some MPs from the North of England disliked it because they felt that it would effectively discriminate against regions that were not to have similar assemblies. In order to facilitate the bill's passage, the government announced its agreement to the devolution proposals being submitted to referendums in Scotland and Wales. The bill achieved a second reading (see Chapter 11) but ran into sustained opposition from both sides of the House in committee (taken on the floor of the House) and the government decided to introduce a motion to limit debate (a guillotine motion). The vote on the guillotine maximized the opposition to the measure and with 22 Labour MPs voting with the Opposition (a further 21 abstained from voting), the government suffered an embarrassing defeat.[37]

The government decided not to proceed with the bill as it stood. Instead, it introduced two new bills, the Scotland bill and the Wales bill. The Scotland bill largely retained the proposals incorporated in the original bill, while the Wales bill provided only for a very limited form of devolution to the principality. On this occasion the government achieved passage of both bills, though only after a number of amendments had been carried against the government's wishes. The most important of these stipulated that if 40% of eligible voters did not cast a "yes" vote in the referendum in Scotland, the government was to bring forward a motion for the repeal of the act. A similar provision was inserted in the Wales bill. In this way, MPs created an important and unprecedented hurdle to the achievement of devolved government.

The referendums in Scotland and Wales were scheduled to be held on March 1, 1979 and were preceded by vigorous campaigns in the two countries. In Wales, it appeared that the prospect of devolved government aroused suspicion among non-Welsh-speaking inhabitants and was not gaining overwhelming support. In Scotland, the debate was keenly fought between pro- and antidevolutionists. Some opponents feared devolution would constitute the thin end of the wedge, leading to an eventual break-up of the United Kingdom; supporters argued that it was necessary in order to maintain the unity of the kingdom. On March 1, 956,330 voters in Wales voted "no" to the devolution proposals: only 243,048 voted "yes." The result in the principality was clearly a decisive rejection. In Scotland, the result was a close one: 1,230,937 people voted "yes," and 1,153,502 voted "no." Although a slight majority of those who voted had opted for the devolution proposals, the number voting yes did not constitute 40% of all eligible voters. As a consequence, the cabinet decided not to proceed with devolution, a decision that precipitated Nationalist MPs to withdraw their support from the government. This loss of Nationalist support deprived the government of a majority in a vote of confidence on March 28, 1979. The result was a general election. In the new Parliament, the Conservative government introduced the relevant motions for the repeal of the two acts and both motions were carried.

In the wake of the 1979 general election, it looked as if devolution was no longer an important issue on the political agenda. The SNP won only two seats in the election, as did the Plaid Cymru. The new government was not notably keen to pursue the issue[38] and other matters soon came to the fore. However, as the Parliament progressed, the subject began to reemerge as a feature of debate. Indeed, a number of more radical proposals began to be aired.

The arguments advanced in favor of devolution had centered on both consent and effectiveness. It was argued that decisions taken by elected government based in Scotland and Wales would be more efficient and effective because of a better appreciation of the area and its needs, as well as available resources, and that such an elected government would enhance consent by being closer to the people. This line of reasoning was employed to justify the case for devolution not only to Scotland and Wales but also to English regions. A minority report to the Royal Commission on the Constitution had recommended the creation of five elected regional assemblies in England, additional to ones in Scotland and Wales. This began to emerge as a topic of debate in the early 1980s, as did more radical extensions of the idea. The Liberal party, as we have mentioned, favored and continues to favor some form of federal government. The new Social Democratic party began to press for a comprehensive scheme of decentralized government. Power, it argued, should be devolved to people in their local communities. This entailed not only a scheme of devolved government but also decentralization of the National Health Service and schemes for worker-participation in industry. "The case for decentralizing government," declared an SDP discussion paper, "rests, in essence, on the belief that decisions should be taken as closely to the people who are affected by them as possible. People know what they want, perceive what they need and should be free to choose how to attain their ends."[39] Devolving governmental responsibilities to regional assemblies, it was also argued, would reduce the pressure on central government and on Parliament. Both government and people, it was felt, would benefit.

Despite such advocacy of devolution, there remains important opposition to the proposal. Fears remain that devolving government powers could lead to the break-up of the United Kingdom and furthermore, it is argued, it could introduce another expensive and unnecessary layer of government, one that is not wanted (people are more interested in their needs being met by government—any government—than in being able to elect another governmental body) and that could lead to greater economic inequality among the regions.[40] There is, as even some SDP supporters recognize, a potential incompatibility between the party's twin goals of equality and decentralization.[41] All but one of the political parties most interested in the subject are supporters of some form of devolved government: the one exception is the party in power, which has not shown any recent enthusiasm to pursue the issue—i.e., the Conservative party. The return of a future Labour government or a government dependent on the support of the Liberal/SDP Alliance would greatly increase the likelihood of some form of devolution being introduced, though given the other demands likely to be made of government and any absence of a nationalist upsurge (in 1983 both Nationalist parties appeared in a relatively weak state, the SNP in particular being rent by internal dissent), the chances are not great of devolution occupying the attention of government in the immediately foreseeable future. It is on the agenda of political debate but, at the moment, is not prominent.

Northern Ireland

The problems of Northern Ireland and its form of government are, as I have said, particular to the province.[42] Those problems arouse perplexity, incredulity, and misunderstanding in other parts of the United Kingdom as well as abroad. (Indeed, the failure of some Americans to comprehend the problems of the province has been a bone of contention both within Northern Ireland and in government circles.) Whereas in Britain there is a consensus favoring a certain norm of political behavior—abiding by the rules of the constitutional game even if one favors a change of the rules (or even a new game)—there is no such consensus in Northern Ireland. There never has been. To Britons reared on solving or avoiding disputes by talk and compromise, the vehement and often violent pursuit by opposing communities of mutually exclusive goals is a vexing and near-incomprehensible phenomenon.

The history of Ireland has been a depressing and troubled one extending over many centuries and marked by bitter conflict between the English and the Irish and, within Ireland, between indigeneous Catholic Irish and Protestant Scottish Presbyterian settlers. The Irish uprising in 1916 forced the United Kingdom government to recognize Irish demands for self-determination. In 1920 the Westminster Parliament passed the Government of Ireland Act. It provided for home rule in the country, creating two Parliaments: one for the 6 northern counties, part of the region of Ulster, and one for the remaining 26 counties. The provisions for the southern counties were stillborn. The continuing troubles in the country resulted in the Treaty of Ireland of 1922, which realized the Irish Free State. Ireland was partitioned and the provisions of the 1920 Act applied in the new province of Northern Ireland. A bicameral Parliament was established at Stormont, from which an executive was drawn. The new government of the province exercised a number of devolved powers and in exercising those powers was not much hindered by the Westminster government. British politicians were not keen to be drawn again into the infructuous bog of Irish politics.

The province of Northern Ireland was created at the forceful behest of the Protestant community of the North. Largely derived from Scottish Presbyterian stock, it had no wish to be engulfed within a Catholic Irish state. Within the new province, it was dominant. It was not, though, the only community within the province. One third of the population was Catholic. The religious divide between the two communities was reinforced by social, economic, and educational differences as well as by centuries of ingrained animosity. Catholic children were educated in Catholic schools, were taught Irish history, played Gaelic games, and lived in Catholic communities. Protestant children were taught British history, played non-Gaelic games, lived in Protestant communities, and were taught to look down on Catholics as being lazy and threatening to the existence of the province. Catholics, in turn, looked on Protestants as being gravely in error. The divisions ran deep. The Protestants continued proudly to celebrate the victory of Protestant William of Orange in the Battle of the Boyne in 1690. Indeed, in the new province the anniversary of the victory was made a public holiday.

Northern Ireland after 1922 became for all intents and purposes a one-party province. The Unionist party, representing the Protestants, regularly won two-thirds of the seats at Stormont (there was little alternation of seats from one party to the other) and formed the government, enjoying uninterrupted power. Despite occasional violence by the so-called Irish Republican Army (the IRA), which wanted a united Ireland and was prepared to engage in terrorist activities to achieve it, the Stormont government enjoyed sufficient coercive powers to impose its will and did so in a manner that favored the Protestants. Catholics were discriminated against in the allocation of houses and jobs, and were forced to live in an environment where they felt themselves to be second-class citizens. There was little they could do about it within the existing political structure: unlike American blacks, they had no Bill of Rights or Supreme Court to call in aid and the Westminster government preferred not to get involved.

The position in the province was to change in the latter half of the 1960s. A new, relatively liberal Unionist prime minister, Terence O'Neill, sought better relations with the Republic of Ireland, a move that caused consternation in the more traditional ranks of his party. On the Catholic side, the steps taken by the O'Neill government were seen as being too little and too late. A civil-rights movement sprang up in the province, inspired by the experience of the United States. The Civil Rights Association was formed in 1967, joined the following year by a more revolutionary organization, the People's Democracy. The two groups engaged in tactics designed to provoke a violent response in the hope that this would draw attention to the plight of the Catholic minority in the province. They organized demonstrations and marches. These resulted in a vigorous reaction from the police force, the Royal Ulster Constabulary, as well as from various Protestant groups. Clashes between protesters and their opponents erupted into civil disorder that the police and their auxiliary forces, the so-called B-Specials (despised in the Catholic community), were unable to contain. In August 1969, at the request of the Northern Ireland cabinet, the Westminster government introduced troops into the province to maintain order. In return for such action, the government insisted on phasing out the B-Specials and the introduction of full civil rights for Roman Catholics. Ensuring that the latter demand was complied with was another matter.

The arrival of troops was initially welcomed by Catholics in the province. However, the use of troops to support the civil authorities—in other words, the Protestant government and the police—and the searching of Catholic areas for arms produced a rapid dissipation of that support. A "shooting war" broke out between the IRA and the British army in February 1971. In August, the British government decided to intern without trial suspected IRA leaders. Instead of lessening the violence, the action appeared to exacerbate it: internment aroused greater sympathy for the IRA cause among the Catholic community and the interned leaders were replaced by more extreme followers. At the same time, tension increased between the Stormont and Westminster governments, the former contending that the latter was not doing enough to counter the activities of the IRA. The Stormont government even made a request for troops in the province to be put under its control. The request was denied.

Violence in the province became more marked toward the end of 1971, with more than 100 explosions a month. In the first two months of 1972, 49 people were killed and a further 257 injured as a result of gunshots and bombings. In an attempt to break the deadlock in the province, the Conservative government at Westminster decided to pursue some form of political initiative: pressure for such action had been building up for some weeks, both abroad and at home, including pressure from the Labour Opposition. The government's proposals included periodic plebiscites on the issue of the border, a start to the phasing out of internment, and the transfer of responsibility for law and order from Stormont to London. The last proposal proved unacceptable to the Northern Ireland cabinet, which made clear that it would resign if the proposal was implemented. In consequence, Prime Minister Edward Heath informed the House of Commons on March 24, 1972 that the British government was left with no alternative but to assume full and direct responsibility for the administration of Northern Ireland until such time as a political solution to the problem of the province could be achieved. In order to give effect to the government's decision, the Northern Ireland (Temporary Provisions) bill was quickly passed by Parliament, enjoying the support of the Labour Opposition as well as of the Liberals. The new act suspended the Stormont Parliament and transferred its powers to the Westminster government. A new Northern Ireland Office was established under a secretary of state. The first occupant of the office was William Whitelaw.

The tasks of the new secretary of state were twofold. He had to try to maintain security within the province, doing so in a way that would not alienate either community (the Protestant community by not doing enough, the Catholic community by doing too much), while at the same time seeking a political solution that was acceptable to both. The solution favored by the government, and supported by the Labour Opposition, was the creation of a power-sharing assembly in the province—i.e., an assembly with devolved powers and with power shared among the different parties: in other words, the Catholics were to have some part in government. Mr. Whitelaw held a conference attended by parties from the province and then published a White Paper outlining proposals for an assembly elected by a form of proportional representation. Agreement was also reached with the government of the Irish Republic on the establishment of a consultative council of Ireland to provide what was commonly referred to as "the Irish dimension."

Elections to the new assembly, a unicameral body with 78 members, took place in June 1973. Unionists of different descriptions won 50 of the seats. The second largest number, 19, was won by the predominantly Catholic Social Democratic and Labour party (SDLP). In December, agreement was finally reached on the formation of an executive, comprising six members of the Official Unionist party, four members of the SDLP, and one member drawn from the nonsectarian Alliance party. The executive took office on January 1, 1974. The creation of the power-sharing executive and the council of Ireland was opposed by a large section of the Protestant community. In the February 1974 general election, 11 of the 12 seats in the province went to Unionists of one hue or another who were opposed to power sharing. A province-wide strike was organized by the Protestant Ulster Workers Council. It proved devastatingly effective, for all intents and purposes virtually bringing the province to a standstill. The new Labour government in London was unwilling to employ its coercive powers to try to break the strike. The executive resigned. It had lasted four months.

With the collapse of the executive, the province reverted to direct rule from London. Two months later, the government published a White Paper proposing an elected constitutional convention as a medium for political leaders in the province to seek an acceptable settlement. The White Paper made clear the government's own continuing commitment to the principle of power-sharing. In elections to the convention, held on May 1, 1975, 46 of the 78 seats went to Unionists opposed to power-sharing. Only 5 members representing the pro-power-sharing Unionist party of Northern Ireland were returned. The convention was a failure. It issued a report favoring a Stormont-type cabinet government—i.e., a majority party exercising all governmental powers unhindered by any sharing of such powers with minority parties. The British government rejected the report and asked the convention to reconvene and reconsider. The reconvened convention failed to reach any new agreement. Recognizing that no further progress could be made, the British government introduced the necessary order to bring the convention to an end. It was dissolved on March 6, 1976.

For the next three years, the government pursued the approach of trying to maintain order in the province while encouraging its people and their leaders to reach agreement among themselves. Some modest proposals for a nonlegislative assembly were made, only to be rejected by the parties in Northern Ireland. Various attempts by the Conservative secretary of state appointed in 1979, Humphrey Atkins, to find some acceptable compromise among the parties failed. A conference he convened at the beginning of 1980 was boycotted by the Official Unionist party. The parties that did attend disagreed on the form of government they favored for the province. A proposal by Mr. Atkins to create an advisory council of elected officials drawn from the province, to fulfil advisory and reporting functions until such time as a more durable settlement could be reached, was stillborn. It was overshadowed by the hunger strikes of IRA prisoners in the Maze prison (demanding various concessions, including the reintroduction of "political status") and by a recommendation from former prime minister James Callaghan that the province develop into a "broadly independent State."[43] The problem of Northern Ireland remained intractable.

The government continued to pursue policies that sought to maintain order and move in the direction of a political settlement, but in so doing ran the risk of alienating both communities within the province. Its refusal to give in to the demands of the IRA hunger strikers forced an end to the strike but the strikers had aroused sympathy for the IRA cause among a large section of the Catholic community. One hunger striker, Bobby Sands, was elected as an MP in a by-election in Fermanagh and South Tyrone. He died a month later. Protestants for their part were extremely suspicious and dismayed by meetings between Mrs. Thatcher and her opposite number in the Irish Republic, meetings that resulted in the agreement on the formation of an Anglo-Irish intergovernmental council. The council was to involve regular meetings at ministerial and official level to discuss matters of common concern between the two governments. Protestants were also highly critical of the government's security policy in the province, considering it to be inadequate. In November 1981, a Unionist MP, Robert Bradford, was assassinated. The leader of the Democratic Unionist party, Ian Paisley, accused the prime minister of being a traitor to Northern Ireland.[44] He also threatened to make the province "ungovernable." For the government, the problem appeared to be getting worse rather than better.

In 1982, a political initiative was launched by the new secretary of state for Northern Ireland, James Prior. The scheme became known as one of "rolling devolution." Under Mr. Prior's proposals, a 78-member assembly was to be elected by a method of proportional representation. Where the scheme differed from earlier ones was in the internal organization and powers of the assembly. It was to have a committee system based on government departments. Each committee was to have a salaried chairman and up to two salaried deputy chairmen. The chairmen and deputy chairmen would be chosen so as to reflect the party composition of the assembly. The committees would have powers to make reports to the assembly and to the secretary of state. The concept of "rolling devolution" was introduced by allowing the assembly to propose at any time the transfer of executive responsibilities for any particular department to its own jurisdiction. It would thus be possible for certain departments to be devolved, assembly members taking over as ministers, while other departments remained the responsibility of the secretary of state. The ultimate objective was to be full devolution, but achieved at a pace made possible by the assembly itself. As a Conservative party publication pointed out, even if the proposals succeeded only in part, they would not hamper further achievements later on. If partial devolution went wrong, "the Assembly can survive without jeopardizing the scheme as a whole."[45]

Although the concept of rolling devolution appeared to have much to commend it, Mr. Prior's scheme began to run into trouble as the year progressed. He encountered some opposition from Ulster Unionist and some Conservative MPs during the passage of the necessary legislation through Parliament. (The Labour Opposition did not oppose the bill, seeing it as broadly in line with its own policy.) More importantly, reaction in the province itself did not bode well for the new assembly. Its success depended on the willingness of the main parties, both Protestant and Catholic, to contest seats and to play an active part in its workings. In August, the main Catholic party, the SDLP, announced that it would contest the assembly elections but would boycott the assembly itself. Whereas the death knell of the previous attempts to establish a power-sharing assembly had been sounded by the Protestant Unionists, this time it appeared to have been sounded from the Catholic side.

The elections to the assembly in October 1982 proved to be even more disastrous from the British government's perspective than had been expected. The Sinn Fein party, the political wing of the Provisional IRA, garnered one-tenth of the first-preference votes cast and, more importantly, saw five of its candidates elected. It constituted a publicity coup for the party. Both the SDLP and Sinn Fein assembly members declined to participate in the body to which they had been elected. The elections, opined *The Times*, were "inopportune."[46] The deputy leader of the SDLP described them as a "ghastly failure."[47] When the assembly met, it comprised Unionist members, divided between Official Unionists and Democratic Unionists.

Despite the protestations of Mr. Prior, few commentators considered the new body to have much chance of realizing the minister's aims.

The apparent stillbirth of the assembly was, in many respects, unsurprising. It was predictable given the problems of the province and the perceptions of those problems by the Westminster government. Successive British governments, Labour and Conservative, proceeded on the basis that problems were solvable by rational people gathering round a table to discuss and resolve their differences. The approach adopted was thus either to leave it to the people of the province to sort out the problem for themselves or else to impose a power-sharing assembly that would force the two sides to work together. Both attempts failed because they sought to create a consensus where the basis for none existed. To some extent they constituted attempts to reconcile the irreconcilable. There is insufficient common ground between the two sides to allow for an acceptable solution. The British government is faced with factions within the province (and interests outside) that pursue mutually exclusive goals, feelings within the divided province being bitter and running deep. Each year brings events that tend to exacerbate the bitterness rather than alleviate it.

For the British government, the situation presents a perplexing and irritating conundrum. The government seeks to find a constitutional settlement for the province. But there is none that is acceptable to the various bodies involved. There are at least nine different constitutional options that have been canvassed. Each one is unacceptable to one or more interested parties. *Direct rule* has little attraction to any party as a permanent solution: it is recognized for what it is—a temporary expedient. *Self-government* within the United Kingdom, akin to the pre-1972 position, is favored by a majority of the Unionists but not by the Catholics, the British and Irish governments, or, for that matter, opinion within the United States. *Integration* within the United Kingdom, analogous to the position of, say, Scotland and Wales, finds favor among some Unionists but is unacceptable to a majority of Catholics as well as to the British government: the problems peculiar to the province are thought to require a constitutional framework distinct from that of the rest of the United Kingdom.

A *power-sharing assembly* is supported by the British government but is opposed by a significant and influential fraction of Unionists, who object to sharing power with a minority not committed to the maintenance of the union with Britain, and is increasingly unacceptable to the SDLP, which considers that it does not go far enough: the SDLP now wants any settlement to be within the context of an "Irish dimension." *Unification* with the Republic of Ireland is sought by the Irish Government and by Catholics in the North and in the long term has a certain appeal to the British government. It is totally opposed by the Protestant majority in the province. An absolute majority voted to maintain the union in a plebiscite in 1973: 99% of those who voted—58% of the total electorate—voted for retention.

A *federal Ireland* is unacceptable to the majority of Protestants, as it is to the IRA: the Protestants consider that such a solution would go too far, the IRA that it would not go far enough. A *redrawing of the boundary* between Northern Ireland and the Republic has been canvassed by some writers but is unacceptable to a majority of both Protestants and Catholics. A redrawing of the boundary would solve little and would almost certainly create new problems, including the possibility of a refugee problem (few Protestants would wish to remain in Fermanagh if it became part of the Republic). The creation of an *independent Northern Ireland* has been advocated by some politicians, notably James Callaghan, but finds little favor among Catholics, Protestants, the British and Irish governments, and other countries. It would be unlikely to be able to sustain itself as an independent entity.

The one other solution which has been raised is for the *withdrawal of British troops,* allowing the competing forces within the province to sort out, or rather fight out, the destiny of the province. It has a certain appeal to opinion within Britain, tired of the terrorist activities conducted by the IRA both within the province and on the British mainland, but is not acceptable to the government. Successive governments have accepted responsibility for the province, admitting the need to try to maintain order and to create the framework for a solution, and making clear a commitment to maintain the Union so long as a majority of the people of Northern Ireland wish to maintain it. There is also the realization that to withdraw troops could pre-cipitate a bloodbath within the province, with the conflict spreading into the Republic and possibly onto the British mainland as well. As much as Britain would like to be rid of the problem, it accepts that it cannot just wash its hands of the difficulty.[48]

In summary, then, Britain is faced with a problem that admits of no obvious or easy solution. It has tended to proceed on the basis of a settle-ment premised on traditional British assumptions and for that very reason its efforts have tended to be unsuccessful: it is faced with a very non-British problem. It is a problem that annually takes more lives within the province and sometimes, in quite horrific attacks of violence, on the mainland as well. It is a problem that Britain would like to be free of but Britain is not prepared to give in to men of violence. The one thing that prevents the IRA from achieving its goal of a united Ireland is the very violence they pursue in order to achieve it. The problem of Northern Ireland is one riddled with paradox—and there is no obvious solution.

SUMMARY

Below the level of national government in Britain, the picture is a complex one. Scotland, Northern Ireland, and Wales each has a multi-functional government department largely responsible for the administration of the territory. At a regional level (which usually means regions within England, plus Scotland, Wales, and Northern Ireland), there are disparate and discrete public bodies, such as the regional water authorities and the regional health authorities, while at the level of counties and towns there are elected councils.

Despite this complexity, these bodies have one thing in common. They are subordinate units of government. What powers they enjoy are granted at the discretion of Parliament, which means in practice (or largely so) that of the government. As resources have diminished, central government has proved increasingly willing to rein in some of the activities of these subordinate units. Squeezed between the demands and expectations of local electors and those of central government, local government, particularly in the 1980s, is not in an enviable position.

In terms of political authority, local government can be seen to be encountering problems in raising resources to meet its commitments to the local community, hemmed in by the demands of local ratepayers and the limitations imposed by central government, and to be having difficulty in maintaining the consent of citizens. Massive increases in rate demands, increases in recent years exceeding 100% in some authorities, tend to contribute to civic indifference. Attempts to maintain political authority by the creation of national or regional assemblies, bringing some decision-making closer to the people, have not come to fruition or else, in the unique case of Northern Ireland, have failed. There is no consensus among political leaders as to what the next step should be.

NOTES

1. The secretary of state for Scotland is vested with similar powers under the Local Government (Miscellaneous Provisions) Scotland Act 1981.

2. *The Times,* August 2, 1983.

3. On the constraints imposed by legislation, see E. Page, "Laws and Orders in Central-Local Government Relations," *Studies in Public Policy No. 102* (Centre for the Study of Public Policy, 1982).

4. *Politics Today,* No. 11, June 7, 1982 (Conservative Central Office, 1982), p. 199.

5. M. Beloff and G. Peele, *The Government of the United Kingdom* (Weidenfeld & Nicolson, 1980), p. 267.

6. The attendance allowance covers travelling and other expenses. The maximum full daily allowance that could be claimed in 1983 (though authorities could set a lower rate) was £15.07 (approximately $22).

7. The functions and proximity of local councils make certain officials and committee chairmen more likely targets for attempts at corruption by bodies seeking preferential treatment than is the case at the more distant levels of central government.

8. See G. W. Jones, "The Functions and Organisation of Councillors," *Public Administration,* Summer 1973, pp. 140–41; and R. E. Jennings, "The Councillor as a Point of Access to Local Government," paper presented at the annual conference of the American Political Science Association, Washington, D.C., 1980.

9. Cited in P. Norton, *The Constitution in Flux* (Martin Robertson, 1982), p. 27.

10. See F. F. Ridley, "View from a Disaster Area: Unemployed Youth in Merseyside" in B. Crick (ed.), *Unemployment* (Methuen, 1981), p. 26.

11. A. King, "The Problem of Overload" in A. King (ed.), *Why Is Britain Becoming Harder to Govern?* (BBC, 1976), p. 9.

12. Government Green Paper, *Alternatives to Domestic Rates,* Cmnd. 8449 (Her Majesty's Stationery Office, 1981).

13. *Rates: Proposals for Rate Limitation and Reform of the Rating System,* Cmnd. 9008 (Her Majesty's Stationery Office, 1983).

14. *The Times,* August 2, 1983.

15. See B. W. Hogwood, "Introduction" in B. W. Hogwood and M. Keating (eds.), *Regional Government in England* (Oxford University Press, 1982), pp. 10–12.

16. B. W. Hogwood, "The regional dimension of industrial policy administration" in Hogwood and Keating, pp. 106–7.

17. Ibid., p. 115.

18. C. Gray, "The Regional Water Authorities" in Hogwood and Keating, p. 143.

19. Ibid., pp. 159–60.

20. Ibid., p. 162.

21. C. Ham, *Health Policy in Britain* (Macmillan, 1982), pp. 27–28 and 109–12.

22. Ibid., pp. 28–29.

23. S. C. Haywood and H. J. Elcock, "Regional Health Authorities: Regional Government or Central Agencies?" in Hogwood and Keating, p. 131.

24. See H. J. Elcock and S. Haywood, *The Buck Stops Where? Accountability and Control in the National Health Service* (University of Hull Institute for Health Studies, 1980).

25. See. B. W. Hogwood and P. D. Lindley, "Variations in regional boundaries" in Hogwood and Keating, pp. 21–49.

26. M. Keating and A. Midwinter, *The Government of Scotland* (Mainstream Publishing, 1983), p. 14. This section draws largely on this work.

27. Ibid., p. 17.

28. Ibid., p. 17.

29. See ibid.

30. For the relationship between the United Kingdom and Stormont, see D. Birrell and A. Murie, *Policy and Government in Northern Ireland* (Gill and Macmillan, 1980).

31. See ibid., pp. 82–86 and 312. This section draws heavily on this work.

32. Ibid., p. 84.

33. D. Steel refers to the commitment to such a policy stemming from Gladstone's pamphlet of 1886 arguing for a reform of government consistent with the aspirations of the individual nations in Great Britain. D. Steel, "Federalism" in N. MacCormick (ed.), *The Scottish Debate* (Oxford University Press, 1970), p. 81.

34. A. H. Birch, *Political Integration and Disintegration in the British Isles* (George Allen & Unwin, 1977).

35. See Norton, *The Constitution in Flux,* pp. 175–76.

36. See ibid., pp. 178–79.

37. *House of Commons Debates,* Vol. 926, col. 1361–66.

38. See Norton, *The Constitution in Flux,* pp. 180–81 and 286.

39. R. Maclennan, "Decentralisation of Government," *SDP Discussion Paper No. 1,* Social Democratic Party Conference, 1981.

40. See G. Smith, "Back on the devolution trail," *The Times,* July 13, 1982.

41. See I. Bradley, *Breaking the Mould?* (Martin Robertson, 1981), p. 135, and Maclennan.

42. This section is based largely but not wholly on Norton, *The Constitution in Flux,* Ch. 10, and P. Norton, *Conservative Dissidents* (Temple Smith, 1978), pp. 82–90, 135–37 and 156–58.

43. *House of Commons Debates,* Sixth Series, Vol. 7, col. 1050.

44. See Norton, *The Constitution in Flux,* p. 199.

45. "Northern Ireland," *Politics Today,* 10, May 24, 1982 (Conservative Research Department, 1982), p. 178.

46. *The Times,* editorial, October 27, 1982.

47. S. Mallon, "Ulster: Time to Face Reality," *The Times,* October 27, 1982.

48. This summary is derived from Norton, *The Constitution in Flux,* pp. 199–209.

The European Communities

Government beyond the Center

PRIOR TO THE 1970s, the United Kingdom had entered into various treaty obligations with other nations. It was a founding member of the United Nations Organization. It had joined the North Atlantic Treaty Organization (NATO). It signed, though did not incorporate into domestic law, the European Convention on Human Rights. At no time, though, did it hand over to a supranational body power to formulate regulations that were to have domestic application within the United Kingdom and be enforceable at law.

This was to change on January 1, 1973. On that date, the United Kingdom became a member of the European Communities. Forty-two volumes of legislation promulgated by institutions of the European Communities were incorporated into British law and, under the provisions of the 1972 European Communities Act, future legislation emanating from the Communities was to be incorporated as well. The United Kingdom entered into a relationship for which the United States has no parallel.

THE EUROPEAN COMMUNITIES

The European Communities comprise the European Steel and Coal Community, the European Atomic Energy Community (Euratom), and the better-known European Economic Community (the EEC). The Steel and Coal Community was formed in 1951 under the Treaty of Paris. It placed iron, steel, and coal production in member countries under a common authority. Euratom and the EEC were created under the Treaty of Rome and came into being on January 1, 1958. Euratom was designed to help create a civil nuclear industry in Europe. The EEC formed a common market for goods within the community of member states. The three bodies were merged in 1967 to form the European Communities (the EC).

Britain declined to join the individual bodies when they were first formed. The Labour government in 1951 found the supranational control of the Steel and Coal Community to be unacceptable. The succeeding Conservative government was not initially attracted by the concept of the EEC. The economic and political arguments for joining, which weighed heavily with the member states, did not carry great weight with British politicians. Britain was still seen as a world power. It was enjoying a period of prosperity. It had strong political and trading links with the Commonwealth. It had a "special relationship" with the United States. It had stood alone successfully during the Second World War. Lacking the experience of German occupation and the need to recreate a polity, Britain was not subject to the psychological appeal of a united Europe, so strong on the continental mainland.[1] Neither main political party was strongly attracted to the idea of a union with such an essentially foreign body. The Conservatives still hankered after the idea of Empire, something that had died as a result of the war (Britain could no longer afford to maintain an empire and the principle of self-determination had taken root) and for which the Commonwealth now served as something of a substitute. Labour politicians viewed with distrust the creation of a body that they saw as inherently antisocialist, designed to shore up the capitalist edifice of Western Europe and frustrate any future socialist policies that a Labour government in Britain would seek to implement. It was one of the few issues about which the leader of the Labour party, Hugh Gaitskell, found himself in agreement with left-wingers within his own party.

The attitude of the British government toward the EEC, at both ministerial and official level, was to undergo significant change in 1960. Britain's economic problems had become more apparent. Growth rates compared poorly with those of the six member states of the EEC (i.e., France, Germany, Italy, and the Benelux countries). There was a growing realization that having lost an empire, Britain had gained a Commonwealth. That Commonwealth, however, was not proving as amenable to British leadership as many Conservatives had hoped, nor was it proving to be the source of trade and materials that had been expected. Even the special relationship with the United States was undergoing a period of strain. The "special" appeared to be seeping out of the relationship. Some anti-Americanism lingered in Conservative ranks following the insistence of the White House that Britain abort its operation to occupy the Suez Canal zone in 1956, a distrust still not wholly dispelled. The sudden cancellation by the United States administration in 1960 of a missile, the Blue Streak, that Britain had ordered and intended to employ as the major element of its nuclear defense policy awakened British politicians to the fact that in the Atlantic partnership, Britain was very much the junior partner. The United States administration itself began to pay more attention to the EEC, and President Kennedy made clear to his friend and distant relative, Prime Minister Harold Macmillan, "that a British decision to join the Six would be welcome."[2] The option became one that had an increasing attraction to Britain.

Politically, the EEC was seen as a vehicle through which Britain could once again play a leading role on the world stage. Economically, it would provide a tariff-free market of 180 million people, it would provide the advantages of economy of scale, and it was assumed that it would encourage greater efficiency in British industry through more vigorous competition. Political and economic advantages were seen as inextricably linked. Economic strength was necessary to underpin the maintenance of political authority.[3] "If we are to meet the challenge of Communism, . . ." Macmillan wrote to President Kennedy, "[we must show] that our modern society—the new form of capitalism—can run in a way that makes the fullest use of our resources and results in a steady expansion of our economic strength."[4] On July 31, 1961 he announced to the House of Commons that Britain was applying for membership.

The first application for membership was vetoed in January 1963 by the French president, General de Gaulle. He viewed British motives with suspicion, believing that Britain could serve as a vehicle for the United States to establish its dominance within the EEC. A second application was lodged in 1967, this time by the Labour government of Harold Wilson.[5] Agreement to open negotiations was reached eventually in 1969. Negotiations began under the newly returned Conservative government of Edward Heath in 1970. Relations between the British and French governments on the issue were now more amicable, de Gaulle having resigned the presidency in 1969, and no French veto was imposed. Negotiations were completed in 1971, and the British government recommended entry on the terms achieved. On October 28, 1971, following a six-day debate, the House of Commons gave its approval to the principle of membership on the terms negotiated. Voting was 356 votes in favor, 244 against.[6] Both parties were badly divided. Of Labour members, 69 voted with the Conservative government in favor of entry and a further 20 abstained from voting. Of Conservatives, 39 voted with the Labour Opposition against entry, a further 2 abstaining.[7] It was the most divisive vote of the Parliament.

At the beginning of 1972, the Treaty of Accession was signed and the European Communities bill, to give legal effect to British membership, was given a second reading on February 17. In order to ensure its passage, Mr.

Heath made the vote one of confidence. Despite that, the majority of the bill was a slim one of only eight,[8] Opposition MPs having largely united against the measure. Despite sustained opposition from Labour members and a number of dissident Conservatives, the bill passed its remaining stages, being given a third reading on July 13.[9] The United Kingdom became a member of the European Communities on January 1, 1973.

Implications of Membership

Membership in the EC added a new dimension to the British Constitution. Under the provisions of the European Communities Act, existing EC law was to have general and binding applicability in the United Kingdom, as was all subsequent law promulgated by the Communities. Clause 2(1) of the act gives the force of law in the United Kingdom to "rights, powers, liabilities, obligations and restrictions from time to time created or arising by or under the Treaties." Clause 2(4) provides that directly applicable EC law should prevail over conflicting provisions of domestic legislation. The net effect of membership and the provisions of the act was to introduce two new decision-making bodies into the ambit of the British polity (the Council of Ministers and the European Communities Commission), to restrict the role and influence of Parliament in matters that came within the competence of the Communities, to inject a new judicial dimension to the Constitution (disputes concerning the treaties or legislation made under them to be treated by the British courts as a matter of law, with provision for their referral to the European court for a ruling), and to allow for British representation in the European Parliament, a body with limited but not unimportant powers.

Membership has also had significant economic implications. It has provided a tariff-free market, whence comes the popular term for the EEC as the "Common Market." The effect of membership has been to increase substantially trade between Britain and its new European partners. Between 1973 and 1981, British exports to EC countries increased by 27% a year, compared with a 19% average annual growth in the country's exports to the rest of the world. In 1980, British trade with EC countries produced a positive trade balance of £700 million (about $1,050 million).[10] By 1982, 43% of British exports went to EC countries, a further 14% going to European countries that had trading agreements with the EC. The extent of the dependence on EC trade in the 1980s was emphasized by the European Democratic Group (the group in the European Parliament formed and dominated by British Conservative members): it estimated, in 1982, that the jobs of no fewer than 2.5 million workers in Britain were dependent on trade with the EC.[11]

Administration by the EC of different funds has also had important economic effects. The agricultural guarantee and guidance fund is used to finance the EC common agricultural policy (the CAP). The basis of the policy is to ensure a secure food supply. However, it has proved to be a contentious issue, the CAP favoring price supports for farmers rather than cheap food, and hence working more in favor of member states that are net agricultural exporters and have large farming communities. Britain is a net importer with a small but efficient farming sector (see Chapter 1). Although the policy has benefited other countries more than Britain, most notably France, its supporters nonetheless maintain that it has proved useful in helping secure supplies for consumers at relatively stable prices. Less contentious has been the operation of the regional development fund, proposed in 1973 and established in 1975 to help the poorer regions of the EC. The fund can be used to contribute up to 50% of national expenditure on a given scheme if it is for the relief of agricultural poverty, for industrial change, or for the provision of infrastructure.[12] Between 1975 and 1979, Britain received about £250 million ($375 million) in assistance from the fund, including aid for building a reservoir in the North of England and for a variety of smaller projects in Wales. Similarly, various allocations have been made to Britain from the social fund, established to improve employment prospects for workers in the Community. Since 1973 it has been used to help agricultural workers who are leaving the land, workers obliged to leave textile and other industries, migrant workers requiring language or vocational training, handicapped workers, and those who are unemployed or in need of some form of training. Relative to the EC budget the fund is a relatively small one, though in 1978 it amounted to £381 million (about $570 million): of this, £75 million ($112 million) went to Britain, the second largest allocation after that to Italy.

The EC also administers a number of other funds and programs. It provides assistance for various energy projects and has an energy research and development program: this has a modest budget and supports shared-cost contracts, paying half the cost along with the organization concerned. There is also the European Investment Bank, created under the Treaty of Rome, which operates on a nonprofit basis to grant loans and guarantees that facilitate the financing of new investment and projects concerned with modernization. By 1979, Britain had benefited from over £1,000 million ($1,500 million) in low-interest loans from the Bank, most of the loans being used to support projects in the regions, such as water-supply schemes in Scotland and South Wales.

The net effect of these developments has been substantial in economic terms for Britain. However, that effect has not been totally beneficial. Overproduction in a number of agricultural sectors has led to a greater proportion than was previously envisaged of EC funds being devoted to the CAP, the result being that only limited funds are available for the schemes from which Britain derives more obvious benefit. Furthermore, the income of the EC comes from member states. Under the terms of British membership, Britain's net annual contribution to the EC increased during the 1970s. By 1979, the *net* annual contribution was £947 million (nearly $1,500 million).[13] This imbalance between contributions and receipts produced a political controversy, with the incoming prime minister in 1979, Mrs. Thatcher, denouncing the position as unjust and demanding a restructuring of the EC budgetary arrangements. She pursued the issue at summit meetings with other heads of government and an interim agreement was reached, after much acrimony, in May 1982 when a refund of £490 million ($735 million) was agreed for 1982 and the need to consider a long-term settlement was conceded.

The debate surrounding Britain's contribution was a politically contentious one. Membership of the EC has obviously had other important political implications as well. Transferring some decision-making powers to the EC has had important consequences for British government in terms not only of the locus of decision-making (the council and the commission) but also of the demands made of ministers and of officials. The continuing debate surrounding membership after 1973 resulted in a constitutional innovation, a national referendum in 1975, and the commitment of membership produced a new level of elections, to the European Parliament, in 1979. Britain's membership in the EC remains a controversial issue in the 1980s, the political parties in Britain, as we have seen (Chapter 6), taking very different positions on the issue. These implications can be briefly sketched under the headings of EC decision-making, constitutional developments, and the current debate.

EC Decision-Making

The decision-making competence of the EC covers subjects stipulated by the Treaties of Paris and Rome as well as various subjects that have been added by agreement at summit meetings or at meetings of the Council of Ministers, or which have evolved under the Rome Treaty. In addition to responsibility for removing trade barriers and administering the agricultural, regional, and social funds, the EC is charged with seeking to ensure the free movement of persons, services, and capital within the Community and with generating policies on external trade, overseas aid, energy, and consumer affairs. In order to eliminate barriers to the development of a common market, it has power to adjust national legal rules through what is known as harmonization procedures—in other words, to ensure that rules are standardized throughout the EC. Such harmonization procedures occupy a substantial amount of EC time and extend to a number of important areas, including taxation and commerce.

Within the EC, the main bodies are the Council of Ministers, the European Communities Commission, the Committee of Permanent Representatives, and the European Parliament (see Figure 10.1). In addition, there is the European Court of Justice, which ensures that EC law is observed in the

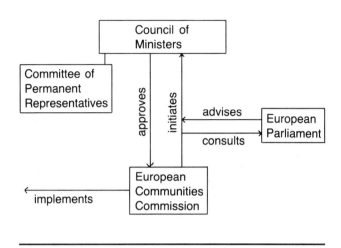

FIGURE 10.1   European Communities legislative process.

interpretation and application of the treaties, and itself can interpret EC law. The court's judgments are binding on member states and enforceable through the national courts.

The commission constitutes the bureaucracy of the European Communities. It is headed by fourteen commissioners. They are drawn from the member states (two from each of the larger countries of France, Britain, West Germany, and Italy; one from each of the smaller countries), though each takes an oath not to seek to represent national interests. From their number, a president is chosen to serve a two-year, renewable term. The commissioners head a large bureaucracy with a developed infrastructure. It now has 20 directorates-general covering all aspects of EC activities and employs a total of 11,000 people (a quarter of whom work in nuclear research establishments).[14] It is responsible both for the administration and the initiation of EC policy.

The policy-making process within the EC is basically as follows: The commission will propose a particular policy, which usually has evolved within one of the directorates. Once the policy has been adopted by the commission in the form of a "proposal," it is then sent to the secretariat of the Council of Ministers and is referred to the European Parliament. The role of the Parliament is largely though not exclusively a consultative one.[15] (It has the power to reject the EC budget and to dismiss *en bloc* the commission.) It works through a series of committees, and after Parliament has commented on the proposal, the proposal is put before the Council of Ministers. The council will take note of the proposal, passing it on to the council's subsidiary body, the Committee of Permanent Representatives (known as COREPER), which has responsibility for preparing the work of the council and for carrying out tasks assigned to the council. COREPER comprises, as the name suggests, official representatives (classified often as ambassadors) from the member states, each assisted by a staff of diplomats and officials seconded (released from regular duty and temporarily assigned elsewhere) from the national civil service. COREPER studies the proposal on behalf of the council, isolating any problems associated with it. If the committee reaches agreement it is usual for the council to adopt the proposal without further discussion.

The Council of Ministers is the body responsible for approving the proposal. The council comprises the ministers from the member states whose portfolios cover the subject under discussion. Thus, a proposal concerning agriculture will be considered by the council comprising agriculture ministers. (In practice, it would be more appropriate to refer therefore to *councils* of ministers.) The demands made of the council vary according to the subject. The Council of Foreign Ministers and the Council of Finance Ministers meet more often than do the others.[16] The council seeks to proceed on the basis of consensus and tacit agreement. Under the treaties, some decisions require unanimous assent; others may be reached by absolute or qualified majority. In a vote by absolute majority, each member state has one vote and a simple majority decision is binding. A qualified majority entails a weighting of the votes: each of the four larger states (France, Britain, West Germany, and Italy) has 10 votes, Belgium, Greece, and the Netherlands each have 5 votes, Denmark and the Republic of Ireland have 3 each, and Luxembourg has 2. (Denmark and the Republic of Ireland became members at the same time as the United Kingdom—January 1, 1973. Greece became a full member on January 1, 1981.) Out of the total of 63, 45 votes constitute a majority. Provisions for majority voting are rarely applied and decisions are usually postponed if one or more countries object in cases where unanimous votes are required. Once the council has reached agreement, it is then the task of the Commission to ensure or rather supervise the implementation of its decision: the actual implementation is left to the member states.

The structure and procedures, as well as the formal powers, of the EC have important implications for British government as well as Parliament. Policy-making takes place, so to speak, at one remove from domestic policy-making. The government is but 1 of 10 involved in the process and its most important power is a negative one: that is, the power to object to a proposal in the Council of Ministers. Furthermore, policy-making is a process that tends to favor civil-service influence. Much of the work is done by officials, both within the EC and in conjunction with those in member states. By the time a proposal comes before ministers, most of the preliminary work will have been completed.[17]

Once the council has given its assent to a measure, it then constitutes EC law. This can take different forms. It can be issued in the form of regulations, which apply directly as law in the member states; as directives, which bind the member states as to the results to be achieved, but not as to the means; or as decisions, recommendations, or opinions, none of which is binding. In Britain, Parliament can seek to influence the government prior to discussion in the Council of Ministers (both houses have committees to consider draft EC legislation), but once a regulation has been issued, there is nothing that members of Parliament can do about it. Assent to the measure has, in effect, been given in advance under the provisions of the 1972 European Communities Act. There is also the problem of ensuring effective scrutiny of draft legislation, given its extent and diversity, and with keeping abreast of its progress within the EC.[18] Insofar as a sustained attempt is made to subject the proposals of the commission and the council to scrutiny and influence, it is undertaken now more by the directly elected European Parliament than it is by the national assemblies of the member states.

Constitutional Developments

By the mid 1970s, British government was enmeshed in the work of the European Communities. Supporters of British membership in the Communities argued that Britain's place in the EC was further cemented by two important events of constitutional significance, both politically contentious, which took place in 1975 and 1979: respectively, the referendum on continued EC membership, and the election by popular vote of members of the European Parliament.

The Labour party was badly divided in the 1970s on the issue of British membership in the European Communities. In the 1974 general elections, in an attempt to maintain some semblance of unity on the issue, the Labour party committed itself to renegotiating the terms of British membership and then submitting the new terms to the British people, either at a general election or through the medium of a referendum.[19] Following the Labour return to office, the foreign secretary undertook the task of renegotiation, achieving some modification in the terms of Britain's membership. (A correcting mechanism "of a general application" was agreed for Britain's budget contribution, some concessions were achieved for the access of New Zealand dairy products to Britain,[20] and satisfactory assurances were deemed to have been given on the subject of regional aid.) The negotiations came to an end in March 1975. By that time the cabinet had decided to consult the electorate by means of an advisory referendum. Once the renegotiated terms were known, it recommended that electors cast a "yes" vote in favor of Britain's remaining within the EC on the basis of those terms. The Conservative and Liberal parties made a similar recommendation. On April 9, 1975, the

House of Commons approved the recommendation of the government to continue Britain's membership, doing so by a majority of 226 votes, though Labour members were deeply divided on the issue.[21] On June 5, the United Kingdom experienced its first national referendum: 17,378,581 electors voted "yes" and 8,470,073 voted "no" to Britain remaining within the EC on the renegotiated terms. Supporters of Britain's membership could point to an overwhelming majority in favor of British membership. Opponents had the consolation of pointing to a low turnout: only 64.5% of eligible Britons cast a ballot.

Prior to 1979, members of the European Parliament had been appointed by the member states. In Britain, the members had been drawn from existing MPs and peers. After some delay, the intention to elect members of the European Parliament (MEPs) was realized, with elections being held throughout the EC in June 1979. In the new directly elected Parliament, the United Kingdom was allocated 81 seats. For the election of the 78 members from Britain, the plurality method of election was employed. Because of the circumstances peculiar to Northern Ireland, a method of proportional representation was used for the return of the 3 members from the province. The remaining EC countries all employed some form, albeit not uniform, of proportional representation.[22] (The exception was Denmark's use of the plurality vote in Greenland.) Coming within three weeks of the Conservative victory in the May general election, the British elections witnessed a remarkable success for Conservative candidates. From the Conservative party, 60 MEPs were elected (see Table 10.1), capturing more than 50% of the votes cast. Labour came a poor second, capturing only 17 seats and 33% of the votes cast. For supporters of the EC, the elections marked another step on the road to European unity and marked a significant move in the

TABLE 10.1
British Elections to the European Parliament, 1979

Party	Seats Won	Total Votes	Percentage of Votes
Conservative	60	6,508,472	50.6
Labour	17	4,253,207	33.0
Liberal	0	1,690,598	13.1
Scottish National	1	247,836	1.9
Plaid Cymru	0	83,399	0.6
Ecology	0	17,953	0.1
Others	0	72,369	0.6

Northern Ireland: Fought under a system of proportional representation, one Democratic Unionist was elected, as were one Social Democratic and Labour party (SDLP) candidate and one Official Ulster Unionist.

direction of bringing electors closer to the Community, enhancing consent for the institutions that it embraced. Opponents could again point to a low turnout. Fewer than one in three of eligible electors (32.7%) bothered to go to the polling stations to cast a vote.[23]

By the beginning of the 1980s there were clear grounds for taking Britain's membership in the European Communities as a well-established fact. Britain had been a member of the EC for more than seven years, it was playing its full role in the institutions of the Communities, it was increasingly dependent on member states for trade, it had had its membership confirmed by the British electorate in a national referendum, and it had elected members to the European Parliament. Britain now appeared to be inextricably linked to the Communities. Nonetheless, however well-established a fact was Britain's membership, it was not a fact that was accepted with overwhelming enthusiasm by the population in Britain: public opinion on the issue over the past decade has often been indifferent or hostile, despite the outcome of the 1975 referendum. Continued membership was opposed by a significant fraction of the population as well as by a number of politicians. The Labour party became committed to a policy of British withdrawal. Britain's membership remained an item on the agenda of political debate.

THE CURRENT DEBATE

Although not occupying quite as central a position in political debate in the 1980s as it did at the beginning of the 1970s, the question of Britain's membership of the EC has remained a controversial one. It retains its supporters, especially at the elite level, but dissatisfaction with continued membership continues to be expressed by a significant section (currently, a majority) of the population, according to Gallup Polls. The relationship with the European Communities is not altogether a harmonious one.

Defenders of British membership can, as we have seen, point to various benefits that they ascribe to being a member of the EC. Britain's trade with EC countries has increased at a faster rate than its trade with other countries. Furthermore, membership is thought to have contributed to a wider choice of consumer goods available, to the enjoyment of Community-wide benefits (for example, the right to health care throughout the Community), to the securing of agricultural supplies at relatively stable prices, and to facilitating cooperation on developing energy resources. To counterclaims of the high cost of membership, the European Democratic Group has claimed that the British contribution to the Community is less than 0.5% of all United Kingdom public expenditure. One report states, "The total placed last year on bets in Britain amounts to more than the whole Community budget."[24] Remaining within the EC provides Britain with the opportunity to play a leading role in world affairs and to take part in a movement toward greater political and economic cooperation, thus underpinning growth and stability in Western Europe. To withdraw from the EC would be politically and economically disastrous: Britain would be isolated politically, and exports and growth would be placed in serious jeopardy. The country would be squeezed economically among the giants of the United States, the EC, and Japan. There would no longer be any alternatives similar to the EC to which Britain could turn, Commonwealth and European Free Trade Association countries having now diversified their trading arrangements. Withdrawal would leave Britain out in the cold. Furthermore, the cost of withdrawal would be significant. It could not be achieved without great upheaval: the economic and political links are now such as to make withdrawal most likely a slow and painful process. Indeed, what would happen to all the EC law incorporated into British law under the provisions of the 1972 European Communities Act? In practice, it would prove difficult to sweep away at one go, and sifting it to determine what should stay and what should go would prove a laborious and time-consuming exercise. For better or worse, supporters argue, Britain is a member of the European Communities and might as well remain so, a view that appeared to be confirmed by the results of the 1975 referendum.

Opponents of British membership continue to argue the case for withdrawal. They contend that Britain has not reaped the political and economic fruits of membership that proponents had suggested would exist. Britain had joined just before the oil crisis of 1973 and the subsequent recession, and it was no longer possible to enjoy the same fruits of membership as had the original six member states in the 1960s. There was a case for saying that Britain had missed the boat.[25] The country was being called upon to make a disproportionate contribution to the Community budget, an argument that, as we have seen, found favor in 1980 with Mrs. Thatcher, who demanded a greater degree of equity between contributions and receipts. Her insistence on this point at EC summit meetings exasperated other European leaders, who felt she was demanding too much. Gallup Polls revealed that most Britons felt that she should have been even tougher.[26] Far from achieving a position of leadership within the Communities, opponents contended, Britain was being engulfed within the machinery of the EC, hegemony being enjoyed by the commission and its officials. Furthermore, the operation of the EC was seen as strengthening further the influence of bureaucrats, both within the EC and within Whitehall. "The Common Market," declared Tony Benn, "is a mandarin's paradise."[27]

Opponents consider the limited political and economic benefits of membership insufficient to justify the transfer of decision-making powers from Westminster to the Council of Ministers, the European Communities Commission and, to a lesser extent, the European Parliament. Although the doctrine of parliamentary sovereignty remains formally intact, the 1972 Act being repealable by Parliament (plus the fact that the British courts would enforce any act of Parliament that expressly overrode a provision of EC law),[28] the practical effect of membership has been to undermine parliamentary government in Britain. In the areas of EC competence, Britain is no longer master of its own destiny, being dependent instead on decisions taken by supranational bodies over which it has only limited influence. As the institutions of the Communities have developed (in 1979 the European Parliament flexed its political muscle by rejecting the draft Community budget), Parliament and government in Britain have been further overshadowed. Britain has committed itself to be subservient to a foreign document, the Treaty of Rome, which constitutes almost a written constitution. On constitutional grounds, opponents considered and still consider British membership in the European Communities to be totally unacceptable.

In their opposition to EC membership, proponents of British withdrawal can cite in aid public opinion. Although the 1975 referendum revealed a reluctant acquiescence in Britain's remaining within the Communities, the referendum constituted a high point of support for British membership. Before and since, public opinion has been notably more hostile. "Throughout 1981," reported Webb and Wybrow, "the British continued to view the EEC mainly with antipathy and dissatisfaction"[29] (see Table 10.2). Those who considered the EC to be a "bad thing," they recorded, had for many years been in a distinct majority over those who approved it. In May 1981, 50% of respondents said they would be relieved to be told that the Common Market had been scrapped, 28% said they would be indifferent to this, and only 16% said that they would be sorry at such an occurrence.[30] Of polls carried out within the EC, it emerged that Britain was clearly the country most hostile to the Community, followed by Denmark, "the remaining eight countries showing a much more pro-Market

TABLE 10.2
Public Opinion on the European Communities, 1981

Question: Generally speaking, do you think British membership in the Common Market is a good thing, a bad thing, or neither good nor bad?

	October	*May*	*April*
A good thing	27%	21%	24%
A bad thing	41%	50%	48%
Neither good nor bad	27%	21%	24%
Don't know	5%	8%	4%

SOURCE: N. Webb and R. Wybrow, *The Gallup Report: Your Views in 1981* (Sphere Books, 1982), p. 99. Copyright 1982 Gallup, U.K. Reprinted by permission.

point of view."[31] One thing supporters of British membership cannot cite in aid of their view is domestic enthusiasm.

A more critical attitude toward the EC also developed in the latter half of the 1970s among the two main parties. The Labour party, badly divided on the issue and having zigzagged in its official stance, became more hostile toward Britain's continuing membership. The 1979 Labour manifesto offered "the prospect of bringing about fundamental and much-needed reform of the EEC."[32] At its 1980 conference, the party voted for a policy of withdrawal from the Communities,[33] a decision that served as a crucial impetus for the breakaway of several leading members to form the Social Democratic party. Labour remains the only major party actually advocating withdrawal (see Table 6.1). Although remaining committed to membership, the Conservative party ceased to display the zeal for the Communities that it had witnessed under Mr. Heath's leadership. The party came to favor a number of reforms within the EC, notably of the common agricultural policy, and once in office Mrs. Thatcher tried to alleviate some of the burden of Britain's budgetary contributions. By the beginning of the 1980s, the only enthusiasm for the European Communities was shown by the Liberal party, joined in 1981 by the Social Democrats: as Ian Bradley observed, continued membership was the most widely and strongly held of the policies to which SDP leaders and activists adhered.[34] It was an issue on which the new party was apparently out of tune with popular feelings.

In summary, then, British membership of the European Communities has had a substantial impact in political, economic, and constitutional terms. The extent to which those terms are advantageous to Britain is a matter of dispute. Membership in the Communities was confirmed by a referendum in 1975, but public opinion toward membership has since become more hostile. As dissatisfaction has grown, Britain has become more deeply enmeshed in the Communities. Even if leaving the EC was thought desirable by the government, realization is growing that the actual process of withdrawing would be a difficult and painful one. Supporters of continued membership also argue that it would be unnecessary. On the positive side, they contend that the country has derived both economic and political benefits from membership. On the negative side, they point out that there is no available alternative to the EC. Overall, the general view would appear to be that, like it or not, Britain is and is likely to remain, a member of the European Communities. Most Britons appear not to like it.

NOTES

1. See A. King, *Britain Says Yes* (American Enterprise Institute, 1977), pp. 2–7.

2. M. Camps, *Britain and the European Community 1955–1963* (Oxford University Press, 1964), p. 336.

3. See the comments of E. Heath, *Our Community* (Conservative Political Center, 1977), p. 4.

4. H. Macmillan, *Pointing the Way* (Macmillan, 1972), p. 310.

5. On the first two applications, see R. J. Lieber, *British Politics and European Unity* (University of California Press, 1970) and U. Kitzinger, *The Second Try* (Pergamon, 1968).

6. *House of Commons Debates,* Vol. 823, col. 2211–18.

7. See P. Norton, *Dissension in the House of Commons 1945–74* (Macmillan, 1975), pp. 395–98; U. Kitzinger, *Diplomacy and Persuasion* (Thames and Hudson, 1973), Ch. 13 and Appendix 1; and, for full details of the voting, *The Political Companion,* 9, October–December 1971.

8. *House of Commons Debates,* Vol. 831, col. 753–58.

9. See P. Norton, *Conservative Dissidents* (Temple Smith, 1978), pp. 64–82.

10. *Yorkshire Post,* August 31, 1981.

11. *European Democrat Brief 1* and *European Democratic Brief 2* (R. Jackson MEP for the European Democratic Group, 1982).

12. A. Daltrop, *Politics and the European Community* (Longman, 1982), pp. 97–98. See also European Democratic Group, *A Guide to Finance in Europe for British Businesses and Organisations* (European Democratic Group, 1981), pp. 28–33.

13. Conservative Research Department, *The Campaign Guide 1983* (Conservative Central Office, 1983), p. 400.

14. S. Henig, "The European Community's Bicephalous Political Authority: Council of Ministers–Commission Relations" in J. Lodge (ed.), *Institutions and Policies of the European Communities* (Frances Pinter, 1983), p. 11.

15. See V. Herman and J. Lodge, *The European Parliament and the European Community* (Macmillan, 1978). On the Parliament's developing powers, see the concluding chapter in J. Lodge and V. Herman, *Direct Elections to the European Parliament* (Macmillan, 1982), especially pp. 286–92.

16. Daltrop, p. 58. Other information in this paragraph is drawn from Daltrop, p. 59.

17. See Lord Crowther-Hunt, "The Case for Civil Service Power," *The Listener,* January 13, 1977.

18. See P. Norton, *The Commons in Perspective* (Longman, 1981), pp. 160–64.

19. The February 1974 Labour manifesto promised a "fundamental renegotiation. of the terms of entry." See D. Butler and U. Kitzinger, *The 1975 Referendum* (Macmillan, 1976), pp. 26–27.

20. See generally J. Lodge, *The European Community and New Zealand* (Frances Pinter, 1982).

21. On a free vote, more Labour MPs voted against it than for it. See P. Norton, *Dissension in the House of Commons 1974–1979* (Oxford University Press, 1980), pp. 58–62.

22. See F. W. S. Craig and T. T. Mackie (eds.), *Europe Votes 1* (Parliamentary Research Services, 1980).

23. Out of an electorate of 41,152,763, 13,446,083 votes were cast. See D. Butler and A. Sloman, *British Political Facts 1900–1979,* 5th ed. (Macmillan, 1980), p. 211. See the same page for the 1975 referendum results.

24. *European Democrat Brief 2.*

25. See P. Norton, *The Constitution in Flux* (Martin Robertson, 1982), p. 167.

26. N. L. Webb and R. Wybrow, *The Gallup Report* (Sphere Books, 1981), p. 79.

27. T. Benn, *Arguments for Democracy* (Penguin, 1982), p. 61.

28. Norton, *The Constitution in Flux,* p. 143.

29. N. Webb and R. Wybrow, *The Gallup Report: Your Opinions in 1981* (Sphere Books, 1982), p. 98.

30. Ibid., p. 99.

31. Ibid.

32. *The Labour Party Manifesto 1979* (Labour Party, 1979), pp. 31–32. *Note:* It is still common practice in Britain to refer to the "EC" as the "EEC" or "Common Market."

33. *The Labour Party Conference Report 1980* (Labour Party, 1980), pp. 125–32. Voting was 5,042,000 to 2,097,000.

34. I. Bradley, *Breaking the Mould?* (Martin Robertson, 1981), p. 124.

Scrutiny and Legitimation

11

Parliament
Commons and Lords

THE UNITED STATES has a bicameral legislature. In legislative matters, each house is the equal of the other.[1] Both houses are chosen by popular vote, albeit by differently defined constituencies. They are elected separately from the executive, and members of the two houses are precluded by the Constitution from holding any civil office under the authority of the United States. There is a formal separation between the executive and the legislative branches not only in personnel but also of powers. Congress displays the characteristics of what Michael Mezey has aptly termed an "active" legislature: its policy-making power is strong and it enjoys popular support as a legitimate political institution.[2] Each house is master of its own timetable and proceedings.

In their behavior, not least in their voting behavior, senators and members of the House of Representatives are influenced by party, more so than is sometimes popularly supposed.[3] Nonetheless, while party is an important influence, it is not an exclusive one. Members of Congress are responsive to other influences. The political landscape bears the bodies of senators and representatives who, regardless of party, fell to the wrath of their electors because of their neglect of their constituencies or because of their stance on a particular issue. Although the initiative in policy-making has passed largely to the executive, Congress remains an important part of the policy-making process. As Professor Mezey writes, "Even though a decline in the power and authority of the Congress has been announced on several different occasions, it remains today one of the few legislative institutions in the world

259

able and capable of saying no to a popularly elected president and making it stick."[4]

The United Kingdom has also a bicameral legislature, but there the similarity ends. Of the two houses, only one—the House of Commons—is popularly elected. Members of the Upper House, the House of Lords, serve by virtue of birth, by appointment for life, or because of the positions they hold. The two houses are no longer equal: the House of Commons as the elected chamber enjoys preeminence and can enforce its legislative will over the Upper House under the provisions of the 1911 and 1949 Parliament Acts (see Chapter 3). The executive, or rather the political apex of the executive (i.e., ministers), is drawn from Parliament—there is no separate election—and its members remain within Parliament. The executive dominates both the business program (deciding what will be debated and when) and the voting of Parliament, party serving as the means of that domination. Party cohesion is a feature of voting in the House of Commons. (The same is largely true of the House of Lords, though fewer votes take place there.) Party is the determining influence in an MP's election and party is normally the determining influence in his or her parliamentary behavior. Parliament exhibits the features of what Mezey has termed a "reactive" legislature: it enjoys popular support as a legitimate political institution but enjoys only modest power, if that, in policy-making. Discussion of "the decline of Parliament" has been a characteristic feature of political discourse in Britain in recent years. Not surprisingly, MPs have on occasion been known to look with envy across the Atlantic at the power and influence of their American counterparts.

The reasons for executive dominance of the legislature in Britain have been sketched already (Chapter 3). For part of the nineteenth century, Parliament exhibited the characteristics of an "active" legislature. The 1832 Reform Act helped lessen the grip of the aristocracy and of the ministry on the House of Commons (seats were less easy to buy, given the size of the new electorate), allowing MPs greater freedom in their parliamentary behavior. Debates in the House could influence opinion and the outcome of votes was not a foregone conclusion. This period was short-lived. The 1867 Reform Act and later acts created a much larger and more demanding electorate. With the passage of the 1884 Representation of the People Act, a majority of working men were enfranchised. Electors were now too numerous to be bribed, at least by individual candidates. The result was that "organized corruption was gradually replaced by party organization,"[5] as one observer puts it, and both main existing parties were developed from small cadre parties to form mass-membership and complex organizations. Party organization made possible contact with the electors. To stimulate voting, candidates had to promise something to electors, and electoral promises could be met only if parties displayed sufficient cohesion in parliamentary organization to ensure their enactment.

Institutional and environmental factors combined to ensure that the pressures generated by the changed electoral conditions resulted in a House of Commons with low policy influence. Competition for the all-or-nothing spoils of a general election victory, the single-member constituency with a plurality method of election, and a relatively homogeneous population (relative to many other countries) would appear to have encouraged, if not always produced, a basic two-party as opposed to a multiparty system. One party was normally returned with an overall parliamentary majority. Given that the government was drawn from and remained within Parliament, the electoral fortunes of MPs depended primarily on the success or failure of that government. Government was dependent on the voting support of its parliamentary majority both for the passage of its promised measures and for its own continuance in office. Failure of government supporters to vote against a motion expressing "no confidence" in the Government or, conversely, not to vote for an important measure that the Government declared a "matter of confidence" would result in a dissolution. Within the House of Commons, party cohesion quickly became the norm.

A willingness to defer to government by MPs was encouraged also by internal party pressures. A member was chosen as a party candidate by his local party and was dependent on it for renomination as well as for campaign support. Assuming local party loyalty to the party leadership (an assumption that usually but not always could be made), local parties were unlikely to take kindly to any consistent dissent from "their" members. The norms of the constitution and of party structures also encouraged acquiescence. There were no career channels in Parliament alternative to those of government office, and a place in government was dependent on the prime minister, the *party* leader. Achieving a leadership position in the House meant, in effect, becoming a minister.

The nature of government decision-making as well as the increasing responsibilities assumed by government also had the effect of moving policy-making further from the floor of the House. The conventions of collective and individual ministerial responsibility helped provide a protective cloak for decision-making within cabinet and within departments. Only the conclusions of discussions could be revealed. Furthermore, as government responsibilities expanded and became more dependent on the cooperation of outside groups (see Chapter 7), government measures came increasingly to be the product of negotiation between departments and interest groups, those measures then being presented to Parliament as packages already agreed on. As the demands on government grew, these "packages" increased in extent and complexity. The House of Commons was called on primarily to approve measures drawn up elsewhere that it had neither adequate time nor resources to submit to sustained and informed debate.

Parliament thus came to occupy what was recognized as a backseat in policy-making. This is not to say that it ceased to be an important political body. The government remained dependent on Parliament for its support and both houses continued to provide significant forums of debate and scrutiny. In an important article in 1975, Nelson Polsby distinguished between transformative legislatures (enjoying an independent capacity, frequently exercised, to mold and transform proposals into law) and arena legislatures (providing a formal arena in which significant political forces could express themselves).[6] The British Parliament can most appropriately be described as having moved from being a transformative legislature in the second third of the nineteenth century to an arena legislature in the twentieth. The United States Congress, by contrast, has remained a transformative legislature.

THE HOUSE OF COMMONS

The events of the nineteenth century that served to transfer power from Parliament to the executive served also to ensure the dominance of the House of Commons within the triumvirate of Monarch, Lords, and Commons. The Commons constitutes the only body of the three that is popularly elected. Indeed, its dominance has become such that there is a tendency for many to treat "House of Commons" and "Parliament" as almost synonymous terms. The attention accorded it by the media and outside observers is far more extensive than that accorded the House of Lords, and more importance is attached to the functions it is expected to fulfill.

Parliament provides the personnel of government—i.e., ministers. By convention, most ministers, including the prime minister, are drawn from the Commons. This function is best described as a passive one. The House itself does not do the choosing. The outcome of a general election determines which party will form the government, and the prime minister, in practice, chooses who will fill which ministerial posts.

The most important functions requiring action on the part of the House are those of legitimation and of debate. Government requires the formal assent of Parliament both for the passage of legislation and for the grant of money. Given the government's control of a parliamentary majority, such assent is normally forthcoming. The giving of this assent, however much it may be taken for granted, fulfills an important symbolic role. It constitutes the elected assembly giving the seal of approval on behalf of the electoral populace. It remains significant also because the House retains the formal power to deny its assent. It may not use that power, but the option to do so remains.

The function that occupies the most time of the House and is the most obvious manifestation of its position as an arena legislature is that of debate. As a representative assembly, the House provides an authoritative forum in which the views of the political parties can find expression. It also provides a forum in which MPs individually can raise the concerns and specific problems of constituents.

Through debate, the House or elements of it can seek to influence government. Formally, it retains the sanction of denying assent to measures. In practice, the publicity accorded debates provides the House with its greatest leverage. Governments are sensitive to the subjection of their measures or specific actions to criticism. If that criticism is effective, especially if it comes from government supporters, then ministers may respond to it. The House provides the forum for their response—hence its importance.

The House, through debate, can thus seek to subject government to a process of scrutiny and influence. The means of "debate" available to the House to achieve this are varied. They can be divided into those used to discuss and scrutinize legislation and those employed to discuss and scrutinize executive actions.

Legislation

Legislation is subject to a well-defined procedure once it has been submitted to the House (see Table 11.1). First reading constitutes the formal introduction of a bill. At this stage it is not debated. Indeed, it does not even exist in printed form. Once formally introduced, it is then set down for its second reading. Compared with the analogous legislative procedure in the United States Congress, the second reading is distinct in two significant respects. First, it is the government that determines when the debate will take place. (On all days, with the exception of certain Fridays and 19 "Opposition days," the government has control of the parliamentary timetable, deciding what will be debated.) Second, the debate precedes the committee stage. On second reading, the principle of the bill is debated and approved. Only after it has received its second reading is it referred to a committee for consideration of its specific provisions.

At committee stage, bills are considered by standing committees. The name is a misnomer: they are appointed on an ad-hoc basis. A committee will be appointed to consider a specific bill and then, having completed its deliberations, ceases to exist in that form. (Committees are known by letters of the alphabet—e.g., Standing Committee A, and once a committee with the letter A has finished its deliberations, a new Standing Committee A will be appointed to consider another bill—but the members of the committee will be different.) The committees will each have a membership of between 16 and 50 members. They meet for the purposes of discussing bills clause by clause. In practice, their ability to amend and influence the content of measures is circumscribed. Once the House has approved the principle of the measure, a committee cannot then make any changes that run counter to the principle embodied in the bill. The greatest constraints, however, are

TABLE 11.1
Legislative Stages in the House of Commons

Stage	Where Taken	Comments
First Reading	On floor of the House	Formal introduction only. No debate.
Second Reading	On floor of the House (noncontentious bills may be referred to a second reading committee)	Debate on the principle of the measure.
Committee	Standing committee (constitutionally important and certain other measures may be taken in Committee of the Whole House.)	Considered clause by clause. Amendments can be made.
Report	On floor of the House (there is no report stage if the bill reported is unamended from Committee of the Whole House.)	Reported to the House by the committee. Amendments can be made.
Third Reading	On floor of the House (there is no debate unless six members submit a motion beforehand.)	Final approval of the bill. Debate confined to bill's content.
Lords Amendments	On floor of the House	Any amendments made by the House of Lords are considered, usually on a motion to agree or disagree with them.

SOURCE: P. Norton, *The Commons in Perspective* (Longman, 1981), p. 86. Copyright 1981 Martin Robertson and Longman. Reprinted by permission.

political. The format adopted at committee meetings is an adversarial one: government MPs sit on one side, Opposition MPs on the other. Debate is usually along party lines, as is voting. The result is that the amendments that are carried are almost always those introduced by ministers. (The relevant minister is usually appointed to the committee.) Of 907 amendments introduced by ministers at committee stage in the three sessions of 1967–1968, 1968–1969, and 1970–1971, 906 were accepted; of 3,510 amendments moved by other MPs in the same three sessions, only 171 were accepted.[7] Since most bills discussed by standing committees are introduced by the government, the main purpose of introducing government amendments is to correct drafting errors, improve the wording, or, more substantially, to meet points made by outside groups or to meet points made by MPs that the government find acceptable.

Standing committees thus differ considerably from their American counterparts. They have no power to summon witnesses or evidence, they are presided over by an impartial chairman (an MP drawn from a body of MPs appointed for their ability to chair such meetings), and are confined in their deliberations solely to the content of bills. They have no power to undertake enquiries or to discuss anything other than the bill before them. The government's majority on a standing committee is in proportion to its majority in the House as a whole. Hence, as long as it has a majority in the House, it is assured a majority on such committees. The result is that bills emerge from committees relatively unscathed. Unlike United States congressional committees, standing committees are not a burial ground for bills. Rather, they serve as temporary transit points in their passage.

Once a standing committee has completed its deliberations, a bill is then returned to the House for the report stage. At this stage the House may make further amendments. This stage is not dissimilar to the committee stage and the government may use it to introduce amendments that it had not been able to introduce in committee (for example, to meet points raised in committee but for which it had not had time to formulate a precise amendment). The outcome of votes on amendments is the same as in committee. Government amendments are normally carried. Amendments introduced by private members are usually defeated, unless they find favor with the government. Of 865 government amendments introduced in the three sessions mentioned above, 864 were approved. (The exception was an amendment that was withdrawn.) Of 688 amendments moved by private members, 39 were approved.[8]

All bills considered in standing committee go through a report stage. Certain important bills, such as those introducing constitutional change (for example, reform of the House of Lords), have their committee stage on the floor of the House. If they emerge from this stage without amendment, there is no report stage. In 1972, for example, the European Communities bill was taken on the floor of the House and was not amended. It thus proceeded directly to third reading.

The final stage is that of third reading, at which the House gives its final approval to a measure. Under a procedural reform introduced in 1967, no debate takes place at this stage unless six members put down in advance a motion for debate. (On bills of any political significance, such a motion is usually submitted.) Any debate that takes place must be confined to the content of the bill. Suggestions for amendments are out of order.

Once the House has approved third reading, a bill is then sent to the House of Lords. (The exceptions, of course, are any bills that originate in the Lords.) If the Lords make any amendments, these are then sent to the Commons. The House debates these amendments, usually on a motion to agree or disagree with them. If the House disagrees with a Lords amendment, this fact—along with the reasons for the disagreement—is communicated to the Upper House. The House of Lords then usually concurs with the Commons and does not press its amendment. Once a bill has passed both Houses, it then proceeds for the Royal Assent.

Government bills dominate the legislative timetable. This is hardly surprising given the onus placed on government to initiate measures and the fact that the government controls the timetable. Between 50 and 70 government bills are introduced and passed each year. Opportunities for private members to introduce bills of their own are extremely limited.[9] Certain Fridays each session (usually 10) are set aside to discuss private members' bills. So limited is the time available and so great the number of members wishing to introduce bills that a ballot is held each parliamentary session (that is, each year). The 20 members coming top in the ballot have priority in introducing bills. In practice, only about the first six whose names are drawn out will stand much chance of getting their bills discussed, and even then there is no guarantee of the bills being passed. The opportunities available for a bill to get through all its stages during private members' time on Fridays are very small. A substantial bill will normally need more time than is available and will be dependent on government's finding time in its own timetable. The government is thus in a position to determine the fate of most private members' bills. It can deny such bills the necessary time to complete the required legislative stages or it can persuade its supporters to defeat them in a parliamentary vote. Because of this, most private members' bills cover matters that are not politically contentious and are unlikely to arouse the opposition of government. A further important constraint is that such bills cannot make a charge on the public revenue: only ministers can introduce bills that make such a charge.

Hence, the scope for legislative initiative by private members is extremely limited. Nonetheless, it is not nonexistent. Occasionally, a private member may introduce a bill on an important issue toward which the government is sympathetic and for which it is prepared to find time. This was the case notably with a number of social reform issues in the 1960s. Because the Labour government did not wish to take responsibility for certain reforms that might prove politically unpopular, possibly with some of its own supporters, the Labour government left it to backbench MPs to introduce private members' bills on subjects such as abortion, divorce, homosexuality, and the death penalty. Where necessary, the government found time to allow the House to reach a decision on these measures but otherwise adopted a "hands off" approach. The consequence was that a number of substantial social reforms were introduced through the medium of private members' legislation.[10] Such occasions, however, are rare.

The number of days the House spends in session each year is given in Table 11.2. About one-third of its time is taken up with debate on govern-

TABLE 11.2
The House of Commons: Sittings and Parliamentary Questions, 1974–1980

	Parliamentary Sessions					
	1974–1975	1975–1976	1976–1977	1977–1978	1978–1979*	1979–1980
Number of days sitting	198	191	149	169	86	244
Number of hours sitting	1,849	1,759	1,371	1,485	739	2,177
Average daily hours:minutes of sitting	9:20	9:13	9:12	8:47	8:35	8:55
Number of parliamentary votes (divisions)	405	432	234	324	110	500
Parliamentary questions:						
Oral	3,611	3,199	2,481	10,226[†]	5,470[†]	12,453[†]
Written	33,447	39,121	29,058	28,630	12,952	39,912

*Short parliamentary session because of calling of general election 1979.
[†]Figures for 1977–1978 onwards are for the total number of questions tabled for oral answer. Figures for preceding sessions are the number actually answered.

ment bills. Less than 5% of its time is spent discussing private members' bills.[11] Most of the remainder of parliamentary time is given over in one form or other to debate and scrutiny of government actions.

Executive Actions

Ministers and civil servants will spend most of their time pursuing and administering policies and programs for which legislative authority has already been given or for which such authority is not necessary (for example, policies pursued under prerogative powers). Hence, the formal approval of Parliament is not required. Nonetheless, the House of Commons seeks to subject such executive actions to scrutiny and debate. There are various procedural devices available. These may be identified as Question Time, debates (of different types), and, away from the floor of the House, select committees, correspondence, and the submission of Early Day motions.

Question Time is a feature of the House of Commons for which there is no United States parallel. It entails the regular appearance of ministers and the head of government in the House to answer questions submitted by backbench MPs. (The rough equivalent in the United States would be for cabinet secretaries and the president to appear regularly on the floor of the House or Senate to answer questions, such sessions taking place several times a week.) Question Time in the House of Commons takes place each parliamentary sitting day, Monday to Thursday. It occupies between 45 and 55 minutes at the beginning of each day (the House commences its business at 2:30 P.M.) and is subject now to well-defined procedures.[12] Ministers answer questions on a rotating basis, the more important ministers coming up for a Question Time about once every three weeks. The prime minister has a regular twice-weekly slot in Question Time, answering questions for 15 minutes between 3:15 and 3:30 P.M. on Tuesdays and Thursdays. Each MP is restricted in the number of questions he or she can hand in (eight in any 10 sitting days and no more than two on any given day), though the number submitted remains substantial (see Table 11.2). After being submitted, questions are published on the Order Paper of the House (see Figure 11.1). At Question Time, the MP who has the first question rises and says to the Speaker "Number one, sir." The relevant minister then rises to answer the question. Having been sent a copy of the question immediately after its submission, the Minister is armed with relevant information compiled by his or her Department and will normally give a prepared answer. Once the answer has been given, it is normal practice for the Speaker to call the member who asked the question to put a supplementary, or follow-up question. It is at the Speaker's discretion as to how many such supplementaries are permitted. Having allowed one or more supplementary questions, the Speaker then calls the MP in whose name the second question on the Order

No. 25   WEDNESDAY 20TH JULY 1983   **459**

ORDER PAPER

QUESTIONS FOR ORAL ANSWER

Questions marked § relate to EEC matters and will start not later than 3.10 p.m.

✱ 1 **Dr M. S. Miller** (East Kilbride):   To ask the Secretary of State for Foreign and Commonwealth Affairs, whether he has any plans to visit Israel or Arab states in the near future.

✱ 2 **Mr Sydney Chapman** (Chipping Barnet):   To ask the Secretary of State for Foreign and Commonwealth Affairs, if he will report recent progress at the disarmament negotiations presently taking place.

✱ 3 **Mr George Foulkes** (Carrick, Cumnock and Doon Valley):   To ask the Secretary of State for Foreign and Commonwealth Affairs, if the United Kingdom is party to any international agreements concerning extra-terrestrial bodies.

✱ 4 **Mr Ivan Lawrence** (Burton):   To ask the Secretary of State for Foreign and Commonwealth Affairs, what progress has been made in the area of human rights at the Helsinki Review discussions in Madrid.

✱ 5 **Mr Geoffrey Lofthouse** (Pontefract and Castleford):   To ask the Secretary of State for Foreign and Commonwealth Affairs, if he will make a statement about the relations of the United Kingdom with Chile.

✱ 6 **Mr James Lamond** (Oldham Central and Royton):   To ask the Secretary of State for Foreign and Commonwealth Affairs, when he last discussed with the United States government the situation in Central America.

✱ 7 **Mr Neil Thorne** (Ilford South):   To ask the Secretary of State for Foreign and Commonwealth Affairs, if he has had any discussions with a view to achieving early implementation of the Israel-Lebanon agreement ; and, if so, what assurances he has received that Syrian forces and Palestine Liberation Organisation terrorist groups will withdraw from the Lebanon at the same time as Israeli forces.

✱ 8 **Mr Dennis Canavan** (Falkirk West):   To ask the Secretary of State for Foreign and Commonwealth Affairs, whether he will seek to meet representatives of the Falkland Islands Company to discuss Government policy on the Falkland Islands.

✱ 9 **Mr Tom Cox** (Tooting):   To ask the Secretary of State for Foreign and Commonwealth Affairs, what plans he has to visit Cyprus.

✱ 10 **Mr Kenneth Warren** (Hastings and Rye):   To ask the Secretary of State for Foreign and Commonwealth Affairs, if he will make representations to the United Nations Organisation to request that they should exert further influence on Argentina to acknowledge the formal cessation of hostilities in the South Atlantic.

✱ 11 **Mr Ernie Roberts** (Hackney North and Stoke Newington):   To ask the Secretary of State for Foreign and Commonwealth Affairs, if he will publish the advice given by his Department to British businessmen and tourists visiting each of the Arab states concerning local regulations and religious restrictions.

✱ 12 **Mr David Winnick** (Walsall North):   To ask the Secretary of State for Foreign and Commonwealth Affairs, if he will make a statement on the Government's policy towards improving relations between the Soviet Union and the United Kingdom.
    2 N

FIGURE 11.1   Questions on the House of Commons' Order Paper, July 20, 1983. Questions continue on subsequent pages of the Order Paper. (*Copyright 1983 by the Crown. Reprinted by permission of the Controller of Her Majesty's Stationery Office.*)

Paper appears. The MP rises, says "Number two, sir," and the process is repeated. This continues until 3:30 P.M., when questions automatically cease, regardless of how many remain on the Order Paper. Questions not answered during Question Time receive instead written answers that are published in *Hansard*, the official report of proceedings that also includes the verbatim transcript of debates as well as of Question Time.

MPs have the option also of tabling (see glossary) questions for written answer. These are more numerous than questions tabled for an oral answer at Question Time (see Table 11.2). The answers, along with the questions, are published in *Hansard*. Tabling written questions is popular especially as a means of eliciting statistics and other material that cannot easily be given in oral form. Oral answers, by contrast, are used to elicit statements and comments on government policy and matters that MPs think might embarrass (or, if the MP is on the government side, help) government or generate favorable attention back in the constituencies.

There are various types of *debate* held on the floor of the House. The most important can be classified as general debates, held to discuss particular government policies. These can be anywhere between three and seven hours in duration. They take place on motions tabled by the government (for example, on motions to take note or approve particular policies or government policy documents) or, on 19 "Opposition days," by the Opposition. General debates are also held at the beginning of the parliamentary session on the Debate on the Address. Following the Queen's Speech at the beginning of each session, outlining the government's program for the year, a debate extending over several days is held. Ostensibly the debate is on an address to the Queen, thanking her for her gracious speech, but in practice it covers particular government policies: one day, for example, is normally given over to a discussion of foreign policy.

The other main type of debate is the adjournment debate. In practice, there are two forms of adjournment debate. One is the same essentially as a general debate; the only difference is that no substantive motion is before the House. Instead, a motion to adjourn is put down as a way of allowing debate to range freely on a topic for which the government has no specific policy or action that it wishes to be approved. In short, it is a useful means of sounding out the opinion of the House. At the end of such debates, the motion to adjourn is generally negatived without a vote. The other type of adjournment debate is known as the half-hour adjournment debate and is held at the end of each day's sitting, usually from 10:00 to 10:30 P.M. on Mondays through Thursdays (2:00 to 2:30 P.M. on Fridays). These debates allow an MP, chosen usually after a ballot, to raise an issue, usually of constituency interest, for about 15 minutes, and allow the relevant minister (traditionally a junior minister) about 15 minutes to respond to the points made. After exactly 30 minutes have elapsed, the House is automatically adjourned. These short debates take up little time but are extremely popular with backbench MPs, allowing them to raise constituency problems or important but nonparty issues (for example, problems such as gambling, drug misuse, or the transferability of pensions).[13] MPs raising the issues normally give ministers advance information of the points they intend to raise, thus allowing for a full reply to be prepared.

There are one or two other forms of debate, the most important but rarely employed being that of the emergency debate. A member can ask leave to move the adjournment of the House "for the purpose of discussing a specific and important matter that should have urgent consideration." If the MP can convince the Speaker that the matter (a) deserves urgent attention, (b) falls within the responsibility of government, and (c) cannot be raised quickly by another procedure, then the debate may be granted.[14] If the debate is granted, it takes place the next day (or the following Monday if granted on a Thursday) or, if the Speaker considers the urgency of the matter justifies it, that same evening at 7:00 P.M. In practice, the Speaker tends to dislike the interruptions to scheduled business caused by such debates, and few are granted: on average, only about four a session. They nonetheless constitute a useful safety valve function, allowing members to discuss an important topic on occasion that the government had not proposed to have discussed. In 1980, for example, an MP successfully applied for an emergency debate on the government's decision to apply sanctions retrospectively against Iran. Aware that it might be in difficulties in the vote at the end of the debate (the retrospective element of the sanctions being unpopular in the House), the government changed its policy before the debate was held.[15]

Of these various types of debate, general debates take up the most time. About 10% of the House's time is taken up with debates on government motions. The format of such debates is similar to that of second reading debates. A government minister moves the motion, an Opposition front bench spokesman speaks (each probably for half-an-hour or more, the minister in particular reading from a prepared brief), then backbench MPs speak, called alternately from each side of the House, then an Opposition front bench spokesman winds up for the Opposition and a minister concludes for the government. Ministers and Opposition front bench spokesmen tend to dominate not only in terms of the time they take but also in the audience they attract. Few MPs remain to listen to the speeches of backbench MPs. Instead, they tend to leave the Chamber, returning when the final front bench speeches are being made and in time for the vote (if there is to be one). In practice, any debate thus takes place among very few members. Indeed, it is a misnomer to refer to "debates." Most speeches are delivered from prepared notes and often have little relevance to the speeches that have preceded them. Nonetheless, any member wishing to have a speech appear in *Hansard* has to be present, catch the Speaker's eye, and deliver it. There is no procedure in debate analogous to the United States' practice that allows for material to be inserted in the official record without it having been presented verbally in the Chamber.

Away from the floor of the House, the most important device employed for the scrutiny of the executive is that of *select committees*. These committees have responsibility for maintaining scrutiny of particular departments or sectors of government responsibility, though they have no responsibility for the formal scrutiny and approval of legislation (that is the function of the separate standing committees, unlike the procedure in the United States, where the two responsibilities are combined in congressional standing committees). Select committees have been variously utilized in past centuries[16] but not on any consistent or comprehensive basis. Only two such committees have existed as important committees for any length of time. One is the Public Accounts Committee, first appointed in 1861 to ensure that public expenditure was properly incurred on the purpose for which it had been voted. Over time the committee has interpreted more widely its terms of references, conducting value-for-money exercises and investigating possible negligence. The committee has developed a reputation as a thorough and authoritative body, its recommendations resulting either in government action to implement them or to provide a reasoned response to them. Traditionally, the committee is chaired by an Opposition MP. The other important committee was the Estimates Committee: unlike the Public Accounts Committee, it no longer exists. It was first appointed in 1912 and, after being suspended from 1914 to 1921, existed until 1971. It was appointed to look at the annual estimates and to consider ways in which policies could be carried out more cost-efficiently. It was not supposed to consider the merits of policies but after 1945 began to venture into areas that could not be described as solely administrative. However, it was hampered by limited resources both in staff and in terms of the information presented to it by government.[17] In 1971 it was replaced by a larger committee, the Expenditure Committee, itself divided into functional subcommittees. This committee disappeared in 1979, when a new system of committees was introduced.

The Select Committee of Nationalized Industries was established in 1955 and a number of similar committees were established in the late 1960s and early 1970s. This latter development began in 1966, when Labour politician Richard Crossman was appointed as leader of the House (i.e., the minister with responsibility for the government's business program in the House). Encouraged by a number of reform-minded Labour MPs, he instigated the creation of a Select Committee on Agriculture and another on science and technology. Later committees included ones to cover education, overseas development, Scottish affairs, and race relations.[18] The committees had limited impact on government. The Agricultural Committee encountered opposition from the Foreign Office when it wanted to go to Brussels to pursue an inquiry and, after it had operated for only two years, Richard Crossman decided not to put forward the necessary motion to renew its existence. The new committees, as one observer recorded in 1970, "have so far exerted only the most minor influence on policy-making and administration."[19] In 1978, a Commons' procedure committee recommended that if Commons' scrutiny of the executive was to be effective, a new system of committee was necessary, created on a systematic and continuing basis. Pressure for the creation of such a committee system built up within the House, and in 1979 the new Conservative leader of the House, Norman St. John-Stevas, brought forward motions for the appointment of the recommended committees. By 248 votes to 12, the House approved the creation of 12 committees to "examine the expenditure, administration, and policy of the principal Government Departments . . . and associated public bodies."[20] In addition to the 12 committees approved, it was agreed subsequently to establish also a Committee on Scottish Affairs and another on Welsh Affairs. The 14 new committees are listed, along with other pertinent data, in Table 11.3.

The new committees have faced a variety of problems. Of necessity they have had to be selective in their choice of topics for investigation (and whether or not to opt for long- or short-term studies, whether to concentrate on the estimates or on policy, and so on), they have had limited resources (usually one full-time clerk each and up to four specialist advisers paid on a per-diem basis), they have had no formal powers other than the power to send for "persons, papers and records" (a power that does not extend to cabinet ministers and cabinet papers), and they have had problems in determining their relationship with the House as such. There is no automatic provision, for example, for any committee report to be debated by the House. Yet despite these limitations, the committees have proved to be major improvements on their predecessors. They have proved to be more extensive and more thorough in their scrutiny, have operated as identifiable units, and have attracted the enthusiasm of Members: they are well-attended and there is demand to join them. (There were 80 applicants for two vacancies on the Defense Committee in 1982, for example.) They have attracted more extensive media attention than their predecessors and they have become the target of representations from outside groups, something that never happened before.[21] As bodies of scrutiny, they not only have served as independent critics of government but also, by issuing reports with or without comment, they have helped inform debate on particular subjects. By examining witnesses and receiving evidence, they have provided authoritative forums in which outside groups can make their views known (especially useful to promotional groups; see Chapter 7). By their questioning of civil servants, they have served also to open up a little more to public scrutiny the activities of government.

The remaining two devices, available to all members, are those of *correspondence* and submitting or signing Early Day motions. Members can and do write to ministers, normally for the purpose of eliciting information or action in pursuit of some constituency casework. On average, a member may write between 5 and 25 such letters a week (ministers are among those writing, sending letters in their capacity as constituency MPs), the Depart-

TABLE 11.3

Select Committees in the House of Commons, 1982–1983

Select Committee	Chairman	Number of Members	Average attendance (December 1979– February 1982)	Number of meetings (April 1, 1981– March 31, 1982)	Number of reports (to July 28, 1982)	Total number of witnesses examined from Government Departments (to June 18, 1981)
Agriculture	Sir William Elliott, Conservative	9	82%	27	4	29
Defense	Sir Timothy Kitson, Conservative	11	62%	39	9	73
Education, Science, and Arts	Christopher Price, Labour	9	74%	48	14	74
Employment	John Golding, Labour	9	69%	32	11	14
Energy	Ian Lloyd, Conservative	11	70%	46	8	15
Environment	Reg Freeson, Labour	11	69%	24	5	6

Foreign Affairs	Sir Anthony Kershaw, Conservative	11 (5)†	74% (67%)†	64*	15	99
Home Affairs	Sir John Eden, Conservative	11 (5)†	83% (91%)†	56*	15	86
Industry and Trade	Sir Donald Kaberry, Conservative	11	79%	33	16	33
Scottish Affairs	David Lambie, Labour	13	82%	32	6	33
Social Services	Mrs. Renee Short, Labour	9	71%	43	9	19
Transport	Tom Bradley, SDP	11	70%	35	12	16
Treasury and Civil Service	Edward du Cann, Conservative	11 (7)†	89% (73%)†	60*	19	50
Welsh Affairs	Donald Anderson, Labour	11	80%	28	3	28

*Includes Sub-Committee meetings.
†Sub-Committee.

ment of Health and Social Security being the most notable recipient of such letters: it receives on average about 2,000 letters a month.[22] Letter-writing is a popular device for pursuing casework, undertaken free of party considerations, and often evokes the desired information or response from departments.[23] In many cases, all that members and their constituents are after is an authoritative explanation of a particular official action. Such letter-writing provides, in conjunction with the letters written by MPs to constituents, the most structured and direct contact that many citizens have with government. About 8% of constituents communicate with their MPs.[24] Of these, according to one survey, about 75% reported a "good" or "very good" response. Of citizens in the United States communicating with their congressmen, a somewhat higher 90% reported a "good" or "very good" response.[25]

Early Day motions are motions put down by members, technically for debate "on an early day." In practice, there is no available time to debate them. Rather, given that they are published, they serve as means of expressing a written opinion. Members can and do add their signatures to such motions and the number of names a motion attracts serves as some indication of opinion within the House.[26] Their impact is limited by the number tabled, often several hundred each session, and by the range of topics covered. Some are essentially flippant or congratulatory (congratulating some prominent figure on a recent achievement, for example), while others express opinions on important issues of policy. Members are free to submit and to sign as many motions as they like. Some rarely do so; others have a reputation for signing every motion with which they have some sympathy. (At least one has been known to sign two motions that were mutually exclusive.) As a result, the significance of such motions is limited.

These, then, constitute the primary devices available to members of Parliament to debate and scrutinize the actions of government. Most such devices are long-standing ones, though used more often in recent years than they were previously. Given the developments that have taken place in government and the nature of policy-making, there has been considerable debate as to whether these parliamentary devices remain sufficient to subject government to effective scrutiny. As we shall see, some critics consider that the House of Commons does not perform well even as an arena assembly, let alone as one that can influence or mold legislation. As the locus of policy-making has moved further away from the House, the House has not moved much to try to close the gap.

THE HOUSE OF LORDS

The House of Lords was gradually forced in the nineteenth and early twentieth century to accept a subordinate position in its relationship with the

House of Commons. The reason for this is clear. It was well stated by the Earl of Shaftesbury during debate on the 1867 Reform Act. "So long as the other House of Parliament was elected upon a restricted principle," he declared, "I can understand that it would submit to a check from a House such as this. But in the presence of this great democratic power and the advance of this great democratic wave . . . it passes my comprehension to understand how an hereditary House like this can hold its own."[27] Although not altogether swept away by this "great democratic wave," the House was at least to be swamped by it. It could not maintain a claim to equal status with the elected House, a House elected on an ever-widening franchise.

That the House of Lords cannot sustain a claim to being a representative chamber is clear. Peers represent no one but themselves: their writs of summons are personal. No member serves by virtue of election. A peer is a member of the Upper House either by virtue of birth (hereditary peers), by virtue of appointment by the Crown on the advice of the prime minister (life peers and hereditary peers of first creation), or by virtue of position (Lords of Appeal in Ordinary, the Archbishops of Canterbury and York, and the 24 senior Bishops of the Church of England). They are divided into the Lords Temporal and the Lords Spiritual. The Lords Temporal are the hereditary and life peers, comprising (in order of seniority) the ranks of Duke, Marquess, Earl, Viscount, and Baron. There are hereditary peers of all ranks, life peers being created only as Barons. The Lords Spiritual comprise the two Archbishops and the 24 senior Bishops representing the established Anglican Church, the only members of the House who may be deemed to sit in some albeit tenuous form of representative capacity.

Currently, there are more than 1,000 members of the House (1,174 in 1980), making it the largest legislative assembly in the world. In practice, many peers do not bother to attend. About 800 attend one or more sittings of the House a year, with an average daily attendance of about 275. As a proportion of their total number, life peers are more active than hereditary peers. Life peerages were introduced under the provisions of the 1958 Life Peerages Act and made possible the introduction of new blood to the Upper House, especially that drawn from the ranks of those who disliked the hereditary principle (notably Labour party supporters). Life peerages also served to prevent the inflation of membership, the title—and eligibility to sit in the Lords—dying with the holder. There are approximately 300 life peers, and elevation to the House of Lords is in practice now usually by the conferment of a life peerage. Labour Prime Minister Harold Wilson suspended the conferment of hereditary peerages in 1964, a suspension continued by his successors until 1983. In June 1983, Mrs. Thatcher created two hereditary peerages. However, neither peer had a male heir so the effect was the same as conferring life peerages.

Given that it is not an elected body and occupies a subordinate position in relation to the House of Commons, what functions are performed by the

House? For one thing, as we have seen, it provides some of the personnel of government. No fewer than two but usually no more than four peers are chosen to be cabinet ministers. Up to 10 more may be chosen as junior ministers, with a further six or seven being appointed as government whips.

The other functions may be subsumed under the broad rubric of scrutiny and influence (of legislation and of executive actions), of providing a forum for public debate, and, formally, of legitimation. The House also has a unique judicial function as the highest domestic court of appeal, a function in practice now exercised by a judicial committee (see Chapter 13). These may be identified as the main functions of the House. Of them, one—that of legitimation—has been circumscribed both by the provisions of the Parliaments acts and by the acceptance by peers of their politically subordinate status.

Recognizing their undemocratic nature, as well as their one-party dominance (the House has a permanent Conservative majority), the Lords has refrained from seeking to challenge the House of Commons. There have been occasional periods of bad feeling between the two houses, notably in the period of Labour government from 1974 to 1979, but the Upper House rarely seeks to press an amendment—let alone delay a measure—when it is clear that the Commons is not prepared to support it. As a result of an agreement between the two front benches in the 1945–1950 Parliament, the official Opposition in the Lords does not force a vote on the second reading of any bill promised in the government's election manifesto. A government is usually assured of the Upper House approving the principle of any measure it proposes.

Given the Lords' reluctance to challenge the government on the principle of measures, the House concentrates instead on scrutinizing the specific provisions of such measures. Bills pass through the same legislative stages as in the Commons, though committee stage is taken on the floor of the House rather than in standing committee. Consideration of a bill in the Lords allows for discussion of many provisions that may not have been debated fully in the Commons, for what may be termed technical scrutiny (ensuring that the specifics of a measure make sense and that they are correctly drafted), and for the introduction of further amendments. Of amendments made to bills during their passage through the House, the majority are initiated by the government. Not surprisingly, therefore, most amendments made by the Lords prove acceptable to the Commons. Of those that do not, the Lords rarely seeks to press any.

Under the rubric of scrutiny of legislation may now be included scrutiny of draft legislation emanating from the European Communities (see Chapter 10). It is a function shared with the House of Commons, but one that the Lords is generally credited with fulfilling most effectively. The function is fulfilled primarily through the Select Committee on European Communities and its seven subcommittees. The subcommittees cover different subjects and make greater use than does the Commons of specialist advisers and outside witnesses. Peers who are not members of the subcommittees may attend to offer the benefit of their knowledge and experience in particular cases. These factors, coupled with the fact that the Lords concentrates on the legal and administrative (as opposed to the political) implications of draft proposals and can comment on their merits, has meant that the House has achieved a more formidable reputation than its Commons' counterpart in scrutinizing EC legislation.[28]

Apart from the scrutinizing bills introduced by government (and draft EC legislation), the House seeks also to scrutinize the actions of the executive. The procedures available to do this are similar to those employed in the Commons: debates and questions. The House spends about one-fifth of its time on general debates, though not all are confined to discussion of government actions and policy (see below). The procedure for asking questions differs somewhat from Commons' procedure. At the start of the day's business, only four oral questions may be asked, though supplementary

---

NOTICES AND ORDERS OF THE DAY

Notices marked † are new

WEDNESDAY THE 12TH OF MARCH

At half-past Two o'clock

Introduction —
The Lord Archbishop of Canterbury
will be introduced.

*The **Lord Brockway** — To ask Her Majesty's Government what were the conclusions of the UNESCO-sponsored International Commission for the Study of Communication Problems and how far there was agreement between the representatives of the West, the Communist countries and the Third World countries.

*The **Lord Gainford** — To ask Her Majesty's Government whether they are considering any schemes for preserving postage stamps on letters and parcels in view of the increased interest by stamp collectors in British postage stamps.

*The **Earl of Selkirk** — To ask Her Majesty's Government whether Tanzanian troops are stationed in the Seychelles or anywhere else outside their Territory.

*The **Lord Donaldson of Kingsbridge** — To ask Her Majesty's Government whether they are aware of the strength of feeling of the musical world, the distress of students of music and the disappointment of listeners at the cuts forced on the BBC, which are to be met in part by cutting the regional orchestras.

The **Earl of Listowel** — To call attention to the Report of the Independent Commission on International Development Issues (the Brandt Report), and to the need for Her Majesty's Government to review their policy in relation to developing countries; and to move for Papers.

The **Lord Hylton** — To ask Her Majesty's Government whether they are giving favourable consideration to certain modest but significant proposals for improving the financial arrangements affecting residential homes and care generally for the elderly who are frail or handicapped.

FIGURE 11.2   Questions on the House of Lords' Order Paper, March 12, 1980. (*Copyright 1980 by the Crown. Reprinted by permission of the Controller of Her Majesty's Stationery Office.*)

questions are permitted. At the conclusion of a day's business, what are termed "unstarred questions" are taken (see Figure 11.2). These are questions (previously submitted, as with all questions) on which a short debate may take place before a minister replies. As in the Commons, written questions may also be put down, the answers being published in the Lords' *Hansard.* (For the number tabled, see Table 11.4). In the Lords, unlike the Commons, all questions are addressed to Her Majesty's government and not to individual ministers.

Except for its work in the sphere of European Communities draft legislation, the House makes little use of committees. It has a number of what may be termed domestic committees, covering the internal administration of the House and its privileges, but it has rarely employed select committees as tools of scrutiny. Nonetheless, it has recently made some tentative moves in the direction of such committees, establishing the Select Committee on Unemployment ("to consider and make recommendations on long-term remedies for unemployment") and one on science and technology with a general brief to consider the topic.

The other main function that may be ascribed to the House is that of providing a forum for debate of important public issues. A similar function, of course, may be ascribed to the Commons. The difference between the two is that the Lords allows greater scope for the discussion of important topics that are not the subject of contention between parties. The Commons concentrate on partisan issues, with little time for discussion of subjects outside the realm of party debate.

The Upper House has not only the time and the inclination to debate important but essentially nonpartisan issues, it can also claim the expertise to do so. Whereas MPs are essentially professional politicians (even though they may have expertise derived from preparliamentary employment), many peers hold—indeed are often ennobled on the basis of holding—leading positions in industry, the trade unions, finance, and the arts. Being a member of the House of Lords is usually a secondary pursuit to another activity or interest. Indeed, given that peers are paid only an expense allowance and receive no salary (see Table 11.5), there is little incentive for them to be full-time members of the House. The consequence is that there are frequently a number of peers who are experts in a particular field and who will attend debates only on those occasions when their subject of expertise is under discussion. The result, according to some observers, is informed and interesting debate. Many view favorably this perceived combination of expertise and lack of party bickering. Detractors would draw attention to the fact that Lords' expertise in certain areas is not replicated in other fields, producing superficial and often dull debate, and, more significantly, calling into question what attention is paid to Lords' debates by government and outside bodies.

Possibly the most significant role played by the House in acting as a

TABLE 11.4
The House of Lords: Sittings and Parliamentary Questions, 1974–1980

			Parliamentary Sessions			
	1974–1975	1975–1976	1976–1977	1977–1978	1978–1979*	1979–1980
Number of days sitting	165	155	105	126	59	206
Number of hours sitting	930	970	596	737	345	1,268
Average daily hours:minutes of sitting	5:40	6:20	5:40	5:50	5:50	6:10
Number of parliamentary votes (divisions)	119	146	45	96	21	305
Parliamentary questions:						
Oral (starred)	560	553	385	439	217	765
Oral (unstarred)	35	41	36	46	23	68
Written	350	517	380	544	432	1,277

*Short parliamentary session because of the calling of the general election 1979.

TABLE 11.5
Parliamentary Salaries

	1964	1972	1977	1979	1982	1983
	MPs Pay for Selected Years					
MP's salary	£3,250	£3,500	£6,270	£9,450	£14,510	£15,308*
	($4,875)	($5,250)	($9,405)	($14,175)	($21,765)	($22,962)
Secretarial/research allowance	none	£1,000	£3,687	£4,520	£8,752	£11,364†
		($1,500)	($5,530)	($6,780)	($13,128)	($17,046)
Allowance for living away from main residence	none	£750	£1,814	£3,064	£4,903	—
		($1,125)	($2,721)	($4,596)	($7,354)	
London supplement (for London MPs)	none	£175	£385	—	£709	—
		($262)	($577)		($1,063)	

Peers' Allowances, 1983

Day subsistence and travel allowance	£16 ($24) per day of attendance
Overnight subsistence	£40 ($60) per day of attendance
Secretarial allowance	£17 ($25.5) multiplied by number of days' attendance (according to certain formula)

Dollar conversions at July 1983 exchange rates.
Dash indicates no rise that year. Ministers, who receive salaries as ministers, receive only part of their salary as MPs.
*Rising by installments to £18,500 in 1987.
†£12,000 in subsequent years.

forum of debate is as a safety valve. By avoiding replication of the party debate in the Commons, it allows for the occasional public debate on topics that might otherwise not receive an airing in an authoritative public forum. For some outside interests, making their voices heard through such a forum is all that they desire. The House of Lords has achieved a reputation especially for discussing important social issues (notably so in the 1960s) and for helping ease onto the political agenda topics that might otherwise have been kept off. In recent years, for example, it has proved a valuable forum for those seeking to introduce a bill of rights.[29]

The House not only debates political topics, it is itself a topic of political dispute. The debate about the House has centered not on whether it fulfills the functions outlined above, or on whether they are the functions most appropriate to a British second chamber, but rather on whether the House of Lords is the body that should constitute the second chamber and discharge those functions. At the heart of the problem is the hereditary basis of the

House. It is seen by many as the remnant of a feudal age, one that can no longer be justified in a political system based on rational-legal rather than traditional authority. It is often seen as a wonderful anachronism that has survived by dint of inertia and by a failure to agree on what, if anything, should replace it.

Schemes for reform of the House are common. "On summer evenings and winter afternoons, when they have nothing else to do, people discuss how to reform the House of Lords," wrote Janet Morgan. "Schemes are taken out of cupboards and drawers and dusted off; speeches are composed, pamphlets written, letters sent to the newspapers. From time to time, the whole country becomes excited."[30] The problem has been one of translating the desire for reform into a tangible and generally acceptable measure. The most important attempt at reform since the passage of the Parliament acts was that made by the Labour government in 1968 and 1969. The government introduced the Parliament (No. 2) bill, which sought to reform rather than replace the existing House. It proposed a two-tier House with voting members (life peers) and nonvoting members (hereditary peers), the House having a six-month delaying power over nonmoney bills. Nonvoting membership was to be confined to the existing hereditary peers, their successors not being entitled to seats in the House. As a result, the hereditary element was to be slowly removed. Under the bill's provisions, the government of the day would be provided with a working majority. The result, according to the White Paper that preceded the bill, would be a move in the direction of ensuring that the Upper House played a role "complementary to but not rivalling that of the Commons." It was envisaged that closer cooperation between the two Houses and a review of the Lords' functions would follow once the changes were implemented.

In any event, the bill was not enacted. Although support for it in the House of Commons was broad—the bill followed interparty talks on the issue—it was not deep. There was bitter opposition to it from a number of Labour MPs, led by Michael Foot, who wished to abolish the House of Lords altogether and from a number of Conservative MPs, led by Enoch Powell, who wished to leave it as it was. This unholy alliance, as it was generally described, fought to delay the bill, and that delay proved successful. The government appeared to lose heart in the measure and many MPs who favored reform found fault with its specific provisions. The committee stage of the bill was taken on the floor of the House, and the government whips had increasing difficulty in keeping sufficient MPs present in order to carry closure motions. Debate began to eat into time that the government preferred to utilize for other measures. In April 1969, the government decided not to proceed with the bill.

The experience of the 1969 bill deterred succeeding governments from seeking to tackle the problem. Nonetheless, debate surrounding the future of the House of Lords was not stilled. Various Labour politicians sought to keep it on the agenda of political debate, proponents of root-and-branch reform becoming more vocal in recent years. In the 1980s, the House of Lords remains an issue of political debate.

THE CURRENT DEBATE

In historical perspective, debate on parliamentary reform has tended to be more intense—and to generate the introduction of more measures of reform—when focused on the House of Lords. In recent years, both Houses have become targets of radical proposals for change.

The House of Commons

Although literature advocating reform of the House of Commons can be found littering the historical landscape, it has tended to be significant primarily in periods of national economic decline. The reasons for this we have touched on already. As the political system has failed to cope adequately, or been perceived as having failed to cope, a number of critics have sought an explanation for that failure in the nation's political institutions. Such has been the case in the past decade or so. Prescriptions for limited procedural reform of the House of Commons have competed with more radical proposals for change.

In the 1960s, a number of Labour MPs and academics, notably Professor Bernard Crick, were active in pressing for parliamentary reform and especially for procedural change. The dominance of the government over Parliament, they argued, was too great. The House of Commons lacked the facilities to subject the government to sustained scrutiny; MPs were too badly paid, lacked adequate research facilities, and were constrained by archaic procedures.[31] Even as an arena assembly, the House was performing badly. What was needed, they argued, were reforms that would allow the House to engage in more effective scrutiny through investigation and debate. To such an end, they advocated the greater use of select committees, longer sittings of the House, better pay and research facilities for members, and modernization of parliamentary procedure, the broadcasting of debates, and more opportunities for emergency debates. Such reforms, it was contended, would allow the House the opportunity to subject government to public scrutiny and to keep it responsive to public feeling, thus maintaining consent for the political system (the House doing the job expected of it) without jeopardizing the effectiveness of government (the government retaining its parliamentary majority). A strong government, declared Professor Crick, was compatible with a strong Opposition.[32]

In the 1970s, pressure for limited internal reform of the House began to give way to calls for more radical change. A convergence of two developments may help explain why this happened. One was the failure of a number of internal reforms implemented in the latter half of the 1960s and early 1970s. The extended use of select committees had little impact on government and on policy-making. As an experiment, the House began to meet in the morning on two days a week. However, votes could not be held during these sittings and members, especially Conservative members (many of whom had outside interests), showed little interest in them and rarely attended. The morning sittings were abandoned. Pay for MPs was increased and more offices were made available, but the improvements were relative: MPs remained poorly paid (see Tables 11.5 and 11.6) and had little by way of research facilities, other than the library of the House. The relationship between the House and the part of it that formed the government remained essentially unchanged—hence an impetus for more far-reaching reform. This was reinforced by a second development. The 1970s witnessed greater economic and political turmoil than had existed in the previous decade (see Chapter 3). The country's economic position worsened, and the two general elections of 1974 produced governments elected with less than 40% of the votes cast and an apparent and significant shift away from the two main parties (see Chapters 5 and 6). A combination of these developments fostered more rigorous and critical analyses of the House of Commons and its relationship to the country's economic and political malaise.

The radical reformers, led by academics such as S. E. Finer and S. A. Walkland, were intent on ripping away what they saw as the inaccurate and misleading gloss placed on the role of the House by previous writers.[33] They assailed the House as having clung to nineteenth-century practices and beliefs during a period that witnessed major economic and social change (the welfare state and the managed economy), the swelling of bureaucracy, and the trend toward a corporate economy. It had failed to adapt and to keep pace with such developments. The electoral system encouraged the return of one party with a majority of seats, and party discipline within the House assured the resulting party government of a parliamentary majority for whatever it proposed. The result was a malfunctional parliamentary system. It was a system that undermined rather than reinforced political authority. The House was incapable of subjecting government to scrutiny, let alone have any tangible impact on public policy.

Such an analysis led reformers to advocate electoral reform, a move supported by academics such as Professors Finer and Walkland, by the Liberal party, by a number of Conservative MPs, and by some Labour Members, most of whom subsequently defected to join the Social Democratic party.[34] The basis of their argument and its implications was discussed in Chapter 5. Electoral reform would produce, according to its exponents, a more representative House of Commons. On the basis of existing voting behavior, no one party would achieve an overall majority, thus forcing a

TABLE 11.6
MPs' Pay and Allowances: International Comparisons, 1975

Legislature	Salary	Rent and Subsistence	Offices	Secretarial Expenses
United Kingdom House of Commons	£5,750	£1,350 London supplement, £340	Shared or single offices for most MPs at Westminster.	£3,200
United States House of Representatives	£18,023	(£1,272 of salary tax deductible)	Three-room suite of offices. Allowance for up to three constituency offices.	Clerk-hire allowance of £77,445
French National Assembly	£10,058	None	Every member has a room.	£317–£423 per month
Australian House of Representatives	£11,256 Electorate allowance of £2,307	£21 for each overnight stay on official business	Single or shared office in Parliament House. Usually two-room office in constituency.	Full-time secretary in constituency. Pool of secretaries at Parliament House.
Canadian Lower House	£7,657	£3,403	Two adjoining offices. Assistance in renting constituency offices.	Provision to employ two secretaries. £2,552 allowance for staff in constituency.
West German Bundestag	£7,820	£3,232	One office per member.	£5,368 plus secretarial pool.

Salaries based on exchange rates prevailing at various points in 1975.
SOURCE: J. Morgan, *Reinforcing Parliament: Sources and Facilities for Members of Parliament, Some International Comparisons* (Political and Economic Planning, No. 562, 1976). Copyright 1976 Political and Economic Planning. Reprinted by permission.

coalition of the political center or a minority government responsive to other parties in the House. The House of Commons would continue to provide most of the personnel of Government, to subject government to (more effective) scrutiny and influence, and to legitimate the government and its measures. The most significant difference would be that the House itself would have a greater claim to legitimacy in fulfilling those functions and would, in its behavior, be more consensual.

Despite a swelling of their ranks in the latter half of the 1970s, those who advocate electoral reform have not yet found themselves in a position to implement such a measure. As we have seen (Chapter 5), they are opposed by a majority of MPs in both parties. They have been opposed also, on less self-serving grounds, by a number of writers. Some have contended that such change is not necessary. In the late 1960s, writer and journalist Ronald Butt argued that Parliament by means of party continued to keep the government responsive to the wishes of the electorate. If the government went too far, its own backbenchers would put a warning shot across its bows.[35] Similar sentiments have continued to be expressed in recent years by MPs such as Michael Foot and Enoch Powell.[36] Parliamentary debate, declared Mr. Foot in the late 1970s, can have a "very considerable effect on what Governments dare to propose and what Governments are capable of getting through."[37] Others have continued to favor internal reform as a means of realizing a more effective scrutinizing chamber. They have tended to advocate, in particular, the more extensive use of investigative select committees and place much weight on the new system of select committees established in 1979.[38] Finally, there is the approach associated with the writer of this work, an approach subsumed elsewhere under the appellation of the "Norton view."[39]

This approach allows for the maintenance of government effectiveness, the political process remaining executive-centered, while on the other side making possible an effective House of Commons, the House fulfilling and being seen to fulfill the function of subjecting governmental actions and measures to scrutiny and influence. The balance between executive and Commons would be maintained, and this balance could be jeopardized by the implementation of a new electoral system (see Chapter 5). The approach posited by this author makes possible such a balance. It draws on recent experience as the basis for arguing not only what should be but also what can be. It stipulates the need for an attitudinal change on the part of MPs as a prerequisite to effective procedural reform.

The approach derives its strength and much of its impetus from changes in parliamentary behavior in the 1970s. In that decade, policy disagreements and, in the 1970–1974 Parliament, Edward Heath's manner of prime ministerial leadership resulted in government backbenchers being willing, for the first time this century, to enter the opposition lobby and deprive the government of its majority.[40] Such willingness resulted in 6 defeats for Mr. Heath's Conservative government (a Parliament in which the government had a clear working majority) and 23 defeats under the Labour government of 1974–1979. In addition, there were 17 government defeats in the short 1974 Parliament because of Opposition parties combining against a minority government, and 19 defeats in the 1974–1979 Parliament for the same reason.[41] The convergence of these developments (backbench willingness to cross-vote and minority governments) produced a total of 65 government defeats in the seven-year period from 1972 to 1979. For a similar number of defeats in a similar period, one has to go back to the 1860s.

These defeats were important not only in themselves—they took place on many significant issues, including income tax and the government's major constitutional proposal of the 1974–1979 Parliament, devolution—but also for their impact on MPs' perceptions of what they could achieve. The defeats and their aftermath served to dispel many myths about constraints presumed to operate on MPs in their voting behavior. Apart from an explicit vote of no confidence, no government felt compelled to resign because of such defeats. Government backbenchers who helped deprive the government of its majority in parliamentary votes were not subject to expulsion by their parliamentary or constituency parties. As understanding of such realities of political life began to dawn, so members' attitudes began to change. A deferential attitude toward government was gradually discarded in favor of a participant one.[42] It was this change of attitude that impelled members to press for the creation of more effective select committees. Pressure from backbenchers built up from 1978 onward, pressure that, coupled with a reforming leader of the House (Mr. St. John-Stevas), effectively overcame cabinet reluctance in 1979, making possible the new select committees approved by the House in June of that year. The committees differed from their predecessors in that they owed their creation to the House as a whole and not to government and they owed their vigor and continuation to the willingness of MPs to sustain them.

The view of this author is that such developments point to the direction in which the House not only should but can go in order to ensure that it fulfills the role expected of it. Members can ensure effective scrutiny and influence of government if they have the political will to do so. A House in which the government of the day can normally be assured a majority, but a majority it cannot take for granted, is the most practical way of ensuring the existence of a government that can govern, but one that is responsive to the House of Commons. If the House is seen publicly to be fulfilling its limited but not unimportant role, it will be achieving as much as one could hope.[43]

The House of Lords

The debate on parliamentary reform has not been confined to the House of Commons. The House of Lords continues in its accustomed role as the subject of disparate proposals for change. The hiatus following the failure of the 1969 Parliament (No. 2) bill has given way to pressure for radical change, including total abolition, from a number of Labour politicians and for less radical surgery from Conservatives and others. The views now expressed on Lords' reform may be summarized for convenience under four heads, the "four Rs": retain, reform, replace, and remove altogether.

Many who find unacceptable the hereditary basis of the House of Lords often express amazement that there are people other than hereditary peers who are prepared to defend the House as it currently exists. Yet a number of observers are prepared to make a case for the retention of the House in its current form, doing so on grounds of principle and of practicality.[44] They contend that the hereditary principle provides peers who are able to render an opinion free of external pressures, being beholden to no party or patron, and that it provides peers with not only a wide range of experience but also a wide range of views. The House boasts not only a large number of independent peers (known as "crossbench" peers because of the benches they occupy in the House, no such benches existing in the Commons), it also has a Communist member, Lord Milford. Members give freely of their services in order to ensure that the House fulfills its functions, and defenders contend that those functions are well fulfilled. In the absence of an acceptable alternative, so defenders contend, why not leave well enough alone? The House does its job and there is little public pressure for change.

Reformers take a different view. Many Conservatives and some Labour supporters (notably a number of Labour peers) are of the opinion that if the Upper House—indeed, any second chamber—is to survive, the existing House must be reformed or replaced; otherwise, it may fall victim to the onslaught of Labour abolitionists. Change is sought in order to conserve. Moderate reformers seek change based on the existing House. They favor a measure on lines similar to those of the 1969 bill. Such a measure was proposed by a working group of Labour peers in 1980. Other reformers seek to replace the existing House either with a completely new elected or appointed chamber or one that forms something of a hybrid between the existing chamber and an elected House. Two Conservative committees have recommended a House chosen mainly or wholly by election.[45] Such election, it is argued, would enhance the legitimacy of the second chamber and, in so doing, create a chamber that had an acceptable basis to act as a safeguard against an over-mighty House of Commons.

Other radical proposals for replacement have included a House based on regional representation and one based on functional representation. A House comprising representatives of the regions of the United Kingdom, a proposal popular with those who support devolution, is seen as a means of providing a countervailing force against the centralizing tendencies of government. A House formed of representatives of groups such as the trades unions and industry would allow for the cooption of sectional groups into the formal political process, enhancing the consent of such groups.[46]

The most radical step—to abolish the House of Lords and not replace it at all, creating a unicameral legislature—has been advocated by some politicians for many years. It has gained strength in recent years. In 1977, the Labour party conference approved a motion in favor of "an efficient single-chamber legislating body," reaffirming its commitment in 1980. One leading

Labour politician, Tony Benn, has made it clear that he believes abolition should be the first task of any future Labour government. A second chamber, however composed, is seen as a potential obstacle to the passage of Socialist legislation. The case for doing away with it has been most succinctly put by Labour Peer Lord Wedderburn: "Either the second chamber is less democratic than the Commons in which case it should not be able to delay legislation," he said, "or it is just as democratic, then there is no point in having two chambers."[47] The functions of the Upper House, so abolitionists argue, could be transferred to a reformed House of Commons.

Although at the national level, defenders of the existing House of Lords are in a minority, those who favor reform have difficulty in finding a measure on which they can agree. Each reform proposal has its detractors: an appointed House would be little better than the existing House; an elected chamber would either duplicate the Commons or (if elected by a procedure different from that for the Lower House) be a potential obstruction to measures emanating from it; a House based on functional representation would further enhance the position of already over-powerful groups; and the absence of a second chamber would generate too many pressures for the remaining chamber, as well as doing away altogether with a necessary constitutional safeguard. It has been such disagreement among those who favor change that has resulted in no significant change taking place. The only measures affecting the Upper House that have been passed in the past 30 years have been those providing for the creation of life peers—a development that has breathed new life into the chamber—and for hereditary peers to disclaim their titles should they so choose. Although such changes are more radical than any made affecting the Commons, the House has undergone no fundamental change. Defenders of the House see this as no bad thing. Others believe that the longer it remains unreformed, the greater the pressure for it to be swept away altogether. The great democratic wave identified by Shaftesbury may yet swell and sweep it away.

SUMMARY

Parliament continues to enjoy popular support as a legitimate political institution. Its output, by virtue of the doctrine of parliamentary sovereignty, is binding upon all and cannot be struck down by the courts. It is the institution from which the political apex of government is drawn and from which government derives its legitimacy as an elected body. It has the characteristics of an arena assembly, seeking through debate to subject government to scrutiny and some measures of influence, and providing the broad limits within which government may govern.

Recent years have witnessed a growing realization that neither popular support for it as a legitimating political body nor its modest powers has been as great as was previously believed. The mode of election and the adversary relationship between two parties have been identified as undermining the claim of the House of Commons to be a representative assembly. The hereditary basis of the Lords continues to be used as sufficient reason for denying the House any claim to be considered an appropriate political institution. Party hegemony has been identified as constricting Parliament's ability to exercise even the modest powers ascribed to it. A consequence has been pressure for significant reform, seeking to restore to Parliament both popular support and the political will to exercise modest powers in the making of public policy. What has been lacking among reformers has been agreement as to what form change should take. Although many may agree on ends, agreement as to means is notably absent. Electoral reformers seek to generate a parliamentary system that reflects and seeks to generate consensus. In their preference for their own scheme of reform, consensus is the one thing they lack.

NOTES

1. Although, under Article I, section 7(1), of the Constitution all revenue-raising bills must originate in the House of Representatives.
2. M. Mezey, *Comparative Legislatures* (Duke University Press, 1979), Ch. 2.
3. See J. Turner, *Party and Constituency: Pressure on Congress,* rev. ed. by E. V. Schneier, Jr. (John Hopkins, 1970), Ch. II.
4. Mezey, p. 37.
5. R. H. S. Crossman, "Introduction" to W. Bagehot, *The English Constitution* (Fontana, 1963 ed.), p. 39.
6. N. Polsby, "Legislatures" in F. I. Greenstein and N. Polsby (eds.), *Handbook of Political Science,* Vol. 5 (Addison-Wesley, 1975).
7. J. A. G. Griffith, *Parliamentary Scrutiny of Government Bills* (George Allen & Unwin, 1974), p. 93.
8. Ibid., p. 159.
9. See P. Norton, *The Commons in Perspective* (Longman, 1981), pp. 99–102.
10. See P. G. Richards, *Parliament and Conscience* (George Allen & Unwin, 1970).
11. Figures derived from R. L. Borthwick, "The Floor of the House" in S. A. Walkland and M. Ryle (eds.), *The Commons Today* (Fontana, 1981), p. 66.
12. See Norton, pp. 111–14. See also D. N. Chester and N. Bowring, *Questions in Parliament* (Oxford University Press, 1962).
13. See Norton, p. 121.
14. See ibid., p. 122.
15. Ibid., p. 123.
16. S. J. Downs, "Select Committees in the House of Commons: An Ineluctable Development?" *Hull Papers in Politics No. 32* (Hull University Politics Department, 1983).
17. See Norton, p. 128.

18. Ibid., pp. 130–31.

19. D. Shell, "Specialist Select Committees," *Parliamentary Affairs,* 23 (4), Autumn 1970, p. 380.

20. Standing Order 86A. See Norton, p. 134.

21. Norton, p. 134.

22. P. Norton, "The Importance of MP-to-Minister Correspondence," *Parliamentary Affairs,* 35 (1), Winter 1982, p. 62.

23. Ibid.

24. B. Cain, J. Ferejohn, and P. Fiorina, "The Roots of Legislator Popularity in Great Britain and the United States," *California Institute of Technology: Social Science Working Paper 288* (October 1979), p. 6.

25. Ibid., p. 7.

26. See Norton, *Commons in Perspective,* pp. 115–17; H. B. Berrington, *Backbench Opinion in the House of Commons 1945–1955* (Pergamon Press, 1973); and S. E. Finer et al., *Backbench Opinion in the House of Commons 1955–1959* (Pergamon, 1961).

27. *Parliamentary Debates (Hansard),* Vol. 188, cols. 1925–26 (1867).

28. See C. Moore, "The Role of the House of Lords in the Scrutiny of EEC Legislation," third-year undergraduate dissertation, Hull University Politics Department, 1979.

29. See P. Norton, *The Constitution in Flux* (Martin Robertson, 1982), p. 246.

30. J. Morgan, "The House of Lords in the 1980s," *The Parliamentarian,* 62 (1), January 1981, p. 18.

31. B. Crick, *The Reform of Parliament* (Weidenfeld & Nicholson, 1964).

32. Ibid.

33. S. E. Finer (ed.), *Adversary Politics and Electoral Reform* (Wigram, 1975), and S. A. Walkland, "Whither the Commons?" in S. A. Walkland and M. Ryle (eds.), *The Commons Today* (Fontana, 1981).

34. An electoral reform group was formed among Labour MPs in the 1970s. All but one subsequently joined the SDP. The exception was Austin Mitchell, MP for Grimsby.

35. R. Butt, *The Power of Parliament* (Constable, 1967).

36. Norton, *The Commons in Perspective,* pp. 217–18.

37. *First Report from the Select Committee on Procedure 1977–1978,* Vol. 2: *Minutes of Evidence* (HC 588-2,) p. 64.

38. See B. George and B. Evans, "Reforming Parliament—The Internal View" in D. Judge (ed.), *The Politics of Parliamentary Reform* (Heinemann, 1983).

39. Norton, *The Commons in Perspective,* Ch. 9.

40. P. Norton, *Conservative Dissidents* (Temple Smith, 1978).

41. P. Norton, *Dissension in the House of Commons 1974–1979* (Oxford University Press, 1980).

42. S. H. Beer, *Britain against Itself* (Faber, 1982), p. 190.

43. This argument is developed in P. Norton, "The Norton View" in Judge, *The Politics of Parliamentary Reform.*

44. See, e.g., Lord Boyd-Carpenter, "Reform of the House of Lords—Another View," *The Parliamentarian,* 59 (2), April 1978, pp. 90–93.

45. Report of the Conservative Review Committee, *The House of Lords* (Conservative Central Office, 1978); and Report of the Constitutional Reform Commit-

tee of the Society of Conservative Lawyers, *House of Lords Reform?* (Macmillan, 1978).

46. Norton, *The Constitution in Flux,* pp. 123–24.

47. Quoted in H. Hebert, "The Lords under the Microscope," *The Guardian,* March 1, 1979.

12

The Monarchy
Strength through Weakness

IN THE UNITED STATES, the head of state is the president. In the United Kingdom, the head of the state is the monarch. Both fulfill certain formal duties associated with the position. Beyond that there is little similarity between the two. In terms of history, determination of incumbency, powers, and current responsibilities, the United States presidency and the British monarchy have virtually nothing in common. The president is both head of state and political head of the administration. He operates directly and personally at the heart of the political decision-making process. The monarch, as head of state, stands above political decision-making. In political terms, he or she serves not to decide but, primarily, to perform a symbolic role. The president serves by virtue of election; the monarch reigns by virtue of birth.

The monarchy is the oldest secular institution in Britain. It predates Parliament by some four centuries and the law courts by some three centuries, the present monarch being able to trace her descent from King Egbert, who united England under his rule in 829 A.D. The continuity of the institution has been broken only once, during the period of military rule by Oliver Cromwell. There have been various interruptions in the direct line of succession, but the hereditary principle has been preserved since at least the eleventh century. The succession itself is governed by certain principles of common law and by statute. The throne descends to the eldest son, or in the absence of a son, the eldest daughter. By the Act of Settlement of 1700, affirmed by the Treaty of Union in 1707, the Crown was to descend to the

294

heirs of the granddaughter of James I, Princess Sophia; this has been confirmed by later acts.[1]

For several centuries, there was no separation of powers: executive, legislative, and judicial power was exercised by the king. With the growth of Parliament (and its power of the purse) as well as the courts, the direct exercise of these functions progressively declined. As we have seen (Chapter 3), the conflict between King and Parliament in the seventeenth century resulted in the Settlement of 1688 and the establishment of what was essentially a limited constitutional monarchy. The monarch nonetheless remained at the head of government, in practice as well as formally. Those responsible for the Bill of Rights of 1689 wanted "a real, working, governing king, a king with a policy,"[2] albeit a king governing with the consent of Parliament. The centrality of the monarch to governing was to decline in the eighteenth century with the king's increasing dependence on his ministers. During this century, one can see the divorce of the positions of head of state and political head of government, formerly united in the person of the king. The former remained with the king, the latter in practice became vested in his chief minister. The withdrawal of the monarch largely but by no means exclusively from active participation in political life was to be a marked feature of the succeeding century. Queen Victoria's reign (1837–1901) marked the transition from a monarch still active in political life to one fulfilling primarily a formal role, part of what Bagehot had identified as the "dignified" part of the Constitution.[3] The twentieth century has realized the move toward a politically neutral monarchy, standing now well removed from the partisan fray of party government.

The years since 1688 have witnessed various landmarks on this path toward a neutral monarchy, divorced from active partisan decision-making. The last occasion a monarch vetoed a piece of legislation was when Queen Anne did in 1707, the last time a monarch dismissed a ministry was in 1834, and the last occasion on which the monarch clearly exercised a personal choice in the selection of a prime minister was Queen Victoria in summoning Lord Rosebery in 1894. (Monarchs have on occasion subsequently had to exercise a choice in the selection of prime ministers but, as we shall see, have acted under advice.) The last monarch to attempt to veto cabinet appointments, with some measure of success, was Queen Victoria. She was also the last monarch to be instrumental in pushing successfully for the enactment of particular legislation: on at least two occasions she virtually initiated legislation, the 1874 Public Worship Regulation Act and the 1876 Royal Titles Act.[4] She may also be described as the last monarch to indulge, albeit within a limited circle, in partisan expression. Initially a Whig, she became for all intents and purposes a vehement Conservative; she clearly adored her Conservative prime minister, Disraeli, and made little secret of her utter disdain for the Liberal leader, William Gladstone. Partisan expression declined significantly under her successors. Indeed, according to

Frank Hardie, this was a notable feature of the first half of the twentieth century: "Since 1901 the trend towards a real political neutrality, not merely a matter of appearances, has been steady, reign by reign."[5]

The result of these developments has been that twentieth-century monarchs have come to occupy a position in which they are called on to fulfill two primary tasks. One is to represent the unity of the nation. The other is to carry out certain political functions on the advice of ministers. The weakness of the monarch in being able to exercise independent decisions in the latter task has ensured the strength of the monarchy in fulfilling the first.

The Crown in Britain is the symbol of supreme executive authority. It serves essentially as a substitute for the concept of the State, a concept not well developed in Britain and one that has not made an impact on the national consciousness. The monarch is the person on whom the Crown is constitutionally conferred. Various public duties are carried out in the name of the Crown (for example, public prosecutions) and, as the person in whom the Crown vests, the monarch's name attaches to both government and the armed forces. The armed services are Her Majesty's Services. Her Majesty is Commander-in-Chief. People go to war to fight for "Queen and Country." The government is Her Majesty's government, ministers are Her Majesty's ministers. Even the Opposition in Parliament is titled Her Majesty's Loyal Opposition. Postage stamps and coins bear the Queen's image. (British postage stamps are unique: the monarch's head substitutes for the name of the nation.) The Queen personifies what for Americans is represented by the Stars and Stripes. The pageantry associated with the monarchy serves as a living expression of national unity. It provides the opportunity for citizens to indulge in that expression of unity and to escape from the drudgery of everyday life: it gives expression to pride in being British.

In order that the Queen may embody the unity of the nation, it is imperative that she not only abstain from partisan activity but be seen to abstain, indeed be seen to transcend political activity. The political functions she performs, such as the appointment of the prime minister, the appointment of ministers, the dispensing of honors, and the assent of legislation, are governed by convention. She acts on the advice of her ministers and is recognized as so acting. When the Queen's Speech is read from the throne on the opening of Parliament, the speech is handed to the Queen by the Lord Chancellor and subsequently handed back to him, signifying that it is the government's responsibility. Government is carried on in the name of the Queen and not by the Queen.

The formal exercise of political functions by the monarch serves a useful purpose. It provides a sense of duty for government (fulfilling duties as Her Majesty's ministers is a reminder that they are in office to perform a service to the nation) and it provides a significant sense of continuity. Governments may come and governments may go, but the Queen continues to reign. When Queen Elizabeth II ascended to the throne in 1952, Winston Church-

ill was prime minister. She has been served by eight separate prime ministers. By being the person to whom prime ministers submit their resignations
and who summons the new premier, the monarch gives a sense of continuity, one that arguably could not be provided by any other form of head of
state in a free society.

The continuity provided by the monarch has another and, from the
perspective of government, very useful aspect. Each prime minister has a
regular audience with the Queen, usually at least once a week when the
sovereign is in London. Her Majesty sees all cabinet papers in advance. She
receives the minutes of cabinet meetings and of cabinet committee meetings. She receives copies of all important Foreign and Commonwealth Office
telegrams. She is reputed to be an assiduous reader of all such papers. Apart
from more than 30 years' experience of meeting with her Prime Ministers,
she has spent much of her reign traveling and meeting with other heads of
state. This being the case, she has an unparalleled wealth of experience.
That experience she can and does bring to bear in her meetings with the
prime minister, doing so in a nonpartisan context and in an environment
where the prime minister does not have to deal with an opponent or potential rival. The audience provides the premier with a unique opportunity, as
Sir Ian Gilmour expressed it, "to explain decisions and policies to a disin-
terested observer in the fullest privacy."[6] Successive prime ministers have
attested to the value of such meetings.

Prime ministers have reason also be to grateful to the monarch for the
fulfillment of various formal duties. In the United States, the president as
head of state has to fulfill a number of time-consuming tasks, including
receiving new ambassadors, presenting medals, and attending a number of
formal nonpolitical functions. The president is not trained to carry out these
tasks and the time given over to them is at the expense of time that could be
used for running the administration. In Britain, the formal tasks are carried
out by the monarch or, in some cases, by other members of the royal family.
The physical distinction between head of state and head of government
allows for ceremonial duties to be carried out by someone schooled for the
task and avoids the conflicting time demands faced by any political leader
cum head of state.

By being scrupulously neutral in performing her duties, the Queen is
able to fulfill her task of representing the unity of the nation. The hereditary
principle in this context is a benefit rather than a hindrance. It helps provide
a monarch trained for the task, one free of the partisan implications that
would inhere in any election of a head of state. A hereditary monarchy, as a
number of observers have pointed out, serves also to prevent the growth of
competing dynastic families. By fulfilling her duties in the way that she does,
the Queen serves also to overcome any perceptions of incompatibility between a hereditary monarchy and a presumed democratic society. Indeed,
there are those who see the monarch as fulfilling an essential role to protect

democratic institutions. In the unlikely event of any attempt to impose military or otherwise nondemocratic government, the monarch would be the most effective barrier to its realization. A monarch, as Gilmour observed, can engage the affections and loyalty of the armed forces more easily than can a President.[7] Almost paradoxically, the monarchy serves as a backstop, an ultimate safeguard, to protect those political institutions that have superseded it as the governing force in the United Kingdom.

THE CURRENT DEBATE

The two main areas of debate concerning the monarchy have been those of (a) the existence, pageantry, and upkeep of the monarchy; and (b) the exercise by the monarch of certain political powers not clearly governed by the convention. The first involves some criticism, and the second, speculation.

The continued existence of the monarchy has been challenged by the occasional republican voice. The institution has been attacked as anachronistic and costly, and a bastion of privilege and conservatism. The best-known of republican vocalists is William Hamilton, the Labour MP for Fife Central. He has attacked the monarchy as being indefensible in a free society. "My objection to the monarchy," he declared in the House of Commons, "is that it is at the apex of the class structure of our society. It is the top of the pecking order in our society, with everybody knowing his or her place in the order of things."[8] He, along with a number of colleagues, has regularly voted against increases in the Civil List, the money paid to the Queen from public funds to meet the expenses incurred in fulfilling her duties as head of state.[9] A number of Labour MPs have spoken in support of a presidential system, though on the lines of the West German rather than the American model[10]—that is, they favor separate election of the head of state and the head of government.

The supporters of the monarchy have defended it on the grounds that it enjoys national support, is efficient and not costly, and performs functions that could not be done as well by a nominated or elected head of state. That the monarchy enjoys popular support is clear. In their survey of working-class voters in the early 1960s, McKenzie and Silver reported that questioning on the need for reforming the monarchy "elicited very few expressions of fundamental hostility and almost no evidence of abolitionist sentiment."[11] A Gallup Poll in 1973 found that 80% of respondents would prefer to retain a king or queen as head of state, only 11% indicating a preference for a president.[12] In a public opinion survey in 1983, 93% of respondents said that they thought that the Queen did a good job (Table 12.1). Open expression of support for royal occasions suggested that support for the institution of the monarchy is deep as well as broad. Abolition or fundamental reform is not an issue on the agenda of political debate.

TABLE 12.1
Opinion on the Queen's Work

Question: Does the Queen do a good job?

	All	Men	Women	Under 35	Over 35
Yes	93%	90%	96%	88%	96%
No	5%	9%	2%	10%	3%
Don't know	2%	1%	2%	2%	1%

SOURCE: Public Opinion Survey conducted on April 11, 1983, published in *The Sun*, April 24, 1983. Copyright 1983 News Group Newspapers, Ltd. Reprinted by permission.

The arguments as to cost and social position are more common. The monarchy is by its nature at the top of the social pyramid in Britain, and those close to the monarch are often drawn from the upper echelons of the aristocracy. Against this is set the argument that much of the snobbery associated with royal functions has been obviated. "It has been firmly demonstrated," wrote Max Nicholson, "that the modern monarchy does not need and indeed may be rather bored by the survivals of a traditional court and its numerous hangers-on, social and commercial."[13] Traditions such as the presentation of debutantes at the beginning of the social season have been done away with. The Queen and other members of the royal family spend much time visiting local communities and going on royal "walk-abouts"—chatting with people in the crowds who have turned out to greet them. Furthermore, as the much-traveled head of the commonwealth, the Queen is well placed to mix with people of all social classes from countries in different parts of the globe. She has carried out her task as head of the commonwealth with obvious dedication and, according to Paul Johnson, "with an acute responsiveness to change."[14]

Expenditure for the exercise of the Queen's public duties is met from the Civil List.[15] This covers such items as staff costs, the upkeep of royal residences, the cost of state dinners and other functions, and transportation to official functions. Provision is also made for the expenses incurred in fulfilling public duties by other members of the royal family to be met from public funds. Increases in the Civil List are often criticized as extravagant or unnecessary at times of economic hardship for the country. Some of the money voted to other members of the royal family—especially to Princess Margaret, the Queen's sister—is criticized as unjustified, some of those involved being considered "hangers-on" at public expense. Critics contend that the upkeep of the monarchy, with all its ceremony, is not necessary and that money could be saved if the Queen's personal wealth was subject to taxation, which at the moment it is not. Defenders of the monarchy retort that, if one takes into account income from Crown Lands (surrendered to the state by the monarchy in return for regular provision under the Civil List) as well as the intangible benefits that accrue from having a monarch rather than a president (for example, increased tourism and international goodwill), then the country makes a net profit from the institution. Furthermore, increases in the Civil List, often referred to as the "Queen's pay rises," are usually to meet increased staff costs. Whether serving a monarch or a president, employees have to be paid. In 1975, the then Chancellor of the Exchequer, Denis Healey, pointed out that the total annual expenditure by the Exchequer or the taxpayer on the monarchy was about equal to the cost of holding one general election.[16] The prevailing opinion would appear to be that, on balance, the expenditure is justified.

The debate surrounding those of the Queen's powers not clearly governed by convention is of a different nature. As we have seen, the exercise of most of the political powers vested in the monarch is governed largely by convention. In most cases, this entails the Queen's acting on the advice of her ministers. However, certain important powers remain vested in the monarch that on occasion may require a choice among alternative options, a choice not clearly dictated by convention. The most obvious and important power involved here is that of choosing a prime minister.

It is a convention of the constitution that the Queen will select as prime minister that person whom she considers capable of ensuring a majority in the House of Commons. In practice, this usually creates no problems. If a party obtains an overall majority in a general election, the Queen summons the leader of that party. But what happens if there is no party leader to be summoned or if no party is returned with an overall majority at a general election? The first possibility no longer faces the Queen, though until recently it did. Until 1965, the Conservative party had no formal mechanism for choosing a leader (see Chapter 6). The leader was expected to "emerge" following soundings of one sort or another within the party. In the event of a Conservative prime minister's retiring with no successor immediately apparent, or with different contenders for the succession, the choice was left to the monarch. In 1957, the Queen was faced with summoning someone to succeed Sir Anthony Eden as prime minister. After consulting with senior statesmen, she sent for Harold Macmillan instead of, as many assumed she would, R. A. Butler. In 1963, she was confronted with the difficult task of appointing a prime minister in succession to Mr. Macmillan. After taking the advice of her outgoing prime minister, she summoned Lord Home (or Sir Alec Douglas-Home, as he quickly became after renouncing his title in order to seek a seat in the House of Commons). The choice was a controversial one[17] and, though the decision was essentially that of Mr. Macmillan, it embroiled the Crown in political controversy. The prospect of any repetition was avoided when the Conservative party introduced a procedure for the election of the party leader in 1965. The party was thus in a position to elect a leader and avoid the Queen's having to make a selection on its behalf.

The second possibility, a party having no overall majority, is one over which many commentators have mused in recent years. What should the Queen do in the event of no party having a parliamentary majority? It became an important topic of debate in 1981 and 1982. The formation of the Social Democratic party and academic analyses of changing electoral behavior pointed to a "hung" Parliament (one with no party enjoying an overall majority) as a real possibility at the next general election. In any event, the possibility was not realized, but the relative electoral positions of the SDP/Liberal Alliance and the Labour party in the 1983 general election (see Chapter 5) fueled speculation as to the possibility of future "hung" Parliaments. If the Conservatives were returned at a future election with a plurality of seats but not an absolute majority, the third party holding the balance of power refusing to support the Conservatives under their existing leader, what should the Queen do? Should she summon a Conservative who would be acceptable to that third party, or should she automatically summon the leader of the second largest party in the House? There is no clear convention to guide the Queen. She would be saddled, as David Watt observed, "with a highly controversial and thankless responsibility."[18] It is one she would almost certainly prefer to do without.

One other power that has produced a similar debate is the power to dissolve Parliament. The usual practice is for the prime minister to recommend a dissolution to the Queen and for Her Majesty to accede to the request. There is some doubt, though, as to whether it is considered a convention for the Queen automatically to concede a dissolution. Various hypothetical circumstances have been postulated to demonstrate a case for arguing that it should not be so considered. In the event of a cabinet's breaking up (possibly after two general elections in close succession) and the prime minister's preference for a dissolution rather than a coalition with another party being opposed by most ministers, would the Queen be justified in withholding her consent to her prime minister's request? Lord Blake has argued that in such or similar circumstances the Queen would not be obliged to grant a dissolution.[19] When the Tribune Group, a group of Labour MPs, argued in 1974 that the prime minister had an absolute right to determine the date of an election, a senior minister responded, "Constitutional lawyers of the highest authority are of the clear opinion that the Sovereign is not in all circumstances bound to grant a Prime Minister's request for a dissolution."[20] The problem is one of determining the circumstances that would justify the Queen's denying a dissolution, and whether, whatever the circumstances, such an action could be taken without seriously damaging the Queen's reputation for being above the partisan fray. "For the monarch," wrote Kingsley Martin, "the only safe rule is always to follow the

Premier's advice."[21] If that rule was to be accepted as a convention, it would strengthen rather than weaken the position of the Queen. As we have seen, any involvement, however unwilling, in the political fray could jeopardize the ability of the monarchy to fulfill its central role of embodying the unity of the nation.

One alternative, recommended by Mr. Tony Benn, is for the power of dissolution (indeed, all prerogative powers) to be transferred to the Speaker of the House of Commons.[22] This, Mr. Benn noted, would avoid the Queen's being drawn into the heart of political debate, transferring instead the power to someone who "knows the Commons intimately and is therefore specially qualified to reach a judgment about the appropriate moment for granting a dissolution and who is most likely to command a majority."[23] The recommendation has been variously rejected, some critics of Mr. Benn viewing it as a disguised attempt to take a step on the road of abolishing the monarchy altogether.[24] Others have argued that it would unnecessarily reduce the Queen to a limited figurehead role, there being no instance of a modern monarch actually abusing the prerogative powers.[25] It is assumed that the hypothetical situation of one political crisis is insufficient to justify such a constitutionally radical move.

In summary, then, the Queen fulfills the task of representing the unity of the nation as well as carrying out certain political functions largely but not exclusively governed by convention. Her role as a political actor is circumscribed, necessarily so in order for her to fulfill her unifying role, and any real choice she is called on to exercise in political decision-making is the product of circumstances and unclear conventions and not of any personal desire on her part. The monarchy occupies a central position in the British polity, a real and valuable one in embodying the unity of the nation, and a formal but nonetheless necessary one in fulfilling certain political duties. In the eyes of some, it is the most efficient element of the constitution. It is certainly the most popular.

NOTES

1. This paragraph is based on *The Monarchy in Britain,* Central Office of Information Reference Pamphlet 118 (Her Majesty's Stationery Office, 1975), p. 1.

2. F. W. Maitland, *Constitutional History of England,* quoted in H. V. Wiseman (ed.), *Parliament and the Executive* (Routledge and Kegan Paul, 1966), p. 5.

3. W. Bagehot, *The English Constitution* (Fontana, 1963 ed.), p. 61.

4. F. Hardie, *The Political Influence of the British Monarchy 1868–1952* (Batsford, 1970), p. 67.

5. *Ibid.,* p. 188.

6. I. Gilmour, *The Body Politic,* rev. ed. (Hutchinson, 1970), p. 317.

7. Gilmour, p. 313.

8. *House of Commons Debates (Hansard),* Vol. 828, cols. 351–52.

9. See, e.g., P. Norton, *Dissension in the House of Commons 1945–1974* (Macmillan, 1975), pp. 400–02, and P. Norton, *Dissension in the House of Commons 1974–1979* (Oxford University Press, 1980), pp. 51–52 and 130–31.

10. See, e.g., the comments of C. Soley, *House of Commons Debates,* Sixth Series, Vol. 2, col. 1241 (April 10, 1981).

11. R. McKenzie and A. Silver, *Angels in Marble* (Heinemann, 1968), p. 149.

12. *The Gallup International Public Opinion Polls: Great Britain 1937–1975* (Random House, 1976), p. 1249.

13. M. Nicholson, *The System* (McGraw-Hill, 1967), p. 159.

14. P. Johnson, *Daily Express,* April 17, 1976.

15. Private expenditure as sovereign—e.g., gifts to visting dignitaries—is met from the Privy Purse (the income from the Duchy of Lancaster), and personal expenditure as an individual, such as wedding or Christmas gifts to other members of the family, is met from her personal wealth.

16. *House of Commons Debates,* 887, col. 628.

17. See R. Churchill, *The Fight for the Tory Leadership* (Heinemann, 1964); I. Macleod, "The Tory Leadership," *Spectator,* January 17, 1964; and P. Norton and A. Aughey, *Conservatives and Conservatism* (Temple Smith, 1981), pp. 243–45.

18. D. Watt, "If the queen has to choose, who will it be?" *The Times*, December 11, 1981.

19. Lord Blake, *The Office of Prime Minister* (Oxford University Press, 1975), pp. 60–61.

20. E. Short, quoted in Blake, p. 60.

21. K. Martin, *The Crown and the Establishment* (Penguin, 1963).

22. Written in *New Socialist,* August 1982. Reported in *The Daily Telegraph,* August 27, 1982.

23. Ibid.

24. See the editorial in *The Sunday Express,* August 28, 1982.

25. Editorial, *The News of the World,* August 28, 1982.

Enforcement and Feedback

13

Enforcement
The Courts and the Police

THE UNITED STATES SUPREME COURT, as one American expert observed, is neither a court nor a political agency: "it is inseparably both."[1] This special status derives from the court's power of constitutional interpretation, a power effectively read into the constitution by Chief Justice John Marshall in his opinion in *Marbury* v. *Madison* in 1803. "It is emphatically the province and duty of the judicial department," declared Marshall, "to say what the law is." The Constitution amounts to a paramount law and, in the event of the ordinary law conflicting with it, the Court must resolve the conflict: "This is of the very essence of judicial duty."[2]

The chief justice's reasoning did not go unquestioned.[3] Nonetheless, acceptance of the Court as the arbiter of constitutional disputes was underpinned by the Lockean philosophy inherent in American society[4] and has been reinforced by reasons of practicality (somebody has to perform the task) and of history (the judiciary has, in effect, always performed it). When Richard Nixon's attorney, James St. Clair, sought to argue in the case of *United States* v. *Nixon* (1974) that the president should interpret his own powers under the Constitution, he was more than one-and-a-half centuries too late in putting such an argument. Acceptance of the court's power of constitutional interpretation was too well established to be overthrown. The court remains the judicial arbiter of a document that is inherently political and one that by its own declaration constitutes the supreme law of the land—hence the Court's dual and inseparable roles.

The position of the British judiciary in the political process is signifi-

307

cantly different from that of its American counterpart. There are two principal reasons for this. For one thing, there are inherent difficulties in seeking to interpret a constitution the boundaries of which are not clearly delineated. For another, the judiciary labors under the self-imposed doctrine of parliamentary sovereignty. The courts have no power to declare unconstitutional an act of Parliament. If the judicial interpretation of an act conflicts with the intentions of Parliament, a new act may be passed making explicit Parliament's wishes: the courts are duty-bound to enforce the new act. The last word, in short, rests with Parliament.

These difficulties are crucial to an understanding of the American and British courts. They serve to explain why the United States Supreme Court (indeed, the United States judiciary, given that any court can declare an act unconstitutional) may be deemed to form part of the political decision-making process in the United States, whereas the judiciary would not form part of that process in Britain. Nonetheless, such differences should not be overstated. A number of caveats need to be entered to the distinctions that have just been drawn.

On the American side, it is important to record that the Supreme Court will decide a case on the basis of constitutional interpretation only where it cannot be resolved by statutory interpretation. A random sample of cases in a recent 60-year period (1912–1972) reveals that only a minority of cases are resolved by resorting to constitutional interpretation.[5] The Court itself will seek to avoid, especially on grounds of nonjusticiability, those cases it considers to be political. Nor is it free of the constraints imposed by other political bodies. Congress can limit, and on occasion has limited (as in the instance of *Ex Parte McCardle*), the Court's appellate jurisdiction. The Court itself is dependent on the executive for the enforcement of its decisions. While it may seek to give a lead to or conversely to restrain the actions of Congress or the president, it will rarely beat a path too far ahead or too far behind what is politically acceptable. And in practice it has rarely struck down federal legislation. Between 1789 and 1975, in a total of 110 cases, 116 provisions of federal law were struck down as unconstitutional, and this was out of a total of some 75,000 public and private laws passed.[6] (The Court was somewhat more active in striking down state law.) Although the power to strike down a measure serves as "an omnipresent and potentially omnipotent check upon the legislative branches of government," it is a power that, as Henry Abraham observed, "courts are understandably loathe to invoke."[7]

On the British side, the courts retain the power of statutory—and common law—interpretation and can determine, in any case brought before them, whether the purported exercise of a power is authorized by law. As a result, the executive actions of ministers and administrative authorities can, when challenged, come within their purview. The determination of the courts in such cases can always be overridden by a new act of Parliament authorizing that which the courts have struck down, but by having to determine such cases, the courts are brought into the political limelight. This relative prominence has been especially evident in recent years, when the higher judiciary has been active in reviewing a number of important executive actions. Furthermore, British entry into the European Communities has added a new judicial dimension to the Constitution (see Chapter 10). The 1972 European Communities Act provided that, in the event of a conflict between the provisions of EC law and domestic law, the former was to prevail. Section 3(1) of the act provided that any disputes as to the interpretation, effect, and validity of the EC Treaties, or of any legislation made under them, was to be treated by British judges as a matter of law. Cases that reached the House of Lords (the highest domestic court of appeal) had, under the provisions of the Rome Treaty, to be referred to the Court of Justice of the European Communities for a definitive ruling, and request could be made from lower courts to the European Court for a ruling on the meaning and interpretation of the treaties. The act created a new role for the British judiciary.

The British judiciary clearly cannot be described as standing divorced totally from the political fray. Nonetheless, despite the foregoing qualifications, the basic difference between the United States and British courts remains. Courts in the United States have the power, however rarely exercised it might be, to strike down legislative measures and executive actions as unconstitutional. British courts have no such powers, however much they might like to have it. It is this fundamental difference that explains why United States courts are accorded a more prominent place in analyses of American politics than is the case with British politics. In studies of British politics, the judiciary constitutes but a marginal consideration.

THE JUDICIAL SYSTEM

The administration of justice is one of the prerogatives of the Crown, but it is a prerogative that has long been exercisable only through duly appointed courts and judges.[8] Apart from a number of specialized courts and various tribunals, the basic organizational division within the court system is that between criminal and civil. There is no such distinction in the United States court system. A simplified outline of the court system in England and Wales is provided in Figure 13.1. (Scotland and Northern Ireland have different systems.) The Court of Appeal, the Crown Court, and the High Court together constitute what is known (confusingly, from the perspective of the American student) as the Supreme Court. At the apex of the structure sits the House of Lords.

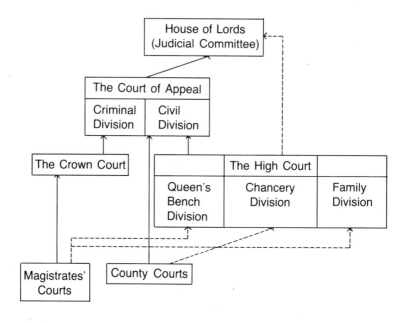

FIGURE 13.1 The court system in England and Wales. Appeals possible to higher courts as shown by arrows, usually through the immediate superior court or, in certain cases (shown by dotted lines), through another route. Tribunals and specialist courts are omitted.

Criminal Cases

Minor criminal cases are tried summarily in magistrates' courts. The courts, presided over by unpaid lay magistrates (except in the case of one or two of the largest cities, which have legally qualified, full-time, paid magistrates known as stipendiary magistrates), have the power to levy fines and, depending on the offense, impose a prison sentence not exceeding six months. Stipendiary magistrates sit alone. Lay magistrates sit in a bench of between two and seven and are normally advised on legal points by the legally qualified clerk of the court. Cases dealt with by magistrates cover such matters as motoring offenses, assault charges, and offenses against public order (for example, breach of the peace). The courts also have a limited civil jurisdiction, primarily in matrimonial proceedings, and have semiadministrative functions in the licensing of public houses, betting shops, and clubs.

    More than 95% of all cases are heard and determined by magistrates, a total of about 2 million cases a year. Appeals from magistrates' courts are possible to the Crown Court or, in certain cases, to the High Court (to the Queen's Bench Division on points of law and to the Family Division in matrimonial cases). Serious criminal cases—indictable offenses—are tried before a jury in the Crown Court. In 1980, magistrates committed just over 74,000 people for trial on indictable offenses at the Crown Court. The Crown Court has nearly 100 centers, divided into six court circuits. Cases in the Crown Court are heard either by a High Court judge (who will normally preside over the most serious cases), a Circuit judge, or a Recorder. Circuit judges are full-time, salaried judges; recorders are part-time and salaried, and when not presiding at court, pursue their normal legal practice. Judges and Recorders are legally qualified and to be eligible for appointment must have practiced for at least 10 years as either solicitors or barristers.

Appeals from the Crown Court may be taken on a point of law to the Queen's Bench Division of the High Court but usually are taken to the Criminal Division of the Court of Appeal. Appeals against conviction are possible on points of law (as of right) and on a question of fact (with the leave of the trial judge or Court of Appeal). The Appeal Court may quash a conviction or uphold it: it can also vary the sentence imposed by the lower court. Appeals against sentence, if not a sentence fixed by law, are also possible with the leave of the Appeal Court. The Appeal Court comprises a presiding judge known as the Master of the Rolls, 17 Lord Justices of Appeal, and a number of *ex officio* members. Three members of the court normally sit to hear a case.

From the Court of Appeal, an appeal to the House of Lords is possible if the court certifies that a point of law of general public importance is involved and it appears to the court or the House that the point ought to be considered by the highest court of appeal. For judicial purposes, the House of Lords does not comprise all members of the House. Instead, the task is undertaken by an appellate committee that will comprise usually five but sometimes as many as seven peers drawn from the Lord Chancellor, Lords of Appeal in Ordinary (life peers appointed for the purpose of undertaking such tasks), and such peers as hold or have previously held high judicial office. The committee meets in a Committee Room of the House of Lords, though its judgment will still be delivered in the full chamber. In 1966, the Lords of Appeal in Ordinary announced that they would no longer consider themselves bound by their previous decisions, the House now being prepared to depart from a previous decision when it appears right to do so.[9]

Civil Cases

In civil proceedings, minor cases involving small sums of money (£100 [$150] or less in small claims procedure; £1,000 [$1,500] or less in contract and tort cases) are heard by county courts, more important cases going to the High Court. The High Court comprises the Queen's Bench Division, covering mainly matters of common law; the Chancery Division, dealing mainly with Equity cases; and the Family Division, for cases of divorce and custody. County courts are presided over by Circuit judges. The High Court comprises the Lord Chief Justice, who presides over the Queen's Bench Division; the Lord Chancellor, who is nominally president of the Chancery Court but who never sits (a Vice-Chancellor, in practice, presides); the President of the Family Division; and up to a total of 75 judges known as Puisne (pronounced *puny*) judges. In civil cases the judges normally sit alone, though a Divisional Court of two or more judges may be formed, especially in the Queen's Bench Division, which has important responsibilities in the issuing of writs of habeas corpus and orders of mandamus, certiorari, and prohibition. As with other senior judicial posts, Puisne judges are appointed from among eminent laywers of long standing.

Appeals in certain instances may go to the High Court. Appeals from county courts in bankruptcy cases are heard by a Divisional Court of the Chancery Division. Appeals against the decisions of magistrates' courts in matrimonial proceedings are heard by a Divisional Court of the Family Division. And appeals on points of law may be taken from a magistrate's court to a Divisional Court of the Queen's Bench Division.

Appeals from county courts (those not going to the High Court) and from the High Court go to the Civil Division of the Court of Appeal and, from there, may go to the House of Lords. In exceptional cases—on a point of law of exceptional difficulty calling for a reconsideration of a binding precedent—an appeal may go directly (with the leave of the House) from the High Court to the House of Lords. In the instance of European Communities law, any case that reaches the House of Lords has, under the provisions of the 1972 European Communities Act, to be referred to the Court of the European Communities for a definitive ruling.

The Judiciary

Concerning the judiciary itself—its recruitment, appointment, and relationship to and with the executive—a number of important points are deserving of mention. Magistrates' courts, with the exception of those presided over by stipendiary magistrates, are staffed by lay magistrates, known as Justices of the Peace, of which there are currently about 19,000. They are not legally qualified, though they do now receive some basic training, and usually constitute prominent local citizens. They are appointed by the Lord Chancellor. Any citizen can recommend the name of an individual for appointment as a magistrate, though in practice, recommendations tend to come from local political parties and civic bodies.

Above the level of magistrates are the legally qualified judges. They are drawn from the ranks of the legal profession. Lawyers in Britain are divided into solicitors and barristers; there is no equivalent distinction in the United States. (There are also far fewer lawyers per head of population in Britain than there are in the United States.)[10] A solicitor is a lawyer who undertakes ordinary legal business for clients. A barrister gives expert legal advice to solicitors and their clients and conducts cases in court: barristers have an exclusive right to appear before certain courts. There is statutory provision as to how long one must have served as a solicitor or barrister before being eligible for appointment as a judge. Usually, judges are drawn from the ranks of barristers (occasionally a solicitor is appointed as a Recorder, but none has been appointed to higher judicial office) and have generally been in legal practice for longer than the minimum period required. Those appointed are regarded as the outstanding members of their profession. The status (an the pay) of a judge is high and is superior to that of a judge in the United States. Elevation to judicial office is regarded as a step up the professional ladder, something to be sought after, rather than a position one settles for if unable to establish oneself as a leading corporate lawyer.

Although judges are recruited from the ranks of well-qualified lawyers and are usually appointed or promoted on the basis of legal merit, their appointment is made by members of the executive branch. Formally, all judges are appointed by the Crown. By convention, senior judicial appointments, those above the level of Puisne judges, are made by the Crown on the advice of the prime minister. Other judicial appointments are made by the Crown on the advice of the Lord Chancellor. In making recommendations, the prime minister will usually consult the Lord Chancellor. Although not unknown, it is rare for judicial appointments to be the subject of political controversy.[11] Such appointments are not subject to any form of parliamentary approval.

The method of appointment of judges, coupled with the unusual position of the Lord Chancellor and of certain senior judges, may raise doubts as to the independence of the judiciary. The Lord Chancellor is living proof that the separation of personnel exercised in the United States between branches of government is not rigidly adhered to in the United Kingdom. The Lord Chancellor is a member of the cabinet, he presides over the House of Lords (though his position as presiding officer is not dissimilar to that of the vice-president with relation to the Senate in the United States),[12] and he is the head of the judiciary. He not only advises the Crown on the appointment of judges and magistrates, he also is himself a judge, as Lord Chancellor. He is a member of the judicial committee of the House of Lords and if he takes part in hearing an appeal, which sometimes he does, then he presides. Furthermore, he is not the only person in government who occupies a position in the judicial hierarchy. The positions of Attorney-General and Solicitor-General, as well as those of Law Officers for Scotland (Lord Advocate and Solicitor-General for Scotland), are political appointments and form part of the government. Also, as already mentioned, the Lords of Appeal in

Ordinary are life peers. As members of the House of Lords, they are free to take part in parliamentary proceedings.

Despite this overlap, and despite the ability of Parliament to overrule the courts through new legislation, the judiciary in Britain is independent. This independence is achieved in a number of ways, by statute, common law, parliamentary rules, and an acceptance by government that the rule of law requires abstention from interference with the conduct of litigation. Judges of superior courts (the High Court and above, with the exception of the Lord Chancellor) cannot be removed except for misbehavior in office, and their salaries are fixed by statute in order to avoid annual debate. They serve in office until they reach a statutory retiring age of 75 years. They enjoy immunity from civil proceedings for anything said or done while acting in a judicial capacity. Judges of lower courts are also immune if acting within their jurisdiction. By custom, questions are not asked in either House of Parliament about the conduct of courts in particular cases, reference may not be made in debate to matters awaiting or under adjudication before the courts[13] (*sub judice* rules also prevent media comment on pending cases), and reflections may not be cast in debate upon the character or motives of a judge.[14] Judges are not eligible for election to the House of Commons, and those who are members of the House of Lords, with the obvious exception of the Lord Chancellor, abstain from party political activities.

Two authors have suggested that another fact that promotes judicial independence is that judges "are all drawn from the bar after successful careers as barristers, a profession which tends to foster self-confidence and independence of mind."[15] Also, service as a judge is not seen as a stepping stone to other things. One makes a career in the law, a career in which one's standing with colleagues and superiors is important and is essentially independent of political (certainly partisan) implications.

The degree to which judicial independence has been maintained is reflected in the fact that since judges of superior courts were accorded security of tenure under the Act of Settlement of 1700, only one judge has been removed from office—an Irish judge in 1830. He was found to have misappropriated money belonging to litigants and to have ceased to perform his judicial duties many years previously![16] In 1973, 180 Labour MPs signed a motion calling for the dismissal of the judge who presided over the new (and, in the event, short-lived) National Industrial Relations Court, a Court regarded by the MPs as a political court set up to restrain the trade unions. In any event, the motion was never debated and it was very much the exception that proved the rule.

Although, as we shall see, the judiciary has not been free of criticism, the principle of judicial independence is a feature of the British Constitution and, in interpreting and applying the law, judges are generally more skilled and better regarded than their American counterparts (especially those that serve in the state courts) and maintain probably a greater degree of judicial decorum in the proceedings before them. The rules and ethics of the legal profession also prevent much of the degrading touting for business by lawyers that is a feature of many American courts.[17]

Nonetheless, some of the problems experienced by the American judicial system find reflection, albeit not quite on such a grand or obvious scale, in Britain. The use of plea bargaining generates similar problems.[18] There are delays in bringing defendants to trial. In 1980, about one in eight defendants committed into custody for trial at the Crown Court had to wait for more than 20 weeks before trial. About one in three released on bail had a similar delay. Although there are now various schemes, including legal advice centers, to provide advice to less well-off individuals, the cost of legal advice and various legal services (not least some straightforward legal services on which solicitors enjoy a monopoly) is a problem for many citizens.[19] For those citizens involved in law suits, it can be an expensive business.

The Current Debate

During the course of the past decade or so, the judiciary has on occasion entered the political limelight. This has been occasioned, on one hand, by the exercise of power already vested in the courts and on the other, by various calls for the judges to be vested with new powers. The powers exercised and the powers proposed have implications for the maintenance of political authority.

The courts have the power to review executive actions to determine whether they are carried out within the limits of the relevant authorizing act. If the action is deemed by the courts to be *ultra vires* (beyond the powers), it is void. A court may also declare void an action if it deems that the principles of natural justice have not been observed or if the action has entailed the abuse or unreasonable exercise of power. The power to declare an action *ultra vires* is a corollary of the principle of parliamentary sovereignty. The power to void an action for failing to observe the principles of natural justice is derived from common law. Until the 1960s, neither power was much used. In part, this may have been due to the realization that the executive dominated the legislature and could thus obtain legitimation of past or proposed actions; it may concomitantly have been due to a lack of will on the part of judges. They were, and more recently have been, accused of not being too sympathetic to the claims of the individual when those claims were pitted against the demands of government.[20] Denied the power to question acts of Parliament and unwilling to exercise their powers over acts of the executive, few judicial decisions entered the realms of controversy. This was to change in the period from the mid-1960s onward.

Professor John Griffith has referred to "the emergence of a period of judicial activism or intervention which began in the early 1960s and has been growing in strength every since."[21] A number of judges, apparently concerned at the encroachment of executive power in the field of individual liberties, became more assertive in the exercise of their common-law power to review the executive actions of ministers and administrative authorities. In four cases during the 1960s, the courts adopted an activist line in reviewing the exercise of powers by administrative bodies and, in two instances, by ministers.[22] The courts maintained their activist stance in the 1970s and early 1980s, in a number of controversial cases holding that ministers had exceeded their powers. Thus, for example, a 1981 decision by the environment secretary to reduce the central government grant to certain London boroughs was quashed by the High Court on the grounds that he had failed to listen to representations made late on behalf of the authorities and in so doing had not validly exercised his discretion under the provisions of the relevant act of Parliament. Nor were cases involving ministerial actions the only ones in which the courts rendered politically contentious decisions. Again in 1981, for example, in the *Greater London Council* (GLC) case, the Court of Appeal quashed an extra rate levied by the Labour-controlled GLC to pay for its policy of reducing fares on London Transport's bus and underground services: the Court held the GLC's action to be an abuse of its powers and *ultra vires*. The Court's judgment was upheld by the House of Lords.[23]

The foregoing cases proved politically contentious not only for the holding of the courts in each case but also, in a number of instances, because of the *obiter dicta* (incidental remarks) of the judges. In particular, the comments of the Master of the Rolls, Lord Denning, in two cases provoked fears that the courts were seeking to usurp the functions of government and Parliament. In one case, Lord Denning declared that the Attorney-General's discretion to refuse consent to a particular action (a relator action) was not unfettered. If the Attorney-General takes into account things he should not take into account, or fails to take into account things he should, "then his decision can be overridden by the courts. Not directly, but indirectly."[24] In the *GLC* case, his Lordship declared that a manifesto issued by a political party (the Labour party had fought the GLC elections on a manifesto that included its cheap fares proposal) "was not to be regarded as a gospel. It was not a covenant."[25] His Lordship, declared *The Economist*, was "demonstrating his popular thesis that judges are a higher form of animal than politicians."[26] Labour politicians were somewhat more disparaging.

In such cases, the exercise by the courts of their powers brought them into the realms of political controversy. They were to enter the sphere of political debate also as a consequence of proposals to extend their powers. As we have mentioned already, the European Communities Act of 1972 ensured a new judicial dimension to the British Constitution. Some politicians and jurists sought to extend that judicial dimension further through the enactment of a bill of rights.

Pressure for the enactment of a bill of rights, if possible with some element of entrenchment (that is, with extraordinary provisions to limit the possibility of amendment), built up during the latter half of the 1970s. A number of jurists considered Parliament no longer capable of resisting the encroachment of government on rights previously considered inviolate. Britain, according to one leading lawyer and politician, Lord Hailsham, labored under an "elective dictatorship."[27] If the rights of the individual were to be protected, some new means of protection was necessary to supplement or to replace that provided by Parliament. The answer, according to a number of politicians (especially on the Conservative side) and jurists, was a bill of rights stipulating the rights of the individual, possibly a bill akin to that of the United States. Such a measure would then be subject to interpretation by the courts, which, if the bill enjoyed a degree of entrenchment, would be able to strike down conflicting measures as being contrary to its provisions. It is not axiomatic that the courts would enjoy such a power. Nonetheless, that is the clear intention of those who advocate such a measure. They seek to put certain rights beyond the reach of government, those rights being put into the care of the courts. Lord Scarman, a Law Lord, in 1974 imputed to society a wish for judges to defend the liberties of the individual from arbitrary acts of government.[28] The power to quash legislation, he envisaged, would rest with a new Supreme Court to be formed with appellate jurisdiction. What he wanted, he said, was a new constitutional settlement.

Both the exercise of the power to review ministerial and administrative actions and the proposal for a judicially protected bill of rights met with criticism from a number of sources, not least from Labour politicians. The actions of the courts, and the *obiter dicta* of Lord Denning, were seen as justifying the impression that senior judges were conservative and potentially dangerous figures. The top 30 or so judges, argued Professor Griffith, had "by their education and training and pursuit of their professions as barristers, acquired a strikingly homogenous collection of attitudes, beliefs and principles, which to them represent the public interest."[29] The public interest was usually construed to favor law and order and the interests of the state (in time of perceived threat) over the rights of individuals, property rights were upheld more assiduously than personal human rights, and their perception involved usually "the promotion of certain political views normally associated with the Conservative Party."[30] The latter, Griffith argued, was reflected in cases involving trade unions, race relations, and the striking down of ministerial decisions in the period from 1975 to 1977. It was a view reinforced by the *GLC* case in 1981. When the House of Lords upheld the Court of Appeal, Labour MP Norman Atkinson assailed the judgment as "an extra-parliamentary political instrument . . . in order to further the politics of the Conservative Party."[31]

Such perceptions of the attitudes and actions of judges fueled opposition to the introduction of a bill of rights. To an American weaned on an entrenched bill of rights interpreted by independent magistrates, opposition to an entrenched bill of rights is difficult to comprehend. Britain, however, lacks those characteristics that have underpinned the American's acceptance of constitutional interpretation by the United States Supreme Court. "Federalism apart," one analyst writes, "judicial review as it has worked in America would be inconceivable without the national acceptance of the Lockian creed."[32] Such a creed has not found universal assent in Britain.

Weaned on the doctrine of parliamentary sovereignty, Britons have come to regard constitutional disputes as matters for resolution by political debate and not litigation. Whereas constitutional interpretation by the courts in the United States may serve as a support of the political system, in Britain it could serve to undermine it. The courts, according to a number of their critics, would make poor defenders of the rights of the individual. "I should hate to rely upon the appointed judiciary rather than upon the elected members of a legislature for the rights of the people," declared an MP, perhaps not altogether disinterestedly.[33] If the courts are seen as not being impartial arbiters and become what Sir Keith Joseph has termed "a party political football"—a possibility even more likely in the event of being empowered to interpret a bill of rights, the provisions of which would be politically contentious—then respect for judges and the judicial process is undermined.

Whereas Americans may be largely if not wholly agreed on the provisions of the Bill of Rights, there is no such agreement in Britain as to what should be included in a British bill. It would be a politically contentious document and anybody vested with the responsibility of its interpretation would be drawn inexorably into the political fray. Some jurists would not be averse to being drawn into that fray. Many politicians and some judges would prefer to defend the judiciary from the perils of such a course. Despite some pressure in favor of a bill of rights from some senior judges and some members of the House of Lords (categories that are not mutually exclusive), the chances of its realization are slim.[34]

THE POLICE FORCE

Respected by many at home, admired abroad, the British police force has been regarded for many years as a paragon among police forces. In recent years, however, it has become a topic of public debate because of the problems of police accountability, the relationship between the police and certain elements of the community, and accusations of police corruption. There is, in the words of one solicitor, "a crisis of confidence in the police force."[35] And lack of confidence in the police force undermines their ability to perform the tasks expected of them.

In Britain, there are 43 police forces. Outside the London Metropolis, each force is under the direction of a chief constable. The Metropolitan Police Force, with its headquarters at New Scotland Yard, is under the control of a commissioner. (There is a separate City of London force.) In England and Wales, the size of the police force has grown from 41,900 officers in 1900 to 120,323 in 1982; in Scotland, it has grown from 4,900 officers in 1900 to 11,800 in 1977.[36] There is approximately one police officer for every 400 people in England and Wales, roughly the same ratio as in the United States. It relies for its effectiveness on the consent and the cooperation of the community. As far as possible, it has sought to operate as a part of the local community. Police officers live in the community they serve (that is, they live in local houses rather than in barracks), they have limited but original powers, and for many years they patrolled their allotted beats on foot. Remarkable in American terms is the fact that, with certain exceptions, they are not armed: police constables on beat patrol carry only a truncheon (a wooden baton). Although in some parts of the community the police have always been treated with suspicion, popular trust in the police has been a feature of recent British history, a view fostered by the police: children have often been taught to look up with respect to the local policeman on the beat, often portrayed as a kindly figure, ready to pass the time of day with residents and obligingly telling children the time or seeing them safely across the road.

It has also been a nonpolitical force in that it has been kept largely at one remove from direct governmental control. (Only the Special Branch, which carries out arrests on behalf of the intelligence services, could be described as fulfilling a political role.) The fear of a national police force under government control has prevented the creation of such a force. The public body to which each force is accountable is the Police Authority. Each authority comprises local councillors, who constitute two-thirds of the members, and magistrates. The exception is in London, where the Police Authority is the Home Secretary. A chief constable, the head of each force, has to submit an annual report to his authority, and the authority can require him to supply a report on any topic, other than on the operational deployment of his force (or anything which could be against the public interest, as confirmed by the Home Secretary). The authority also appoints senior officers above the rank of Chief Superintendent. Of the funding for the police force, 50% is provided by the local authority, the other 50% coming from central government. This funding provides, or could provide, both the police authorities and the Home Secretary with leverage in seeking to ensure police accountability. In practice, chief constables have tended to achieve autonomy in their activities, local authorities being more concerned with the provision of funds than the policies for which those funds are intended.

Pitted against the fear of centralized government control has been the desire for greater operational efficiency. Problems arising from the existence of too many autonomous police forces (such as the 40,000 police forces that exist in the United States) has encouraged the amalgamation of forces, reducing the number from a little under 200 in the 1920s to the present 43. Perceptions of the police force as a local, well-trained force (all officers undergo a standard training) that is free of political direction, combined with a crime rate considered low by international standards (not least when compared with the United States) helped produce the positive view of the police force held at home and abroad, particularly in the 1950s and, to a lesser extent, the 1960s.

In recent years, essentially since the latter half of the 1960s, the public attitude toward the police has undergone some change. In part, this is attributable to certain changes in the police force itself. From being the local constable on the beat with nothing more than a whistle to summon assistance, the policeman was transferred to driving a car (known as panda cars because of their appearance) and was equipped with a personal radio. By being in a car, able to respond more quickly to calls for assistance (the rationale for the move), the police officer had less direct contact with the local citizenry. By having a personal radio he or she was able to summon the assistance of colleagues: there was less need to appeal to local citizens or pursue a diplomatic approach in handling quarrelsome characters. There also emerged a new breed of more professional chief constable, more self-assertive and imposing his own views on policing onto his own forces.

The police force also came under pressure as a result of an increase in the crime rate, or at least an increase in the number of offenses known to the police. Indictable offenses in England and Wales known to the police in 1960 totaled 797,500. This figure rose to 1.6 million in 1971 and to nearly 2.7 million in 1980 (Table 13.1). In 1981, it was 2,964,000. Of these latter cases, only a little over 1 million were classified as having been cleared up.[37] Public concern at the rise in crime, or perceived rise in crime, generated what has been termed a "moral panic."[38] The police were increasingly hard-pressed to deal with the situation, and their operational methods came in for criticism. Many observers felt that policemen were more effective by being on beat patrol, thus acting as visible deterrents, than they were in cars responding to an event after it had happened. Also, a number of television series (some American imports, some home-produced) portrayed police behavior as more aggressive than the image previously conveyed.

The crisis of confidence in the police force emerged toward the end of the 1970s and in the early 1980s as a result of a number of sometimes interrelated factors. One that probably caused the most widespread concern was accusations of police corruption (particularly bribery), primarily in the Metropolitan and City of London forces and, within those forces, the Criminal Investigation Department (the plain-clothed investigative branch). Between 1972 and 1977, the Metropolitan Police Commissioner, Sir Robert Mark, removed from his force more than 450 officers. A new specialist department known as A10 was created to investigate complaints. The 1976 Police Act also estab-

TABLE 13.1
Serious Offenses Recorded by the Police in England and Wales

Serious Offences Recorded	1971*	1980*,†
Violence against the person	47,000 (82%)	97,200 (77%)
Sexual offenses	23,600 (76%)	21,100 (74%)
Burglary	451,500 (37%)	622,600 (26%)
Robbery	7,500 (42%)	15,000 (29%)
Theft and handling stolen goods	1,003,700 (43%)	1,463,500 (39%)
Fraud and forgery	99,800 (83%)	105,200 (75%)
Criminal damage	27,000‡(34%)	359,500 (28%)
Other offences	5,600 (92%)	4,100 (91%)
Total serious offenses	1,665,700 (45%)	2,688,200 (40%)

*Clear-up rates are in parentheses.
†For comparative purposes, 1980 figures have to be treated with caution since they are based on slightly different counting procedures from those used in 1971.
‡Figures for 1980 include offenses of criminal damage valued at £20 ($35) and under (of which there were 167,607). Such offenses are not included in the 1971 figures.
SOURCE: Central Statistical Office, *Social Trends 12* (Her Majesty's Stationery Office, 1981), p. 205. Copyright 1981 Social Trends. Reprinted by permission.

lished a Police Complaints Board. Nonetheless, allegations of corruption were such that the Home Secretary established a special investigation, known as "Operation Countryman," to inquire into corruption within the police force in London. Manned by officers from provincial forces, it proved expensive and resulted in few criminal charges and even fewer convictions. Many observers, as well as members of the Operation Countryman team, ascribed the low number of charges to an inability to obtain tangible evidence and to obstruction by senior London officers rather than to an absence of corruption.[39] Continuing allegations affected both police morale and confidence in the police. In May/June 1981, the Gallup Poll found that "one in three people felt uneasy about the police force due to recent happenings," those happenings including corruption, allegations of brutality, and the handling of the Yorkshire Ripper case, a case involving a rapist and murderer who was eventually caught after a lengthy and often mishandled investigation by police. Of respondents, 45% believed that there were cases of corruption and violence in the police force albeit very scattered, while 16% believed that "cases of corruption and violence occur too often."[40]

Other happenings that raised questions about the police were riots in Bristol at the beginning of 1980, followed by more extensive outbreaks of public disturbance in various cities in the summer of 1981, especially in parts of London (notably Brixton) and cities such as Liverpool. A number of riots, such as those in Bristol and Brixton, had racial overtones. Inquiries into the cause of the disturbances and the police reaction to them raised two separate but related questions. One was the question of the relationship between the police and the black community in certain areas. The other was the question of police accountability.

One of the reasons attributed to the riots in certain areas was the attitude taken by the local police toward black communities. There were allegations of racism on the part of some police officers and of a heavy-handed approach by the police generally in dealing with black suspects. Police officers were accused of picking on black youths and detaining them under the so-called "sus" law—a law permitting arrest on suspicion of someone's being about to commit a crime. One unit of the Metropolitan Police, the Special Patrol Group, came in for particular criticism because of the aggressive tactics it was alleged to employ in responding to public disturbances. The police were thought to lack good communication with local black communities and to be a notably white force: in 1980, a total of only 293 police officers were drawn from ethnic minority groups.

In the wake of the riots, and following a report on the Brixton riots by Lord Scarman,[41] greater efforts were made to establish better liaison between police and local black communities. Some attempts were also made to recruit more blacks into the police force. One problem in attempting such a recruitment was resistance on the part of many young blacks. Another problem was that many lacked the minimum educational requirements to join the force. Various proposals were advanced to try to overcome this problem. One suggestion was to employ a quota system and another, not incompatible, was to provide special tuition for young black police cadets in order to bring them up to the necessary educational standards. Despite such efforts, relationships between police and local black communities remained tense in a number of areas, particularly in London.

Some of the police operations alleged to have contributed to tension between police and blacks, and inadequate consultation with Police Authorities by a number of chief constables (notably Kenneth Oxford in Liverpool) following the riots in 1981, raised questions of police accountability. This debate was fueled by controversy over policing methods in general: the panda car versus the foot-patrol officer was a point of particular contention. There were allegations that the Police Complaints Procedure was too bureaucratic and too insular, with an insufficient independent element in its operation. The controversy was added to by a tendency on the part of some chief constables (such as Chief Constable Alderton in Greater Manchester) to adopt a high public profile and to comment on issues of public policy. All these developments generated a vigorous debate as to the accountability of chief constables and of their forces. It was a debate that gained partisan overtones. Various Labour politicians who viewed the police as authoritarian defenders of established privilege were accused of working to place the police under the control of local police authorities. "I want the police to be more accountable to the Labour Movement. I want the police to be instruments of Socialism," declared one Labour parliamentary candidate.[42] The 1981 Labour party conference approved a proposal that police policies must be approved by police authorities. A similar proposal was adopted by the Liberals at their 1982 conference. Perceiving a left-wing attack, the Conservatives responded by defending the police force. The police began to emerge more as a topic of partisan conflict.

What many reformers wanted was to ensure a greater degree of public accountability on the part of chief constables. Various proposals have been put forward to ensure a greater degree of accountability, extending in some cases to the Labour proposals for control over police policy. In 1979, a Labour MP introduced a bill (unsuccessfully) to empower police authorities to decide "the general policing policies for their areas." Other proposals have included improving the police complaints procedure and improving accountability to the public through the creation of liaison committees comprising police officers and members of local communities. One problem faced by reformers is that even if a greater degree of accountability is achieved with relation to chief constables, there is still the problem of the degree of control exercised by them over their men. Many police officers are resistant to any changes that they, or their union (the Police Federation), do not think are in their best interests.

Some attempt to deal with the problem of police complaints procedure, consultation with local communities, and powers to deal with the rise in crime was made by the Conservative government in 1982 with the introduction of a Police and Criminal Evidence bill. An omnibus measure, the bill sought to strengthen police powers to enter and search premises and to stop and search a person in a public place if they had reasonable suspicion that the person was carrying stolen goods or offensive weapons, and it provided that suspects could be detained in police custody for a maximum of 24 hours without being charged. It sought also to reform the police complaints procedure and to place the onus on police authorities to make suitable arrangements for public consultation on police matters. The bill was attacked by the Labour Opposition on the grounds that the extension of police powers went too far while those to extend police accountability did not go far enough. The Labour spokesman on Home Affairs, Roy Hattersley, argued that the bill would have the effect of further alienating the police from the community.[43] The 1983 general election was called before the bill had completed its parliamentary stages and the bill was hence lost. After the election, the bill was not immediately reintroduced, though the Home Secretary indicated that he intended to bring forward a similar bill at some stage in the parliamentary session.

Thus, despite some efforts by Government to respond, the identified problems remain. Relations between the police and the local community remain a problem in certain inner-city localities such as London, corruption within the Metropolitan and City of London police forces remains a cause for concern and inquiry, and the number of indictable offenses known to the police continues to grow. Many policemen consider that their ability to deal with crime is hampered by politicians' attempts to constrain them, attempts that lower police morale.

There is also much public concern at what are considered lenient sentences in cases of serious crimes. There remains majority support, among both the public and the police force (though not within Parliament) for the return of the death penalty for murder, abolished in 1965. The Gallup Poll in 1981 found that more than 80% of respondents favored the restoration of capital punishment for one form of murder or another.[44] Since 1965, Parliament has consistently voted against such a reintroduction, the last occasion being in July 1973.[45]

Nonetheless, the problems should not be overstated. According to the Gallup Poll, a majority of respondents (58% in 1981, compared with 55% in

TABLE 13.2
Police and Crime: United States–United Kingdom Comparisons

	Police Forces	
	United States	Britain
Number of forces	~40,000	43
Number of police officers per 1,000 inhabitants	~2.4 (1973 figure)	~2.4 (1982 figure, England and Wales)
Armed/unarmed	Armed	Unarmed

	Selected Crime Statistics*	
	United States (Thousands)	England and Wales (Thousands)
Number of burglaries	2,540.9 (1973)	451.5 (1971)
Clear-up rate	18%	37%
Number of robberies	382.7 (1973)	7.5 (1971)
Clear-up rate	27%	42%
Aggravated assault/violence against the person	416.3 (1973)	47 (1971)
Clear-up rate	63%	82%
Number of murders	19.5 (1973)	0.4 (1973)
Total offenses recorded	8,638.4 (1973)	1,665.7 (1971)

*For comparative purposes, figures must be treated with caution: offenses included within a particular classification are not identical in the two countries.

SOURCES: Adapted from *Crime in the United States, 1973*, F.B.I. Uniform Crime Reports (Federal Bureau of Investigation, 1974) and Central Statistical Office, *Social Trends 12* (Her Majesty's Stationery Office, 1981).

1979) consider that the police "are efficient and do the job well,"[46] the problems of poor police–community relationships and corruption appear to be largely confined to certain urban centers, and the incidence of crime, though rising and seen as a serious problem, is not as extensive as it is in the United States (see Table 13.2). The United States has a homicide rate that at times has been as much as 49 times greater than West Germany's, Britain's and Japan's put together.[47] In Britain in 1981, though the number of offenses of violence against the person increased, the homicide figure was actually lower than it was in 1979 and 1980. In recent years, police recruitment has improved (after declining in the late 1970s, it has improved markedly in the past four years), and more policemen are being returned to foot patrol. Training methods for new recruits have been revised. And for anyone with experience of American police forces, especially those in a number of the larger cities, the British police force remains a body to be admired.

NOTES

1. J. J. Magee, "Constitutional Vagaries and American Judicial Review," *Hull Papers in Politics No. 10* (Hull University Politics Department, 1979).

2. Marshall, C. J., *Marbury* v. *Madison*, 1803, 5 U.S. (1 Cranch), 137 2 L. Ed. 60. H. W. Chase and C. R. Ducat, *Constitutional Interpretation* (West Publishing, 1974), p. 26.

3. See the cogent argument advanced by J. Gibson in his dissenting opinion in *Eakin* v. *Raub*, 1825, Supreme Court of Pennsylvania, 12 S. & R. 330. Chase and Ducat, pp. 27–33.

4. See L. Hartz, *The Liberal Tradition in America* (Harcourt, Brace & World, 1955), especially p. 9.

5. Taking cases in which the Court rendered a full opinion, all cases in every twentieth volume of the *U.S. Reports* were analysed, starting with Volume 230 (the Court's October term 1912). Of the 10 terms covered, in only 3 did the number of cases determined by constitutional interpretation outnumber those determined by statutory interpretation. Of the total of 471 cases studied, 264 were decided by statutory interpretation and 207 by constitutional interpretation. (Drawn from research undertaken by the author while a Thouron Scholar at the University of Pennsylvania.)

6. H. J. Abraham, *The Judicial Process*, 3rd ed. (Oxford University Press, 1975), pp. 280 and 286.

7. Abraham, p. 280.

8. O. Hood Phillips and P. Jackson, *O. Hood Phillips' Constitutional and Administrative Law*, 6th ed. (Sweet and Maxwell, 1978), p. 377.

9. E. C. S. Wade and G. Godfrey Phillips, *Constitutional and Administrative Law*, 9th ed. by A. W. Bradley (Longman, 1977), p. 311.

10. There is approximately one lawyer for every 600 people in the U. S. A., compared with one for every 1,600 people in Britain (*The Economist*, November 5, 1977, p. 45). Another difference is that barristers and solicitors (they take different

examinations) have to meet one set of national standards in Britain. In the United States, there is some variety in the standards set by the 50 State Bar Associations.

11. The appointment by Mrs. Thatcher in 1982 of Lord Donaldson as Master of the Rolls aroused controversy. The judge had presided over the short-lived National Industrial Relations Court set up under the provisions of the 1971 Industrial Relations Act and was regarded as a political enemy by the Labour party and by trade unions.

12. Like the vice-president, the Lord Chancellor exercises few powers as presiding officer—the Lords have minimal rules of procedure and all Lords who wish to participate in debate do so, having signed up to speak in advance of the debate—and so often hands over the task of presiding to one of a panel of peers appointed for the purpose.

13. Subject to the right of Parliament to legislate on any matter. See *Erskine May's Treatise on the Law, Privileges, Proceedings and Usage of Parliament,* 19th ed., edited by Sir D. Lidderdale (Butterworths, 1976), pp. 368 and 427.

14. *Erskine May,* p. 428 and footnote (d).

15. T. C. Hartley and J. A. G. Griffith, *Government and Law,* 2nd ed. (Weidenfeld & Nicolson, 1981), p. 181.

16. Wade and Phillips, p. 371. Judges of inferior courts may be removed by the Lord Chancellor on grounds of incapacity or misbehavior, and magistrates may be dismissed by the Lord Chancellor as he thinks fit. Occasionally, magistrates have been dismissed for failing to fulfill their duties, and in 1977 a Scottish sheriff (a judicial not a police position) was dismissed for engaging in political activities.

17. On this, see L. Downie, Jr., *Justice Denied* (Penguin, 1971).

18. See P. Knightley and E. Potter, "How Lawyers Bend Justice," *Sunday Times,* July 11, 1982, pp. 33–34.

19. P. Knightly and E. Potter, "How Solicitors Get Rich," *Sunday Times,* July 18, 1982, p. 25.

20. See, e.g., J. A. G. Griffith, *The Politics of the Judiciary,* 2nd ed. (Fontana, 1981), Ch. 9.

21. Griffith, p. 210.

22. *Ridge* v. *Baldwin* (1964), *Anisminic* v. *Foreign Compensation Commission* (1968), *Conway* v. *Rimmer* (1968) and *Padfield* v. *Minister of Agriculture, Fisheries and Food* (1968). See P. Norton, *The Constitution in Flux* (Martin Robertson, 1981), pp. 136–38.

23. Norton, *The Constitution in Flux,* pp. 138–42.

24. Quoted in Griffith, pp. 130–31.

25. *The Times,* Law Report, November 11, 1981.

26. *The Economist,* November 14, 1981, p. 19.

27. Lord Hailsham, *Elective Dictatorship* (B.B.C., 1976).

28. Sir L. Scarman, *English Law—The New Dimension* (Stevens, 1974), p. 86.

29. Griffith, p. 193.

30. Griffith, p. 195.

31. *House of Commons Debates,* Vol. 15, col. 447–49.

32. Hartz, p. 9.

33. *House of Commons Debates,* Vol. 2, col. 1256.

34. See Norton, *The Constitution in Flux,* Ch. 13, pp. 244–60.

35. Said by a solicitor at a seminar attended by the author. It is a phrase variously echoed in writings on the police force. See, e.g., Kenneth Warren MP and David Tredinnick, *Protecting the Police* (Conservative Political Centre, 1982), p. 7.

36. D. Butler and A. Sloman, *British Political Facts 1900–1979*, 5th ed. (Macmillan, 1980), p. 292.

37. B. Whittaker, *The Police in Society* (Eyre Methuen, 1979), p. 82, and *The Daily Telegraph,* March 13, 1982.

38. A. K. Bottomley and C. Coleman, "The problem of 'law and order': facts and fallacies." Paper presented to Hull University Politics Department, October 1982.

39. Allegations made by the former head of the Countryman Operation in the television program "World in Action," August 2, 1982. See also "D. P. P. and the Yard answer accuser," *The Guardian,* August 4, 1982.

40. N. Webb and K. Wybrow, *The Gallup Report: Your Opinions in 1981* (Sphere Books, 1982), p. 123.

41. *The Brixton Disorders, 10–12 April 1981.* Report of the Rt. Hon. Lord Scarman (Cmnd. 8427) (Her Majesty's Stationery Office, 1981).

42. Quoted in Warren and Tredinnick, p. 9.

43. *House of Commons Debates,* Vol. 33, col. 161.

44. Webb and Wybrow, p. 121.

45. *House of Commons Debates,* Vol. 45, col. 892–996. Several votes were held, but the majority against the reintroduction of the death penalty in each was no fewer than 81.

46. Webb and Wybrow, p. 123.

47. Whittaker, p. 81.

Communication and Feedback

The Mass Media

COMMUNICATION IS AN ESSENTIAL AND INTEGRAL part of any
society. It is a necessary if not always well-used tool of the politician's trade.
To influence others, one must communicate. With the advent of a mass
electorate, politicians have had to communicate with a large audience. In the
eighteenth century, when affairs of state were the concern of an aristocratic
elite, communication by word of mouth or by letter was often sufficient in
order to reach those with political influence. In the nineteenth century, the
newspaper became more important as a medium of communication, especially toward the end of the century. (The only other medium of mass
communication, or at least one capable of reaching a large audience, was
political pamphleteering.) In the twentieth century, newspapers have remained important but have been supplemented by radio and more recently
have been overshadowed though not quite supplanted by television.

Other forms of communicating by a single medium to a large number of
people have also been developed. These now include records, videocas-
settes (a recent phenomenon in Britain), films, and books. Although some of
these have served as vehicles for political communication and, more especially, influence, their impact is limited. They are rarely used to fulfill
such functions and their audiences are relatively small. Book-reading and
cinema-going are minority interests. In Britain, as in the United States, the

primary *mass* media for communicating political information remain television, radio, and newspapers. It is with these three media that this chapter is concerned.

PRESS AND BROADCASTING IN BRITAIN

Despite an increase in the sophistication of mass communication, the sheer size and diversity of the United States has militated against the development of "national" newspapers. The number of daily newspapers with anything other than a geographically limited readership can be counted probably on the fingers of one hand. Even the titles of the exceptions—*The Washington Post, The New York Times, The Wall Street Journal*—imply specific parochial interests. In Britain, by contrast, factors of geography and demography have tended to encourage the development of a national daily press. The country is geographically small, with most of the population living in England, the greatest concentration living in the nation's capital. Despite some exceptions, the press in Britain is London-based and national (which often means London) in its orientation. The newspaper emerged as a medium of political information and influence at the turn of the century and has remained an important medium since. By international comparison, Britons remain great newspaper-readers.

The advent of "popular" newspapers, those designed to appeal (in both content and price) to artisans and the lower middle class, took place in the 1890s, a development made possible by advances in adult literacy and in printing technology. The first such newspaper was the *Daily Mail*, founded in 1896 by Alfred Harmsworth (later Lord Northcliffe). It was followed by the *Daily Express* in 1900, the *Daily Mirror* in 1903, and the *Daily Sketch* in 1908. They built up mass readerships not enjoyed by the more sedate and serious newspapers such as *The Times*, the doyen of influential newspapers founded in 1788; the *Morning Post* (merged with the *Daily Telegraph* in 1937); or the *Manchester Guardian*, one of the few significant newspapers with a regional orientation. The mass circulation of the new popular "dailies" attracted advertisers, and income from advertising came to constitute a (and in some cases, the) main form of revenue, thus allowing the publishers to keep down the cost of their papers. Harmsworth boasted that he was able to sell a one-penny paper for half-a-penny.[1] The newspapers themselves were largely in the hands of a few wealthy individuals, known in the early decades of the century as the "press barons." The Harmsworth family was especially influential (owning the *Mail*, the *Mirror* and, from 1908 to 1922, *The Times*), as was the Canadian Max Aitken (Lord Beaverbrook), who acquired control of the *Daily Express* in 1916. Although the papers were run as essentially commercial enterprises, proprietors were not averse to using their newspapers in attempts to influence political developments. In the early 1930s, the Conservative leader, Stanley Baldwin, bitterly assailed the press barons for seeking to engineer his removal from the party leadership. This attempt was one that many critics of the press would regard as the tip of a very large iceberg. Overt political partisanship remains a feature of Britain's newspapers.

Newspaper circulation continued to grow in the first decades of the century. By 1945, the circulation of the main daily newspapers had reached nearly 13 million. Throughout the 1950s, it exceeded 16 million, dropping to below 16 million in the 1960s and to below 15 million in the 1970s.[2] However-er, given that each copy of a newspaper is usually read by more than one person (and most households order only one daily paper), the figures reveal that a majority of adults in Britain continue to read a daily newspaper. In 1964, the national daily newspapers reached over 80% of households, a higher proportion than that in any other country.[3] The circulation of newspapers relative to the population was 66% greater than it was in the United States. For morning newspapers, it was three times as great.[4]

Of the national newspapers currently available, there is in terms of numbers a relatively wide choice. This is supplemented by a variety of national Sunday newspapers, weekly magazines of news and current affairs, and regional daily newspapers, as well as a host of local daily and weekly papers: hardly any community is without its "local" publication. Table 14.1 lists the main national newspapers available in 1983 along with their 1980 circulation figures and their 1983 partisan preferences.

Although journalists may differ in their political beliefs, the individual newspapers tend to adopt a particular though not always committed editorial position in support of a political party or general political persuasion. The party that benefits most from editorial preferences is the Convservative party. The *Daily Telegraph* is generally regarded as *the* Conservative newspaper and its editorials and columns are read widely in Conservative circles. The *Daily Mail*, *Daily Star*, *Daily Express* and *The Sun* (formerly a Labour supporter) also tend to fall within the Conservative camp, though not always giving editorial support to specific Conservative policies (the *Express*, for example, was a long-standing opponent of British entry into the European Communities). *The Times* is often considered a Conservative-leaning newspaper, though many Conservatives now consider it to be supportive more of the Social Democratic party than the Conservative. The *Daily Mirror* is the only mass-circulation daily newspaper that remains a consistent supporter of the Labour party. *The Guardian* (now national in its orientation) is a radical newspaper that currently tends to favor the Social Democratic party or at least the principle of social democracy. The *Morning Star*, with a small national circulation (about 25,000), is the paper of the Communist party.

Critics on the left ascribe the Conservative bias of the press to the nature of ownership, newspapers being part and parcel of a capitalist system,

TABLE 14.1
Main National Daily and Sunday Newspapers in Britain

	Average Circulation, 1980 (Millions)	Estimated Readership, 1980 (Millions)	Partisan Preference, 1983
Daily newspapers			
Daily Express	2.3	6.2	Conservative
Daily Star	1.0	3.6	Independent Conservative
Daily Mail	2.0	5.2	Conservative
Daily Mirror	3.6	10.9	Labour
The Sun	3.8	11.5	Conservative
The Times	0.3	0.8	Independent Conservative/SDP
The Financial Times	0.2	0.7	Independent Conservative
Daily Telegraph	1.4	3.6	Conservative
The Guardian	0.4	1.2	SDP/Liberal
Morning Star	0.02*	—†	Communist
Sunday newspapers			
Sunday Times	1.4	3.9	Independent
Observer	1.0	2.9	Independent Alliance
Sunday Telegraph	1.0	3.0	Conservative
Sunday Express	3.0	7.8	Conservative
News of the World	4.3	11.5	Independent
Sunday Mirror	3.8	11.2	Labour
The Mail on Sunday	—‡	—‡	Conservative
The People	3.8	10.9	Independent

*Estimated.
†Not known.
‡Not in existence in 1980.

with more and more newspapers coming within the control of fewer hands. More than 90% of national daily and Sunday newspaper circulation is controlled by the five leading companies in the sector.[5] A similar concentration is to be found in other media, with a considerable overlap of ownership.

Whereas newspapers, being owned by private concerns, are free to express their partisan preferences (and do so), the broadcasting media are more constrained. Initially, a monopoly on radio and television broadcasting was enjoyed by the British Broadcasting Corporation (the BBC), a quasi-autonomous state corporation that came into being on January 1, 1927. (It succeeded an independent company, the British Broadcasting Company Ltd.) It was granted a license to broadcast under Royal Charter and it was and remains financed by a license fee levied originally on radio receivers (abolished in 1971) and subsequently—from 1946 onwards—on television sets. The first scheduled public television service was started in 1936, though suspended for the period of the war. The 1950s witnessed the growth of television, more sets being purchased and more services becoming available.

In 1954, the BBC's monopoly was ended with the creation of the Independent Television Authority. This body was authorized to license program-contracting companies to transmit in certain areas of the country and to finance their operations by carrying paid advertisements. The first commercial independent television (ITV) channel was broadcast in 1955. Television was well established in Britain by the 1960s (more than 10 million television licenses were issued in 1960) and witnessed further expansion both in that and succeeding decades. In 1964, a second BBC channel, BBC2, began transmission, catering more for minority tastes, especially in the spheres of culture and education. In 1967, the BBC began experimenting with local radio stations to supplement their (by then) four national services, 20 new stations being established within six years. In the 1970s, the establishment of independent local radio stations was authorized for the first time, 19 such stations being established in 1976. In November 1982, a fourth television channel (Channel 4), in independent hands, began transmission and early in 1983 both the BBC and, on independent television, a new franchise (TV-AM) began early morning transmissions—"breakfast television." By mid-1983, the viewer or listener was offered what was, by British standards, a considerable variety of programs emanating from different television channels and radio stations, though the two main television channels—BBC1 and ITV (divided up into regional networks)—retained the mass audiences.[6] Significant inroads into their viewing figures were apparent, but were more the product of an increase in the use of videorecorders (and of fewer people watching television) than to a large shift of viewers to Channel 4 television or to an increase in radio listening.

In their coverage of politics, both the BBC and the independent stations—television and radio—are required to be impartial. The concept of equal time has been applied to the two main parties, though the advent of significant third parties (and of more fringe candidates in parliamentary by-elections) has created problems in determining the allocation of time to other parties. During general election campaigns, no paid political advertisements are permitted on radio or television, though both media carry an agreed number of party election broadcasts (the number agreed between the parties and the broadcasting authorities), which are scripted and presented by the parties themselves, the broadcasting media transmitting them without comment.[7]

The BBC and the independent companies come under the control of separate semi-autonomous bodies—the BBC Board of Governors and the Independent Broadcasting Authority—which position themselves as a cushion between the broadcasting companies and the government of the day. Although some critics see the media (and the BBC in particular) as unduly subservient to government, the broadcasting authorities appear to pride themselves on their independence of government, an independence that sometimes, as in the Falklands War of 1982, may generate tension between the two.

POLITICAL INFLUENCE

The mass media, by the content and method of their communicating or failing to communicate information, can exert tremendous political influence. Political evaluations and actions of politician and citizen are based on receipt of information. How that information is portrayed and transmitted can significantly affect both the evaluation and the action taken on the basis of that evaluation.

The political information transmitted by the mass media is, of necessity, limited. Newspapers have not the space nor broadcasting media the air time to transmit comprehensive coverage of daily events (nationally or worldwide) of political significance. Nor do they have the inclination to do so. Although newspapers and the broadcasting media constitute the primary means of transmitting political information to a mass audience, they do not exist exclusively or indeed even primarily to fulfill such a function. Television and radio are essentially media of entertainment. Newspapers may make some claim, by virtue of the written word, to be more a medium of information, but the information transmitted is not usually on the subject of political behavior. Although the so-called quality newspapers (*The Times, Daily Telegraph,* and *Guardian*) devote a significant porportion of space to reporting and commenting on political events, the mass readership papers do not.

Indeed, the trend has been away from covering political items to what publishers consider human-interest stories.[8] This is in line with what are seen as consumer demands at a time of intense competition among newspapers for readers. A survey in the 1960s found that newspaper-readers were most likely to read thoroughly (that is, from beginning to end) articles covering tragedies and celebrities as well as cartoons and letter columns. More readers (41%) read thoroughly the horoscopes than they did stories on home politics (37%) or international politics (29%).[9] In the 1970s and 1980s, as the circulation war among newspapers became more intense, *The Sun* and the *Daily Star* competed against one another to publish pictures of half-naked females and most of the popular dailies sought to attract new readers through running competitions offering large cash prizes.

Nonetheless, the role of the mass media in transmitting political information remains of vital significance. Indeed, the significance of newspapers and television as media of communication has increased in the twentieth century not only because of the increase in the size of the audiences but also because of the increase in sophistication of communication technology. Television, in particular, is important not only for the content of what it conveys but also for the method and speed by which it conveys that content. Not only can various happenings—a bomb blast in Northern Ireland, candidates addressing meetings, politicians arguing with one another—be portrayed visually and in sound (and, nowadays, in color), but they can also be transmitted shortly after or even at the time of happening. Receiving information with such immediacy, and in such a form, can affect viewers' evaluations in a way not possible when this medium of communication did not exist. As Hedley Donovan queried once in *Time* magazine: "Could the Civil War have survived the 7P.M. news? Could George Washington have held his command after a TV special on Valley Forge?"[10] Media coverage of the Vietnam War clearly affected the American public's perception of the wisdom, or lack of it, in such an action. In Britain, recognition of the implications of media coverage influenced the government in its actions and its control of information during the Falklands War in 1982. The government controlled the means of transmitting news from the Task Force to Britain, and facilities for the quick transmission of television pictures were not made available. To have shown on television during the conflict "pictures of the sort of realism that the Americans had during the Vietnamese war," to be seen by servicemen's families, would, in the words of one commanding officer, "have had a very serious effect" on troop morale.[11] Media coverage of particular events such as riots may extend beyond constituting an impartial recording of those events to being an alleged instigator of them. The activities of the media themselves may constitute political issues.

The way in which information is channeled, then, is not neutral in its effect. The mass media, in short, exert political influence. This influence may be primary, affecting the recipient of the communication, or it may be secondary, affecting a party independent of the communication process (e.g., a politician whose capacity to achieve a particular action is limited by public reaction to news of a certain event as, for instance, President Johnson in the Vietnam War).[12] The influence of the media may be seen as especially important in terms of the legitimacy of the political system, the partisan support of electors, and the behavior of politicians. The influence exerted in each case may be described as that of enhancing, of reinforcing, and of constraining, respectively.

The media fulfill a function of latent legitimation of the political system. By operating within that system and accepting its norms, newspapers and television help to maintain its popular legitimacy. When a political crisis arises, journalists and TV reporters descend upon ministers and MPs for comment, hence accepting and reinforcing the legitimacy of those questioned to comment on the matter at hand. There is regular coverage of parliamentary proceedings. What political leaders and members of the royal family do in a public and often in a private capacity is considered newsworthy. By according this degree of status to such figures and to the institutions they occupy and represent, the media serve to reinforce the legitimacy of such bodies. Where a body does not enjoy popular legitimacy, the media probably could not create it. Where it does exist, however, they can and do reinforce it by the very nature of their activities.

At times, certain media may also fulfill the more conscious role of overt legitimation. Coverage of the activities of the royal family, for example, may go beyond reporting to a clear statement of editorial approval. At times of national crisis, some newspapers consider it not only their duty but that of their readers to support the national effort, and vigorously exhort their readers to provide such support. The most recent and obvious example was that of a number of national newspapers, most notably *The Sun*, during the Falklands War in 1982. Reporting of the war was merged with vigorous, not to say crude, editorializing in support of the British effort, any critics being roundly condemned as unpatriotic. The broadcasting media, by virtue of their charters, sought to take a more detached position.

On party political preferences, the media may be seen as having primarily a reinforcing effect. This is in line with the findings of various studies of the effect of mass communication. Persuasive mass communication, as Klapper noted, tends to serve far more heavily in the interests of reinforcement and of minor change than of converting opinions.[13] There is a marked tendency for the recipients of communications to indulge in a process of selective exposure, perception, and retention.[14] This would appear to be borne out by the Butler and Stokes study in Britain of the effects of newspaper-reading.[15] Most readers chose a newspaper whose partisan stance was in line with their own stance or, for young people, with that of their parents; when the children absorbed and accepted the preferences of their parents, they continued to read the same newspaper.

The effect of reading any given partisan newspaper was characterized by Butler and Stokes as "magnetic": "Readers who are already close to their paper's party will tend to be held close; those at some distance will tend to be pulled towards it."[16] By adopting a critical stance of the party with which it is associated, a newspaper may have a "demagnetizing" effect, helping lessen the degree of partisan support of its readers. This demagnetizing effect may be seen to be of particular importance in recent years, the Labour party having witnessed the loss of *The Sun* to the Conservative cause and with liberal newspapers such as *The Guardian* becoming more associated with the Social Democratic party. This is not to argue that such shifts in support by newspapers have *by themselves* served to convert partisan support; rather, they have served to loosen the partisan grip of the reader and to facilitate a change for which the seeds had already been sown.

Media coverage also serves to have a constraining effect on politicians' behavior. In order to achieve their aims, politicians must be able to communicate with others, at what may be described as the horizontal level (i.e., with fellow politicians, civil servants, and other policy-makers) as well as the vertical (i.e., politician to the public), and they must also at times ensure the noncommunication of material. Most politicians crave the attention of the media. Such attention enhances their legitimacy and provides them with the means to influence others. Political behavior may often be geared, in consequence, to the needs of television and newspapers. Press conferences are now *de rigueur* during election campaigns. (They are not so necessary at other times, because Parliament provides ministers with an authoritative and structured forum for communicating their views, an important facility not available to the president and cabinet secretaries in the United States.)[17] Texts of speeches are given in advance of delivery to journalists and TV reporters. Meetings are organized so as to present a good televisual effect and also timed in order to meet newspaper deadlines or in order to get onto the early evening news on television. The effect or presumed effect of the televizing of particular politicians may even influence the careers of political leaders. A politician whose words in print may be persuasive may, on television, come across as hesitant and bumbling; he or she may physically not be photogenic. The Conservative leader in the 1964 general election, Sir Alec Douglas-Home, suffered badly from coming across as a poor performer on television; his Labour opposite number, Harold Wilson, came across as a confident, dynamic young leader. (There are certain parallels with the American public's perception of the television performances of Richard Nixon and John Kennedy in the 1960 presidential election campaign.) Politicians are thus constrained not only in how they behave in seeking to put across a particular message but also in how they look and how they present themselves before the television cameras.

The media may constrain a politician also in terms of what substantive actions or policies he or she may wish to pursue. Knowledge that one's activities may be observed and reported may deter a minister, for example, from engaging in a policy or particular action that is thought to be unpopular or likely to incur the wrath of one's colleagues or supporters. In the Falklands War in 1982, the British policy-makers were keen to achieve a quick military victory with as few casualties as possible. They were conscious that reports of heavy losses or a long-drawn-out and indecisive campaign could have an effect on public morale similar to that of media coverage of the Vietnam War on morale in the United States. Civil servants and other public officials may decide not to pursue a particular line, albeit a secret one, for fear that details may be leaked to the press and television. The effect of media reporting may thus limit the options that policy-makers believe are open to them.

Thus despite not seeking primarily to act as channels of political information and influence, the mass media in Britain constitute an integral part of the political process. Through reading newspapers and watching television (or listening to radio), citizens receive information that helps shape and reinforce their political attitudes and that, by its presentation, reinforces the legitimacy of the political system and may at times help modify their attitudes. By similarly reading newspapers and watching news and current affairs programs, politicians are aware of the material that is being communicated to the public. Their perceptions of the likely impact of this material may influence their behavior, even if the communication does not have the impact expected.

The media also serve to communicate information to political leaders on how particular policies and programs are being received. Investigative work by journalists or television researchers may present new public evidence on a particular issue—a feature of television programs such as "TV Eye" (ITV) and "Panorama" (BBC). The reporting of evidence researched by others, the coverage of demonstrations, or the publication of opinion polls commissioned by the newspaper or program serve to inform both the public and political leaders of attitudes and responses to policies and the actions of policy-makers.

That the media are intrinsically significant and influential in the political process is a statement of fact. Whether the effect and influence of the media are desirable is another question and a point of current contention.

CURRENT DEBATE

The media serve to convey information. They also form part of contemporary political debate. This stems in part, especially in the case of national newspapers, from their own operation and internal practices.

Newspapers have been criticized for being free with their advice on industrial relations while themselves having one of the worst records of management–employee relations in Britain. Bad management and uncooperative unions have helped produce sour relations between management and workforce, with chronic overmanning in the print rooms of Fleet Street (where most of the major newspapers are based) and a refusal to use new technology to produce and print the papers. On occasion, disputes have resulted in the temporary suspension of publication. In December 1978, *The Times* suspended publication for several months, during which period its future was in some doubt, until a dispute over manning levels and the use of new machinery was resolved.

The activities of the popular press particularly in obtaining stories has also proved a cause of some controversy in recent years. The harassment of individuals by journalists and television crews—camping outside their homes, constantly telephoning, pursuing them down the street whenever they venture out—has been a cause of serious complaint, ranging from pursuit of aged and innocent relatives of figures in the public eye to the engulfing of the then-Lady Diana Spencer whenever she appeared publicly following speculation as to her likely engagement to the Prince of Wales. Following her marriage, press pursuit of the Princess reached such a level—especially during the period of her pregnancy—that Fleet Street incurred the public displeasure of the Queen, who summoned editors to Buckingham Palace to request that the privacy of the Princess be respected. The use of money to elicit exclusive stories has similarly incurred public criticism, particularly in instances when it has been employed to obtain evidence from witnesses involved in pending court cases.

In their political influence, the media have also attracted disparate criticism. Their effect as legitimizers and as supporters or alleged supporters of the Conservative party has come in for particular complaint.

Fulfilling a function of latent legitimation has attracted criticism from left-wing bodies opposed to the existing political system. They see the media as buttressing opposition to change. Radical critics such as the Glasgow University Media Group have argued that rather than devoting space to the activities of the royal family or to interviewing MPs, television and newspapers should give greater coverage to the activities and the opinions of factory workers and the unemployed.[18] Such criticism from the left of the political spectrum is an enduring feature of debate, but on occasion criticism is leveled by government and other elements of the existing political system. Such criticism often stems from media coverage of bodies and activities that are opposed to the existing political order. In particular, reporting on the Irish Republican Army (IRA) in Northern Ireland, and especially the interviewing of IRA leaders and sympathizers, generates a strong reaction from political leaders in Britain. By communicating details of IRA activity, by using to some extent IRA terminology (including its name), and by showing IRA leaders and activities (the firing of guns over the coffin of a dead IRA member, for example), the media are seen as giving legitimation to an illegal organization.[19] The response of the media, especially the broadcasting media (which are most sensitive to criticisms from government sources), is that coverage does not imply approval and that to fail to report what is going on in the province would constitute a form of censorship. Nonetheless, such criticism has probably resulted in a more cautious approach to the coverage of IRA activity in the province.

Criticism of the media function of legitimation has extended, more obviously, to its overt attempts to reinforce the legitimacy of particular institutions or of specific actions. Opponents of the monarchy decry the extent not only of the coverage given the royal family by the media but also the editorializing and some degree of sycophancy in its support. Those who opposed sending the British Task Force to retake the invaded Falkland Islands in 1982 found themselves at the receiving end of intense press criticism, being characterized as unpatriotic or (if foreign) villianous. The conflict was portrayed, especially by the *Sun* newspaper, in terms of a clear contest between right and wrong, between the British and the anti-British.

And just as the media may be accused of indulging in overt attempts at legitimation, they are accused also of seeking to deny the legitimacy of certain bodies and types of activity. Among bodies or activities portrayed as being in some respect not legitimate, and hence deserving of public disapproval, are strikes (and, some critics suggest, trade unions generally), Communists, homosexuals, large demonstrations by certain groups, and individuals who manage to obtain more social security payments than they are entitled to (dubbed "social security scroungers").[20] A number of Labour politicians on the left, such as Mr. Tony Benn, also consider themselves as falling within this broad category.

On occasion, the media have also come under pressure from the government of the day for failing to indulge in more overt approval of particular actions. This has been notable at times of national crisis, especially when British troops have been in action abroad: for example, during the Suez crisis in 1956 and the Falklands War in 1982. In the latter instance, though some newspapers were enthusiastic in their support of the British action, some media—notably television—were accused of treating Argentinian news releases as being on a par with those of the British and of seeking to present in a neutral fashion both sides of the dispute. The BBC came in for especial condemnation from Conservative MPs when a "Panorama" program devoted itself to a study of the Conservative critics of the action. Such programs were taken by some Conservatives as reinforcing their belief that the BBC was manned by left-wing sympathizers.

The media have also come under much criticism from Labour politicians, especially on the left-wing of the party, for consciously favoring the Conservative party and, more recently, the Social Democrats. The partisan preference of the national daily newspapers I have recorded already. Many Labour politicians consider the broadcasting media to share a similar bias, albeit one less consciously expressed. The result is seen as a consensus among the media in support often of Conservative and certainly of conservative policies, whether introduced by a Conservative or Labour government.[21] More recently—and here, there is some measure of agreement between Conservative and Labour politicians—the media have been accused of treating sympathetically and certainly uncritically the new Social Democratic party. "The Social Democrats," declared Tony Benn, "have been the beneficiaries of the greatest display of media support ever given to any group of MPs in recent history. . . . [They] were launched upon their venture with a fanfare of publicity that rivalled the coverage accorded to the American space programme or a royal tour."[22] To many established Labour and Conservative politicians, the publicity-conscious SDP was essentially a media creation.

That newspapers do indulge in political bias has not generally been a point of contention. No one, least of all the more vociferous newspapers, has sought to deny it. Rather, the newspapers have been attacked by opponents for the views they have expressed and not for making claims to be objective. The position is somewhat different with the broadcasting media, which do make a claim to be neutral and objective. Their defense to charges of bias has tended to take the form of pointing out that they have been criticized by politicians both on the political left and on the right (Mrs. Thatcher has been a well-known critic of the BBC) and that this, in some way, implies that they have pursued a neutral course. Such a defense has had little effect on their critics. Labour activists, as Mr. Benn put it, "feel that the BBC is an instrument being used by the centre against the left—and it is no answer to be told that Mrs. Thatcher does not like the BBC either."[23]

The argument that the SDP is purely a media creation cannot be proven. Although extensive media coverage facilitated the new party in getting its message conveyed to a mass audience (and the claim that much of the coverage was at first fairly uncritical may be justified), the Social Democratic party was produced by pressures independent of (though highlighted by) the media. In any event, the party was unable to maintain a high level of support despite continuing media coverage. According to opinion poll data, support for the SDP peaked in December 1981 and had begun to decline well before the Falklands crisis forced the activities of the SDP to assume a low priority in the eyes of journalists and the broadcasting media.[24] Lack of extensive media coverage may have exacerbated the decline in SDP support, but it does not appear to have been the cause of it.

The failure of extensive and allegedly sympathetic coverage of the SDP to maintain public support for the party is important also in responding to claims that the media, when combining on a particular issue, can determine popular attitudes on that issue. It is the case, as a number of Labour critics have noted, that the media may express the same opinion on a particular issue—for example, supporting continued British membership of the European Communities in the 1975 referendum and supporting Denis Healey against Michael Foot in the contest for the Labour party leadership in 1980.[25] However, while such support may clearly or presumably be useful to the causes in question, it does not follow that the support has been either necessary or sufficient to influence public opinion (or the opinion of the audience in question) toward supporting the line advocated. In 1980, despite media support, Denis Healey failed in his bid to become leader of the Labour party. Earlier, in the February 1974 general election, all major national newspapers but one supported the return to office of Edward Heath's Conservative government. As it happened, the leader of the Labour party, Harold Wilson, was summoned to form a minority government.

Other criticisms of media influence have centered on their ability to set the agenda of political debate and on the extent to which events may be manufactured for the benefit of media coverage. The former is an important but possibly overstated point. By selecting certain material and events to cover, newspapers and news programs can influence the agenda of political debate. However, in order for that debate to be sustained, the media have to find some apparently solid base on which to pursue it and it has to be considered a salient issue by those who participate in the debate. If an issue fails to elicit a response or, worse still, produces a counterproductive response (readers or viewers objecting to the line taken), then media coverage may be affected accordingly—that is, the issue may not be pursued or the editorial policy may be changed. In the case of newspapers, it is important to recall that their primary concern is to sell copies. Taking an unpopular political line that could jeopardize sales of the newspaper would be unlikely to find favor with the proprietors. Although the significance of the media in helping set the agenda of political debate is great, the preceding qualification is important. They can rarely help influence that debate by operating in a political vacuum.

Finally, the accusation that events are created for the benefit of media coverage is an important and contemporary one. Clearly, politicians and others, as we have seen, modify their actions in order to try to ensure media coverage. Where controversy arises is the cases of violent demonstrations or specific acts of violence being carried out, allegedly, in order to attract media attention. By being present on the streets of Belfast or, in the summer of 1981, in the streets of Liverpool or Brixton, television crews were regarded as encouraging—not actively, but passively, by virtue of their presence waiting for something to happen—the stoning of troops or police by rioters. Again, it is important to stress that rioting is unlikely to take place merely for its own sake (so-called "copycat" riots in other parts of Britain in the summer of 1981 quickly subsided), but had camera crews not been present, the incidents that occurred might not have been as extensive or as violent as they were. The problem for the media, primarily the broadcasting media, is deciding what to do in such circumstances. Once rioting has begun, they can hardly ignore it. Yet, once present at the scene, they are open to claims that their presence served to instigate continued or renewed rioting. For producers and reporters, it remains a delicate problem.

In summary, then, the mass media in Britain play a significant, indeed vital, role in the political process. They serve to communicate information to a mass audience. By virtue of the way in which they present that information, they can and do exert influence on attitudes toward the political system, on partisan support, on attitudes toward particular issues, and on politicians' behavior. They help set the agenda of political debate. Not only do they help communicate contemporary political debate, they are themselves in part the subject of that debate. They remain the subject of criticism, especially on grounds of political bias, from politicians on the political left and sometimes on the right of the political spectrum. Nonetheless, their role and influence, though great, should not be exaggerated: as we have seen, various qualifications need to be entered. Not least, it is important to record that, though constituting the primary means for communicating political information to a mass audience, the national newspapers and the broadcasting media remain first and foremost commercial concerns intent on maintaining readership and viewing figures. In order to achieve a large audience they must remain media of entertainment. As we have seen, the most thoroughly read stories in newspapers are those dealing with tragedies and with celebrities (the celebrities attracting most interest almost certainly being members of the royal family). The most consistently popular program on television for the past two decades, with a regular audience of 8 million or more, has been "Coronation Street," a soap opera. Current affairs programs (as opposed to news programs, which do appear) rarely make an appearance in the TV ratings.

NOTES

1. J. Whale, *The Politics of the Media* (Fontana, 1977), p. 86.

2. D. Butler and A. Sloman, *British Political Facts 1900–1979,* 5th ed. (Macmillan, 1980), pp. 449–50.

3. D. Butler and D. Stokes, *Political Change in Britain,* 1st ed. (Penguin, 1971), pp. 281–82.

4. Ibid., p. 282 note.

5. J. Curran and J. Seaton, *Power Without Responsibility* (Fontana, 1981), pp. 108–09.

6. The most popular ITV programs in mid-1983 had audiences in excess of 10 million viewers and the most popular BBC1 programs, in excess of 8 million viewers. Popular BBC2 programs rarely attracted as many as 5 million viewers (usually 3 million or fewer), and Channel 4 programs rarely attracted as many as 3 million viewers.

For the week ending July 24, 1983, the most popular programs on television were Coronation Street (ITV, Monday), 12.85 million viewers; Coronation Street (ITV, Wednesday), 12.3 million viewers; and the A-Team (ITV), an American import, 10.85 million viewers.

7. In the 1979 general election, the allocation of election broadcasts was five to the Conservatives, five to Labour, and three to the Liberals. On broadcasting in the 1979 election campaign, see M. Pilsworth, "Balanced Broadcasting" in D. Butler and D. Kavanagh, *The British General Election of 1979* (Macmillan, 1980), pp. 200–230.

8. Curran and Seaton, p. 123.

9. See ibid., p. 124.

10. "Fluctuations on the Presidential Exchange," *Time,* November 9, 1981, p. 60.

11. *The Handling of Press and Public Information During the Falklands Conflict,* First Report from the Select Committee on Defense, Session 1982/83, Vol. 1: Report and Minutes of Proceedings, HC 17–1 (Her Majesty's Stationery Office, 1982), p. xiv.

12. See C. Seymour-Ure, *The Political Impact of the Mass Media* (Constable, 1974), p. 22.

13. J. Klapper, *The Effects of Mass Communication* (Free Press, 1960), pp. 15–18.

14. Ibid., pp. 19–26.

15. Butler and Stokes, pp. 281–300.

16. Ibid., p. 291.

17. On this, see the conclusion of C. Seymour-Ure, *The American President: Power and Communication* (Macmillan, 1982).

18. See the Glasgow University Media Group, *Bad News* (Routledge & Kegan Paul, 1976) and *More Bad News* (Routledge & Kegan Paul, 1980). Channel 4 television has provided a regular program for the presentation of "alternative" news.

19. See generally R. Clutterbuck, *The Media and Political Violence* (Macmillan, 1981).

20. See, e.g., S. Cohen and J. Young (eds.), *The Manufacture of News,* rev. ed. (Constable, 1981), passim.

21. This point is developed in T. Benn, *Arguments for Democracy* (Penguin, 1982), Ch. 6, especially p. 115.

22. Ibid., p. 111.

23. Ibid., p. 110.

24. See the summary of Gallup Poll findings for January 1981 to March 1982 in *The Political Companion,* 32, Spring 1982, p. 70, and above, Chapter 6.

25. See Benn, p. 115.

Conclusion

15

Flux and Strength
A Book with Two Themes

MOST POLITICAL SCIENCE TEXTS develop particular themes or arguments. This book is no exception. Indeed, it has two themes. What is unusual is that only one of these themes derives explicitly from what I have written in the body of the text. The other theme is drawn from what is absent in my earlier pages. "Listen, Watson." "I hear nothing, Holmes." "Precisely." The first theme, clear from the chapters, is that of a constitution in flux. The second, the hidden or covert, theme is that of the continuing strength of the political culture.

CONSTITUTIONAL FLUX

The period of the past 10 to 15 years has been notable for actual and demanded change in the institutions and practices of British government. There have been reforms and more especially advocacy of radical reforms in existing institutions such as the civil service, the judiciary, the House of Lords, and the structures of regional and local government. Demands have increased for the introduction of what would constitute new dimensions to the Constitution: an entrenched bill of rights, membership in the European Communities, federal or regional government, and the regular use of referendums.[1] Some of these demands have been met; others, as we have seen, have been stoutly resisted by government.

347

The result of these developments is that the constitutional landscape in Britain in the 1980s is not what it was at the beginning of the 1970s. Britain is now a member of a supranational body with legislative powers, the European Communities. Northern Ireland is governed directly by the United Kingdom government. Referendums are no longer alien to constitutional practice. Local government has been reformed. Direct elections have been held for members to serve in a supranational Parliament. (The next elections will be held in June 1984.) For the election of members of the European Parliament from Northern Ireland, a system of proportional representation has been employed.

The period of the 1970s was notable also for attempts by government to introduce elected assemblies in Scotland and Wales, attempts thwarted in large part by a more assertive House of Commons and the unprecedented conditions it imposed for the holding of referendums on the issue. Various practices and constitutional norms also underwent modification. The convention of collective ministerial responsibility was variously undermined. The assumption that a government defeat on an important issue in the House of Commons, and not just on an explicit vote of confidence, necessitated the government resigning or requesting a dissolution was shown to be a myth. Members of Parliament became more assertive in their behavior, imposing defeats for which there were not twentieth-century precedents. For two periods, the government was in a minority in the House of Commons, surviving from 1977 to 1978 on the strength of a "Lib–Lab Pact," the Liberal Parliamentary party being consulted on government measures in return for supporting the government in parliamentary votes. By the turn of the decade, texts on the Constitution written less than 10 years previously were well and truly out of date.

Indeed, books on constitutional law written by lawyers started to give way to books on the Constitution written by political scientists.[2] By the latter half of the 1970s not only had the Constitution changed but so too had the nature of constitutional debate. The Constitution had been drawn into the realms of political controversy. Constitutional changes were implemented as possible means of resolving some of the nation's political problems. Other changes were advocated as a means of providing a partial solution to Britain's economic and social as well as her political ills. Most notable among the reforms proposed was that of a new electoral system. Others, as we have seen, included devolved or regional government and an entrenched bill of rights.

As the Constitution became drawn into the maelstrom of political debate, different approaches to constitutional change began to be discernible. The prevailing, rarely articulated consensus gradually disintegrated. By the beginning of the 1980s, six separate approaches could be identified. The High Tory approach favored the existing constitutional framework, arguing for things to be left as they are. The Socialist approach argued for a constitutional reformulation that would permit a strong party-dominated central government to fulfill a party program free of external constraints. The Marxist approach largely rejected institutional change, regarding it as an attempt by the ruling state elite to maintain the interests of finance capital; it waited instead for the crisis of capitalism to result in a collapse of the existing political system. The group approach sought the more extensive incorporation of groups into the governmental process. The liberal approach (not confined to the Liberal party) sought constitutional reform that would defend the individual in society and allow for the generation of consensus-building constitutional rules. The sixth and final approach, the traditional approach, sought limited change in order to maintain a balance between strong government and an effective Parliament, the emphasis being on the maintenance of parliamentary sovereignty and parliamentary (and party) government.[3] These approaches were not all well developed nor were they coterminous with existing political parties. Their more obvious emergence and articulation served to generate a vigorous but confused debate about the structure and the future of the British Constitution.

By the early 1980s, the description of the Constitution as being in a state of flux would thus appear both apt and accurate. That it should be in such a state is not surprising. As the nation's economic condition worsened and as economic and political remedies failed to have the desired effect, attention began to turn to institutional change as a possible solution. As this author stated elsewhere, "When Britain enters a period of economic travail, when government has difficulty in maintaining effectiveness and/or consent, there is a tendency to look to constitutional change as a palliative or a means of dealing with the problem, of producing a system capable of being effective and maintaining consent. In this there is nothing new."[4] Britain has experienced similar periods of economic malaise and demands for constitutional change, most notably but not exclusively in the 1930s. The implications of the Depression for the Constitution were noted at the time by Conservative leader Stanley Baldwin. "There is bound to be unrest when more questions are being put than statesmen can answer," he said in 1930. "Within the House of Commons itself there is a growing sense of the need for overhauling the ship of State."[5] Disappointment with the working of representative government, he said, was no new thing. "It recurs periodically and we are in one of the fermenting periods now. It may be uncomfortable but it is not surprising."[6]

In short, the demands for constitutional change in recent years have been significant but, in historical perspective, they are not unusual. From the perspective of the languid 1950s they may appear surprising, but historically, the 1950s constitute a decade more atypical than that of the 1970s. Pressure for political and constitutional change has littered the historical landscape, an observation borne out by a study of the development of parliamentary government in Britain (Chapter 3). Demands for constitutional change may be more virulent in some decades than in others, but rarely have such demands been totally absent from the agenda of political debate. Even in the 1950s and early 1960s, the period from which many generalizations have been drawn about British political behavior, modest constitutional changes were carried out by government (the introduction of life peerages, for example). Less modest proposals, not least concerning the House of Lords, were being put forward by more radical reformers.[7] Given the apparent failure of the political system in the 1970s to meet demands and expectations that it had appeared capable of meeting in earlier decades, it is hardly surprising that the pressure on the institutions of government became much greater, the Constitution being dragged back into the fray of political debate as it had been in the 1930s and earlier.

Thus, that the Constitution in the 1970s should be a matter of political controversy is not something that should be a cause of wonder. Apprised of the contemporary debate, the appropriate response should be "Oh yes, only to be expected" and not "Good heavens, how surprising." And yet there does remain something that *is* remarkable about the constitutional ferment of the past decade. Given the problems faced by the nation, problems worse than those faced by many other Western industrialized nations, it is amazing that the force for change has not been greater. The basic constitutional structure remains intact. Pressure for change has not overwhelmed or gone beyond the Constitution—that is, the people have not taken to the streets to demand action. (For those who might query this assertion, read on.) Indeed, looked at from this perspective, what emerges as being far more deserving of attention than what has happened over the past decade is what has *not* happened over the past decade. Why has the political system proved relatively resilient at a time of acute stress? Why have demands for reform not been more strident? Why have such demands been channeled through largely conventional avenues rather than through more radical action? The explanation, I suggest, lies in the continuing strength of the political culture.

THE STRENGTH OF THE POLITICAL CULTURE

For the past 10 to 20 years, Britain has faced serious economic problems. Various explanations have been offered as to the cause of these problems (Chapter 3). Economic problems have generated political and social problems. Government has lacked the resources it had previously to meet rising demands and expectations. Its failure to meet those demands has led to demands for political and institutional change as well as to social tension. As we have seen, the 1970s witnessed a relative desertion by voters of the two main parties, and demands for a new electoral system and for new forms of government in Scotland, Wales, and (in some quarters) the English regions.

In the early 1980s, public order broke down in a number of cities, starting in the St. Paul's district of Bristol early in 1981 and followed that summer in Liverpool, London, and other cities, with occasional sporadic outbursts of public disorder since that time. Government has had difficulty in imposing its wishes upon the plethora of groups on which it depends for the successful implementation of its policies, those groups standing out for the results that will favor their own interests, if not the public good. Hence, one has the problems of recent years. All of which is true.

According to some analyses, these problems both reflect and are in part the product of a decline in the "civic culture" in Britain. In particular, Samuel Beer has contended that the growth of technocratic and populist attitudes, the latter engendered by a "romantic revolt in politics," has served to undermine the hierarchic and organic values that formed the civic culture in Britain. The consequence has been a decline, indeed a collapse, in the civic culture, producing distrust in government and demands for more radical participatory democracy. This, coupled with pluralist stagnation, provides an explanation for political fragmentation and immobilism in Britain.[8] All of which, I would suggest, is not true.

Let me first of all express the thrust of my own argument before explaining why Professor Beer's well-expressed points are wrong. In Chapter 2, I argued that the strength of the political culture lay in the convergence of the orientations toward problem solving, the political system, cooperation and individuality, and other people. Those orientations, I suggested, were congruent with one another and had been molded and reinforced by the experience of history. Recognition of the apparent strength of the political culture, certainly of the corollary of having a culture and a political system that worked and was different from that of other countries, reinforced pride in the political system and encouraged a rather romanticized teaching of its attributes. Indeed, I would suggest that these developments imparted to the political culture a momentum that has resulted in a strengthening of that culture over past decades, not a weakening. The events of more recent years point to its continuing strength. Viewed from a deeper historical and cultural perspective than that of the 1950s and 1960s, the political and social tensions of the 1970s are unusual only in that they were not more severe. Certainly, they can be understood and should be understood within the context of the well-established civic culture.

Consider the following quotation. It is a lengthy one but, important for the purposes of my argument, it could have been much longer:

> In 1919, following demobilisation, serious rioting occurred throughout the country. In May and June there were race riots in South Wales, the East End [of London,] and Liverpool when whites attacked blacks. In Cardiff three people were shot dead. In July the Peace Day celebrations were attended by riots in Wolverhampton, Salisbury, Epsom, Luton,

Essex, Coventry and Swindon. In Luton the town hall was destroyed by arson. Police and firemen were attacked by bricks, stones and bottles and there was widespread looting. On the first of August the police in Liverpool went on strike, and severe rioting and widespread looting began, continuing for four days and nights. Steel helmeted troops and tanks were sent in. There were bayonet charges and shooting. In July and August there were also riots and battles between police and youths in London: in Greenwich, Hammersmith, Tottenham, Edmonton, Wood Green, Barking and Brixton.[9]

This was not an isolated period in British history. There were clashes before the First World War between the police and the suffragettes (demanding votes for women) and between police and strikers. On a number of occasions, troops were called out to assist the police. During a railway and dock strike in 1911, the Home Secretary, Winston Churchill, actually sent a gunboat up the River Mersey. He despatched troops to guard Manchester railway stations. According to one newspaper, he sent troops "hither and thither as though Armageddon was upon us."[10] There was rioting on various occasions in the 1920s and 1930s. There were clashes between police and demonstrators during the General Strike of 1926. In 1931, thousands of unemployed demonstrators fought with the police in Glasgow. There was extensive damage. Violent clashes took place for two days between demonstrators and police in Birkenhead, resulting in many injuries.[11] Public disorder, in short, is not unknown in Britain in the twentieth century.

Various caveats must now be entered. The violence and disorder in the early part of the century were significant but (a) they were less common than in the eighteenth and nineteenth centuries,[12] (b) they were less extensive than in many other Western countries, and (c) they remained exceptional. For an illustration of the second point, one need look no further than the United States. In the three-year period 1902 to 1904, about 200 people were killed and 2,000 injured in the United States in the violence that accompanied various strikes and lockouts.[13] In 1914 in the so-called Ludlow Massacre, National Guardsmen killed a number of striking coalminers and set fire to their tents. There were 16 deaths in the Little Steel Strike of 1937.[14] Lynch-mob violence remained a feature of the American South and race riots occurred in the North. Between 1915 and 1919, there were 22 racial disturbances in United States cities, the most violent being in Chicago in 1919: 15 whites and 23 blacks were killed.[15] Violent clashes have been far more a feature of the American than the British historical landscape.

That the clashes in Britain were exceptional is significant and central to my argument. The early part of the century was marked by the orientations identified in Chapter 2. A desire to reach agreement, "to work things out," and to accept established authority remained predominant features of the political culture. Despite clashes between police and demonstrators, most strikes and demonstrations were peaceful. Every year there were several hundred industrial stoppages involving several hundred-thousand work-ers.[16] Despite clashes during the General Strike of 1926, the most notewor-thy feature of the dispute was its peacefulness and the desire to reach some form of agreement. "Paradoxically," wrote A. H. Halsey, "the General Strike of 1926, which may reasonably be described as a moment of tense confrontation between the two main classes, . . . provides unmistakable evi-dence of a consensual political culture."[17] He discerned this consensus as much in the actions of the political elite as in the activities of police and strikers. The union leaders were keen not to be seen as threatening the Constitution. Prime Minister Stanley Baldwin, for his part, was keen to heal any social wounds caused by the dispute. He discouraged his supporters from seeking further to restrict the unions once the strike was over, invoking in the House of Commons the prayer "Give Peace in our time, O Lord."[18] What disputes there were tended to be conducted more often than not in a very British fashion, according to accepted norms. Winston Churchill pro-vided an idiosyncratic but nonetheless British response when berated by a fellow cabinet minister for having sent troops to northern cities. "Now, Charlie," he said, "don't be cross. It was such fun."[19]

My contention, then, is that the orientations of the political culture, as identified in Chapter 2, were well developed by the beginning of the twen-tieth century and became more marked as the century progressed. This development was reflected in the decline in violent clashes and public disor-der. The strength of the political culture helps explain both the nature and the extent of the political conflicts and the public disorder of the 1970s. The orientation toward the political system ensured that the controversies sur-rounding the institutions of government were essentially disparate (few com-prehensive schemes for constitutional change were advanced) and were con-ducted according to the accepted "rules of the game." Those parties seeking radical constitutional change, the Liberal and Social Democratic parties, were prepared to seek that change through the existing electoral and parlia-mentary framework. Despite the Conservative and Labour parties becoming more polarized in the policies they advocated, both parties remain wedded to the essentials of British parliamentary government. Left-wing politician Tony Benn is as ardent a parliamentarian as is Mrs. Margaret Thatcher. Parliament remains the accepted legitimate forum in which political battles must be fought. Left-wing Labour MPs are among the most assiduous atten-ders of parliamentary debates. Advocacy of extra-parliamentary action—in essence, of taking to the streets to press for change—remains remarkable for its rarity and for the fate of those who pursue it. Few advocate it, and even fewer appear to try it (see below and Table 15.3). Public demonstrations are popular but in this, as in clashes between competing groups, there is nothing new. What remains unusual is the reluctance to consider action that goes beyond the norms of the political culture—for example, the use of violence or of political strikes.

Trade union leaders retain the fear that characterized their predecessors of the 1920s—that of taking "political" as opposed to "industrial" action. Industrial action in Britain continues to take the form of wage militancy rather than political militancy.[20] When a one-day "Day of Action" (in effect a general strike) was called, rather half-heartedly, to protest against government policies in 1980, it was a failure.[21] Despite being implacably opposed to government economic and industrial policies, trade union leaders remain prepared to talk to government, including through the established forum of the National Economic Development Council: attempts to persuade union leaders to withdraw from the NEDC in 1983 in protest at government policies were successfully rebuffed.

Despite the riots of 1981, violence and public disorder remain uncommon to contemporary Britain. Even during the riots, serious violence was rare. The only fatality was a youth struck by a police vehicle. (Compare this with the experience of race riots in Miami.) There is also no monocausal explanation of the riots. Some appear the product of mounting tension between police and black youths, others of spontaneous violence between white gangs and blacks.[22] The riots themselves, at least in Liverpool, appeared to follow well-ordered patterns, with a clear "us" and "them" division between the police and the rioters, members of the public being allowed to stand on the side and spectate. One anecdote by a Liverpool resident reflects the British nature of the rioting. As a gang of predominantly black youths was marching up one street, setting fire to a number of buildings, a local white resident rushed out to try to persuade them not to set fire to the local squash club building on the grounds that it was of architectural importance. Apparently, the gang and the resident were engaged in discussion for several minutes before the decision was taken that the building should be burned.[23] Such an exchange is hardly conceivable in the context of riots in, say, Miami, Los Angeles, or Chicago.

It is possible that at this stage some readers, looking at the problem from a United Kingdom rather than a British perspective, are getting irritated with my line of argument. What, they may well ask, is the position in Northern Ireland? Is that not an example of a society in which violence is rife and in which political strikes have been held, most notably that of the Ulster Workers Council in 1974 (the strike that effectively brought down the new Northern Ireland Executive)? Indeed yes, but this reinforces rather than undermines my argument. The *British* political culture is precisely that: British. The culture and history of Northern Ireland, as I sought to show in Chapter 9, is totally distinct. It is precisely because of this gulf between the British and Northern Ireland cultures that the problems of Northern Ireland are so incomprehensible to the British mind. It also helps explain why, as I suggested in Chapter 9, the British government has had difficulty in knowing how to handle the problem, policy often being premised on the British assumption that problems can be solved by discussion, by reasonable people gathering round a table to resolve their differences.[24] The British political culture also helps provide a partial explanation for the continued presence of troops in Northern Ireland. Opinion polls have shown that most people in Britain would prefer to withdraw troops from the province.[25] They remain, in part, because of the sense of responsibility shared by political leaders, persuading them that to pursue a policy of withdrawal would result in a bloodbath.

So much, then, for a basic statement of my argument. Let me now pursue it further, from a negative perspective, by dissecting the threads of Professor Beer's argument. A confluence of technocratic and populist attitudes, he argues, have undermined the values of the traditional civic culture, thus explaining a decline in deference, class decomposition, and lack of trust in government. The changes, he claims, are sufficient to argue that the decline in the civic culture can be described as a "collapse."[26] In fact, the changes he claims to discern are relative and have so far effected no fundamental change in the political culture.

Let us consider briefly the different elements, both the new attitudes and their presumed effects, that Professor Beer identifies. The assertion of *technocratic values*, he concedes, had a limited impact on the populace and is presented in his work primarily in order to help isolate and characterize the more powerful influence of populist values.[27] Nonetheless, he contends that "the technocratic attack," "an exaggerated assertion of the scientific ethos," helped shape in critical ways the behavior of the political elite: it found reflection in the reform of the civil service following the Fulton Committee report in 1968 and in Edward Heath's managerial approach as prime minister, with the introduction of Program Analysis and Review (PAR) and the Central Policy Review Staff (CPRS). Yet even this is to state too much. As previous chapters have shown, primarily Chapter 8, those reforms failed to overcome the self-interest and incremental-policy style of government, a style facilitated by the existing political culture. Far from the reforms having a significant impact on the traditional processes of government, those processes in effect smothered the new managerialism. The CPRS and PAR exist no longer, and the managerialism of Edward Heath was short-lived, Mr. Heath being replaced by a leader who adheres to a philosophy that, taken to its logical conclusion, has an antimanagerial bias.

What, then, of the *romantic revolt?* Professor Beer concedes that the reasons for the occurrence of this "revolt" and for the method of its occurrence are not clear. Possible explanations that he discusses, but does not fully align himself with, are post-material reaction to affluence, a reaction to the failure of government to meet expectations, and a reaction to a centralized bureaucratic state.[28] Whatever the causes, the new romanticism took the form of emphasizing cultural values as well as demanding wider and more intense participation. It was also radically decentralizing.

It was a revolt that found reflection in the cultural and political upheavals of the 1960s. It had to be seen within the context of a wider far-reaching assault on the values of society. "The ethos was the same in all spheres," Professor Beer writes. "No explanation of political developments can satisfy that does not recognise this connection."[29] On the left of the political spectrum, Marcuse and the New Left writers had a major impact on young students. Beer continues, "No one who was a university teacher in those days [the 1960s] can doubt the power of a book, such as Brown's *Life Against Death* or Marcuse's *Eros and Civilisation*, to work a 'conversion.'"[30] But the new populism reached wider. Pop music served as one transmission belt for new messages that broke with established values. The songs of the Beatles are accorded special attention. "I doubt," writes Beer, "that they ever used the word 'democratic' or 'participation' in a song, but it would be hard to find a stronger case against exclusion than *Eleanor Rigby* or in favor of inclusion than *Sergeant Pepper*. And if you are looking for a secular hymn to agape, *All You Need is Love* should do. The localism of their songs is fundamental."[31]

The romantic revolt, the new populism, extended into the 1970s, con-stituting a new orthodoxy of dissent. It found reflection in workers' attitudes, emphasizing principles rather than material benefits when striking, and has had an impact on the political parties. There has been a populist thrust within the Labour party, stressing participation and being less willing to accept established authority within the party. Within the Conservative par-ty, it has found reflection in the rise of neoliberalism and in a decline in the traditions of deference, authority, and acceptance of an organic society. There has been, declared Beer, "a waning of Toryism."[32] The parties most in tune with and benefiting most from this new romanticism—with its em-phasis on values, participation, and decentralization—have been the Liberal party, and after 1981, the new Social Democratic party.

Possibly the kindest comment that can be made about this thesis is that it is vague. The more you try to come to grips with it, the more the sand seeps through your fingers. The threads of the argument are thin and ten-uous, resting on little empirical verification. In asserting that no university teacher in the 1960s could doubt the power of writings such as those by Marcuse and Brown to work a "conversion," Professor Beer is clearly draw-ing on his own recollections as a university teacher. This, with all due respect, tells us little about changes in the political culture. I, as an under-graduate in the very late 1960s, can put forward the conflicting assertion that few British students were "converted" by any such works and that few students had read Marcuse and even fewer had heard of Brown. Such anec-dotal assertions take the argument not very far forward. Far more relevant, and observable, is the comparative behavior of students in different coun-tries during the 1960s. While students were facing National Guardsmen on campuses in the United States and rioting students in France came close to toppling the French government, British students were mostly getting on with their studies and a number at a minority of campuses were engaging in occasional bouts of public disorder. What needs to be explained is not why there were sit-ins and demonstrations by students in some British universities but why those students did not emulate their foreign counterparts. The answer, I would suggest, is to be found in the continuing strength of the political culture.

As for the relevance of the pop music of the 1960s, one reviewer of *Britain Against Itself* wrote "I cannot take seriously a discussion of the lyrics of the Beatles, although I'm willing to admit that the rock, pop and teenage culture generally are symptomatic of a change."[33] Some of the music of the period may indeed have served to convey messages that broke with established values. However, the interpretation of their meaning by Beer is not necessarily the interpretation given by those responsible for the music, nor is it necessarily the same as that rendered by those who listened to the music. Music means different things to different people. *Eleanor Rigby* had quite an impact on this writer, but how I interpret it bears no resemblance to Beer's interpretation. Because music that conveys a message of change or a challenge to existing values is popular does not mean necessarily that the message has won approval.[34] If the pop culture of the 1960s is symptomatic of change, there is little empirical evidence to demonstrate what that change is, other than a change in musical tastes and behavior. Certainly, there is little to demonstrate a connection between the lyrics of Beatle songs and Beer's "new populism."

Moving to more relevant ground, the assertion of the new populism in workers' behavior and in the political parties is not sufficient to bear the weight that Beer gives it. There may indeed have been a greater fragmentation in the union movement in the 1960s and early 1970s, local groups starting to regulate their own behavior, but the cause of this was not some new populism that was sweeping across the land but rather the failure of government to meet the demands of the unions. When union leaders became unable to produce the goods for their members, local groups began to get what they could for themselves, and in that there is nothing surprising. Such changes may have engendered some change in attitudes, but not to an extent that has threatened the existing political culture. Union attitudes and behavior, looked at in broad historical perspective, have not departed dramatically from those of earlier periods. In taking strike action, workers may indeed, as Beer suggests, emphasize the importance of the principles at stake ("Money doesn't count when you're fighting for principle," he quotes one striker as saying), but he presents no evidence that such expressions are new. One might be forgiven for suggesting that it would be surprising if such assertions were not made. If one is out on strike for any length of time, ending up losing more money through lost wages than the amount that would be gained by the claimed pay rise, how is one to justify one's action? Furthermore, looked at from the perspective of member participation, the greater demands for participation that form part of the romantic revolt can hardly be said to have swept through the trade union movement. The prevailing ethos remains one of nonparticipation.

As for the political parties, the attempts within the Labour party to introduce populist themes are hardly new to the traditions of the party. In considering the *Labour Programme 1976*, Beer claims to discern "a sense of the new values in the background."[35] What is more obvious are demands that find root in British Labour party history. An emphasis on the individual, on electing regional authorities (responsible for planning), on opening up civil-service decision-making to "much greater scrutiny and political control," on liberalizing the Officials Secret Act, and on moving toward employees' control and self-management—the items in the program singled out by Beer—have well-established lineages. They may have become more pronounced but they are best understood within the context of the strands that form the Labour party and the divisions between those strands that have existed since the party's formation (see Chapter 6).

Beer's argument concerning the Conservative party is similarly overdrawn. As we have seen (Chapter 6), neoliberalism is one well-established strand of Conservatism. It has become more prominent in recent years, especially since the election of Mrs. Thatcher as party leader, but its significance should not be exaggerated. The party, as I said in Chapter 6, now has a leader more identified with the neoliberal wing than was the case before, but the government she heads has not pursued a vigorous neoliberal policy nor has the Conservative party as a whole become neoliberal. Outside of its economic policy, the government has pursued many traditional Tory policies, and on economic policy most of the parliamentary party remains agnostic (that is, in the event of neoliberal policies failing, it will turn to support other policies). Beer's claim to substantiate the "waning of Toryism" rests largely on the writings of two Conservatives (one of the works a somewhat idiosyncratic one and, as its author conceded to this writer, somewhat self-indulgent) and their failing to address themselves to the issues of deference and authority.[36] Within the Conservative party, deference and attitudes toward authority may be less marked than in the 1950s, but any change is relative. Deference and the relationship between leaders and led within the party remain fundamentally unchanged.[37]

So much, then, for the supposed "romantic revolt." This is not to say that some of the changes mentioned by Beer have not taken place (neoliberalism clearly is more prominent in the Conservative party than it was previously), but the changes will not bear the weight of the analysis given them. What, then, of the developments that Beer hypothesized were the result of his supposed romantic revolt?

Class decomposition is discussed primarily in terms of the decline in the class–party nexus.[38] This decline I have charted in Chapters 5 and 6. The decline is significant but, as argued in Chapter 6, class remains the most important predictor of voting behavior. Although class may have declined in significance, class-related factors, notably home ownership, have grown in importance. If one goes beyond the class–party nexus, class remains fundamental to British society (see Chapter 1). There is greater social mobility than before, as Goldthorpe has shown, and a "service class" may be emerging, but to contend as Beer does that there has been class decomposition and a reintegration of the working class into competitive society by a new plurality of groups is again to take the argument further than the empirical evidence will allow. It is also to emphasize the economic over the social. Class provides a social orientation for which groups have provided no substitute.

As for a *decline of leadership* and *weakening of party government*, these are not unique to contemporary Britain. Indeed, the assertion of a decline in leadership at the beginning of the 1980s is clearly open to question. As I interpret Beer's thesis, leadership decline results from the failure of government to mobilize consent and to impose policies on disparate groups. If this interpretation is correct, I would make three simple points. First, it is arguable (and supporters of the present government would argue) that any such drift has been at least halted, possibly reversed, under Mrs. Thatcher's leadership. (Enoch Powell, for example, implicitly makes this point in his review of Beer's book.)[39] Second, it can be contended that there was an absence of leadership during the collectivist era of the 1950s, the product of an unwillingness to break from the collectivist consensus and give a lead. (If this is the case, what has leadership "declined" from?) Third, a failure to mobilize consent and impose policies on groups is not exclusive to the 1970s and is apparent at different periods in British history—for example, in the first two decades of this century. It may have been more marked in recent years, but it is explicable in terms of the existing political culture. As for a weakening of party government, that again is not exclusive to the past decade or so of British history. As to strong two-party government and the functions attributed to it (choice, aggregation, consensus), the period from 1945 to 1970 is as much atypical in modern British history as is the period since 1970. It is also relevant to remind ourselves of Nevil Johnson's observation (cited in Chapter 6) that a decline in voting support for one or both main parties is not, in itself, proof of a decline in support for a two-party system.

Finally, what of *trust in government?* Beer cites a decline in such trust as empirical verification of a waning of the deference that underpins the positive orientation toward government. He calls in aid the analyses of Alan Marsh and Vivien Hart (the latter using the findings of the Royal Commission on the Constitution: see Chapter 9), who interpret a decline in trust as reflecting a change in values.[40] The biggest change, according to Beer, being a decline or a collapse in deference.

Let us consider first the evidence. Both Marsh and the Royal Commission detected a significant fraction of the population expressing distrust in government. The responses to the Royal Commission question on the pre-

TABLE 15.1
Trust in Government (1), 1970

Question: Which of these statements best expresses your opinion on the present
system of running Britain?

"Works extremely well and could not be improved"	5%
"Could be improved in small ways but mainly works well"	43%
"Could be improved quite a lot"	35%
"Needs a great deal of improvement"	14%
"Don't know"	4%

SOURCE: Royal Commission on the Constitution, Research Papers 7, reproduced in V. Hart, *Distrust and Democracy* (Cambridge University Press, 1978), p. 60. Copyright 1978 Cambridge University Press. Reprinted by permission.

sent system of running Britain are given in Table 15.1. As it shows, only 5% of respondents thought the existing system worked extremely well and could not be improved. Marsh found that when asked "How much do you trust the government in Westminster [sic] to do what is right?," 47% responded with "Only some of the time" and 10% responded "Almost never."[41]

That there was a significant level of distrust in government in the late 1960s and early 1970s, as defined by these researchers, I do not seek to deny. In fact, I do not find it surprising. It is surprising to Beer and others because of the assumptions that they make about the political culture. However, if one accepts that the deference accorded government is contingent, not certain (Chapter 2), then the failure of government to meet expectations could be expected to produce a greater expression of distrust in government than was the case in the heady days of Almond and Verba's research for *The Civic Culture* (1963). What should be considered surprising, given Beer's assumptions about the political culture, is the proportion of respondents who did not express any distrust in government and, much more importantly, the fact that distrust did not appear to increase during the 1970s. A survey by Louis Moss of adults in England and Wales in 1978 revealed responses very similar to those obtained in 1970 by the Royal Commission on the Constitution (Table 15.2). Questions similar to those asked by Marsh also elicited no increase in the proportions giving nontrusting responses.[42]

Other surveys in the 1970s of attitudes toward specific elements of the constitutional structure, such as the House of Commons, also failed to elicit the negative response expected by some critics. A National Opinion Poll (NOP) undertaken for Granada Television in 1973 on the attitudes toward Parliament "failed to demonstrate the extent of disaffection they expected. So in the end they discarded the poll and used the dissatisfaction of many MPs and civil servants as their framework."[43] (Of those questioned, 55% had said that "Parliament works very well or fairly well." Only 8% thought that

TABLE 15.2
Trust in Government (2), 1978

Respondents were asked their opinion "on the present system of running the government of this country."

"On the whole it works well and probably could not be improved"	4%
"It could be improved in small ways but mainly works well"	53%
"It could be improved a lot"	30%
"It needs a great deal of improvement"	11%

SOURCE: L. Moss, "Attitudes Towards Government," *SSRC Research Report HR 5427* (1980), Appendix, p. 28. Reprinted by permission.

their MPs were doing "a poor job.") A MORI poll carried out for *The Sunday Times* in 1977 on how well institutions performed found that "Parliament emerges with surprisingly little egg on its face," only 8% of respondents considering that Parliament did "a bad job."[44] Nor did polls in this period suggest that dissatisfaction with government had swelled to the level of demanding significant institutional change. Indeed, an Opinion Research Centre (ORC) poll in 1977 found that respondents gave constitutional change "a very low priority" in relation to other issues.[45] People were more concerned that government should deal with problems such as rising prices and unemployment.

For those who claim to detect a collapse of trust in government, the foregoing constitute inconvenient pieces of data. Let me add two more. A Harris Poll taken in 1973 resulted in 82% of those interviewed agreeing with the statement that 'On the whole, the British system of government works pretty well." Only 15% disagreed.[46] Second, there are no comparable data that permit us to compare the lack of trust in government expressed in the 1970s with that of the earlier decades of the century. That it should have declined in the 1960s and early 1970s compared with the 1950s is not surprising, but has it declined compared with the 1920s and 1930s? From my earlier observations on public disorder during those decades, I suspect not. There are no survey data that would dispel this suspicion.

Indeed, when one puts the debate in a historical framework, a great deal of recent survey evidence begins to look decidely suspect. For example, much has been made by some writers of the findings of Barnes, Kaas, et al. (as well as Marsh) about the preparedness of the British public to engage in direct action (see Table 15.3). These findings, we are told, "even considering the fraility of the comparative data base," suggest that significant micro-level political changes have occurred "since the mid 1960s."[47] "Indeed, perhaps the most startling finding of these studies was the proportion of the mass population willing to undertake direct political activities such as boycotts,

TABLE 15.3
Willingness to Engage in Direct Action

The preparedness of the British public to engage in direct action

| | Percentage Answering | | | | |
Action	"Have done"	"Would do"	"Might do"	"Would never do"	Missing data
Petitions	22	31	22	21	4
Lawful demonstration	6	25	24	42	4
Boycotts	5	17	23	47	7
Rent strikes	2	10	20	65	4
Unofficial strikes	5	7	15	69	3
Occupying buildings	1	6	13	77	3
Blocking traffic	1	7	15	74	2
Damaging property	1	1	2	95	2
Personal violence	0	1	4	93	2

SOURCE: Barnes, Kaas, et al., *Political Action* (1979), reproduced in D. Sanders and E. Tanenbaum, "Direct Action and Political Culture: The Changing Political Consciousness of the British Public," *European Journal of Political Research*, 11, 1983, p. 47.

demonstrations, and strikes in situations where these activities had hitherto been deemed 'illegitimate' or 'unacceptable.' "[48] Put in historical perspective—that is, going back some way beyond "the mid 1960s"—the most startling thing about the figures is quite the reverse. Table 15.3 is remarkable for the proportion of people who "would never" engage in activities that are lawful and have not been considered illegitimate or unacceptable, never mind the overwhelming proportion who would never engage in more dubious activities. Bearing in mind the extent of public disorder in the early part of this century, Table 15.3, if anything, supports my argument as to the continuing strength of the political culture, not its erosion.

In short, then, the arguments advanced by Beer and others are not sufficient to justify the claim that there has been a collapse of the civic culture. That is not to say that some of the changes identified by Beer are not significant. Clearly they are. But they are insufficient individually and collectively to bear the weight of his argument. His analysis does not and cannot explain many of the inconvenient pieces of data outlined above. His narrow, time-bound focus has obscured the wider reality.

The wider reality is the continuing strength of the political culture. The various orientations identified in Chapter 2 have converged to form the political culture in Britain, and that culture has influenced and been reinforced by the experiences of history, generating a certain momentum.

Throughout the twentieth century, government has proved capable of meeting expectations, victory in the Second World War and the availability to government of resources to meet demands in the 1950s serving to reinforce trust in and allegiance to the political system. With a decline in resources available to government in the 1960s and 1970s, the degree of trust has declined but that decline, like the decline in resources, is relative. Indeed, what is remarkable, as I have suggested, is that the decline in trust has not been greater. It is that phenomenon, not the extent of the decline since the 1950s, that is deserving of most attention.

CONCLUSION

In concluding Chapter 3, I argued that the political culture may have helped facilitate some structural problems but that nonetheless the culture also helped provide a breathing space for government in attempting to deal with Britain's basic problems, problems that I would suggest are essentially economic. The orientations toward problem-solving and cooperation have encouraged the incremental and now complex style of policy-making that exists in Britain and that some observers have seen as part of Britain's problems. The effects of the orientations and the complexity of government have made it increasingly difficult for government to govern and to initiate radical change. This was as much a feature of Beer's collectivist era of the 1950s as it was of the 1970s. The fragmentation of groups was compatible with, and indeed if anything was encouraged by, the orientations mentioned. The significant change between the 1950s and the 1970s was in the resources of government to meet the demands of groups rather than in the demands or attitudes of such groups.

The longevity of the political system and the orientations mentioned have also contributed to some of the other structural problems, allowing for the growth piecemeal of disparate political institutions that make for a confused political system. That, I trust, emerges from the previous chapters. As more demands are made of institutions, the less able they are to cope because of the reduction in resources available to them—hence, in Anthony King's analysis, the problem of government overload.[49]

How, then, to deal with Britain's basic ills? The answer lies not so much with institutional changes, though such changes are possible, but with resolving the country's economic problems and hence increasing resources *and/or* reducing the expectations and demands made of government. It is not my purpose to propose solutions for the former. Rather, I want to draw attention to the importance of the political culture in providing a breathing space for a government, any government, intent on pursuing a determined policy to resolve Britain's economic ills. Such policies may fail, they may be disastrous, but the opportunities are there. The British orientation to problem-solving, to the political system, and to cooperation make such an attempt possible. To some extent, we are seeing this in the experience of the Thatcher government. The structural obstacles are there: the incrementalism, the fragmentation of groups, the complex governmental structure. However, pluralist stagnation provides no insuperable obstacle; indeed, it can be used to the government's advantage and to some extent is being so used. Favoring their own interests, groups have proved unwilling to join with others in the interests of "solidarity" (the union equivalent of the "public good") to resist government imposing its policy on particular groups. The orientation to problem-solving allows policy experimentation, not on grounds of ideology but on the basis of seeking a policy that works. Probably few people in Britain have much knowledge of monetarism, let alone support it, but a great many, sufficient to give Mrs. Thatcher a parliamentary majority, would seem to be prepared to give the government a chance "to see if it works." The orientation to cooperation also gives government a head start in seeking to impose a policy. Those affected by such a policy are reluctant to rush to oppose it in any form that extends beyond discussion and parliamentary opposition. Such opposition may well prove successful, as it did in 1969 when the Wilson government abandoned its proposals to reform industrial relations, but if the government persists, groups are unsure how to react. Thus, it is significant that trade-union leaders continue to talk with government in 1983 and to use such discussion as the primary means of seeking to effect a change in government policy.

What strengthens the government's position is, as Beer emphasizes, the mobilization of consent. In a sense, existing structures militate against that but the orientations of the political culture provide no insuperable bar to its realization. Indeed, the greatest success of the Thatcher government has been not the achievement of policy goals but rather the (further) lowering of public expectations. The empirical approach to problem-solving has made this possible. As economic growth has slowed, people have been persuaded to scale down their expectations.[50] The results of the 1983 election helped give the lie to the adversary politics thesis. A partial explanation of Labour's failure to win the election, despite more than 3 million unemployed people in Britain, was not that the party did not offer enough but that it appeared to offer too much. Electors did not believe that it could deliver on its promises.

Thus, one has the contradictions of the British political culture. It militates against decisive leadership but if such leadership is attempted, it provides the potential for the popular support for its realization. However, government itself does not exist independently of the political culture and is itself constrained by the reciprocal relationship between governors and governed (see Chapter 2). It can only go so far and at the end of the day, its policies need to bear fruit. But the political culture is stronger and may permit of more determined government than many have been prepared to admit.

NOTES

1. P. Norton, *The Constitution in Flux* (Martin Robertson, 1982).

2. See, e.g., P. Bromhead, *Britain's Developing Constitution* (George Allen & Unwin, 1974) and, more especially, N. Johnson, *In Search of the Constitution* (Pergamon Press, 1977); G. Peele, "The Developing Constitution" in C. Cook and J. Ramsden (eds.), *Trends in British Politics Since 1945* (Macmillan, 1978), Ch. 1; M. Beloff and G. Peele, *The Government of the United Kingdom* (Weidenfeld & Nicolson, 1980), Ch. 1; and Norton, *The Constitution in Flux.*

3. Norton, *The Constitution in Flux,* Conclusions.

4. Ibid., p. 27.

5. S. Baldwin, *The Torch of Freedom,* 4th ed. (Hodder & Stoughton, 1937), p. 50.

6. Ibid.

7. See, e.g., A. W. Benn, *The Privy Council as a Second Chamber,* Fabian Tract 305 (Fabian Society, 1957); and Lord Chorley, B. Crick, and D. Chapman, *Reform of the Lords,* Fabian Research Series 169 (Fabian Society, 1954).

8. S. H. Beer, *Britain against Itself* (Faber, 1982).

9. S. Field and P. Southgate, *Public Disorder,* Home Office Research Study No. 72 (Her Majesty's Stationery Office, 1982), pp. 4–5.

10. A. G. Gardiner in the *Daily News,* quoted by S. Reynolds, book review, *Punch,* July 13, 1983, p. 60.

11. Field and Southgate, p. 5.

12. Ibid.

13. *To Establish Justice, To Insure Domestic Tranquility,* the Final Report of the National Commission on the Causes and Prevention of Violence (Bantam Books, 1970), p. 52.

14. Ibid.

15. Ibid.

16. D. Butler and A. Sloman, *British Political Facts, 1900–1979,* 5th ed. (Macmillan, 1980), pp. 340–41.

17. A. H. Halsey, *Change in British Society,* 2nd ed. (Oxford University Press, 1981), p. 70.

18. Quoted in ibid., p. 71.

19. Reynolds, p. 60.

20. A. W. Cox, "Strikes, Free Collective Bargaining and Public Order" in P. Norton (ed.), *Law and Order in British Politics* (Gower: in press).

21. It was estimated that fewer than 10% of Trades Union Congress members responded to the TUC's call for action. D. Shell, "The British Constitution in 1980," *Parliamentary Affairs,* 34 (2), Spring 1981, p. 150.

22. See, e.g., J. Rex, "Law and Order in Multi-Racial Areas: The Problems After Scarman" in Norton (ed.), *Law and Order in British Politics* (in press).

23. Recounted to the author on a visit to Liverpool in 1982.

24. See above, Chapter 9, and Norton, *The Constitution in Flux,* Ch. 10.

25. R. Rose and I. McAllister, *United Kingdom Facts* (Macmillan, 1982), p. 121.

26. Beer, p. 119.

27. Ibid., p. 120. This paragraph is based on pp. 120–26.

28. Ibid., pp. 143–48.

29. Ibid., p. 134.

30. Ibid., p. 137.

31. Ibid., p. 142.

32. Ibid., pp. 169–80.

33. B. M. Jones, book review, *Teaching Politics,* 12 (2), May 1983, p. 262.

. 34. Thus, for example, more recently Tom Robinson's *Glad to be Gay* proved quite popular, but apparently many of those who sang along with the words at concerts had little understanding of the message, even though it was quite obvious.

35. Beer, p. 157.

36. Ibid., p. 175.

37. See P. Norton and A. Aughey, *Conservatives and Conservatism* (Temple Smith, 1981), Ch. 5 and especially Ch. 6.

38. Beer, pp. 79–83.

39. E. Powell, book review, *The Sunday Telegraph,* October 24, 1982.

40. Beer, pp. 114–18. A. Marsh, *Protest and Political Consciousness* (Sage, 1977); V. Hart, *Distrust and Democracy* (Cambridge University Press, 1978).

41. Reproduced in Beer, p. 116.

42. Of respondents, 24.8% thought they could trust government to do what was right "all or most of the time"; 68.4% thought they could trust it to do what was right "some of the time"; fewer than 7% responded with "none of the time." L. Moss, "Attitudes Towards Government," *SSRC Research Report HR 5427* (1980), p. 296.

43. Granada TV, *The State of the Nation* (Granada TV, 1973), p. 201.

44. P. Kellner, "Who Runs Britain?" *Sunday Times,* September 18, 1977.

45. Cited in S. E. Finer, *The Changing British Party System 1945–1979* (American Enterprise Institute, 1980), p. 176.

46. Hart, p. 217, note 42. Other polls showing contradictory results can be cited, but they would support rather than detract from the point I am seeking to make—i.e., too much store should not be set by these survey data.

47. D. Sanders and E. Tanenbaum, "Direct Action and Political Culture: The Changing Political Consciousness of the British Public," *European Journal of Political Research,* 11, 1983, p. 46.

48. Ibid.

49. A. King, "The Problem of Overload," in A. King (ed.), *Why is Britain Becoming Harder to Govern?* (BBC, 1976).

50. See J. Alt, *The Politics of Economic Decline* (Cambridge University Press, 1979).

Select Reading List

THIS IS NEITHER a bibliography of works used nor a comprehensive survey of available literature. Rather, it is a *guide* to the main and most useful texts available for student use. Chapter footnotes provide a pointer to further reading for students whose intellectual appetite is not satiated by what follows.

Part I *Introduction*

The Contemporary Landscape. There are various reference works which provide useful facts and figures on contemporary Britain. The most regular and helpful of these are *Britain: An Official Handbook*, published annually by Her Majesty's Stationery Office, London; and *Social Trends*, compiled annually by the Central Statistical Office and also published by Her Majesty's Stationery Office (HMSO), London. Other useful sources include *The Statesman's Year Book*, published annually by Macmillan, London (useful for comparative purposes); R. Rose and I. McAllister (eds.), *United Kingdom Facts* (London: Macmillan, 1982); and D. Butler and A. Sloman (eds.), *British Political Facts 1900–1979*, 5th ed. (London: Macmillan, 1980).

Political Culture. For a succinct introduction, see D. Kavanagh, *Political Culture* (London: Macmillan, 1972). The most significant work is that of G. Almond and S. Verba, *The Civic Culture* (Princeton, N.J.: Princeton University Press, 1963). See also their most recent compilation, which they edited, *The Civic Culture Revisited* (Boston, Mass.: Little, Brown, 1980). On changes in the contemporary British culture, see S. H. Beer, *Britain Against Itself* (London: Faber, 1982) and V. Hart, *Distrust and Democracy* (Cambridge: Cambridge University Press, 1978), both of which should be read in conjunction with the conclusion to this book.

Historical Perspective and Contemporary Problems.   There are a great many works that provide a political history of Britain. The most comprehensive history from Roman Britain to the twentieth century is that provided by *The Oxford History of England,* published in 15 volumes (with different dates of publication and different authors) by Oxford University Press. The most recent volume, also available in a Pelican edition (Harmondsworth: Penguin Books, 1970), is A. J. P. Taylor, *English History* (Oxford: Oxford University Press, 1965).

For works by political scientists that provide a historical perspective and an analysis of post-1945 political developments, see S. H. Beer, *Modern British Politics,* 3rd ed. (London: Faber, 1982)—in practice, a reprint of the 1969 edition—and Professor Beer's more pessimistic *Britain Against Itself* (London: Faber, 1982); R. Dahrendorf, *On Britain* (London: British Broadcasting Corporation, 1982), and, from a more radical perspective, A. Gamble, *Britain in Decline* (London: Macmillan, 1981). Other works providing analyses of Britain's contemporary problems include R. Emmett Tyrell Jr., *The Future that Doesn't Work* (Garden City, N.Y.: Doubleday, 1977); B. Nossiter, *Britain: A Future that Works* (London: Andre Deutsch, 1978); and K. Middlemas, *Politics in Industrial Society* (London: Andre Deutsch, 1979). The Dahrendorf book is the shortest and essentially the most introductory of the foregoing and is useful for identifying and summarizing the position of other works and analyses.

For books that place more emphasis on the political system as a partial explanation of Britain's contemporary ills, see S. E. Finer (ed.), *Adversary Politics and Electoral Reform* (London: Wigram, 1975); A. King (ed.), *Why is Britain Becoming Harder to Govern?* (London: British Broadcasting Corporation, 1976); S. Brittan, *The Economic Consequences of Democracy* (London: Temple Smith, 1977); and D. Coombes, *Representative Government and Economic Power* (London: Heinemann, 1982). These works should be read in conjunction with Chapter 5 of this book.

Part II *The Political Environment*

The Constitution.   There are various introductory texts on the Constitution and constitutional law. Of those by constitutional lawyers, the most readable and useful are A. W. Bradley, *Wade and Phillips' Constitutional and Administrative Law,* 9th ed. (London: Longman, 1977); O. Hood Phillips and P. Jackson, *O. Hood Phillips' Constitutional and Administrative Law* 6th ed. (London: Sweet and Maxwell, 1978); and S. A. de Smith, with the equally originally titled *Constitutional and Administrative Law,* 4th ed. revised by H. Street and R. Brazier (Harmondsworth: Penguin, 1981).

For works on contemporary constitutional debate, two works by political scientists are recommended: P. Norton, *The Constitution in Flux* (Oxford: Martin Robertson, 1982) and N. Johnson, *In Search of the Constitution* (London: Methuen, 1980 ed.); and two by jurists: Sir L. Scarman, *English Law—The New Dimension* (London: Stevens, 1974) and Lord Hailsham, *The Dilemma of Democracy* (London: Collins, 1978).

The Electoral System.   For an introductory text on the British electoral system, G. Alderman, *British Elections: Myth and Reality* (London: Batsford, 1978) can be recommended. On candidate selection, there are two now rather dated books: M. Rush, *The Selection of Parliamentary Candidates* (London: Nelson, 1969) and A. Ranney, *Pathways to Parliament* (London: Macmillan, 1965). The standard works on general elections are those published in the Nuffield election series, authored or co-authored by D. Butler, and published after each general election under the title of *The British General Election of . . . .* (London: Macmillan). On the 1979 election there is also H. Penniman (ed.), *Britain at the Polls, 1979* (Washington, D.C.: American Enterprise Institute, 1981), written for an American audience. For the reader interested in the financing of parties and election campaigns, the best and most recent book on the subject is that by M. Pinto-Duschinsky, *British Political Finance 1830–1980* (Washington, D.C.: American Enterprise Institute, 1981).

Changes in electoral behavior up to 1979 are summarized in S. E. Finer, *The Changing British Party System, 1945–1979* (Washington, D.C.: American Enterprise Institute, 1980). See also the texts listed below under "Political Parties." For the debate surrounding the electoral system, one should consult S. E. Finer (ed.), *Adversary Politics and Electoral Reform* (London: Wigram, 1975); J. Rogaly, *Parliament for the People* (London: Temple Smith, 1976); D. Coombes, *Representative Government and Economic Power* (London: Heinemann, 1982); Sir A. Maude and J. Szemerey, *Why Electoral Change?* (London: Conservative Political Centre, 1982); J. A. Chandler, "The Plurality Vote: A Reappraisal," *Political Studies*, 30 (1), 1982, pp. 87–94; and chapter 12 in P. Norton, *The Constitution in Flux* (Oxford: Martin Robertson, 1982).

Political Parties.   A standard but now sadly dated work on political parties is R. McKenzie, *British Political Parties*, 2nd rev. ed. (London: Heinemann, 1964). On the individual parties, the most recent and comprehensive text on the Conservative Party is P. Norton and A. Aughey, *Conservatives and Conservatism* (London: Temple Smith, 1981), encompassing philosophy, history, organization, electoral support, leadership and recent developments within the party. Other useful works are Z. Layton-Henry (ed.), *Conservative Party Politics* (London: Macmillan, 1980) and, on the party's history, Lord Butler (ed.), *The Conservatives* (London: George Allen & Unwin, 1977). The Norton and Aughey volume has a select reading list that identifies other relevant works. On the Labour Party, the most useful recent book for the student is D. Kavanagh (ed.), *The Politics of the Labour Party* (London: George Allen & Unwin, 1982). H. Pelling, *A Short History of the Labour Party*, 7th ed. (London: Macmillan, 1982) provides precisely what its title suggests. On party doctrine, H. M. Drucker, *Doctrine and Ethos in the Labour Party* (London: George Allen & Unwin, 1979) provides a useful discussion and, for recent developments within the party, D. Kogan and M. Kogan, *The Battle for the Labour Party* (London: Fontana, 1982) constitutes a succinct survey, to be read in conjunction with the contributions to the Kavanagh volume. For students of the Liberal Party, two useful but dated books are J. S. Rasmussen, *The Liberal Party* (London: Constable, 1965) and A. Cyr, *Liberal Party Politics in Britain* (London: John Calder, 1977). The most recent and thorough text is V. Bogdanor (ed.), *Liberal Party Politics* (Oxford: Oxford University Press, 1983). On the Social Democratic Party, the most interesting and readable books are I. Bradley, *Breaking the Mould?* (Oxford: Martin Robertson, 1981) and H. Stephenson, *Claret and Chips* (London: Michael Joseph, 1982). Of the books written by SDP leaders, the most useful to the student is D. Owen, *Face the Future* (Oxford: Oxford University Press, 1981).

On the changes in party support among the electorate, the essential publications are: D. Butler and D. Stokes, *Political Change in Britain*, 2nd ed. (London: Macmillan, 1974); I. Crewe, B. Sarlvik, and J. Alt, "Partisan De-alignment in Britain, 1964–1974," *British Journal of Political Science*, 7 (2), 1977, pp. 129–190; B. Sarlvik and I. Crewe, *Decade of Dealignment* (Cambridge: Cambridge University Press, 1983); and M. N. Franklin and A. Mughan, "The Decline of Class Voting in Britain: Problems of Analysis and Interpretation," *American Political Science Review*, 72 (2), June 1978, pp. 523–534. A valuable analysis of the 1983 general election, by I. Crewe, was published in the *Guardian* newspaper, 13 and 14 June 1983. Also of relevance are D. Robertson, *Class and the British Electorate* (Oxford: Martin Robertson, 1983) and P. Dunleavy, "The Urban Basis of Political Alignment," *British Journal of Political Science*, 9 (4), 1979, pp. 409–443.

An invaluable study of the effect of political parties in office in R. Rose, *Do Parties Make a Difference?* 2nd ed. (London: Macmillan, 1983), providing an effective rejoinder to the thesis advanced in S. E. Finer, *Adversary Politics and Electoral Reform*.

Interest Groups.   On groups in British politics, see S. H. Beer, *Modern British Politics* 3rd ed. (London: Faber, 1982); R. Kimber and J. Richardson (eds.), *Pressure Groups in Britain* (London: Dent, 1974); and J. J. Richardson and A. G. Jordan, *Governing under Pressure* (Oxford: Martin Robertson, 1979). Important but now dated works include H. Eckstein, *Pressure Group Politics* (London: George Allen & Unwin, 1960); S. E. Finer, *Anonymous Empire* (London: Pall Mall, 1958); J. D. Stewart, *British Pressure Groups* (Oxford: Oxford University Press, 1958); and H. H. Wilson, *Pressure Groups* (London: Secker & Warburg, 1961).

Other books include G. Wooton, *The Politics of Influence* (London: Routledge & Kegan Paul, 1963), a now dated case study of British ex-servicemen; B. Pym, *Pressure Groups and the Permissive Society* (Newton Abbot: David and Charles, 1974), dealing essentially with promotional groups on moral issues; P. G. Richards, *Parliament and Conscience* (London: George Allen & Unwin, 1970), covering similar ground but in a more structured manner; and P. Rivers, *Politics by Pressure* (London: Harrap, 1974). Also worthy of mention is R. Kimber and J. J. Richardson (eds.), *Campaigning for the Environment* (London: Routledge & Kegan Paul, 1974), a study of campaigns to protect the environment.

For writings on "peak" organizations, see W. Grant and D. Marsh, *The CBI* (London: Hodder and Stoughton, 1977); G. K. Wilson, *Special Interests and Policy Making* (London: Wiley, 1977); and M. Harrison, *Trade Unions and the Labour Party since 1945* (London: George Allen & Unwin, 1960); and C. Crouch, "The Peculiar Relationship: The Party and the Unions," in D. Kavanagh (ed.), *The Politics of the Labour Party* (London: George Allen & Unwin, 1982).

On the different group theories, one should consult Richardson and Jordan, *Governing under Pressure* (see above) for the group pluralist approach and, for a summary of the Marxist and Weberian approaches, A. Cox, "Corporatism and the Corporate State in Britain," in L. Robins (ed.), *Topics in British Politics* (London: The Politics Association, 1982). See also A. Cawson, "Pluralism, Corporatism and the Role of the State," *Government and Opposition*, 13 (2), 1978, pp. 178–198; R. E. Pahl and J. Winkler, "The Coming Corporatism," *New Society*, 10 October 1974, pp.

72–76; and R. J. Harrison, *Pluralism and Corporatism* (London: George Allen & Unwin, 1980). The Richardson and Jordon volume includes a useful select bibliography covering groups and the policy process.

Part III *Governmental Decision Making*

The Executive. There is no one good single-author text on the contemporary office of the Prime Minister. Instead, one has to have recourse to the aging but still useful compilation of A. King (ed.), *The British Prime Minister* (London: Macmillan, 1969). For a short history of the office, there is Lord Blake, *The Office of Prime Minister* (Oxford: Oxford University Press, 1975). On the Cabinet, including PM-Cabinet relationships, there are various works: J. P. Mackintosh, *The British Cabinet*, 3rd ed. (London: Stevens, 1977); H. Wilson, *The Governance of Britain* (London: Sphere Books, 1977); P. G. Walker, *The Cabinet*, rev. ed. (London: Fontana, 1972); B. Sedgemore, *The Secret Constitution* (London: Hodder & Stoughton, 1980); R. Crossman, *Inside View* (London: Jonathan Cape, 1972); and also by R. Crossman, *The Diaries of a Cabinet Minister*, vols. I, II, and III (London: Hamish Hamilton/Jonathan Cape, 1975, 1976, and 1977), providing an indiscreet insight into the workings of Cabinet and of government generally. All the foregoing authors, from Mackintosh on, were practising politicians (Sedgemore still is one). See also Chapter 1 in P. Norton, *The Constitution in Flux* (Oxford: Martin Robertson, 1982).

On the structure of Departments, there are three relevant articles: Sir R. Clarke, "The Machinery of Government," in W. Thornhill (ed.), *The Modernization of British Government* (London: Pitman, 1975); E. Heath and A. Barker, "Heath on Whitehall Reform," *Parliamentary Affairs*, 31 (4), 1978, pp. 363–390; and J. M. Lee, "The Machinery of Government under Mrs. Thatcher's Administration," *Parliamentary Affairs*, 33 (4), 1980, pp. 434–447.

There are various books and articles on the civil service. One should consult *The Report of the Committee on the Civil Service*, Cmnd. 3638 (London: HMSO, 1968), otherwise known as the Fulton Report. Useful books include Lord Crowther-Hunt and P. Kellner, *The Civil Servants* (London: Macdonald Futura, 1980); B. Castle, *The Castle Diaries 1974–1976* (London: Weidenfeld & Nicolson, 1980); and the Crossman *Diaries* already referred to above. All three works, by former Labor ministers, are essentially critical of the civil service. More objective assessments appear in article or chapter form. These include B. Headey, "Cabinet Ministers and Senior Civil Servants," in V. Herman and J. Alt (eds.), *Cabinet Studies: A Reader* (London: Macmillan, 1975); M. Wright, "Ministers and Civil Servants: Relations and Responsibilities," *Parliamentary Affairs*, 30 (3), 1977, pp. 293–313; and the articles in the special issue of *Parliamentary Affairs*, 33 (4), 1980, grouped under the title of "Government and Public Servants." For a summary of the debate, read chapter 4 in Norton, *The Constitution in Flux*.

Subnational Government. There are various texts on local government in Britain. Two of the most recent and most useful are A. Alexander, *The Politics of Local Government in the United Kingdom* (London: Longman, 1982) and H. J. Elcock, *Local Government* (London: Methuen, 1982). On regional government, the work to consult is B. W. Hogwood and M. Keating (eds.), *Regional Government in England* (Oxford: Oxford University Press, 1982). On the specific example of the National Health Service, there is a succinct and up-to-date work available in C. Ham, *Health Policy in Britain* (London: Macmillan, 1982). The most useful work on the government of Scotland is M. Keating and A. Midwinter, *The Government of Scotland* (Edinburgh: Mainstream Publishing, 1983) and the book that deals most succinctly with the actual government of Northern Ireland is D. Birrell and A. Murie, *Policy and Government in Northern Ireland* (Dublin: Gill and Macmillan, 1980).

There are a number of books available on the issue of devolution. The most important are V. Bogdanor, *Devolution* (Oxford: Oxford University Press, 1979); A. H. Birch, *Political Integration and Disintegration in the British Isles* (London: George Allen & Unwin, 1977); and H. M. Drucker and G. Brown, *The Politics of Nationalism and Devolution* (London: Longman, 1980). One should also refer, selectively, to the extensive Report, vol. I, of the Royal Commission on the Constitution, Cmnd. 5460, published by HMSO in 1973. See also R. Rose, *Understanding the United Kingdom* (London: Longman, 1982).

On the debate surrounding Northern Ireland, see R. Rose, *Governing without Consensus* (London: Faber, 1971) and, by the same author, *Northern Ireland: A Time of Choice* (Washington, D.C.: American Enterprise Institute, 1976). On the constitutional options, consult D. C. Watt (ed.), *The Constitution of Northern Ireland* (London: Heinemann, 1981) and chapter 10 in P. Norton, *The Constitution in Flux*.

European Communities.   On Britain's first application to join the EEC, read R. J. Lieber, *British Politics and European Unity* (Berkeley: University of California Press, 1970) and for details of the second application see the material collected in U. Kitzinger, *The Second Try* (Oxford: Pergamon, 1968). On the domestic and parliamentary debate in the 1970s preceding British entry, one should refer to U. Kitzinger, *Diplomacy and Persuasion* (London: Thames and Hudson, 1973) and, *inter alia*, P. Norton, *Conservative Dissidents* (London: Temple Smith, 1978). On politics and decision-making within the European Communities, see J. Lodge (ed.), *Institutions and Policies of the European Communities* (London: Frances Pinter, 1983), and A. Daltrop, *Politics and the European Community* (London: Longman, 1982). There is a text available now on the problems for British government posed by EC membership—F. Gregory, *Dilemmas of Government* (Oxford: Martin Robertson, 1983).

There are two books that deal with the EC referendum in 1975: D. Butler and U. Kitzinger, *The 1975 Referendum* (London: Macmillan, 1976) and A. King, *Britain Says Yes* (Washington, D.C.: American Enterprise Institute, 1977). For the contemporary debate surrounding membership, read chapter 8 in P. Norton, *The Constitution in Flux*.

Part IV *Scrutiny and Legitimation*

Parliament.   The two most recent and comprehensive texts on the House of Commons are P. Norton, *The Commons in Perspective* (Oxford: Martin Robertson, and New York: Longman, 1981) and S. A. Walkland and M. Ryle (eds.), *The Commons Today* (London: Fontana, 1981). A thorough historical study is S. A. Walkland (ed.), *The House of Commons in the Twentieth Century* (Oxford: Oxford University Press, 1979). The Norton volume includes a guide to further reading.

There is not one good introductory text on the House of Lords. P. Bromhead, *The House of Lords and Contemporary Politics, 1911–57* (London: Routledge & Kegan Paul, 1958) is obviously out of date. J. Morgan, *The House of Lords and the Labour Government, 1964–70* (Oxford: Oxford University Press, 1975) provides an interesting case study. Useful introductory material exists primarily in pamphlet or monograph form, in *Factsheets* issued by the House of Lords Information Office (House of Lords, London SW1A OPW) and in N. Baldwin, "The House of Lords: A Study in Evolutionary Adaptability," *Hull Papers in Politics No. 33* (Hull: Hull University Politics Department, 1983).

As for the debate surrounding parliamentary reform, B. Crick, *The Reform of Parliament*, rev. 2nd ed. (London: Weidenfeld & Nicolson, 1970) constitutes the classic reform tract of the 1960s. For the contemporary debate see especially chapter 9 in Norton, *The Commons in Perspective*, and the various contributions to D. Judge (ed.), *The Politics of Parliamentary Reform* (London: Heinemann, 1983).

The Monarchy. There are numerous biographies and sketches of members of the Royal Family, but few recent works dealing with the role of the monarch in politics. An interesting reformist, but not anti-monarchical, tract is K. Martin, *The Crown and the Establishment*, rev. ed. (Harmondsworth: Penguin, 1965). F. Hardie, *The Political Influence of the British Monarchy 1868–1952* (London: Batsford, 1970) provides a helpful and concise summary. Only a few general works on British politics devote much space to the monarchy. A short but interesting comment appears in an otherwise critical work on British institutions: M. Nicholson, *The System* (New York: McGraw-Hill, 1967), pp. 156–159. The pamphlet, *The Monarchy in Britain*, compiled by the Central Office of Information and published by HMSO (London: 1975), provides much useful basic information.

Part V *Enforcement and Feedback*

The Courts and the Police. There are a number of introductory texts on the British legal system. These include the three texts on constitutional law listed above under "The Constitution." Students may also find helpful G. Drewry, *Law, Justice and Politics* (London: Longman, 1975) and, for comparative purposes, H. J. Abraham, *The Judicial Process*, rev. 3rd ed. (New York: Oxford University Press, 1977). On the current debate surrounding the judiciary, see J. A. G. Griffith, *The Politics of the Judiciary*, 2nd ed. (London: Fontana, 1981); chapter 5 in H. W. R. Wade, *Constitutional Fundamentals* (London: Stevens, 1980); and chapter 7 in P. Norton, *The Constitution in Flux* (Oxford: Martin Robertson, 1982).

As for texts on the police, there is not one work that can be recommended on its own. Among books dealing with the subject are B. Whittaker, *The Police in Society* (London: Eyre Methuen, 1979) and two by former senior police officers: Sir R. Mark, *In the Office of Constable* (London: Fontana, 1978) and J. Alderson, *Policing Free-*

dom (London: Macdonald and Evans, 1979). On the current debate surrounding the police force, one should consult also the report of Lord Scarman, *The Brixton Disorders: 10–12 April 1981*, Cmnd. 8427 (HMSO, 1981); Part 2 of P. Norton (ed.), *Law and Order in British Politics* (Aldershot: Gower, in press) and the forthcoming work on the police by J. L. Lambert (Aldershot: Gower, in press).

The Mass Media.   The main books dealing with the mass media in Britain are J. Curran and J. Seaton, *Power Without Responsibility* (London: Fontana, 1981); J. Whale, *The Politics of the Media* (London: Fontana, 1977); C. Seymour-Ure, *The Political Impact of the Mass Media* (London: Constable, 1974); and, also by Seymour-Ure, *The Press, Politics and the Public* (London: Methuen, 1968). More radical analyses are presented in S. Cohen and J. Young (eds.), *The Manufacture of News*, rev. ed. (London: Constable, 1981) and the Glasgow University Media Group, *Bad News* (London: Routledge & Kegan Paul, 1976) and *More Bad News* (London: Routledge & Kegan Paul, 1980).

The role of the press and television in general election campaigns is covered in each volume in the Nuffield *British General Election* series (see above, "The Electoral System") and, for the 1979 campaign, also in R. M. Worcester and M. Harrop (eds.), *Political Communications: The General Election Campaign of 1979* (London: George Allen & Unwin, 1982) which, though useful, does not live up to the expectations generated by its title.

Part VI *Conclusion*

Flux and Strength.   For anyone wishing to read further on the theme of constitutional flux, the essential works are P. Norton, *The Constitution in Flux* (Oxford: Martin Robertson, 1982) and N. Johnson, *In Search of the Constitution* (London: Methuen, 1980). The Norton volume includes a guide to other material on the subject.

The argument developed in the chapter as to the strength of the political culture is, in part, as the text makes clear, a retort to S. H. Beer, *Britain Against Itself* (London: Faber, 1982). Other works of relevance include J. Alt, *The Politics of Economic Decline* (Cambridge: Cambridge University Press, 1979) and the works listed above under "Political Culture" and "Historical Perspective and Contemporary Problems," in particular, the books by Hart, Tyrell, Nossiter, and Dahrendorf.

Glossary

Backbencher A member of Parliament who is neither a minister for the government nor a spokesperson for the opposition. The name derives from the location of their seats.

Barrister A specialist lawyer who appears on behalf of clients in superior courts and is retainable only through a solicitor (*see text*).

Bobby Colloquial name for a policeman (not used much now) that was derived from the name of the Home Secretary, Sir Robert Peel, responsible for the creation of the (Metropolitan) police force in 1829.

Buckingham Palace The London residence of the Queen.

By-election The election to return a Member of Parliament (MP) in a constituency in which a vacancy has occurred (e.g., because of the death of the incumbent). A vacancy can only be filled by means of an election.

Chief Constable The professional head of each police force except in London, where the Metropolitan and City of London forces are headed by Commissioners.

Collective ministerial responsibility The answerability of all members of the Cabinet as a body for decisions taken in Cabinet (*see text*).

Commonwealth A voluntary association of independent states and territories dependent upon these independent states. The Commonwealth evolved from the British Empire and exists now to provide cultural, sporting and some political links between member states. The Queen is Head of the Commonwealth.

Constituency An electoral area equivalent in nature to a Congressional district. One Member of Parliament is elected from such an area.

Contest an election Run for election.

Conventions of the Constitution Informal constitutional rules treated as binding by those to whom they are directed (*see text*).

CPRS Central Policy Review Staff, also known as the "Think Tank." It was in existence until 1983 (*see text*).

Devolution The conferring of powers by national government on subordinate units (*see text*).

Dissolution The dissolving of Parliament to prepare for a general election, that is, the return to power of a new Parliament.

Empire The British Empire comprised countries under British sovereignty (though some were self-governing), and in 1918, it encompassed well over a quarter of the human race and more than a quarter of the world's land surface. It began to wither as various dominions gained independence. Since the 1920s, it came to be called the British Commonwealth of Nations, now known simply as the Commonwealth.

Field a candidate Put a candidate up for election.

Free votes Parliamentary votes in which parties have not formally requested their members to vote in a particular way.

Front Benchers The front bench on the Government side of the House of Commons (known traditionally as the Treasury Bench) is by custom reserved for ministers. On the Opposition side of the House, the front bench is occupied by the spokesmen of the official Opposition party. Hence, those who occupy the bench are referred to as Front Benchers.

General election The election of a new House of Commons.

Going to the country The Prime Minister's decision to request a general election.

Individual ministerial responsibility The answerability of ministers, to the Crown (formally) and to Parliament (politically) for their official actions and those of civil servants within their Departments (*see text*).

Lord Chancellor A political appointee (a member of the Cabinet) who is head of the judiciary.

Master of the Rolls The presiding judge of the Court of Appeal.

"New" Commonwealth countries A term employed to refer to Asian and African countries that were granted independence in the 1940s, thus distinguishing them from the "old" Commonwealth countries of Canada, Australia, and New Zealand.

Officials Civil servants.

Peer A member of the peerage (i.e., a Lord).

PM Prime Minister.

Premier Alternative term used to refer to the Prime Minister.

Private Members All Members of Parliament who are not Ministers. (The term is not synonymous with backbenchers, since Opposition Front Benchers are Private Members).

QUANGO Quasi-autonomous non-governmental organization (*see text*).

Returned to office The achievement of position usually via election.

Rt. Hon. The Right Honorable. This title denotes a member of the Privy Council which was historically important as an advisory body to the Crown, but is now largely ceremonial in nature. However, membership of the Council is still important because members can receive state secrets. All members of the Cabinet and other senior ministers are sworn in as members of the Privy Council.

Scotland Yard The Headquarters of the Metropolitan police. The name was derived from the location of the original headquarters—Scotland Yard, Westminster.

Second reading Parliamentary debate on the principle of a bill (*see text*).

Solicitor A lawyer who deals directly with the public and handles general legal problems (*see text*).

Speaker The Speaker of the House of Commons, a non-partisan figure selected by the House from among their members. The Speaker has the power to select members in debate, select amendments for debate, and discipline members. After election to the post, the Speaker ceases to be a member of a political party and leads an isolated parliamentary existence.

Tabling The act of submitting a motion for debate. This is a positive move and should not be confused with the American equivalent which means to shelve a motion.

Ulster The northern nine counties of Ireland form the historic region of Ulster. However, the name (Ulster) is often used, especially by Unionists (*see text*), to refer to the northern six counties which now constitute Northern Ireland. Since Northern Ireland was formed, it has been common to refer to it as a province of the United Kingdom.

Upper House The House of Lords. (It is rare, though, to refer to the House of Commons as the Lower House.)

Vote of confidence A formal motion expressing confidence (or no confidence) in the Government *or* a vote on a motion on which the Government has declared that, if defeated, it will resign or request a dissolution.

Vote of no confidence *See* vote of confidence.

Westminster A district of London. The name is usually employed to refer to the Palace of Westminster where the two houses of Parliament are located.

Whipped votes A process in which parties have issued requests (via a weekly written document known as a "whip") to their members to cast their vote on an issue in a particular manner. The request in the whip is given emphasis by means of underlining. The most important votes during which all party members are requested to be present and to vote in unison are designated by being underlined three times. The term "three-line whips" emanates from this practice.

Whitehall London street traditionally housing most government departments. Name still employed to denote the environment occupied by ministers and, especially, civil servants even though most Departments are now located elsewhere.

Whitehall Mandarins The name sometimes employed to refer to the senior civil servants in government departments.

Index